The 1980s

A Decade of Contemporary British Fiction

Titles in *The Decades Series*

The 1970s: A Decade of Contemporary British Fiction, edited by
Nick Hubble, John McLeod and Philip Tew

The 1980s: A Decade of Contemporary British Fiction, edited by
Emily Horton, Philip Tew and Leigh Wilson

The 1990s: A Decade of Contemporary British Fiction, edited by
Nick Hubble, Philip Tew and Leigh Wilson

The 2000s: A Decade of Contemporary British Fiction, edited by
Nick Bentley, Nick Hubble and Leigh Wilson

The 1980s

A Decade of Contemporary British Fiction

Edited by

Emily Horton, Philip Tew and Leigh Wilson

Bloomsbury Academic
An imprint of Bloomsbury Publishing Plc

B L O O M S B U R Y
LONDON • OXFORD • NEW YORK • NEW DELHI • SYDNEY

Bloomsbury Academic
An imprint of Bloomsbury Publishing Plc

50 Bedford Square	1385 Broadway
London	New York
WC1B 3DP	NY 10018
UK	USA

www.bloomsbury.com

Bloomsbury is a registered trade mark of Bloomsbury Publishing Plc

First published 2014
Reprinted by Bloomsbury Academic 2016
First published in paperback 2017

© Emily Horton, Philip Tew, Leigh Wilson and Contributors, 2014, 2017

All rights reserved. No part of this publication may be reproduced or transmitted in any form or by any means, electronic or mechanical, including photocopying, recording, or any information storage or retrieval system, without prior permission in writing from the publishers.

No responsibility for loss caused to any individual or organization acting on or refraining from action as a result of the material in this publication can be accepted by Bloomsbury Academic or the editors.

British Library Cataloguing-in-Publication Data
A catalog record for this book is available from the Library of Congress.

ISBN: HB: 978-1-4411-2649-8
PB: 978-1-3500-0539-6
ePub: 978-1-6235-6350-9
ePDF: 978-1-4411-6853-5

Library of Congress Cataloging-in-Publication Data
A catalog record for this book is available from the Library of Congress.

Series: The Decades Series

Cover design: Eleanor Rose

Typeset by Integra Software Services Pvt. Ltd.

Contents

Series Editors' Preface — vii
Acknowledgements — x
Contributors — xi

Critical Introduction
   Emily Horton, Philip Tew and Leigh Wilson — 1

1 Literary History of the Decade
   The Bomb, Kidnappings and Yuppies: British Fiction in the 1980s
   Emily Horton — 21

2 Special Topic 1
   The Awakening of Caledonias? Scottish Literature in the 1980s
   Monica Germanà — 51

3 Special Topic 2
   The Art of Bad Government: Thatcherism and British Fiction
   Joseph Brooker — 75

4 Postcolonial and Diasporic Voices
   'Black' British Women's Fiction and Literary Institutions in the 1980s
   Susan Alice Fischer — 101

5 Historical Representations
   The Heritage Industry and Historiographic Metafiction: Historical Representation in the 1980s
   Alex Murray — 125

6 Generic Discontinuities and Variations
   Crises of Authority and Innovations in Form and Technique in British Fiction of the 1980s
   Frederick M. Holmes — 151

7 International Contexts (North America)
   The American Reception of British Fiction in the 1980s
   Brian Finney — 175

8   International Contexts (Europe)
    The Romanian Context: Between Realism and Postmodernism
    Ana-Karina Schneider   203

Timeline of Works   228
Timeline of National Events   232
Timeline of International Events   236
Biographies of Writers   239
Index   251

Series Editors' Preface

Nick Hubble, Philip Tew and Leigh Wilson

Contemporary British fiction published from 1970 to the present has expanded into a major area of academic study in the last 20 years and attracts a seemingly ever-increasing global scholarship. However, the very speed of the growth of research in this field has perhaps precluded any really nuanced analysis of its key defining terms and has restricted consideration of its chronological development. This series addresses such issues in an informative and structured manner through a set of extended contributions that combine wide-reaching survey work with in-depth research-led analysis. Naturally, many older British academics assume at least some personal knowledge in charting the field of the contemporary, but increasingly many of these coordinates represent the distant past of pre-birth or childhood not only for students, both undergraduate and postgraduate, but also for younger academics. Given that most people's memories of their first five to ten years are vague and localized, an academic born in the early to mid-1980s will only have real first-hand knowledge of less than half these 40 years, while a member of the current generation of undergraduates, born in the mid-1990s, will have no adult experience of the period at all. The rather self-evident nature of this chronological, experiential reality disguises the rather complex challenges it poses to any assessment of the contemporary. Therefore, the aim of these volumes, which include timelines and biographical information on the writers covered, is to provide the contextual framework that is now necessary for the study of the British fiction of these four decades.

Each of the volumes in this Decades Series emerged from a series of workshops hosted by the Brunel Centre for Contemporary Writing (BCCW) located in the School of Arts at Brunel University, London, UK. These events assembled specially invited teams of leading internationally recognized scholars in the field, together with emergent younger figures, in order that they might together examine critically the periodization of contemporary British fiction by dividing it into its four constituent decades: the 1970s symposium was held on 12 March 2010; the 1980s on 7 July 2010; the 1990s on 3 December 2010; and the 2000s on 1 April 2011. During these workshops, draft papers were offered and discussions ensued, with the aim of exchanging ideas and ensuring both continuity and fruitful interaction (including productive dissonances) between what would become chapters of volumes that would hopefully exceed the sum of their parts.

The division of the series by decade could be charged with being too obvious and therefore rather too contentious. In the latter camp, no doubt, would be Ferdinand Mount, who in a 2006 article for the *London Review of Books* concerned primarily with the 1950s, 'The Doctrine of Unripe Time', complained 'When did decaditis first strike? When did people begin to think that slicing the past up into periods of ten years was a useful thing to do?' However, he does admit still that such characterization has long been associated with aesthetic production and its relationship to a larger sense of the times. As Frank Kermode so influentially argued in *The Sense of an Ending: Studies in the Theory of Fiction*, published in 1967 just before the period covered by this series began, divisions of time, like novels, are ways of making meaning. And clearly both can also shape our comprehension of an ideological *and* aesthetic period that seem to co-exist, but are perhaps not necessarily coterminous in their dominant inflections. The scholars involved in our symposia discussed the potential arbitrariness of all periodizations, but nevertheless acknowledged the importance of such divisions, their experiential resonances and symbolic possibilities. They analysed the decades in question not only in terms of leading figures, the cultural zeitgeist and socio-historical perspectives, but also in the context of the changing configuration of Britishness within larger, shifting global processes. The volume participants also reconsidered the effects and meaning of headline events and cultural shifts such as the miners' strike of 1984–85, the collapse of communism, Blairism and cool Britannia, 9/11 and 7/7, to name only a very few. Perhaps ironically to prove the point about the possibilities inherent in such an approach, in his *LRB* article Mount concedes that 'For the historian ... if the 1950s are famous for anything, it is for being dull', adding a comment on the 'shiny barbarism of the new affluence'. Hence, even for Mount, a decade may still possess certain unifying qualities, those shaping and shaped by its overriding cultural mood.

After the symposia had taken place at Brunel, the individuals dispersed and wrote up their papers into full-length chapters (generally 10,000–12,000 words), revised in the light of other papers, the workshop discussions and subsequent further research. These chapters form the core of the book series, which, therefore, may be seen as the result of a collaborative research project bringing together twenty-four academics from Britain, Europe and North America.

Each volume shares a common structure. Following the introduction, the first chapter of each volume addresses the 'Literary History of the Decade' by offering an overview of the key writers, themes, issues and debates, including such factors as emergent literary practices, deaths, prizes, controversies, key developments, movements and best-sellers. The next two chapters are themed around topics that have been specially chosen for each decade, and which also relate to themes of the preceding and succeeding decades, enabling detailed readings of key texts to emerge in full historical and theoretical context. The tone and context having been set in this way, the remaining chapters fill out a complex but comprehensible picture of each decade. A 'Postcolonial Voices' chapter addresses the ongoing legacy of Britain's Empire and the rise of globalization, which is arguably the most significant long-term influence on contemporary British writing. 'Historical Representations' is concerned not just with historical novels but the construction of the past in general, and thus the later volumes will be considering constructions of the earlier decades so that a complex multilayered account of the historicity of the contemporary will emerge over the series. The chapter on 'Experimental Writing' highlights the interaction between the socio-cultural contexts, established in earlier chapters, and aesthetic concerns. The 'International Contexts' chapters allow the chosen international academics allocated them to write about the key international aspects of the British fiction of the particular decade they are focusing on. This might variously concern how the fiction relates to international ideological, aesthetic and other relevant movements and/or how the fiction influenced international fiction and/or international reader reception. Each decade is different, but common threads may emerge.

In the future it is hoped to expand the Decades Series by adding to the first four planned volumes others that extend the period of 'Contemporary British Fiction': both by covering subsequent decades as they complete their course and by featuring precursory decades, extending the focus of study backwards in time to cover the British fiction of the modern and post-war periods.

Works cited

Kermode, Frank. *The Sense of an Ending: Studies in the Theory of Fiction*. Oxford: Oxford University Press, 1967.

Mount, Ferdinand. 'The Doctrine of Unripe Time.' *London Review of Books* 28(22) (16 November 2006): 28–30, http://www.lrb.co.uk/v28/n22/ferdinand-mount/the-doctrine-of-unripe-time. N.pag.

Acknowledgements

First, we recognise all our contributors' great expertise, patience and generosity in responding to our queries and guidance as this volume gradually took shape. We enjoyed excellent support throughout from the editorial team at Bloomsbury, especially David Avital and Mark Richardson, who have been instrumental in bringing this book – and indeed the whole 'Decades' series – to fruition.

We gratefully acknowledge the support of the Brunel University Research and Knowledge Transfer Committee for providing the funding which enabled the Brunel Centre for Contemporary Writing to host the 'Contemporary British Fiction Decades Seminar Series' during 2010 and 2011, which has led to the publication of the volumes in this book series. Without the support of administrative and catering staff at Brunel these events would not have been so congenial or perhaps even have taken place. We would also like to thank all the academics and postgraduate students who attended and contributed to the discussions at these events.

We would also like to mention the staff at Brunel University Library, the British Library, the National Library of Wales and all other research libraries who have provided support to the contributors to this volume.

Contributors

Joseph Brooker is Reader in Modern Literature at Birkbeck, University of London, where he is Director of the Centre for Contemporary Literature. He is the author of *Joyce's Critics* (2004), *Flann O'Brien* (2005) and *Literature of the 1980s* (2010), and has edited or co-edited special issues of *New Formations*, the *Journal of Law & Society* and *Textual Practice*.

Brian Finney is Professor Emeritus of Literature at California State University, Long Beach. Educated in England, he obtained a PhD from the University of London, where from 1964 to 1987 he taught and arranged extramural courses. Since 1987, he has taught at the University of California, Riverside, University of Southern California, UCLA and California State University, Long Beach. Prof. Finney has published seven books: *Since How It Is: A Study of Samuel Beckett's Later Fiction* (1972), *Christopher Isherwood: A Critical Biography* (1979), which was awarded the James Tait Black Memorial Prize, *The Inner I: British Literary Autobiography of the Twentieth Century* (1985), *D. H. Lawrence: Sons and Lovers: A Critical Study* (1990), *English Fiction since 1984: Narrating a Nation* (2006), *Martin Amis* (2008) and *Terrorized: How the War on Terror Affected American Culture and Society* (2011). He is married and lives in Venice, California.

Susan Alice Fischer is Professor of English at Medgar Evers College of The City University of New York. She is editor of the online journal *Literary London Journal* and co-editor of *Changing English: Studies in Culture and Education*. Her work has appeared in *Tulsa Studies in Women's Literature*, *The Women's Review of Books*, *Critical Engagements*, *Zadie Smith: Critical Essays* and *The Swarming Streets: Twentieth Century Representations of London*. Her research focuses largely on contemporary British literature.

Monica Germanà is Senior Lecturer in English Literature and Creative Writing at the University of Westminster. Her research interests and publications concentrate on contemporary British literature, with a specific emphasis on the Gothic, women's writing and Scottish literature. Her first monograph, *Scottish Women's Gothic and Fantastic Writing*, was published in 2010.

Frederick M. Holmes is Professor of English at Lakehead University in Thunder Bay, Ontario, Canada. His area of expertise is British literature of the twentieth and twenty-first centuries, with special emphasis on contemporary fiction and narrative theory. He is the author of numerous articles and book chapters as well as of two books, *The Historical Imagination: Postmodernism and the Treatment of the Past in Contemporary British Fiction* (1997) and *Julian Barnes* (2009).

Emily Horton is a visiting lecturer in English Literature at Brunel University and at the University of Greenwich. Her research interests include contemporary British and American fiction, specializing in trauma fiction; contemporary genre and popular fiction; and contemporary explorations of globalization and cosmopolitanism. Her first monograph, *Contemporary Crisis Fictions*, is forthcoming, and she has co-edited a volume with Monica Germanà, *Ali Smith: Contemporary Critical Perspectives* (2013).

Alex Murray is Senior Lecturer at the University of Exeter. He has published broadly on Critical Theory and nineteenth- and twentieth-century literature. He is the author of *Recalling London* (2007) and *Giorgio Agamben* (2010) as well as co-editor of several collections of essays. He is currently researching late-Victorian literature and place, writing a monograph with the working title 'Landscapes of Decadence', and, with Jason Hall, has co-edited *Decadent Poetics: Literature and Form at the British Fin de Siècle*, which is forthcoming.

Ana-Karina Schneider is Associate Professor at Lucian Blaga University, Sibiu, holding a PhD in critical theory and Faulkner studies from Lucian Blaga University (2005), and a Diploma in American Studies from Smith College, MA, USA (2004). Her teaching expertise covers mainly English literature from the seventeenth century to the present, alongside literary criticism. She has published a book titled *Critical Perspectives in the Late Twentieth Century. William Faulkner: A Case Study*, and a textbook on the history of Anglo-American literary criticism, as well as an assortment of articles on William Faulkner's novelistic achievement and its critical reception, English prose fiction, literary translation and English Studies in Romanian higher education. Dr Schneider has also been manuscript editor for various publications.

Critical Introduction

Emily Horton, Philip Tew and Leigh Wilson

To an unparalleled extent in the history of post-war Britain, the 1980s were dominated by one political figure and one political ideology, Margaret Thatcher and Thatcherism. This introduction seeks to set out a context for the chapters which follow which explains some of the reasons for this domination, and plots some of its consequences for the novel and for the study of it. As Brian V. Peck notes, when arriving at Downing Street in 1979, Thatcher actually paraphrased rather than quoted St Francis of Assisi thus: 'Where there is discord, may we bring harmony. Where there is error, may we bring truth. Where there is doubt, may we bring faith. And where there is despair, may we bring hope' (24). Retrospectively, her words appear bleakly comic. There was much opposition to Conservative policies, and, across the arts, in novels, film and television and visual art, creators represented the discord and strife that emerged from their imposition. As Miguel Mota points out, film-maker Mike Leigh rose to prominence by 'addressing a British society that had turned its back on the political and social consensus of the previous forty years' (24), this theme informing such films as *Meantime* (1983), *High Hopes* (1988) and *Life Is Sweet* (1990). Likewise, as David Monaghan explains, 'the most effective opposition to the Conservative government that ruled Britain throughout the 1980s was often to be found in the creative arts, particularly in the realm of literature and film' (2). He describes Alan Bleasdale's seminal television drama series *Boys from the Blackstuff*, which takes the unemployed in Liverpool as its main characters:

> Like Thatcher, Bleasdale finds a new position for the unemployed. However, whereas they are marginalized almost to the point of extinction under Thatcherism, the unemployed are located at the very heart of Bleasdale's representation of working-class life. (4)

Equally unconvinced by Thatcherism, many writers and critics resisted her ethos, often using satire and parody to question this. For example, Pete Davies's *The Last Election* (1986) foregrounds the media's domination of the public sphere, while in the background the prime minister, Nanny, seeks re-election for her Money Party. Clearly modelled on Thatcher, Nanny uses her authority to marginalize any opposition, such as when 'following the discovery of subversive literature on their premises, both Help the Aged and Age Concern had been closed down until such time as the DPP had evaluated their cases' (194). Certainly, Thatcher too explicitly represented moneyed interests. According to figures analysed for an Institute of Fiscal Studies briefing by Alissa Goodman and Andrew Shephard, under Thatcher's governments the income growth of the poorest groups in society lagged behind their middle-income and wealthier counterparts considerably (17), so that '[i]ndeed, the income growth of the richest group was over eight times that of the poorest' (16).

Many creative artists and novelists in the 1980s appeared to be appalled by Thatcher and by the dominant realities of her administrations. In particular, they questioned her divisive politics and scorched earth economic policies, which they contrasted to the preceding post-war period of consensus, with its full employment, prosperity and welfarism. While the positive effects of this consensus government had continued at least until the late 1960s, as Suzanne J. Konzelmann, Marc Fovargue-Davies and Frank Wilkinson point out, even by then cracks were beginning to appear, since '[b]y the 1960s and 1970s, it was clear that British industry had become progressively less competitive' (8). Neither did welfarism produce any accord in the 1970s in the public sphere; rather, discord prevailed. This becomes clear, for example, in the various active campaigns against working-class mobilization organized by the consensus government, as well as in the activities of the trade unions in retaliation, as discussed by Philip Tew (48–49), who notes that many among the middle classes were still animated by 'long-held antipathies to other classes' (48). In both of these ways, the nation's experience of dissension under consensus became evident, as was explored not only in politics but as Tew indicates in much of the fiction of the time. A version of history and economics which favoured the interests of the middle class continued, however, into the 1980s, as one can see in a 1989 publication by the Adam Smith Institute, which is clearly entirely sympathetic to Thatcher's reforms. In his contribution to this publication, Norman Gash reflected in 'The Year before Thatcher: June 1978– May 1979' that industrial strife ran rampant prior to her first electoral victory:

> Unemployment (which had been running at just over 600,000 in 1974) rose by the late summer of 1978 to 1.3 million. A thoughtful economist at Sussex University predicted that by the year 2000 it would reach five million. As the summer wore on trade union discontent with the government's policy of limiting wage increases to 5% began to find outlet in acts of defiance. (5)

As Tom Pettinger noted in 2010, having negotiated resolutions to the International Monetary Fund (IMF) crisis of 1976, subsequently James Callaghan, Thatcher's predecessor as prime minister

> faced what could arguably be described as some of the toughest times any Prime Minister has had to face post-war. Having held the three leading Cabinet posts (Home Secretary, Foreign Secretary and Chancellor), he became Prime Minister in April 1976 following Wilson's surprise resignation, inheriting an economy experiencing rampant inflation … (N.pag.)

As Pettinger adds, two key dynamics appeared to be beyond Callaghan's control: 1970s stagflation and post-war Keynesian inflationary economics. Gash details the struggles of Callaghan's government to maintain a central wage control policy, limit inflation and limit the effects of 'widening industrial misrule' (6), culminating in the so-called Winter of Discontent of 1978–79. All of this led to a successful motion of no confidence in the House of Commons in March 1979 and to a subsequent general election on 3 May. The rest, as the cliché goes, is history. However, despite these brief indications of the troubled situation in Britain by May 1979, it is not at all clear that Thatcher ever truly represented, let alone united, the nation as a whole. Even in her party's so-called landslide victories in 1983 and 1987, the Conservatives garnered only 44 per cent of the votes cast and a far lower percentage of the total number of eligible potential votes. Moreover, certain facts suggest that the picture of Thatcher as a successful innovator and saviour of the nation needs to be revised. Take one key headline, the Thatcherite theme of inflation. According to figures from the Office of National Statistics, in 1978 Labour had reduced it to an average of 8.3 per cent. In March 1979 inflation ran at 9.8 per cent. By 1980 it was consistently over 15 per cent, peaking at 21.9 per cent in May 1980. Despite subsequent lower rates by 1989, partly fuelled by far more local pressures than Callaghan had faced, such as inflationary house price rises, inflation under Thatcher was still running at around 8 per cent and consistently over 10 per cent by 1990.

Indeed, according to many later commentators, Thatcher's ideological monetarist solutions to supposedly fundamental problems divided the nation, impoverished huge swathes of working-class people, created an economic recession, led to inner-city riots in 1981 and decimated Britain's industry and massively increased unemployment. Again, according to official figures from the Office of National Statistics, in 1982, for the first time since the 1930s, unemployment topped 3 million at 3,070,621, with one in eight out of work in the country as a whole, nearly 20 per cent unemployed in Northern Ireland, and 16 per cent in most parts of Scotland, the North East and the North West.

In addition, despite the war cry that the Conservatives would roll back the state, public spending actually increased during Thatcher's administrations. The government's first White Paper on the subject published by HM Treasury entitled *The Government's Expenditure Plans 1980-81* (1979) stated, 'Public expenditure is at the heart of Britain's present economic difficulties' (1). Ironically, the increased spending on benefits (a rise of almost 50 per cent) was funded largely by oil revenues, taxes from an industry cultivated and invested in by successive Labour governments. John Hills notes, 'in its last year in office, 1996–97 (the financial year starting in April 1996), the Conservative government devoted almost the same share of national income to the main welfare services as its Labour predecessor had twenty years before' (1). As Kitson and Michie explain:

> Neither the specific problem of deindustrialization nor the consequent general problem of continued relative economic decline were solved in the 1980s... this fundamental problem, a lack of any strong modernizing force, has if anything been exacerbated since 1979. (196)

Moreover, many commentators and historians now question whether Thatcherism even represented a consistent ideology. Beyond its mix of neo-conservatism and neo-liberalism that led to policies such as the privatization of public assets, the selling of council houses and deregulation of the City and banks, it did little to reflect a consistent economic policy line. This seems even truer given that, according to the Institute for Fiscal Studies' tabulations, by 1989 taxation for basic rate taxpayers was not radically lower than it had been a decade previously, while National Insurance rates were rising. Moreover, as Hills notes in terms of welfare, 'the restrictions of public spending began not in 1979, but in 1976 under the then Labour government' (3). Additionally, Hills confirms that 'the overall tax burden was not, in fact, cut under the Conservatives. Income tax *rates* were indeed reduced, particularly for those with the highest incomes, but taxes were raised in other ways, notably from higher VAT and increased National Insurance Contributions (NICs)' (3–4). Nonetheless, while Conservative economics may not have been as radical as Thatcher's governments claimed, the creation of a new ideological rhetoric and cultural context was powerfully obvious. Joseph Brooker explores this in Chapter 3, noting the strong political hold Thatcherism had on 1980s culture, even despite itself. As he puts it, 'one might find writers feeding off it and channelling its energies, even as they sought to criticize many of its effects'. In this sense, Thatcherism was pervasive within the 1980s, incorporating at times even its strongest opponents.

Following the victory in 1982 in the Falklands War – which has since been seen as a somewhat precarious enterprise with a fortunate outcome – another defining moment occurred when, after the Coal Board had built up substantial coal stocks in 1984, Thatcher provoked the National Union of Mineworkers (NUM) and, as James Cooper records, described them to the Conservative 1922 Committee as 'the enemy within' (214, n. 53). John Saville points to an example of an orchestrated campaign against the strikers, an occasion where the television news switched the chronological sequence of a key confrontation, so as to implicate the miners as its initiators rather than admit that the police had made an unprovoked attack:

> the supposed riot at Orgreave: a day of violence which probably more than any other single incident convinced large sections of British opinion that the miners were guilty of mindless violence. It is now (mid August 1985) known to be quite untrue, and a fabrication of the police supported by the mendacious media. (N.pag.)

For a year before the union's capitulation, the government adopted underhand and arguably extra-legal tactics, including coordinating a black propaganda campaign and using police to physically attack miners, and, as Claire Berlinski points out, they had even 'infiltrated MI5 spies into the miners' inner circle' (N.pag.).

Thatcher and her supporters were characterized by self-belief and conviction, not by doubt, which she actively decried. As Linda Leung indicates, Thatcher even 'referred to members of her party as "wets," "waverers and fainthearts" and "moaning minnies"' (36). Not only did she polarize the nation, but she avowed a credo of self-assertion for the successful and powerful. Such egotistical attributes informed other key Thatcherite policies as well, including so-called 'monetarism', a term derived from Friedrich von Hayek's *The Road to Serfdom* (1944); Big Bang deregulation in 1986; the poll tax; and the endeavour to 'free' workers by limiting the power of trade unions, disciplining members to flout majority decisions and outlawing secondary strikes and 'flying' pickets. Konzelmann, Fovargue-Davies and Wilkinson comment of the decade, 'It would also see the (by now familiar) bias towards the City not only continue but increase dramatically, with wholesale deregulation and an expansion of credit that would turn Britain from a nation of shopkeepers into a nation of shoppers' (11). Attitudes towards personal indebtedness thus were transformed. This was part of a wider cultural and social revolution that occurred in the 1980s, and even though its effects upon huge swathes of individuals were negative, individualism blossomed, fuelling a fevered obsession with property ownership and the predominance of the profit motive. The authorization for such attitudinal shifts apparently derived from the power and opinions of the so-called Iron Lady, avowing a share-owning, propertied democracy that would radicalize the nation. Essentially, Thatcher came to embody a set of ideas. Retrospectively judged, at least in domestic terms, her influence can be regarded as remarkable only if winning elections and media spin are the key points of determination, but a judgement based on economic well-being is much less sure, her major legacy being a largely de-industrialized nation.

As suggested above, some of the most powerful voices raised in opposition to Thatcher and her governments came from writers and artists. However, the decade also had paradoxical effects for the novel and the arts more generally. Thatcherite economic policies and the ideologies which supported and surrounded them had little time for a definition of culture beyond the financial, but opposition to Thatcher revitalized the arts in many ways. Indeed, the 1980s have been seen by many critics and commentators as a flowering of the British novel, with Dominic Head identifying it as 'a period of renaissance in English fiction' (45). After the anxieties during the 1970s around the 'death of the novel' from critics such as Bernard Bergonzi in his *The Situation of the Novel* (1970), fiction in the 1980s exploded with renewed formal innovation, political bite and the variety of new perspectives, styles and backgrounds of its authors. As Frederick M. Holmes argues in Chapter 6, 'intellectual strains contributed to a pervasive crisis of authority within the fiction of the 1980s, which revealed itself not only in content and themes but also in generic instability and plurality'. In this way, the decade's stylistic heterogeneity registered its resistance to ideological conformism.

However, it is also the case that the decade saw the industry that produces the novel, literary publishing, change beyond recognition, and become, as Giles Clark has argued, part of the 'larger media leisure industry' (15). The implications and consequences of this change for this generation's reading of the novel, and for the nature of the novel's 'renaissance' in the 1980s, are complex. The shifts within British publishing in the 1980s can be seen both as *producing* the revitalized novel and as helping us to *see* that revitalization in new and more critical ways.

British publishing had struggled in the testing economic climate of the 1970s. In 1974, following the worldwide oil crisis between the autumn of 1973 and the beginning of 1974, during which oil prices quadrupled, the number of new titles fell for the first time in two decades. The price of paper rose by 600 per cent between 1972 and 1980, and printing costs rose by about 30 per cent annually as Randall Stevenson indicates (145). As a consequence, the price of books too rose sharply. Publishers' fortunes were additionally dented through severe cuts to the funding of public libraries in Britain across the decade. As an indication of the serious state of the industry during the 1970s, Penguin, which had transformed publishing through its 'paperback revolution' from the mid-1930s on, made a loss in 1979.

This was the context for one of the most powerful and determining forces to shape the novel in 1980s: the swift and almost total absorption of independent publishers into large, multinational conglomerates. Although this was not completely new – as Stevenson says, *Author* magazine had noted a 'trend towards amalgamation' as early as 1960 (146) and Penguin had been bought by Pearson Longman in 1970 – the speed and comprehensive nature of the changes in ownership were unprecedented. By the 1990s, most of Britain's major publishers had been absorbed into larger companies: either large publishing conglomerates or even larger multinational companies whose interests went far beyond publishing. Publishers including Routledge, Methuen, Chatto & Windus, Bodley Head and Jonathan Cape, all of which had been independent since their origins in the nineteenth and early twentieth centuries, had been absorbed by the end of the decade. By 1990, the number of publishers had been severely reduced, while the size of those remaining had significantly increased.

The reasons for these changes are rooted in the policies of Thatcherism, as well as in the shifts of capitalism globally. The deregulation of the financial markets in the US in the 1970s and the UK in the 1980s provided one of the most significant origins for these changes. As Giles Clark argues:

> The deregulation of the financial markets led to increased availability of long- and short-term equity and debt financing allowing large publishers or their parents to take over medium-sized publishers, and small publishers to expand or start-up. Book publishing was attractive to investors who could see that the industry had consistently ... returned pre-tax profits and return on capital above the average level of all industries ... (15)

While many lamented this loss of independence and what they saw as the reduction in commitment to literary and intellectual value as a consequence, these mergers gave the ailing industry a new lease of life. Such large companies, many of them with more broadly based interests and products, were more able to withstand economic instabilities, and their centralized structures reduced costs in key areas such as distribution, publicity and marketing. However, it is the case too that the new locations for literary publishing entailed changes in focus and priority. As Stevenson argues:

> A more efficient, profitable industry, on the other hand, was not necessarily any more democratically oriented to its choice of texts for publication, nor more

reliable in sustaining a range of literary or cultural forms... Though publishing increasingly benefited from the security and flexibility of corporate finance, this inevitably entailed a primary commitment to corporate profit-seeking. (147–148)

While earlier critics concentrated on the revitalizing of the novel in the 1980s as a critical response to Thatcherism and its consequences, more recent critics have seen the new forms of the novel during the decade as at least in part a *product* of the new economic realities. As Stevenson suggests, the '[c]ombination of innovation and tradition', which he sees in the British novel from the 1980s on, 'could be seen as motivated directly by the need to appeal to a wide audience, though one increasingly well-educated and sophisticated in its literary tastes' (161).

The relations between accessibility and the commercial can also be seen in another aspect of literary culture which changed significantly in the 1980s, that of literary prizes. While the Booker Prize – the leading literary prize for the novel in the UK – began in 1969, a number of critics have seen the 1980s as the period during which this award and prize culture became significant and, according to James English, the moment in which the Booker 'finally achieved real economic importance' (172). As Richard Todd reports, the Booker award ceremony was first televised in 1981, and from that date the shortlisted novels, and even more so the winners, achieved extremely high sales, relative to most literary novels (104–105). Brian Finney's Chapter 7 speaks to this new popularity, as it explores British fiction's reception by American readers and the shift which ensued in its popularity following changes to the way it was read and marketed. As he writes, 'The supra-national trend noted in British fiction during the decade, itself partly the result of American influence, made American novelists pay renewed attention to British fiction, after at least half a century of conscious rejection of the yet earlier ascendancy of British fiction in the United States'. In this way, a new literary market in the 1980s gave British writing a new fascination for American readers.

The mixed fortunes brought by the changes in ownership in literary publishing, and the effects of the place of literary prizes and their central place in the media, are particularly clear when considering the role of other media in the shape and dynamics of publishing during the decade. The relation between books and the television – which had long been seen as a threat to the cultural status of the book, and to the novel in particular – changed through the consequences of such mergers. Many of the large conglomerates which had absorbed Britain's literary publishers also had stakes in television companies, or at the very least, rather than being suspicious of, were highly aware of the medium's potential for marketing and publicity. By 1980, 98 per cent of households in Britain had a TV, and while many saw this as a marker of cultural doom, as Stevenson indicates, polls and surveys during the decade indicated that 'as many as 22 per cent of book-buyers had been influenced by some connection between their chosen volume and television' (128). In less obvious ways, too, as Stevenson argues, the domination of the leisure of the nation by television can be seen as productive for the place and status of the novel:

> The central position of a television set in every living room ensured that fictional worlds were more easily and immediately available than at any time in history, and that late twentieth-century life was daily drenched in narrative. (128)

In Steven Connor's words, television, rather than being seen as a rival, can be seen in the decade as becoming 'largely fiction publishing carried out by other means' (18).

These changes undoubtedly, however, shifted literary publishing from being led by the product to being led by the market. André Schiffin has argued that one consequence of this has been what he calls 'market censorship' (103); that is, that it is no longer the state which controls what can and cannot be published, but profitability. As Claire Squires has argued:

> The reversal of the traditional book economy of long-termism and the backlist towards a short-term, mass-market logic has been profound. Increasing advance levels have meant that publishers make greater initial financial outlay, which demands to be quickly recouped. The shelf life of books is short – worryingly so to many. Short-termism encourages novelty, and the late twentieth century has seen a growing pressure on novelists to produce works of fiction with greater regularity, to counteract short shelf lives and the threat of returns. (189–190)

Such structural demands for accessibility, marketability and commercial success are now being seen as playing at least a part in the aesthetic choices of some of the most celebrated, and ostensibly critical, novelists of the decade, as noted in Chapters 1 and 5 by Emily Horton and Alex Murray, respectively. These shifts were heightened by changes in the selling of books during the decade. Over the 1960s and 1970s, bookshops had found it increasingly hard to make a profit. At the same time, many buyers felt intimidated by bookshops and excluded by their elitist attitudes and associations. The opening of two new kinds of bookshops, Waterstones and Dillons, in the early 1980s radically changed the nature of bookselling. The stores stressed accessibility and comfort for the costumer, and eschewed the traditional divisions between elite and more mass market publishing. Both companies were very soon absorbed into the WHSmith group by the end of the 1980s, an indication that such attitudes to the sector quickly became mainstream. Again, accessibility moved to centre stage in another arm of the literary industry.

As well as being a vital site of the novel's imbrications with the commercial, a number of critics have linked the rise of the literary prize to Britain's postcolonial state. As English has argued about the Booker, 'It was a postcolonial prize by means of which London could – couldn't *not* – reaffirm its domination of the formerly colonized space. And it was paid for by a company eager to put literature in service of rehabilitating an ugly colonial past' (169). The postcolonial as a key factor in the decade goes beyond the nature of literary prizes, though. It is the case that any account of British fiction in the 1980s must necessarily consider the significance of postcolonialism to that period. This is in part because of the new wide-scale critical influence of theorists such as Edward Said, Homi Bhabha and Gayatri Chakravorty Spivak, which both Neil Lazarus (1) and John McLeod in *Beginning Postcolonialism* (24) attribute to making the 1980s the starting point for postcolonial studies. However, it is also because of new developments in British culture and writing itself in this decade, where a new or altered attention to issues of race, place and ethnicity, largely provoked by the reactionary racism of Thatcherite policies, worked to politicize and re-conceive 1980s 'Black Britishness'. Thus, on the one hand, as Lazarus notes, '[b]efore the late 1970s, there was no field of academic specialization that went by the name of "postcolonial studies" ' (1):

> [We]e could argue that 'postcolonial criticism' could not possibly have existed before the 1980s, not because it would have lacked an adequate audience then, but because it would have made no sense at all in the historic-ideological context of the 1970s. (6)

Thus, while the 1970s tended to understand 'postcolonial writing' principally as 'a periodizing term, an historical and not an ideological concept' (4), and where the shift in political economy to the 'New World order' was part of what galvanized theorists to define 'postcolonialism', it was precisely the new influence of theorists such as Said, Bhabha and Spivak, as well as Benedict Anderson, Mary Louise Pratt, Peter Hulme, Henry Louis Gates and V. Y. Mudimbe, which helped to initiate 'postcolonial studies' ideologically in the 1980s, a discipline later brought under fire by critics in the following decades (see McClintock (1994), Dirlik (1999) and Huggan (2001)). As McLeod (2000) comments, these theorists '[s]ensitised ... a new generation of critics' to the importance of theory in contemplating imperial relations (23), and, we might add, in exploring such difficult and necessary concepts as colonial discourse, ambivalence, hybridity, nationalism and subaltern identity. In this way, postcolonial theorists moved scholarship away from 'the earlier, humanist approaches which characterized criticism of Commonwealth literature' and towards a more critical form of reading (23–24).

On the other hand, equally important to this decade is the specific context of Thatcherite Britain and the considerable struggles that immigrant and minority communities confronted within this. Thus, rather than reflecting merely a new framework of emergent critical thinking, which, as Dirlik notes, might also have been accused of 'covering up the origins of postcolonial intellectuals in a global capitalism of which they are not so much victims as beneficiaries' (353), writers in Britain also engaged with a specific *national* context in which the politicization of race under Thatcher made feasible and necessary a notable shift in cultural dynamics. Thus, as Bailey et al. explain, ' "blackness" in Britain means something rather different from what it means in the United States – specifying primarily, particularly in the 1980s, an act of social and political identification' (xxi). Likewise, Mark Christian notes how '[t]he 1980s ushered in great socio-economic despair for Britain's working class and Black communities. Urban disturbances in 1981, that were initiated by both draconian policing methods of Black communities and a distinct lack of economic opportunity for the youths, led to the worst rioting ever witnessed on maintained Britain' (333). And McLeod (2004), somewhat more positively, explains how '[s]ubjected to repeated police harassment, institutionalized racism and discrimination in jobs, housing, and living in some of the most neglected areas in London, many in the black communities organized themselves politically and began forcefully to resist the behaviour of the police who had come to resemble, in A. Sivanandan's stark phrase, "an army of occupation" ' (130). Within this tense context, the importance of 'Black British' fiction was not only to help make visible the discrimination and violence prevalent within 1980s British society against Black communities but also to mobilize and animate a Black British politics and artistry.

Thus, in response to what Stuart Hall et al. (1978) and Paul Gilroy (1987) identified as the 'policing' of African, South East Asian and Caribbean communities, including but not limited to the Nationality Act of 1981 and the antagonism of police prior to and in the 1981 riots, British authors such as Salman Rushdie, Buchi Emecheta, Jackie Kay, Barbara Burford, Joan Riley, Caryl Phillips, Tsitsi Dangarembga and Hanif Kureishi activated a discourse of 'Blackness', which recognized the legitimacy of non-white belonging within contemporary Britain and across a variety of cultural ethnicities. As Prabhu Guptara wrote (in 1986), 'Being "black" is a matter of visibility, with social and political consequences ... In my view, therefore, "black Britons" are those people of non-European origin, who are now, or were in the past, entitled to hold a British passport and displayed a substantial commitment to Britain' (14), a claim quoted in evidence of significant issues of identity by Mark Stein (8). In other words, 1980s Black writers and critics made clear an identification *through race* which was not limited to any single racial background (e.g. in the way that African American politics were in the US). Likewise, Kobena Mercer comments on the significantly non-elite nature of this enactment, wherein 'the new cultural trends of the 1980s – from rap and hip hop or black women's writing in the States, to black British film, fine art and photography – came from the margins, from subjects and spaces historically marginalized from the centres of power and authority in liberal society' (32). In this way, 'Blackness' worked to disrupt and subvert established Conservative social frameworks.

Indeed, what distinguishes this 1980s generation from that which preceded it in Britain, including the 'Windrush generation' of V. S. Naipaul, Sam Selvon, Beryl Gilroy, William Harris and George Lamming, is the recognition of a simultaneous belonging *within* the political category of 'Black British' *and* a multiplicity of Black identities and interests not always aligned to the question of race, an issue Stein touches on (4). Thus, in response to (or in echo of) Hall's essay 'New Ethnicities', which distinguishes how 'black artists and cultural workers now have to struggle not on one but on *two* fronts' in order to recognize political solidarity whilst also admitting 'the immense diversity and differentiation of historical and cultural experience of black subjects' (443–444), authors (including those of various gender, sexual, class, national and ethnic backgrounds) began to explore and differentiate the variable, 'unsettling' and hybridized nature of 'Blackness' in the context of a very diverse 1980s cultural experience (448). As Stein comments:

> What Hall refers to as the 'politics of ethnicity predic[a]ted on difference and diversity' ... is a move towards strengthening the political concept of Black British identity in the plural, precisely by weakening its boundaries, by making it a more pluralist concept. (13)

On a similar note, James Procter writes of how '[t]he late 1980s witnessed a radical re-interrogation of notions of a "unified" black community as a new set of theoretical agendas began to accumulate towards the end of what became termed "a critical decade"' (6). In this way, in Hall's own words, the second half of the 1980s saw a 'recognition that "black" is essentially a politically and culturally constructed category, which cannot be grounded in a set of fixed transcultural or transcendental categories and which therefore has no guarantees in Nature' (443). Black British authors embraced this hybridizing and socially constructed understanding of 'Blackness' in the 1980s, initiating a more diversified, but also contextualized and embedded, Black British writing.

The writers explored in this collection, in particular Rushdie, Emecheta, Burford and Riley, speak to this 'new ethnic' understanding, exploring visions of Black British identity complicated by a particularized awareness of Indian-Pakistani, Nigerian and Jamaican migrant history, as well as (for the three latter writers) a particular focus on Black British *women's* experience, as Susan Fischer explores in Chapter 4. This is so despite Rushdie – through his dismissive response to John Akomfrah's *Handsworth Songs* – having provoked Hall's 'New Ethnicities' essay (448–450). Nevertheless, of course, not all of what is read as 1980s British postcolonial writing is Black British, or indeed even written by authors from a colonial background, as writers such as Timothy Mo and Kazuo Ishiguro make clear. For each of these writers, their texts explore British imperialism and its legacies from outside Black Britain, but with an awareness of both national and global postcolonial immigration. Also significant are the numerous Scottish, Welsh and Northern Irish fiction writers who emerged in the 1980s – such as Iain Banks, Alasdair Gray, James Kelman, Bernice Rubens and Robert McLiam Wilson – who were working *within* a British cultural context, but who wrote overwhelmingly in defence of national devolution. Monica Germanà's Chapter 2 explores this critical emergence in relation to 1980s Scottish writers, who, she argues, were not shy in voicing their antipathy to and disillusionment with Thatcherite nationalism. More generally, the chapters in this volume make evident the wealth of Black British, minority, immigrant and pro-devolution voices which came forward in the 1980s and which put into motion a heterogeneous but in many ways mobilized and integrated anti-hegemonic writing.

The rise of postcolonialism as a theoretical position and critical practice during the decade drew on wider theoretical contexts and debates which themselves shaped both novels and the subsequent readings of them. As we have suggested, by the 1980s, Britain as a society seemed both ailing and divided. As Stephen Brooke and Louise Cameron comment:

> [T]he seventies and early 1980s were marked by crisis: from the 1972 miners' strike to the IMF loan of 1976, through the 'Winter of Discontent' in 1978–79, and inner city riots in the summer of 1981. Inevitably, such crisis was accompanied by the dissembling of the political order, of which the social

democratic or liberal capitalist post-war consensus was the most obvious victim, with Thatcherism on the right and Bennism on the left, and by a heightened sense of social disorder, whether over race relations, industrial disputes, or the unity of the United Kingdom itself. (639)

Where such polarizations prevailed – with a seemingly old-style social democracy and its consensus both under threat by the 1980s – the resulting schisms emerged quite differently in various fields and institutions. From the 1970s, a new generation of literary and humanities scholars had adopted 'theory', an umbrella term which served as shorthand for the deployment of scholarly concepts and ideas drawn from various strands of continental philosophy and sociology. 'Theory' opposed traditional scholarship, which proponents of the former regarded as being based on an unwarranted assumption that art could record accurately an objective world independent of the observer by a system of reference that mirrored reality. The proponents of 'theory' objected to such certainties, and generally supported in contrast structuralism and post-structuralism, both of which regard words and representation as signs that are arbitrarily imposed, having no necessary connection to the world of things. Debates on the academic merits of such divergent approaches became highly politicized and known as 'the theory wars', often an intensely ideological, inter-generational struggle. This was epitomized for many by a particular controversy which occurred at Cambridge University with regard to the teaching of and research into literary studies. In 1981, senior members of the English faculty bitterly contested Colin McCabe's upgrading to a full lectureship after his sabbatical spent in Paris, objecting in part to his subsequent avowal of post-structuralism and championing of the work of, among others, Jacques Derrida, Jacques Lacan, Michel Foucault and Gilles Deleuze. As Francis Mulhern has stated, 'the effect of such a critique, if it were carried to a victorious conclusion, would be to undermine the *authority* of literature and so confound the long standing claim of literary intellectuals to privileged cultural insight' (28). This was part of a wider struggle provoked by new approaches to the subject, which confronted what Nick Peim describes as 'the ideologically loaded nature of English' (5) as a subject for study, while claiming that '[l]iberal ideas held by the advocates of creativity have never been interested in situating the subject within the context of its history as institutionalized discourse' (5–6). The McCabe Affair, accompanied by a veritable media frenzy, followed the young lecturer's departure from Cambridge in the summer of 1981 having failed to win a permanent position, despite ably fulfilling the necessary criteria. In a sense, it was a precursor of the far wider 'culture wars' of the late twentieth century, when the deconstructive approach, in the words of David Lodge, challenged the traditional canon in literary studies. He continues:

> It extended the scope of traditional literary criticism to take in the whole range of cultural production, and it spawned a number of new, nonaesthetic approaches to this material under a bewildering variety of names – the New Historicism, post-colonial studies, subaltern studies, queer theory, and so on, each with its own jargon, periodicals, and conferences. Most of these projects were seen, and saw themselves, as belonging to that even looser and larger phenomenon known as 'postmodernism'. (N.pag.)

A range of post-structuralist and postmodern intellectuals offered apparently fundamental challenges to the very foundations of Enlightenment rationality, exhibiting preferences for the plural and the ludic, endorsing bricolage, the fragmentary and pastiche, the aesthetic possibilities of which influenced many writers who came to prominence in the decade. In Chapter 8, Ana-Karina Schneider explores this influence in relation to two authors not always regarded as experimental, but who, she argues, 'epitomized the current realism–experimentalism dichotomy' for many Romanian readers: that is, Iris Murdoch and John Fowles. As she puts it, 'their ambivalent situation vis-à-vis postmodernism enabled interpretations that were sites where theories of representation played themselves out and were tested'. However, as Schneider also recognizes, the belief that one might retain 'grand narratives', to use the phrase of Jean-François Lyotard, had not disappeared completely. At the end of the decade, Francis Fukuyama published the highly influential and controversial essay 'The End of History?' (1989) amidst the collapse of the Soviet Union and the wider disappearance of communism as a state ideology. Here, Fukuyama challenged postmodern academic cynicism regarding democracy's viability within late capitalism, instead defending liberal democracy as the most sustainable system available. As Jan-Werner Müller suggests:

> Nor was Fukuyama's 'End of History' the naïve, liberal triumphalism it has so often been made out to be in retrospect – and as it has been subject to endless ridicule. Fukuyama, after all, did not predict the end of all conflict and violence; rather, he asserted that there was, in the long run, no attractive alternative way of life or way of organizing human collectives that could rival liberal democracy. He predicted that the world was going to go the way of post-Hitler – that is, 'post-ideological' and therefore 'post-historical' – Western Europe, and that there would in all likelihood be a 'Common-Marketization' of international relations.

> Fukuyama was not afraid of asserting what both the postmodern and the methodological individualism of Hayek and other libertarians had allegedly discredited: a 'grand narrative'. (21)

Fukuyama's work in some ways appeared to run counter to another movement in literary studies towards the end of the 1980s; scholars embraced a 'turn to history', by once again asserting historical and political context as central to criticism, but not necessarily in traditional ways. As Andrew Bennett and Nicholas Royle argue, 'During the 1980s and 1990s, the political dimensions of reading became increasingly central to critical debate' (13). They comment, concerning new historicism:

> [N]ew historicists argue that the production of literary texts is a cultural practice different only in its specific mode or formulation from other practices – from furniture-making to teaching to warfare to printing. No absolute distinction can be made between literary and other cultural practices…Literary texts are embedded within the social and economic circumstances in which they are produced and consumed. But what is important for new historicists is that these circumstances are not stable in themselves and are susceptible to being rewritten and transformed. (115)

In the UK, this politically engaged turn to history, which attempted to see beyond conventional notions of literary value and to self-consciously think through the present's investment in privileging certain versions of the past, was most influentially seen in the work of critics such as Jonathan Dollimore and Alan Sinfield, both at the time at the University of Sussex. In the work they co-edited, *Political Shakespeare: Essays in Cultural Materialism* (1985), they set out a kind of manifesto for their work, which they call cultural materialism, a phrase and practice originated by the Marxist cultural critic Raymond Williams:

> Cultural materialism does not pretend to political neutrality. It knows that no cultural practice is ever without political significance – not the production of *King Lear* at the Globe, or at the Barbican, or as a text in a school, popular or learned edition, or in literary criticism, or in the present volume. Cultural materialism does not, like much established literary criticism, attempt to mystify its perspective as the natural, obvious or right interpretation of an allegedly given textual fact. On the contrary, it registers its commitment to the transformation of a social order which exploits people on grounds of race, gender and class. (viii)

Sinfield's contributions to the collection together constitute a reading of contemporary appropriations of the figure of Shakespeare for right-wing ideological purposes, in particular as a guarantor of Englishness, English history and class privilege. In cultural materialism, the effects of Thatcher's project, the postcolonial state of the country, the rise of theory and a sense of the complicity of both literature and literary criticism with the institutions of power all came together in the 1980s to produce a variety of cultural impulses largely running counter to the period's political zeitgeist.

Works cited

Akomfrah, John. Dir. *Handsworth Songs*. Black Audio Film Collective, 1986.
Bailey, David A., Ian Baucom and Sonya Boyce. *Shades of Black: Assembling Black Arts in 1980s Britain*. Durham, NC: Duke University Press, 2005.
Bennett, Andrew and Nicholas Royle. *An Introduction to Literature, Criticism and Theory*. 3rd ed. Harlow and London: Pearson Longman, 2005.
Bergonzi, Bernard. *The Situation of the Novel*. London: Macmillan, 1970.
Berlinski, Claire. 'Five Myths about Margaret Thatcher.' *Washington Post*. 22 December 2008. http://www.berlinski.com/node/161. N.Pag.
Bleasdale, Alan. *Boys from the Blackstuff*. 10 October 1982–7 November 1982. Producer: Michael Wearing. BBC 2 series, 5 episodes.
Brooke, Stephen and Louise Cameron. 'Anarchy in the U.K.? Ideas of the City and the "Fin de Siècle" in Contemporary English Film and Literature.' *Albion: A Quarterly Journal Concerned with British Studies* 28(4) (Winter 1996): 635–656.
Christian, Mark. 'The Politics of Black Presence in Britain and Black Male Exclusion in the British Education System.' *Journal of Black Studies* 35(3) (January 2005): 327–346.
Clark, Giles. *Inside Book Publishing*. 3rd ed. London: Routledge, 2001.
Connor, Steven. *The English Novel in History 1950–1995*. London: Routledge, 1996.
Cooper, James. *Margaret Thatcher and Ronald Reagan: A Very Political Special Relationship*. Basingstoke and New York: Palgrave Macmillan, 2012.
Davies, Pete. *The Last Election*. London: Andre Deutsch, 1986.
Dirlik, Arif. 'The Postcolonial Aura: Third World Criticism in the Age of Global Capitalism.' *Critical Inquiry* 20(2) (Winter 1994): 328–356.
Dollimore, Jonathan and Alan Sinfield (eds). *Political Shakespeare: Essays in Cultural Materialism* (1985). 2nd ed. Manchester: Manchester University Press, 1994.
English, James F. 'The Literary Prize Phenomenon in Context'. In *A Companion to the British and Irish Novel 1945–2000*. Ed. Brian W. Shaffer. Oxford: Blackwell, 2005, 160–176.
Fukuyama, Francis. 'The End of History?' *The National Interest* 16 (Summer 1989): 3–18.
Gash, Norman. 'The Year before Thatcher: June 1978–May 1979.' In *A Decade of Revolution: The Thatcher Years*. Ed. Madsen Pirie. London: Adam Smith Institute, 1989, 5–8. http://www.adamsmith.org/sites/default/files/images/uploads/publications/ThatDecade.pdf.

Gilroy, Paul. *There Ain't No Black in the Union Jack*. Chicago: University of Chicago Press, 1987.
Goodman, Alissa and Andrew Shephard. *Inequality and Living Standards in Great Britain: Some Facts*. Briefing Note No. 19. London: Institute of Fiscal Studies. December 2002 (research funded by the Nuffield Foundation, as part of the project, *Inequality in the 1990s*, grant number OPD/00111/G).
Guptara, Prabhu. *Black British Literature: An Annotated Bibliography*. London: Dangaroo Press, 1986.
Hall, Stuart. 'New Ethnicities.' In *Stuart Hall: Critical Dialogues in Cultural Studies*. Ed. David Morley and Kuan-Hsing Chen. London: Routledge, 1996.
Hall, S., C. Critcher, T. Jefferson, J. Clarke and B. Roberts. *Policing the Crisis*. London: Palgrave Macmillan, 1978.
Head, Dominic. *The Cambridge Introduction to Modern British Fiction, 1950–2000*. Cambridge: Cambridge University Press, 2002.
Hills, John. *Thatcherism, New Labour and the Welfare State*. CASE paper 13. August 1998. London: Centre for Analysis of Social Exclusion, London School of Economics. http://eprints.lse.ac.uk/5553/1/Thatcherism_New_Labour_and_the_ Welfare_State.pdf.
HM Treasury. *The Government's Expenditure Plans 1980–81*. Cmnd 7746. London: HMSO, 1979.
Huggan, Graham. *The Postcolonial Exotic: Marketing the Margins*. London: Routledge, 2001.
Institute for Fiscal Studies. *Tax Tables*. http://www.ifs.org.uk/fiscalFacts/taxTables.
Kitson, Michael and Jonathan Michie. 'Britain's Industrial Performance since 1960: Underinvestment and Relative Decline.' *The Economic Journal* 106(434) (January 1996): 196–212.
Konzelmann, Suzanne J., Marc Fovargue-Davies and Frank Wilkinson. 'Thatcherism: "A Heavy Hand and a Light Touch."' *Social Science Research Network* (1 March 2012). http://ssrn.com/abstract=2049438.
Lazarus, Neil. 'Introducing Postcolonial Studies.' In *The Cambridge Companion to Postcolonial Literary Studies*. Ed. Neil Lazarus. Cambridge: Cambridge University Press, 2004, 1–16.
Leung, Linda. 'The Making of Matriarchy: A Comparison of Madonna and Margaret Thatcher.' *Journal of Gender Studies* 6(1) (March 1997): 33–42.
Lodge, David. 'Goodbye to All That.' *The London Review of Books* (27 May 2004). http://www.nybooks.com/articles/archives/2004/may/27/goodbye-to-all-that/?pagination=false.
Lyotard, Jean-Francois. *The Postmodern Condition: A Report on Knowledge*. Minneapolis: University of Minnesota Press, 1984.
McCabe, Colin. 'A Tale of Two Theories.' *New Statesman* (26 September 2011). http://www.newstatesman.com/education/2011/09/cambridge-english-kermode.
McClintock, Anne. 'The Angel of Progress: Pitfalls of the Term "Post-colonialism."' *Social Text* 31/32 (Third World and Post-Colonial Issues) (1992): 84–89.

McLeod, John. *Beginning Postcolonialism*. Manchester: Manchester University Press, 2000.
———. *Postcolonial London: Rewriting the Metropolis*. London: Routledge, 2004.
Mercer, Kobena. 'Back to My Roots: A Postscript to the 1980s.' In *Critical Decade: Black British Photography in the 80's*. Ed. D. Bailey and S. Hall *Ten.8*, 2(3) (1992): 32-39.
Monaghan, David. 'Margaret Thatcher, Alan Bleasdale, and the Struggle for Working Class Identity.' *Journal of Popular Film and Television* 29(1) (Spring 2001): 2–13.
Mota, Miguel. 'Mike Leigh's High Hopes: Troubling Home in Thatcher's Britain.' *Film Criticism* 32(3) (Spring 2008): 24–40.
Mulhern, Francis. 'The Cambridge Affair.' *Marxism Today* (March 1981): 27–28.
Müller, Jan-Werner. 'The Cold War and the Intellectual History of the Late Twentieth Century.' In *The Cambridge History of the Cold War, Vol. 3: Endings 1975–1991*. Ed. Melvyn P. Leffler and Odd Arne Westad. Cambridge: Cambridge University Press, 2010, 1–22.
Peck, Brian V. *The Myth of Real Democracy and Other Myths of Modernity*. Bloomington, IN: AuthorHouse, 2011.
Peim, Nick. *Critical Theory and the English Teacher: Transforming the Subject*. London: Routlege, 1993.
Pettinger, Tom. 'Jim Callaghan: A Successful Prime Minister?' *E-international Relations* (7 December 2010): N.pag. http://www.e-ir.info/2010/12/07/jim-callaghan-a-successful-prime-minister/.
Procter, James. *Dwelling Places: Post-war Black British Writing*. Manchester: Manchester University Press, 2003.
Saville, John. 'An Open Conspiracy: Conservative Politics and the Miners' Strike 1984–5.' *The Socialist Register 1985/6* (August 1985): 295–329; *Marxists' Internet Archive*. http://www.marxists.org/archive/saville/1985/08/miners.htm.
Schiffin, André. *The Business of Books. How Conglomerates Took Over Publishing and Changed the Way We Read*. London and New York: Verso, 2000.
Sivanandan, A. *A Different Hunger: Writings on Black Resistance*. London: Pluto, 1962.
Squires, Claire. *Marketing Literature: The Making of Contemporary Writing in Britain*. Basingstoke: Palgrave, 2007.
Stein, Mark. *Black British Literature: Novels of Transformation*. Columbus, OH: Ohio State University Press, 2004.
Stevenson, Randall. *The Oxford English Literary History, Volume 12. 1960–2000. The Last of England?* Oxford: Oxford University Press, 2005.
Tew, Philip. *The Contemporary British Novel*. 2nd ed. London and New York: Continuum, 2007.
Todd, Richard. *Consuming Fictions: The Booker Prize and Fiction in Britain Today*. London: Bloomsbury, 1996.
Von Hayek, Friedrich. *The Road to Serfdom*. London: Routledge, 1944.

1

Literary History of the Decade
The Bomb, Kidnappings and Yuppies: British Fiction in the 1980s

Emily Horton

Given the difficult task of isolating and distinguishing a particular decade of literature from those that precede and follow it, what Colin Hutchinson calls the 'packaged' character of 1980s politics (7), beginning with the elections of Margaret Thatcher and Ronald Reagan in 1979 and 1980, respectively, and closing with the fall of the Berlin Wall and the end of apartheid in South Africa in 1989 and 1991, seems to offer an advantage. Of course, this formulation is itself something of a fiction, discounting the ways in which these events were both precipitated by and antecedent of other historical happenings, not least the 1973 OPEC crisis before and the general prolongation of neo-liberal politics after. Novels like Pat Barker's *Union Street* (1982) and Hanif Kureishi's *The Buddha of Suburbia* (1990) reflect on this continuity, making clear a larger, more graduated historical-political framework. Even so, in so far as this decade did issue a host of new young 1980s authors – highly politicized in their writing and overwhelmingly anti-Thatcherite in their cause – this expression of 'packaged' singularity does retain pertinence, aptly reflecting the decade's fiction's motivated stance against Conservatism.

Granting this, this chapter sets out to examine in detail a specific, historically locatable 1980s British fiction, defined not only in terms of publication date but also, equally importantly, by an explicitly leftist and dissenting political agenda. Thus, in accordance with Dominic Head's idea of a 'renaissance in English fiction' in the 1980s, in which Thatcher's 'radical and divisive political strategy...stimulated outrage from the novelist' (45), I see this period as responding directly to contemporary institutions, rejecting the dominant Thatcherite agenda and upholding against this a critical, collectivist ideology, hostile in many ways to free market individualism. Or rather I wish to qualify this argument in some important respects. I want to argue that what is conceived of as 1980s counter-culture today – including such names as Martin Amis, Salman Rushdie, Ian McEwan, Graham Swift, Kazuo Ishiguro and Jeanette Winterson – while indeed important in articulating and motivating anti-Thatcherite dissent, especially in its creative subversion of dominant Conservative discourses, has nevertheless achieved this status in part through its critical and market appropriation, in a society in which liberal left thinking has become the new literary orthodoxy.

This argument demands some elaboration. Certainly a move to the left in terms of literary criticism is by no means a negative occurrence: the post-war period had been dominated in many ways by a very conservative critical apparatus, which, while recognizing literature's value in influencing social change, understood this in largely elitist terms, as a product of innate truth and natural insight and in this way relevant to all cultures indifferently. What was elitist about this understanding was its implications in terms of how this truth should be arrived at: that is, precisely in accordance with existing tradition-based institutions of class and gender and with hierarchies of ethnicity and nationalist sentiment. Alan Sinfield writes of how 'in the postwar settlement... art and literature were envisaged as good things which (like healthcare and social security) would be generally available within welfare capitalism' (xxxiv). Emphasis was placed on universal application and empathy rather than cultural specificity, and in this way Englishness and patriarchy remained largely unchallenged norms. The 1980s in some senses saw a change to this, with the rise of a post-structuralist and cultural materialist mode of reading which understood literature in textual and *con*textual terms, as linguistically specific and taking part in (rather than separate from) historical and cultural processes – that is, as taking part in the construction of ideology. Steven Connor writes of how

> [b]y the 1980s, only the oldest of old fogeys was still asserting that the greatness of *Ulysses* consisted in the way in which it reduced the world to rule, or transfigured it into form. Everywhere one looked, *Ulysses* was being discovered and proclaimed as the great precursor of postmodernist novels in letting in, or letting itself out into, the multiplicity of things. (69)

Thus historical particularity and multiplicity became dominant literary critical values.

Even so, as Sinfield insists, the marketing of culture as a fungible consumer commodity in the 1980s, valuable primarily for its economic status rather than its cultural critique, empties this perception to some extent of its critical impact, reducing multiplicity and democracy to packaged simulacra and allowing deep-set institutional prejudices to remain intact. Thus, the 'themes [of new-right ideology] are made the more insidious by the way they vary certain radical themes: the libertarian impulse... is reorganised as aggressive individualism; the wish for a collective identification is parodied by racist ideology; the idea that the personal is the political is shrivelled to belief in "the family"' (335). In effect, cultural meaning itself becomes coordinate with the market, as mainstream consumerism finds more and cleverer ways of containing dissidence and explicating injustice in accordance with its own right-wing agenda. While 1980s 'leftist' fiction does not necessarily take part in this manoeuvre, retaining a textual ability to be read in multiple and contrasting ways, nevertheless a tendency within contemporary criticism to read this oeuvre in largely left liberal terms, as the function of a global and class-independent 'postmodern' critique, supports this perception, undercutting fiction's sociological and ideological importance in favour of 'experiment'.

Indeed, part of what is notable about 1980s literary criticism ideologically is its evident departure from the radical ideas of 1960s and 1970s subculture, where what was presented in the latter as a critical imperative towards protest – in the form of identity politics and Marxist dissent – is in the former translated in part into a philosophical ideal, in which meaning is conceived of textually, as a condition of language rather than of lived materiality. Paul Sheehan notes that 'in the absence of fixed identities, the fixity of identity politics is also abandoned'. Meaning is transformed into a 'performance' and, correspondingly, 'reluctance [on the part of critics] to see the symbolic economy as unitary means that collective resistance to it, in the guise of political reform or universal panacea, is also untenable' (34). Protest is remodelled as textual scepticism. Of course, this understanding itself can be conceived of as radical, challenging humanism's mythology of universal reason and making representation itself accountable. In this sense, Derrida's 'there is no outside text' is indeed political. Even so, the obsessive focus in much 1980s literary criticism – from Catherine Belsey's *Critical Practice* (1980) to Patricia Waugh's *Metafiction* (1984), Brian McHale's *Postmodernist Fiction* (1987) and Linda Hutcheon's *The Poetics of Postmodernism* (1988) – on *style*, and in particular on stylistic self-reflexivity, suggests implicitly a departure from materialist preoccupations, moving attention instead to textual aesthetics.

This tendency can also be seen within literary marketing. Thus, appropriating from literary criticism the terminology of 'hybridity', 'heterogeneity' and 'in-between-ness', while at the same time conceiving this in largely 'spectacular' terms – as something to be exalted, prized and debated in the context of postmodernism – reviews and advertisements of 1980s fiction often ignore the implicit classist, patriarchal and ethnic biases espoused by these fictions (or espoused by their own sensationalizing of these fictions), seeing these as irrelevant to larger questions of 'eventfulness' and technical complexity. Thus, James F. English explains:

> The sudden emergence of prizes from the arcane recesses of British literary life into the spotlight of national fascination must be seen as part of this radical reconfiguring of the economic and cultural fields. In particular, the sped-up and intensified appetite of cultural consumers for 'events' or 'happenings', as opposed to cultural works as such, exerted a certain pressure on the literary field to produce its own brand of ephemeral spectacle or excitement. ('The Literary Prize Phenomenon in Context' 168)

In effect, 1980s 'prize culture's' complicity with corporate transnational networks, as a means of granting fiction the cultural capital of television and film, prioritized the criteria of stylistic spectacle as a critical principle, in this way emptying contemporary criticism of its material and ideological bases.

Recognizing these tendencies explicitly, this chapter attempts to identify a handful of these literary and literary critical complicities outright, while at the same time giving credit to genuine radical thought within literature where this exists. My concern in particular is to distinguish where 1980s fiction carried on some of the more far-reaching sub-cultural projects of the 1960s and 1970s, projects which, alongside Greenham Common, the miners' strikes and the critical writings of Sinfield, Stuart Hall, John Berger and Paul Gilroy, for example, appreciate the role of art as a vehicle for dissent. My argument is that while dissidence is indeed theoretically valued by many 1980s writers who are now canonical, and while we as readers are inclined to credit this evaluation today – affirming the anger of 'new young 1980s generation' – this attempt in practice often proves problematic. Deep-set anxieties about the possibilities inherent in dissent continue to be evident, and it remains necessary to look outside the mainstream, or to re-read this against the grain, in order to discover a critical vision which is not assimilated by the centre. In effect, I argue that the mutually reinforcing tendencies of the academy and literary fiction need to be thrown into question and in this way a path cleared for an appreciation of both complicity with the literary/political establishment and radical potential.

*

To provide a background for this analysis, I want to begin by exploring briefly Thatcherite society's understanding of dissidence, taking as my premise that certain more individualistic, libertarian forms of dissidence were allowed precisely so that other more collectivist forms might be contained. Writing on this subject directly, Sinfield notes how the impression that Thatcher liked to give of a 'permissive 1960s', entirely divided from her own Conservative policies and at fault for the failures of society, was a hoax: 'the exuberance and disrespect for traditional authority of the 1960s produced, among other things, a property boom and a more frantic chase for satisfaction through consumption.' In other words, capitalism found an anchor in 1960s individualism, which 'liberated [it] from the fig-leaf decencies of old-style Toryism' and in this way cleared the path for Thatcherite enterprise (317). In the context of Sinfield's analysis, focused on the contradictions within the welfare state, this argument itself suggests most obviously not a reprieve for Thatcherism but on the contrary an indictment of 1960s hypocrisy, where the veneer of welfare state 'socialism' is exposed by its opponents as a 'corporate' form of capitalism. As Sinfield puts it: 'whatever we were saying on the left, we hadn't really worked out a system to supersede welfare-capitalism' (xxxii).

Yet, while acknowledging this direction of analysis, there is another sense in which this deceit can also be flipped around. Thus, if the 1960s turn out to be more conservative than it liked to admit, embracing individualism as a means towards unfettered consumerism, in another sense Thatcherite Toryism itself inversely included certain strategic concessions, not least in the area of capital punishment, sexuality and divorce law (as also noted by Hutchinson 24). Peter Riddell writes: 'To Mrs Thatcher and her allies the problem lay in the permissive 1960s … The legislation of that era – changes in the law on capital punishment, homosexuality, abortion, divorce, and censorship – had created "the impression that there was no need for restraint at all." Yet, significantly, none of this legislation was reversed during the 1980s' (171). My intention in drawing attention to this contradiction is not, as with Riddell, to suggest that Thatcher failed in certain key policy ventures or alternatively to propose that her government was more liberal minded than it seemed – by no means. Rather, I want to suggest that the uptake of Thatcherite 'pragmatism' – that certain 'left liberal' policies were allowed to go unchallenged – may be because such policies were not in fact so antagonistic to Thatcherism as they were initially perceived to be and, as Hutchinson writes, that 'the two impulses came to exist in a relationship of mutual confirmation from which the right drew considerable advantage' (25).

This point deserves some explanation. Thatcherism certainly perceived and presented itself as a populist form of government, echoing the voice of the 'corner shop' and 'people's politics'. Peter Clarke notes how, despite her outspoken disdain for the work of the unions, 'she was confident that she spoke *for* an influential section of the working class and she challenged the stereotypes of the old class system' (380). In effect, she presented her own free market Conservatism as *anti*-elitist, catering to the entrepreneurial/consumerist sentiments of the working-class demographic – it was *old* money which was classist. Nevertheless, given how aggressive she was in tearing down working-class safety nets, and in asserting the overriding importance of individual economic ambition – such that there was 'no such thing as society' (Thatcher, N.pag.) – the authority of this perception remains highly dubious. As David Harvey writes, Thatcherite politics became a hotbed of neo-liberalism, as 'all forms of social solidarity were to be dissolved in favour of individualism, private property, personal responsibility, and family values … "Economics are the method," she said, "but the object is to change the soul." And change it she did, though in ways that were by no means comprehensive and complete, let alone free of political costs' (23).

In economic terms, this shift was decisive, moving away from Keynesian intervention, austerity and political cooperation and instead towards the unbending indifference of the global free market. In effect, consumer capitalism became the rule, leaving a gap between rich and poor which came to define British and indeed global social realities in the 1980s. Even so, in terms of the field of cultural and literary production in Britain, this entailed more ambiguous consequences. Thus, while on the one hand, the commodification of postmodern cultural aesthetics did find its way into 1980s critical and literary writing, not only through 'spectacular' market principles but also through a 'metafictional' endorsement of radical self-reflexivity and the crisis of reference – a paradigm which (especially within criticism) seemed at times to sanction ethical relativism – on the other hand authors and texts also in many ways resisted this tendency, still incorporating self-conscious and experimental devices developed by 1960s and 1970s counter-cultural writers, but with a clear concern to uphold narrative's referential dimension and to respond experientially, intellectually and emotionally to a lived social reality undergoing transition within the emerging global world order. Thus, as Philip Tew writes:

> In fact, recent fiction in Britain retains a subtextual appeal to reality and naturalistic social mores, exploring this intensified realm of value and commodification, an extension of these strands of influence upon the Renaissance, the Enlightenment, and Victorian utilitarianism. (22)

In short, changes to the focus of 1980s criticism and theory – with an increasing value attached to style and more especially self-reflexivity, as above – failed to adequately comprehend 1980s fiction's persisting sociological dimension, in particular in relation to Thatcherite individualism and the new entrepreneurial ethic of the global world order. In Tew's words, increasingly 'postmodernism is being seen as insufficient for explaining or even describing fragmentation, differentiation and plurality'. Its obsession with textuality 'risks prioritizing a secondary [and socially and ideologically indifferent] view of understanding' (23).

Indeed, in doing this, it also overlooks some of the more pressing critical issues attached to 1980s fiction, which relate *not* to experiment or self-consciousness per se but rather to the conflicting political strategies and policies that Thatcher and global capitalism used. Thus, while some fiction continued to assert a largely liberal humanist and universalizing ideological position, unconcerned with elitist, patriarchal and imperialist implications of liberal thinking, by contrast other works explicitly set themselves against this agenda, appropriating experiment and self-consciousness precisely so as to challenge established class, gender, sexual and ethnic prejudices and in this way open a path for a more socially engaged and collectivist vision. Thus, as Tew suggests, a fiction can be identified in the late 1970s and 1980s which builds on 1960s counter-cultural sentiment and which condemns 'middle-class self-obsession and imperial nostalgia and regret', including that of a postmodern variety (24–25). The question is how to identify this fiction given 1980s criticism's larger textualist bent. Tew begins this project, with his emphasis on fiction's sociology, but it demands more analysis.

Indeed, the issue is even more complex than this, for it is often the case that individual texts demonstrate (or can be read to demonstrate) conflicting tendencies and values within themselves, thus supporting both left liberal and anti-liberal messages. Patricia Waugh points to this concern when she writes that

> [m]ost [contemporary writers] have been accused of complicity with what they reveal to be destructive in its effects: power, violence, the irrational, desire. Many are self-professed liberal humanists, yet their work is often a savage indictment of late liberalism for its moral dishonesty and exclusions and its spiritual failings. (*The Harvest of the Sixties* 70)

On a similar note, Hutchinson, writing on the contemporary British social novel, argues that 'ambivalence' (especially with regard to the position of the white middle-class male, who is so often the protagonist of 1980s social fiction) 'appears to have confounded commitment, and it remains unclear as to whether that ambivalence could ever be re-cast in such a way as to act as a substitute for an unattainable revolution and a commitment that cannot escape compromise' (36). Uncertain about the ironic or alternatively liberating implications of its own individual-centred narratives, the avowed radicalism of the 1980s novel remains conceivable but still under question.

In what follows, I hope to build on this understanding critically, looking at five 1980s fictional discourses in particular: history; time; the state of the nation; gender and sexuality; and postcolonialism and nationality. While these by no means cover all aspects of 1980s fiction in terms of its thematic, aesthetic, theoretical and ideological agendas, which must necessarily extend beyond the remit of a single introductory chapter, nevertheless it does offer a broad exploration of certain key debates and issues which occupied literary and cultural thinking during the decade and which mediated fiction's response to larger social and cultural change. My intention, as stated above, is to explore some of the 1980s' more radical possibilities, while at the same time recognizing elements of complicity between the novel and the postmodern critical apparatus in order to provide a new, more critical view of fiction in the 1980s.

*

With respect to the first of these discourses, in the wake of a still-remembered WWII and a currently evolving Cold War crisis, history becomes particularly prominent in 1980s fiction, where a new interest not only in the past itself, a category often sidelined by the Thatcherite political establishment, but also in historical writing and interpretation more generally, understood in textual terms, became the unexpected focus of literary attention, challenging a traditionalist notion of an unalterable historical 'truth' and 'progress' and instead recognizing history's necessarily situated and provisional conceptual nature. One category under which this fiction was classed at the time, coined by Linda Hutcheon, was that of 'historiographical metafiction', which by invoking a shared 'constructedness' between fiction and history, both dependent upon selective human processes, asserts these novels' underlying scepticism towards accepted narrative-historical values, avowing that history and fiction are ultimately, as Hutcheon argued, 'discourses, human constructs, signifying systems, and both derive their major claim to truth from that identity' (93).

The textualist slant of this reading, prioritizing discourse and self-consciousness over reference, takes its cue from 1970s and 1980s post-structuralist theory, where an increasing focus on narrative's (and particularly historical narrative's) deceptive fictional quality – as it attempts to assert and mythologize truth – makes ideas of textual self-awareness and 'discursivity' especially attractive. Thus, Jean-François Lyotard, in *The Postmodern Condition*, challenges history's status as a 'grand narrative', emphasizing instead its multiple and specific 'micro-narrative' condition. Likewise, Michel Foucault, for example in *The Order of Things*, sees history as a series of ruptures and 'epistemes', which rather than exerting change merely shift culture's focus of attention. Equally, postmodernist criticism also reads contemporary history in terms of its uncertain and changeable dimensions, asserting in Hutcheon's words that 'the meaning and shape [of history and literature] are not in the events, but in the systems which make those past "events" into present historical "facts"' (89).

Under this reading, as Daniel Bedggood explains, history becomes 'just another genre of discourse or narrative which imposes order on events through writing, and its particular claim to produce "facts" that illuminate the past is questionable' (205). Bedggood continues:

> References to history in literature, or to historiography 'proper', are equally unable to claim a privileged association with the reality of events: the very reporting and ordering of events reconstitutes them, with the act of writing or representation replacing the event as the subject of history. (205)

This reading thus divests historical narrative of its referential capacity, asserting textuality, and with this relativism, as historical fiction's primary value – in place of knowledge, contemporary writing invokes doubt or 'incredulity'. Julian Barnes's 1980s novels *Flaubert's Parrot* (1984) and *A History of the World in 10½ Chapters* (1989) reflect this conception perhaps most clearly within 1980s British fiction, where a continual emphasis on narrative history's structural organization and fragmentation finally undercuts any clear notion of referential coherence or accessibility. As *A History of the World in 10½ Chapters* describes (in a section entitled 'Parenthesis'):

> We lie in our hospital bed of the present... And while we fret and writhe in bandaged uncertainty... we fabulate. We make up a story to cover the facts we don't know or can't accept; we keep a few true facts and spin a new story round them. Our panic and our pain are only eased by soothing fabulation; we call it history. (164)

The self-supporting historical delusion envisioned here is dire, rejecting any larger possibility of hope or change through historical curiosity. Even so, for other 1980s novels, such as those of Peter Ackroyd, Iain Sinclair, Rose Tremain, Barry Unsworth and Graham Swift, another conception is evident, which engages with postmodern ideas of discursive constructedness and textual reflexivity as explored by Hutcheon, but which nevertheless insists on the value of historical narrative as a means of understanding and engaging with lived reality. Throughout these works, post-structuralist ideas of history's fluidity and textuality are visible, thus reaffirming Hutcheon's 'metafictional' conception – Ackroyd through play with biography, Tremain and Unsworth through a mixture of ironically inflected realism and romance and Sinclair through a unique 'psycho-geographical' historical fiction. Even so, equally pressing is a concern to interrogate contemporary historical ideologies, in this way exploring what Suzanne Keen refers to as 'nostalgic fantasies about the uses of the past... the endogamous Englishness of the past discovered' (215). In order to address this concern more precisely, I want to look at one 1980s novel specifically: Swift's *Waterland*, exploring as I do so the significance of Swift's historical vision as a response to Thatcherite mystifications of historical 'progress'.

Told from the perspective of a history teacher, Tom Crick, made redundant during Thatcherite cutbacks, a motif of institutionalized forgetting is visible from the start of the novel, as Crick's redundancy is, the text makes clear, a consequence of Thatcher's reductive conception of culture and history, which instrumentalizes education, prioritizing maths and science over the humanities, and which understands history as a fact-based, rather than selective and interpretative subject. As the headmaster Lewis explains:

> Equipping for the real world. It just so happens that I think that's what we're here for... Send just one of these kids out into the world with a sense of his or her usefulness, with an ability to apply, with practical knowledge and not a rag-bag of pointless information. (17)

Following Thatcher's utilitarian and pragmatic understanding of history, as a vehicle for wider global economic 'progress', this outlook rejects from the start any conception of historiography's critical or reflective role, confining it to a position of trivia and national heritage.

On the other side of this situation is Crick's students' political radicalism, which by contrast with Lewis dismisses history not because of 'rationalization', in the mould of Thatcher, but rather out of fear, articulating 1980s nuclear anxieties. As one student puts it: 'The only important thing about history... is that it's got to the point where it's probably about to end' (5). Correspondingly, the students institute a revolutionary agenda as a means of inducing social protest: 'We want to pool people's fears', the student Price argues, 'Tell them not to hide it... add it to ours' (206).

This opposition between pragmatism on the one hand and revolution on the other is the starting point for the novel's historiographical inquiry, using metaphors of Fenland flooding and 'drainage' to explore the complex duality of historical knowledge – at once real and representational – and to recognize that it is sometimes difficult to distinguish between the two. The often ironic and self-conscious character of this exploration, which builds on post-structuralist ideas about history's conservative institutional bearing, questioning its reality as anything more than a 'yarn' or children's fairy tale, opens this depiction up to charges (or celebrations) of relativism, where, as Catherine Bernard writes:

> The fragmentation of the diegetic continuum destroys the coherence of the facts as well as of the narration. Each diversion seems to erect a narrative screen before the referent, hides the facts however much it wants to get closer to them. While these narrative departures are introduced to clarify the action, to illuminate the backdrop, they render the representation more opaque, more contradictory. (38, qtd. in and trans. by Craps 80)

Following this reading, *Waterland*'s narrative uncertainty and digression offer a barrier to historical knowledge which ultimately colludes with a relativistic reduction of history to storytelling: 'overly coherent codes…break up in the presence of a referent that always exceeds the limits of representation and defies language' (41). Even so, other aspects of the novel unmistakably resist this reading, situating Crick's insistence on uncertainty pointedly as a response to Thatcherite close-mindedness and nostalgia (in this way evading a co-option with neo-liberal ideals). The metaphor of 'land reclamation' in particular speaks to this reading, where a vision of constant 'slow and arduous' drainage offers a relational metaphor of a more critical, interrogatory historical ideal. As Crick puts it:

> My humble model for progress is the reclamation of land. Which is repeatedly, never-endingly retrieving what is lost. A dogged and vigilant business. A dull yet valuable business. A hard, inglorious business. But you shouldn't go mistaking the reclamation of land for the building of empires. (254)

Set in the present-day context of 'Star Wars' nuclear anxiety, where Crick's students confess to nightmares of nuclear apocalypse and devastation, these ideas repudiate Thatcher's denial of history, emphasizing instead the importance of inquiry as a means to preventing future catastrophe.

Even so, I would continue to question the full impact of these ideas as they attempt to confront crisis through postmodern style. Thus, while the novel evidently lends itself to postmodern notions regarding the constructedness of history and the necessity of storytelling, which facilitate a critical reflexivity, nevertheless, given the enduring uncertainty of Crick's situation – including the haunting memories of his wife's abortion and the knowledge of his own complicity with this and his brother's disappearance/death – it seems unclear to what extent this outlook succeeds in dispensing with doubt or in offering a critical (and ethical) solution. Crick *does* put forward an important memorial ideal, but nevertheless the persisting methodology of storytelling his narrative pursues, which suggests that everything – even the most horrendous trauma – must be remembered, seems to overlook the constructive potential of forgetting. Thus, weighed down by painful personal losses, which evidently *cannot be* ameliorated through storytelling, as Crick's excessive drinking demonstrates, the question remains, how is either Crick or the reader meant to get beyond this tragedy: is endless retelling really a viable response? In this sense, the novel's appeal to postmodern curiosity seems insufficient (and potentially conservative): it suggests that contemporary dissent depends on reliving past trauma when in some cases it instead requires moving forward. In this way, historical cyclicality evades the project of disciplined moral-political re-engagement in Swift's novel.

*

The focus on inquiry in this novel reconfirms the decade's challenge to Thatcherite anti-historical ideals (however problematic the solution offered may sometimes be). Nevertheless, in so far as Swift's novel also jumps between present and past, digressing in its assertions and allowing moments of interruption and simultaneity which complicate its assimilation, another concern is also evident, namely time and narrative temporality.

In the context of a hyper-technologized and mediated late twentieth century, where history itself takes on, in Fredric Jameson's phrase in *Postmodernism*, a 'pastiche' quality (17), and where everyday experience becomes enmeshed in notions of 'acceleration', 'de-synchronization', 'montage' and 'simulacra' most often associated with cinema and information technology, this interest becomes, in some ways, institutional, reflecting in general a disjointed late-century experience. Thus, as Steven Connor argues, the time of contemporary culture, especially 'by the 1980s', is often 'out of step with itself, the past and the future being made present to us in simulation, and the present deferred and distributed into other times' (69, 77). Indeed, in texts like Swift's above, where layers of information, myth and narrative build up in a bricolage fashion, time becomes not only disjointed but also in some ways entropic, unfolding outwards in an often chaotic associative spill. The consequence of this reality for Connor, taking a notably critical view, is a fiction of temporal 'counter-temporality', wherein the text's real-life 'interpenetration' makes it increasingly difficult to 'measure the world and the world-making act of story up against each other' (69). Here, in a notably postmodern argument, 1980s fiction is said to enact a sort of vacuuming aporia, wherein its hyper-real consciousness impedes its historical situating. Again, textualist style becomes a concern. However, I would argue that in a British oeuvre influenced not only by technology but also by the context of Thatcherite Conservatism, where time is connected to authoritarian ideals of 'progress' and domination, a fictional concern for reconnecting with lost personal time and renewing time's libratory potential is also (and perhaps more centrally) apparent, this again opposing more relativist readings.

Various 1980s authors can be listed here, including, alongside Swift, Jeanette Winterson, Christine Brooke-Rose, Salman Rushdie, Angela Carter, Michael Westlake, Martin Amis and Ian McEwan, each exploring time's multidimensional and often uncontainable contemporary ontology. As Jago Morrison notes, several of these writers, especially Rushdie, Winterson and McEwan, incorporate specifically 'New Physical' terminologies, developing in an aesthetic way the 'quantum' science introduced by Max Planck, Niels Bohr and Werner Heisenberg, whose principles of 'indeterminacy' and 'complementarity' offer innovative challenges to traditional linear models. As Morrison explains, these imaginative adaptations 'supplant Newton's universal, abstract, mechanistic time with Relativity's quite different model of a flexible four-dimensional space-time' (26). On a different note, the fictions of Carter, Brooke-Rose, Westlake and Amis invoke instead encyclopaedic and anemnetic temporal injunctions, seeking to either index or alternatively reorganize narrative time's allotted historical causality. The self-conscious and often spiralling nature of these presentations often seems to uphold a postmodern aporetic temporal ideal, replacing coherence with unfettered proliferation. Thus, as Connor writes, 'few things evidence the naturalization of postmodernism more emphatically than the fact that what used to look like disorder now looks like brimming plentitude' (69). Nevertheless, at least in several of these oeuvres, an equally strong sense of postmodern time's potential collusion with the strategies of power – where as Michael Hardt and Antonio Negri note, the absence of 'time clocks' assures that 'the proletariat produces in all its generality everywhere all day long' (403) – complicates this message significantly, placing limits on the value of temporal uncertainty. One work which gives voice to this application is Ian McEwan's *The Child in Time* (1987), often considered a manifesto of New Physics' temporal and scientific ingenuity.

The novel begins with a narrative of crisis, in this case belonging to children's book writer, Stephen Lewis, whose three-year-old daughter, Kate, had been abducted on a visit to the supermarket three years earlier. Since then, Stephen's temporal world has turned upside down: drifting between distraction and paranoia, he contemplates time's 'monomaniacal' denial of 'second chances' and daydreams about what Kate might look like now. Living in solitude and squalor, with 'meaty black flies...empty armchairs...speared plates and old newspapers' (6), his world reflects a death-like existence, unmotivated by hope or change.

This personal crisis is paralleled in the novel by larger social turmoil, as the fictional 1990s setting, conceived of as an extension of third-term Tory government, is depicted as a nightmarish dystopia, complete with licensed beggars, traffic jams, privatized schools and ecological disaster, which reflect an Orwellian distortion of regular social and temporal sensibilities. As Bernard O'Keefe explains: 'McEwan extends and exaggerates some of the right-wing policies he saw in operation in the late 1980s – privatisation, reduction of public subsidy, the encouragement of free enterprise, and the espousal of family values' (3). In this way he makes clear the country's removal from recognized democratic and collectivist ideals. The question then is how forceful this critique is within the novel's exploration of alternative temporalities.

The initial answer to this question comes through Stephen's visit to Julie, his ex-wife, at her cottage in the country. Thus far, Stephen has resisted Julie's example, seeing her effort to confront and mourn Kate's loss as escapist and impractical: 'It was the inertia, the collapse of will, the near ecstatic suffering which disgusted him and threatened to undermine his efforts' (21). Nevertheless, in Stephen's visit to Julie, he twice experiences moments of temporal variation which complicate this attitude, introducing a more complex phenomenal perspective. In one of these, Stephen is confronted with an unusual dreamlike experience. He encounters a pub that is familiar even though he does not remember visiting it, and looking in through a window, he sees a couple he recognizes as his parents before he was born. Making a greeting gesture to his mother, he feels himself going back in time, regressing into a foetal state:

> His eyes grew large and round and lidless with desperate, protesting innocence, his knees rose under him and touched his chin, his fingers were scaly flippers, gills beat time, urgent, hopeless strokes through the salty ocean that engulfed the treetops and surged beneath their roots... (63)

In this seemingly hallucinatory moment, depicting a mystical time travel initially at odds with the novel's otherwise realist aesthetic, the text offers a key theoretical readjustment, depicting a new idea of time and temporality which directly challenges Stephen's previously unbending conception. Gesturing to his mother from the window, Stephen ensures not only his *current* recovery, introducing a more primal, embryonic state which disrupts and challenges his former draconian linearity, but also (more complexly) his *past* survival, this other-worldly gesture apparently convincing his mother to continue with her pregnancy despite his father's protestations. Indeed, when Stephen awakes from his unconsciousness in Julie's bed and shares a brief romantic encounter with her, the future too becomes implicated: 'what was happening now, and what would happen as a consequence of now, was not separate from what he had experienced earlier that day' (67). The ideas of temporal otherness as well as continuity and wholeness this understanding creates, set against Stephen's current grief-stricken psychology, establish an alternative, more redemptive outlook, seeing time as flexible and holistic, offering purpose as well as pain. In this sense, the novel initially seems to redeem postmodern temporality.

Even so, McEwan notably diverges from one dominant postmodern understanding of time, where in place of Lyotard's disconnected and unstable physical reality, for example – defined by 'undecidables, the limits of precise control ... fracta, catastrophes, and pragmatic paradoxes' (60) – what emerges instead is not fracture but integrated wholeness. Thus, as Stephen reflects, 'all the empty waiting had been enclosed within meaningful time, within the richest unfolding conceivable' (235). Building on David Bohm's mystical physics (recognized in the acknowledgements) – which envision an 'implicated order' wherein reality is explained in terms of multidimensional 'folding' and 'flow' (203) – this depiction moves away from textualist invocations of metafictional incredulity, instead embracing an integrationist ideal of pre-ordered purpose. While this itself may appear problematic in other terms – invoking 'a higher order of reality, a higher ground ... [where] matter, space, time, even consciousness itself, would be complicatedly related embodiments, intrusions which made up the reality we understood' (127) – this reading rejects textualist appropriation, instead emphasizing a focus on integration as a means to reaffirming material and affective signifiers – the interpersonal connections and experiences which Stephen's obtuse theorizing ironically ignores.[1]

In relation to my argument, this situates McEwan outside a popular postmodern relativism, and hence outside a market celebration of aporetic time – the absence of purpose. While the novel evidently gestures at modes of temporal thinking comparable to hyper-technology, it backs down from the more atomistic dimensions of this, instead promoting an 'integrated order' as a means to a more dynamic, emotionally, spiritually *and* materially informed temporal outlook. In fact, this may seem conservative in its own right, though in a different way from Thatcherism, as the novel embraces holism and connectedness with some disregard of the dangers of universalism. Nevertheless, I see it instead as coherent with Jameson's critique of post-structuralism in *The Political Unconscious*, wherein he argues that

The current poststructural celebration of discontinuity and heterogeneity is therefore only an initial moment in the Althusserian exegesis, which then requires the fragments, the incommensurable levels, the heterogeneous impulses, of the text to be once again related. (41)

This Marxist proclamation resonates with McEwan's repudiation of postmodern fragmentation in favour of integration, seeing this as a foundation upon which distantly perceived connections between events and experiences, otherwise overlooked within neo-liberalism, might be affirmed.

*

In relation to the parodic bent of McEwan's text, informed by a self-conscious revulsion at Thatcher's 'law and order' and 'family values' campaigns, yet another 1980s concern arises, namely that of 'state of the nation' critique, especially in terms of a rejection of dominant New Right values. The readings offered thus far have already touched on this concern to some extent, in particular in relation to the Cold War and pragmatist social policies, where alternatively fantastic, dangerous and authoritarian institutions betray at once naivety and social disinterest. The consumerist dimensions of these applications, making the market the new locus of social success, establish an anti-collectivist ideology, disregarding the importance of community in favour of uncontrolled individual ambition. Throughout this fiction, a cultural demand for improved socio-political responsibility is evident, thus providing a key basis for a revived contemporary social novel.

In relation to a clearly diverse generic production, including narratives of satire, tragedy, farce, confession and development, as well as more ambivalent contemporary modes, numerous authors might be linked to this 'state of the nation' concern, including the 'trauma fictions' of Graham Swift and Pat Barker; the parodic 'campus novels' of David Lodge and Malcolm Bradbury; the fantasy fictions of Christopher Priest, Clive Sinclair, Alasdair Gray and Iain Banks; the magical realism of Salman Rushdie; and the varying genre mixtures of McEwan, Amis, Winterson, Maggie Gee and Kazuo Ishiguro. In their differing representations of social injustice and inequality, each of these writers offers a clear critique of New Right structures, promoting (at least in theory) collectivism as a basis for change. Even so, the alternative to individualism is perhaps not always as clear as it could be, so that ambivalence and sometimes cynicism regarding social community become a clear critical concern. One work which typifies this is Martin Amis's 1984 novel *Money*, often considered *the* quintessential 1980s novel.

The narrative is told from the perspective of advertising director John Self, a lewd, fat and money-obsessed yob who is in most senses the symbolic embodiment of Thatcherite and Reaganite corruption. Hypnotized by a consumerist ideology of self, wealth and fame, directly reflecting Thatcher's 'monetarist' values, his money-centred principles embody a new social standard, based on extravagance, pornography, alcoholism, sexism and artifice. As he puts it at one point, in a statement replete with parody, 'My food is made of monosodium glutamate and hexachlorophene, my clothes are made of polyester, rayon, and lurex, my brain is gimmicked by a microprocessor the size of a quark, and I'm made of – junk, I'm just junk' (265).

In contrast to works like those of Swift and McEwan above, this voice makes more directly palpable the technologized and consumer postmodernity of 1980s life, contextualizing the narrator by embedding him in a discourse of modern slang. Thus, Self presents himself as trendy and commodified, familiar with 'junkfurters', 'gum gimmicks', 'rug redos', 'jet swells' and 'shitstorms' (1, 29, 40, 30). He knows his brands: he flies 'Airtrak', drives a 'Fiasco' and reads 'Scum magazine' (43, 10, 62). But while on the one hand these details help to situate and bring to life Self's extravagant persona, on the other hand, they also mock his values, making clear that frankfurters are just 'junk', Fiats really 'fiascos' and porn 'scum'. In this way, as James Diedrick notes, Amis adopts an ostensibly Dickensian technique, employing proper names to caricature and satirize an existing world (77–78).

Indeed, Amis's style is more complex than this, for it incorporates not only lingo and brands, but also jokes, misinterpretations and double entendres which vivify Self's ignorance while at the same time making clear a textual rejection of his values. Some of these are pointedly slapstick, as when Self misconstrues 'date-rape' as rape by fruit (22), or when he misunderstands 'genre' as 'John roar', thus fumbling his claims to authorship (100). Nevertheless, as Self reflects on the difficulties he must endure in order to maintain his eroding personal dignity, a more tragic humour emerges, which censures yuppie egotism even as it makes the discombobulated nature of Self's life explicit. Indeed, there is much to draw reader sympathy here, in relation to Self's absorption and abuse at the hands of postmodernity. Self suffers a variety of illnesses, including 'gut-ache', toothache, headache and earache, which, while sometimes repelling the reader's sensibilities, at the same time signal a metaphorical fragmentation which impels compassion. Consumed by 'me society's' commercialized and mediated images, Self's mind and body decompose, leaving him bereft of a positive identity. Perhaps the most powerful figure for this in this novel is Self's unusual, schizophrenic 'tinnitus', distinguishing in particular four voices which haunt him. He lists these as follows:

> First, of course, is the jabber of money, which might be represented as the blur of the top rung of a typewriter – £%¼@!... Second is the voice of pornography. This often sounds like the rap of a demented DJ... Third, the voice of ageing and weather, of time travel through days and days, the ever weakening voice of stung shame, sad boredom and futile protest... Number four is the real intruder... It has to do with quitting work and needing to think about things I never used to think about. It has the unwelcome lilt of paranoia, of rage and weepiness made articulate in spasms of vividness: drunk talk played back sober. (108)

In this invoice of psychological fragmentation, inflections of Thatcherite greed and corruption play it out against a still enduring conscientiousness, the former evidently holding the advantage. The climax of this storyline comes when the fantasy of abstract capital in which Self indulges – where 'the car is on the house. The house is on the mortgage. The mortgage is on the firm' (79) – is uncovered as just that, a fantasy. Self's producer colleague has strategically orchestrated Self's own financing of their ultimately unsellable film. The ambivalent combination of loathing and empathy the reader feels for this character, who only too late realizes the disabling implications of his chaotic lifestyle, suggests a complex denunciation of Thatcherite Britain, where, under her defence of conspicuous consumption, even the so-called 'winners' appear ultimately as losers.

Recognizing the narrative finality with which this message is given, where both Self's professional career and his love life fall apart, and even his suicide is a botch, this ending would appear depressingly sceptical about the availability of alternative, more redemptive political solutions. Indeed, like many of the decade's authors, Amis is pointedly pessimistic in his outlook, preferring disgust to prescription – a 1980s tendency which some readers have been critical of, linking it to a failure of ideological commitment. Thus, for example, D. J. Taylor comments on how 'Amis's chief characteristic is an intense and fascinated disgust, in which the exposure of his characters' appalling behaviour is invariably followed by retribution and, occasionally, outright obliteration... But disgust is not necessarily a moral statement' (189–190). Relatedly, Hutchinson also detects an underlying political 'ambivalence' in Amis's novel, wherein notions of ethical 'complicity' and 'guilt' tied up with Amis's white middle-class background ultimately blockade a more effective collectivist assertion. 'Morality and politics are confounded in ways that occasionally suggest that morality transcends the enmities associated with political conflict' (63), he comments. In this sense, the importance of the individual in the novel would seem problematically to overarch community.

I would argue that the novel does provide responses to these critiques, but ones which themselves are subject to question. Thus, against the contention that Amis's fascination with corruption overrides his moral critique, it is possible to see the ending as moral in a different way. Amis contends: 'I remember telling my father three years ago that the plot of *Money* would all be based on a totally unexplained confidence trick which I meant to be as bald and brutal as possible – absolutely unexplained – and I think that's quite a good analogy for money' (Haffenden 6). In this way, the issue of the plot's inexplicability (its lack of motivation) becomes a way of reflecting on the postmodern condition – the distorted state society has arrived at: it may seem confident, but this is a sham. Likewise, the concern that the novel conflates morality and politics can be answered by calling attention to Amis's so-called 'moral' character, Goodney. Far from embodying judgement or a moralizing voice, as Hutchinson contends, this character reflects vendetta and small-mindedness – the very lunacy of consumer society – which the novel condemns. Amis reflects: '[Fielding Goodney] embodies confidence, which is at last in my novels identified as a psychotic state. The last chapter says that confidence is a wildly inappropriate response to present-day life' (Haffenden 5). In this way, the novel resists any clear-cut retribution.

Even so, the unmistakable confidence of the novel itself as it explores consumer modernity makes this anti-consumerist message hard to credit. Thus, the novel is fuelled by an energy around fashion and entrepreneurialism – in terms of its brand names, its fast pace and its fascination with sexualized women – which celebrates, even as it contests, consumer society: its popular cultural fluency and the stylistic bravado both speak to this. In this way the novel's male-centred and commodity-enthused language subconsciously participates in the spectacle of consumer capitalism. It parodies society's greed and objectification but also thrives on the allure of these practices precisely as a means of stylizing parody. In this way, the novel's politics remain conflicted, balancing critique with an admission of complicity.

*

Recognizing the importance of a specifically 'male' emotional obtuseness and 'female' affectivity in both McEwan's and Amis's novels, yet another decadal concern arises in relation to contemporary representations of gender and sexual identity. Thus, impelled by new ideas in both post-structuralist theory and politics, these categories reflect a central counter-cultural interest of the decade, which gives way to a newly feminist, 'new man' and queer 1980s fiction. In the interest again of mapping dissent and collusion in 1980s novels, especially in relation to postmodern queer techniques and their potential denial of referentiality, several aspects of this project deserve mention.

First, in terms of theory, both French 'second wave' feminism and post-structuralism more generally were an influence in 1980s fiction, the former contributing such concepts as '*écriture féminine*', 'phallogocentrism', 'woman's time' and 'herethics', while the latter complicated this with 'regulative discourses', 'disciplinary regimes' and gender and sexual 'performativity', thus asserting a more historically embedded identity politics.[2] In the 1980s context of retrograde sexual conservatism, where Thatcher denounced both feminism and homosexuality as belonging to a depraved 1960s 'permissive society', the value of *both* of these (very different) critical schools related to their shared celebration of female and gay identity, reaffirming against Conservatism a more open and flexible gendered and sexual apperception.

Literature in the 1980s clearly benefited from these movements, opening itself up to a more self-conscious style and form. Various writers can be connected with this experience, including, amongst feminists, Angela Carter, Jeanette Winterson, Fay Weldon, Emma Tennant, Marina Warner, Janice Galloway and Pat Barker, and amongst queer authors, (again) Winterson, Maureen Duffy, Kay Dick, Alan Hollinghurst and Hanif Kureishi, all of whom make gender and sexuality textually central. Throughout these writings, innovative narrative devices throw off repressive rightist postures, asserting instead a stylistic re-validation of stigmatized gender and sexual categories. Nevertheless, as Patricia Duncker notes, the postmodern emphasis on uncertainty and undecidability in some 1980s queer writing potentially moves away from the radical aims of 1960s and 1970s feminist and gay politics, replacing this with a more ambivalent principle of 'fragmented subjectivity' (78). Thus, under the post-structuralist focus on multiple selfhood, the political activist concern for defined 'political categories, such as woman, Lesbian, Black [became] suspect, self-indulgent, essentialist...based upon the illusion of substantial identity and the apparently sinful belief in the metaphysics of substance' (78). As a consequence, post-structuralist critique came to overshadow important feminist and gay rights commitments, collapsing significant distinctions between gender positions, as well as between sexual identities. One novel which evidences this is Winterson's 1985 *Oranges Are Not the Only Fruit*, winner of the 1985 Whitbread Award for a first novel and an often-celebrated lesbian text.

Drawing in many ways on Winterson's own life, this novel tells the story of 15-year-old Jeanette's teenage discovery of her lesbian identity. Set against a background of evangelical Protestantism, where ideals of sexual 'purity' and moral righteousness linked to the Pentecostal church reflect in the extreme Thatcher's attack on the 'permissive society', the text offers a cutting satire of contemporary political coordinates. Jeanette's matriarchal church demonstrates both prejudice, banning homosexuality from its congregation, and, more interestingly, self-effacement and repression, denying its own complex feminist, sexual and homosexual tendencies in favour of an inhibited doctrinal 'psychosis' (xii). In its final affirmation of a compulsory asexual and repressed religious identity, the church becomes a symbol of Conservative, patriarchal oppression, both historical and current. Nevertheless, as Nick Bentley aptly notes, there are also instances of love and tenderness in the story which suggest the centrality of community, and especially female community, as a source of gender and sexual empowerment (110).

Importantly, in a text which aspires towards a specifically female narrative perspective, this message is given through a mixture of traditional realist and fantasy techniques, combining an overarching *Bildungsroman* structure with passages of dreams, fairy tales and myths, as well as Biblical and literary allusions, which reflect and complicate the narrative's meaning. The novel's chapter titles invoke names of books of the Bible – 'Genesis' introducing Jeanette's beginnings, 'Exodus' her leaving home to go to school, 'Leviticus' the establishment of a textually based church law – thus from the start suggesting a rewriting of Old Testament ideals. Winterson is critical with these designations, satirizing their conventional doctrinal significance by imbuing them with motifs of northern English provincialism and sexual repression which parody their regular sacrosanct authority. Indeed, as Peter Childs points out, she uses not only parody but also a New Testament 'counter-narrative', complete with a virgin 'birth' (through adoption) and beatific sacrifice, which establishes the rebellious Jeanette as an effective Christ figure (266). In the final three chapters of 'Joshua', 'Judges' and 'Ruth', this then produces a reversal of Old Testament narrative, wherein Jeanette frees herself from the strictures of divine law in favour of feminine loyalty and independent thought. In other words, she creates her own new covenant, rejecting Old Testament legalism, as Christ did.

One crucial aspect of this narrative concerns Jeanette's ambivalent relationship with her mother, who provides at once support and betrayal. Jeanette describes her as 'out there, up front with the prophets, and much given to sulking under trees when the appropriate destruction didn't materialise' (4), thus emphasizing her eccentric defiance and female willpower. Similarly, in terms of sexuality, while apparently apathetic in her relationship with Jeanette's father – never sleeping with him for more than an hour per night – she nevertheless lets on to certain hidden sexual attractions and sentiments which complicate her posture of radical puritanism. Thus, she describes her first view of the pastor as 'look[ing] like Errol Flynn, but holy' – 'A lot of women found the Lord that week' (8) – and when questioned about a woman's photograph she has kept, she is elusive, removing the picture from the album. Mrs Jewsbury comments, 'She's a woman of the world, even though she'd never admit it to me. She knows about feelings, especially women's feelings' (104).

Against this intriguing background, Jeanette's mother's conformity to church doctrine invokes a betrayal, denying both her own and her daughter's feminist and lesbian proclivities. Avowing that Jeanette had 'taken on a man's world' both in her ministry and her sexuality, she abjures her own and Jeanette's sexuality, allowing the church's neurosis to decide her own position. Against this revocation of personal integrity, Jeanette expresses her profound disappointment: 'If there's such thing as spiritual adultery, my mother was whore' (131–132).

This set-up provides a complex breakdown of gender and sexual discourses in the 1980s, combining a narrative of self-assertion and increasing political awareness (on Jeanette's part) with a subtler inquiry into the non-normative aspects of status quo identity. Even so, the second half of the novel involves a fantasization of Jeanette's relationships, such that Jeanette's identity becomes gradually dissolved into various conflicting and overlapping personae whose particular political significance remains fundamentally ambiguous. Thus, at one point Jeanette is a woman and at another a man; at one point herself and at another, her mother. For Isabel Anievas Gamallo, this dreamlike logic functions critically, offering an alternative, postmodern textual framework which discards any 'single, autonomous, unitarian model of subjectivity' (127) and so in this way undermines Enlightenment discourses of empirical totality. As she writes, 'In Winterson's text we can find no reliable or unique pattern, historical, linguistic or otherwise, but are forced to remain painfully aware of the instability and lack of finality of any narrative we construct' (127). Even so, as Patricia Duncker argues in her reading of the novel, in the context of the text's 'coming out' narrative, which demands some consideration of sexual solidarity, this section specifically obscures the novel's larger political agenda, making issues of historical collectivism and ideological commitment problematically intangible (83). Thus, in accordance with a critical recognition of the socio-political responsibilities towards collective identity, the novel's postmodern ending, I argue, clashes with its initial contextualized vision, abandoning a defence of lesbian solidarity in favour of textual experiment and an embrace of ambivalence with regard to gender and sexual identity. While in some ways this itself might be seen as an alternative rebuttal of hetero-normative sexual politics, highlighting an important spectrum of negotiable subject positions for gender and sexual engagement, I find myself, nevertheless, frustrated alongside Duncker at the curious desertion of collective politics (through parody) in the final section, in favour of textual ambivalence and what seems in many ways an embrace of ideological uncertainty. Again here, commitment, at a ground level, seems lacking.

*

In the context of Conservatism's prejudice against not only women and homosexuals but also immigrants and minority ethnic communities, who Thatcher declared to be 'swamping' British values (Thatcher 1978), this question of postmodernism's possible compromise with dominant hegemonic systems must also extend to postcolonial, Black British and post-imperial writers, who offered a key reflection on both national and ethnic identity categories. Several names merit mention here, including Salman Rushdie, Buchi Emecheta, Ben Okri, Tsitsi Dangarembga, Caryl Phillips, Hanif Kureishi, Timothy Mo and Kazuo Ishiguro, as well as a number of Scottish, Welsh and Northern Irish writers, such as Iain Banks, Alasdair Gray, Bernice Rubens and Robert McLiam Wilson, who emerged in large part in defence of national devolution. Again the styles used by these writers vary widely, including magical realism, realism, genre parody, fantasy and modernist introspection, in this way making clear a multiplicity of approaches to postcolonial and anti-imperialist questions. Even so, as critics such as Timothy Brennan (1997), Graham Huggan (2001) and Benita Parry (2004) have also commented, the textualist focus in several of these oeuvres (or at least in readings of these oeuvres), prioritizing postmodern ambivalence, hybridity and self-consciousness above directly oppositional politics, means that political complicity again becomes a concern, in particular in relation to an 'exoticized' colonial other. One novel whose readings help to illustrate this is Salman Rushdie's *Midnight's Children*, winner of the Booker Prize in 1981 and the Booker of Bookers in 1993 and the Best of the Booker in 2008, and easily (alongside *Money*) one of the most popular British literary novels of the decade.

It is Indian Prime Minister Jawaharlal Nehru's speech declaring India's secession from imperial Britain on 14 August 1947 which gives the novel its title and which by reference to a new 'mansion of children' as a generational metaphor for post-independence nationhood anticipates its central trope of the miraculous birth. The narrator, speaking in first person and moving between the present and past tenses, is Saleem Sinai – one of two (fictional) Indian children born exactly at midnight – who relates his story to his companion Padma, a local pickle factory employee and a chief representative in the novel of the indigenous working classes. As Damien Grant notes, this set-up provides a focal point and mode of suspense for the novel, whereby in the midst of Saleem's prolix and often digressive narrative, the reader gains 'a point of entry into the novel', and one which 'sustains our interest through its many complications' (39). In terms of its politics, this is also noteworthy, where Padma's 'down-to-earth' and 'unofficial' persona can be understood (somewhat controversially) as a democratization of traditional literary hierarchies, wherein, as Abdulrack Gurnah notes, in contrast to the unequal relationship established between the speaker and audience in *One Thousand and One Nights*, Padma's presence ostensibly introduces a more egalitarian dynamic: 'where Scheherazade had the king, Shahiriya, as her listener', in Rushdie's novel, 'Saleem has Padma: "Thick of waist and somewhat hairy of forearm," who spends her days stirring vats of pickle' (93). This reading has been challenged by other postcolonial critics, who see Padma instead as a secondary figure in the novel, reflecting the privileged condescension of the 'cosmopolitan' author. Thus, 'Padma's functions reinforce her as a mere stereotype', Charu Verma argues: 'She is good only as audience, a receiver, for Saleem is giver' (159). I shall discuss this 'cosmopolitan' contention in more detail below. However, suffice it to say that not all readers see Padma positively in this way, and many (such as Verma and Brennan) question her viability in the novel as a native (or subaltern) authority.

Formally, this conversational set-up involves a combination of narrative devices, which weave together reality and fantasy in innovative ways. Saleem, it is worth noting, is both the narrator and the protagonist of his story, and as such takes on diverging (and intertwining) literary roles. As a narrator, he reflects explicitly on the process of storytelling within the novel, questioning Padma's insistence on plot and linearity, and invoking instead a more dynamic, oral form of telling, founded on a preoccupation with connectivity: 'Things – even people – have a way of leaking into each other', he tells Padma, 'like flavours when you cook … Likewise … the past has dripped into me … so we can't ignore it …' (38). Here Padma's working-class identity is tied to her stubborn linearity such that style becomes a facet of middle-class 'culture'. In effect, Rushdie affirms the capitalist reification of subaltern femininity, tying Padma to a native simplicity and vulgarity which makes any claim to authority hard to credit. Thus, as Brennan explains:

> [S]he is, aesthetically speaking, much more important as an image of the Indian masses' gullibility – a translation of her readerly naivety into social terms... Her guillibility ('folkloric simplicity') is part of the fictional status quo she represents, and is responsible for her failures to challenge the demagogy of India's national leaders. (106)

Thus, Padma invokes the failure of the working-class militancy which, while providing a necessary 'bluff' to the cosmopolitan romanticism, nevertheless falls short of offering a viable oppositional solution: 'Folklore's incessant repetitions mould history itself into a fixed pattern in which there is no escape from injustice and deception because the ones being deceived are unprepared or unwilling to change' (106–107).

This indictment of 'Third-World cosmopolitanism' (viii) is decidedly condemning, connecting the novel to an imperialist and sexist norm, in which Padma functions as both a victim and a scapegoat. Even so, other critics have interestingly revised this 'cosmopolitan' reading, recognizing a more 'vernacular' or 'rooted' understanding within the novel – located in a politics of heterogeneity rather than universalism. One way of articulating this is by looking at the novel's attention to context.

Thus, despite *Midnight Children's* reliance on ambivalent form, which admittedly hampers its claims to radical dissidence, the novel's focus on historical location is compelling. As Stephen Morton points out, the novel is not as de-contextualized as some critics (such as Brennan) have suggested. Rather,

> by focusing on the material effects of national independence in India and Pakistan, Rushdie exposes the violence associated with postcolonial modernity as a counterpoint to what he calls the 'optimism disease' of national liberation. (34)

One way in which this becomes clear is through the 'cracking' of Saleem's body, which literalizes the reality of national oppositions covered over by Nehru's idealism and Indira Gandhi's terror. Morton explains, 'Saleem's bodily disintegration is... linked to the fragmentation of the postcolonial body politic', in this way questioning Nehru's narrative of unified nationhood (45). Additionally, the novel's postmodern 'multiple' perspectives also emerge as unreliable in the text, as Saleem exaggerates and misconceives his own 'multiplicity', thus undermining his claims to 'unify the nation' (45). The variation he speaks of is in this sense disabling rather than empowering: he is unable to construct a politics sufficient to meet his ideal. Thus, I would argue, the text moves away from postmodern ambivalence in any radical sense, instead appropriating irony as a clue to vernacular politics. Indeed, through Saleem's body, the novel denounces practices of corruption and subjugation which underlie India and Pakistan's postcolonial situation; it makes clear that even after Empire, nationalist exclusion and oppression continues to exist. In this way, the novel defies a (now familiar) cosmopolitan reading, not by embracing universalism but instead by exposing the violence implicit in nationalism.

*

Looking back at this decadal production in summary, a retrospective hopefulness might be expressed regarding its significance. On the one hand, its political importance remains problematic: as Hutchinson puts it, 'for British novelists at least, the project of renegotiating a collective history along politically subversive lines remains a task that is attempted but rarely achieved' (35). D. J. Taylor agrees, denouncing the supposed disengagement of 1980s novelists, who 'you feel, did their "research" in the cutting libraries of national newspapers: their observation was of headlines and government statistics' (286). Nevertheless, against these readings, I would insist that 1980s texts do explore some significant political realities; their innovative styles and forms at once denounce Thatcher and introduce new programmes for political reassessment, however tentative or sometimes conflicted. As I have argued, this entails some contradictions: scepticism remains important with respect to certain aspects of postmodern style, in particular textualist uncertainty. Even so, queer, feminist, working-class and postcolonial fictions of the decade do push for social change. Indeed, a left-wing solidarity is visible in numerous fictions of the period, which, despite some moments of ambivalence, do engage with the deceptions of consumer capitalism.

Works cited

Primary texts

Amis, Martin. *Money*. London: Penguin, 1986.
Barker, Pat. *Union Street*. London: Virago, 1987.
Barnes, Julian. *Flaubert's Parrot*. London: Pan, 1985.
———. *A History of the World in 10½ Chapters*. New York: Alfred A. Knopf, 1989.

Kureishi, Hanif. *The Buddha of Suburbia*. London: Faber and Faber, 1990.
McEwan, Ian. *The Child in Time*. London: Vintage, 1992.
Rushdie, Salman. *Midnight's Children*. London: Vintage, 1995.
Swift, Graham. *Waterland*. New York: Washington Square Press, 1985.
Winterson, Jeanette. *Oranges Are Not the Only Fruit*. London: Vintage, 1991.

Secondary texts

Acheson, James and Sarah C. E. Ross (eds). *The Contemporary British Novel*. Edinburgh: Edinburgh University Press, 2005, 203–216.
Anievas Gamallo, Isabel C. 'Subversive Storytelling: The Construction of Lesbian Girlhood through Fantasy and Fairytale in Jeanette Winterson's *Oranges are Not the Only Fruit*'. In *The Girl: Constructions of the Girl in Contemporary Fiction by Women*. Ed. Ruth O. Saxon. London: Palgrave Macmillan, 1999, 119–134.
Batty, Nancy. 'The Art of Suspense: Rushdie's 1001 (Mid-)Nights'. *Ariel: A Review of International English Literature* 18(3) (1987): 49–65.
Bedggood, Daniel. '(Re)Constituted Pasts: Postmodern Historicism in the Novels of Graham Swift and Julian Barnes'. In *The Contemporary British Novel*. Ed. James Acheson and Sarah C. E. Ross. Edinburgh: Edinburgh University Press, 2005, 203–216.
Belsey, Catherine. *Critical Practice*. London: Methuen, 1980.
Bentley, Nick. *Contemporary British Fiction*. Edinburgh: Edinburgh University Press, 2008.
Bernard, Catherine. *Graham Swift: La parole chronique*. Univers anglo-américain. Nancy: Presses universitaires de Nancy, 1991.
Bohm, David. *Wholeness and the Implicate Order*. London: ARK, 1980.
Brennan, Timothy. *Salman Rushdie and the Third World: Myths of a Nation*. Basingstoke: Macmillan, 1989.
——. *At Home in the World: Cosmopolitanism Now*. Cambridge, MA: Harvard University Press, 1997.
Bristow, Joseph. 'Being Gay: Politics, Identity, Pleasure'. *New Formations* 9 (Winter 1989): 61–81.
Caserio, Robert L. 'Queer Fiction: The Ambiguous Emergence of a Genre'. In *A Concise Companion to Contemporary British Fiction*. Ed. James F. English. Oxford: Blackwell, 2006, 209–226.
Childs, Peter. *Contemporary Novelists: British Fiction since 1970*. Basingstoke: Palgrave Macmillan, 2005.
Clarke, Peter. *Hope and Glory: Britain 1900–2000*, 2nd edn. London: Penguin, 2004.
Connor, Steven. *The Cambridge Companion to Postmodernism*. Cambridge: Cambridge University Press, 2004.
——. 'Postmodernism and Literature'. In *The Cambridge Companion to Postmodernism*. Ed. Stephen Connor. Cambridge: Cambridge University Press, 2004, 62–81.

Craps, Stef. *Trauma and Ethics in the Novels of Graham Swift: No Short-Cuts to Salvation*. Brighton: Sussex Academic Press, 2005.
Diedrick, James. *Understanding Martin Amis*, 2nd edn. Columbia, SC: University of South Carolina Press, 1995.
Duncker, Patricia. 'Jeanette Winterson and the Aftermath of Feminism'. In *'I'm Telling You Stories': Jeanette Winterson and the Politics of Reading*. Postmodern Studies 25. Ed. Helena Grice and Tim Woods, New York: Editions Rodopi BV, 1998, 77–88.
English, James F. (ed.). *A Concise Companion to Contemporary British Fiction*. Oxford: Blackwell, 2006.
———. 'The Literary Prize Phenomenon in Context'. In *A Companion to the British and Irish Novel: 1945–2000*. Ed. Brian W. Shaffer. Oxford: Blackwell, 2007.
———. and John Frow. 'Literary Authorship and Celebrity Culture'. In *A Concise Companion to Contemporary British Fiction*. Ed. James F. English. Oxford: Blackwell, 2006, 39–57.
Foucault, Michel. *The Order of Things: Archaeology of the Human Sciences*. London: Routledge, 2001.
Grant, Damien. *Salman Rushdie*. Tavistock: Northcote House Publishers, 1998.
Gurnah, Abdulrack (ed.). *The Cambridge Companion to Salman Rushdie*. Cambridge: Cambridge University Press, 2007.
———. 'Introduction'. In *The Cambridge Companion to Salman Rushdie*. Ed. Abdulrack Gurnah. Cambridge: Cambridge University Press, 2007, 1–10.
———. 'Themes and Structures in *Midnight's Children*'. In *The Cambridge Companion to Salman Rushdie*. Ed. Abdulrack Gurnah. Cambridge: Cambridge University Press, 2007, 91–108.
Haffenden, John. *Novelists in Interview*. London: Methuen, 1985.
Hardt, Michael and Antonio Negri. *Empire*. Cambridge, MA: Harvard University Press, 2000.
Harvey, David. *Neoliberalism*. Oxford: Oxford University Press, 2005.
Head, Dominic. *The Cambridge Introduction to Modern British Fiction, 1950–2000*. Cambridge: Cambridge University Press, 2002.
———. *Ian McEwan*. Manchester: Manchester University Press, 2007.
Huggan, Graham. *The Postcolonial Exotic: Marketing the Margins*. London: Routledge, 2001.
Hutcheon, Linda. *A Poetics of Postmodernism: History, Time and Fiction*. New York: Routledge, 1988.
Hutchinson, Colin. *Reaganism, Thatcherism and the Social Novel*. London: Palgrave Macmillan, 2008.
Jameson, Fredric. *The Political Unconscious*. London: Routledge, 1981.
———. *Postmodernism, or, the Cultural Logic of Late Capitalism*. Durham, NC: Duke University Press, 1991.
Keen, Suzanne. *Romances of the Archive in Contemporary British Fiction*. Toronto: University of Toronto Press, 2002.

Lazarus, Neil. 'Introducing Postcolonial Studies'. In *The Cambridge Companion to Postcolonial Literary Studies*. Ed. Neil Lazarus. Cambridge: Cambridge University Press, 2004, 1–16.

Lyotard, Jean-François. *The Postmodern Condition: A Report on Knowledge*. Trans. Geoff Bennington and Brian Massumi. Manchester: Manchester University Press, 1984 [1979].

McHale, Brian. *Postmodernist Fiction*. London: Routledge, 1987.

Morrison, Jago. *Contemporary Fiction*. London: Routledge, 2003.

Morton, Stephen. *Salman Rushdie*. Basingstoke: Palgrave Macmillan, 2008.

O'Keefe, Bernard. 'Thatcherism, Feminism and *The Child in Time*'. *The English Review* 12.3.2 (2002): 2–5.

Parry, Benita. *Postcolonial Studies: A Materialist Critique*. London: Routledge, 2004.

Riddell, Peter. *The Thatcher Decade: How Britain Has Changed during the 1980s*. Oxford: Basil Blackwell, 1989.

Shaffer, Brian (ed.). *A Companion to the British and Irish Novel: 1945–2000*. Oxford: Blackwell, 2007.

Sheehan, Paul. 'Postmodernism and Philosophy'. In *The Cambridge Companion to Postmodernism*. Ed. Steven Connor. Cambridge: Cambridge University Press, 2004.

Sinfield, Alan. *Literature, Politics and Culture in Postwar Britain*. London: Continuum, 2004.

Taylor, D. J. *After the War*. London: Chatto and Windus, 1993.

Tew, Philip. *The Contemporary British Novel*. London: Continuum, 2004.

Thatcher, Margaret. 'TV Interview for Granada *World in Action*', 27 January 1978, at Margaret Thatcher Foundation, http://www.margaretthatcher.org/document/103485.

———. 'Interview for *Women's Own*', 23 September 1987, at *Margaret Thatcher Foundation*, http://www.margaretthatcher.org/document/106689.

Verma, Charu. 'Padma's Tragedy: A Feminist Deconstruction of Rushdie's *Midnight's Children*'. In *Feminism and Recent Fiction in English*. Ed. Sushila Singh. New Delhi: Prestige Books, 1991, 154–162.

Waugh, Patricia. *Metafiction*. London: Routledge, 1984.

———. *The Harvest of the Sixties*. Oxford: Oxford University Press, 1995.

Notes

1. I explore these concerns in more detail in 'Reassessing the Two-Culture Debate: Popular Science in Ian McEwan's *The Child in Time* and *Enduring Love*', *Modern Fiction Studies* 59:4 (Winter 2013).

2. Some of the prominent texts from which these concepts emerge include Judith Butler. *Gender Trouble: Feminism and the Subversion of Identity*. London: Routledge, 1990; Hélène Cixous. 'The Laugh of the Medusa'. In *Feminism-Art-Theory: An*

Anthology 1968–2000. Ed. Hilary Robinson. Oxford: Blackwell, 2001, and 'The Newly Born Woman'. In *The Hélène Cixous Reader*. Ed. Susan Sellers. London: Routledge, 1994; Michel Foucault, *The History of Sexuality*, vol. I, trans. Robert Hurley. London: Penguin, [1976] 1990; Luce Irigaray. *This Sex Which Is Not One*. New York: Cornell University Press, [1977] 1985; Julia Kristeva. 'Women's Time'. *Signs* 7(1) (1981): 13–35, and 'Sabat Mater'. In *Tales of Love*, trans. Leon S. Roudiez. New York: Columbia University Press, 1987; and Eve Kosofsky Sedgwick. *Between Men: English Literature and Male Homosexual Desire*. New York: Columbia University Press, 1985.

2

Special Topic 1
The Awakening of Caledonias?
Scottish Literature in the 1980s

Monica Germanà

> It has become commonplace to observe that the past two decades have proved the most productive and challenging period in Scottish literary culture since the Scottish Renaissance of the 1920s and 1930s. Indeed, the profusion and eclecticism of creative talent across all genres and all three of the nation's languages has led some to speak not simply of revival, but of a new – perhaps even more 'real' – Scottish Renaissance. (Wallace and Stevenson, 1)

In the aftermath of the disappointing devolution referendum of 1979, the 1980s have been regarded by many as a decade of cultural renewal, as captured by Wallace and Stevenson's reference to a new 'Scottish Renaissance'. As Berthold Schoene has remarked in 'Going Cosmopolitan', from the other side of the millennial threshold, '[a]lbeit thematically often bleak and pessimistic, in terms of quality and sheer volume post 1979 literature rapidly developed into a vibrant and characteristically unruly vehicle for Scottish self-representation' (7). The decade saw the consolidation of important literary figures, such as Liz Lochhead and Edwin Morgan, as well as the emergence of a new avant-garde of novelists eminently represented by Iain Banks, who debuted with *The Wasp Factory* in 1984, and James Kelman, whose novels – *The Busconductor Hines* (1984), *A Chancer* (1985) and *A Disaffection* (1989) – brought a very distinctive Scottish realism into the foreground of Scottish literature. While Kelman's fiction would be followed up by other significant writers, such as Irvine Welsh, Janice Galloway and Alan Warner, to draw more national and international attention to Scottish fiction, another revival – that of the Gothic and fantastic romance – represented the other important trend in the Scottish literary production of the 1980s: 'This early 1980s aesthetic can be described as Gothic', Michael Gardiner rightly observes, 'set against long shadows and empty warehouses, and presaging how hidden languages and experiences would haunt experience' (183). This revival was pioneered, as many critics have suggested, by the publication of Alasdair Gray's *Lanark* (1981), where the 'return to magic', as Douglas Gifford put it, unravels as a parallel strand to realism, a blend explored, in different ways, in the subsequent works of writers such as Iain (M.) Banks, Sian Hayton, Ellen Galford and, in the following decade, A. L. Kennedy, Margaret Elphinstone and Ali Smith. In Gifford's words:

> Major changes took place throughout the 1980s, with writers like Edwin Morgan, Alasdair Gray, and Liz Lochhead,... developing a new kind of imaginative relationship with their country and its culture, a relationship which refused to accept a simple realism of generally bleak and economically deprived urban character... The changes of these writers in approach and ideology, and of the contemporary writers who follow them, have radically altered the directions of Scottish literature, and fiction especially. (17)

What both realist and fantastic strands share in the literary production of the Scottish 1980s is a self-conscious interrogation of the alienated identity and marginal belonging of the Scottish self within Thatcherite Britain and an increasingly globalized political system. Such cultural and psychological investigations are underpinned by the urgent desire to find an authentic voice, an increasing anxiety about parochialism and an intense awareness of the heterogeneous strata comprising late-twentieth-century Scottish culture.

The aim of this chapter is to give an indication of the kinds of preoccupations and aesthetic responses produced throughout the 1980s and with particular references to Gray's *Lanark*, Banks's *The Wasp Factory*, Kelman's *The Busconductor Hines* and Galloway's *The Trick Is to Keep Breathing* (1989). These novels have been selected as representative of the most innovative aspects of the second Scottish Renaissance and can be seen as paradigms of the decade's cultural zeitgeist. Though in many ways exemplary of the variety of distinctive voices that emerged from the 1980s literary production in Scotland, the four novels display similar concerns and shared thematic approaches. Whether urban, suburban or small-town, the environment depicted in these texts presents itself as an elusive, or problematic, space to negotiate: in *Lanark*, the parallel narratives revolve around the two main characters' quests to conquer their own positions in the hostile environments of Glasgow and Unthank; in *The Wasp Factory*, a novel which points to the family home as an uncanny source of danger, Frank Cauldhame is obsessed with controlling the territory of the island, where the house rests; *The Busconductor Hines* unravels as the story of Rab's endless – and aimless – journeys around town; Joy Stone's trauma informs the de-familiarization of domestic and institutional spaces in *The Trick Is to Keep Breathing*. While spatial negotiation is made more complex by the amnesiac consciousness all but Kelman's character share, psychological instability is also implicitly referenced through various conditions (asthma/dragonhide, schizoid and compulsive behaviour, addiction): what Lanark/Duncan Thaw, Frank, Rab and Joy ultimately share is a state of sickness, which, arguably, reflects back on the diseased community – or nation – in which they struggle to belong. In a sense, however, it is the emphasis placed on the marginal characters, abused bodies and alienated minds of these narratives that produces the aesthetic innovation and formal revolution that these novels bring forward. In its playful approach to linear chronology, intertextuality, narrative structure and generic conventions, *Lanark*'s experimentalism makes it, in many ways, the most distinctive novel of the decade. Banks's blend of horror and dark humour epitomizes the revival of the Scottish Gothic. The innovatively hybrid linguistic register employed by Kelman in his first published novel, *The Busconductor Hines*, and subsequent fiction, subverts the politics of the literary novel. Similarly, the formal and textual disruptions of Galloway's prose bring female marginality into the foreground of literary imagination. In different ways, the four novels analysed in this chapter subvert the rule, disturbing the order and stability of literary conventions in the name of innovation.

It is perhaps unsurprising that the rise of a new set of aesthetics arose from the ashes of the Scottish dream of independence: the 1979 referendum, despite a narrow majority, failed to allow Scotland devolution. On one level, the political climate following the debacle was one of utter disappointment and disenfranchisement. Many intellectuals, including, eminently, Alan Massie, felt disenchanted and disillusioned with regard to the possibility of ever achieving cultural autonomy for Scotland. As Massie pointed out in his introduction to a reprint of Edwin Muir's *Scott and Scotland* (1936) published in 1982, 'Scott's Scotland retained a public life; ours has none; or at least none that can invigorate, or prove fertile, to a writer' (xxii). The Thatcher years were particularly hard on Scotland and the North of England, economically as well as politically. In Scotland, the decline of the shipyard industry, already begun in the post-war years, caused unemployment levels to soar. Simultaneously, the gender divide became wider and more difficult to articulate: the clash was between unemployed working-class men and educated women, who faced different problems, producing, in turn, other social repercussions in the negotiation of gender roles in Scotland.

More than anything else, what the referendum created was an introspective reaction, a questioning of national identity and the foundations of nationalism as an ideology perhaps too entrenched in old-fashioned definitions of patriotism, which did not necessarily function in the global context of the late twentieth century. Michael Gardiner suggests that while 'Scottish literature enjoyed a revival, Britain as an idea was collapsing more rapidly than at any time since the eighteenth century' (181); in fact, Scotland, too, appeared to be divided between Scottishness and Britishness; or, rather, the referendum exposed uncomfortable truths about Scotland as a nation characterized not by the cohesive brotherhood of its nationalist ideology, but by a profoundly heterogeneous culture, divided by political and religious sectarianism. As a result, Scottish intellectuals found themselves suspended between the desire to find and maintain a distinctive Scottish character and a simultaneous resistance to both pigeonholing and the parochialism that a minor nation within the British hegemonic system had been suffering for quite some time. The 'watershed' year of 1979 catalysed the rebirth of Scottish literature, a reincarnation that the previous decades had somehow paved the way for, but which undoubtedly blossomed in the 1980s; as Cairns Craig says in *Out of History*, 'what happened in Scotland in the 1960s and 1970s, and what laid the foundation for the enormous creative achievements of the 1980s, was the liberation of the voice' (193).

Scottish history has developed as a history of layers or, as Craig would put it, 'erasures'; John Knox erased what had been medieval Scotland to give birth to modern Presbyterian Scotland; the Acts of Union of 1706 and 1707 put an end to independent Scotland and launched the history of Scotland as dependent upon both Westminster and the sovereign authority of the British monarch. In *The Modern Scottish Novel*, Craig links the notion of Scotland's history of erasures to the impossibility of establishing a coherent literary tradition and the impossibility even to represent Scotland in any kind of monolithic or unitary fashion:

> The constant erasure of one Scotland by another makes Scotland unrelatable, un-narratable: past Scotlands are not gathered into the being of modern Scotland; they are abolished. Modern Scotland thus has no past, since no past Scotland can be related to the actually existing Scotland, and no narrative can be constructed to constitute its continuing identity. Unrelated and unrelatable, Scotland becomes invisible[.] (21)

The notion of Scotland and Scottish identity as a kind of nonentity, or a non-place, emerges in different ways throughout the literary production of the decade: the poetry of Scotland's laureate poets, Edwin Morgan (2004) and Liz Lochhead (2011), shares a similar resistance to reductive notions of national identity, blending tradition with an assertive faith in innovative possibilities of aesthetic expression. In different ways, too, the fiction published by Gray, Kelman, Banks and Galloway deconstruct the view that Scotland – and its culture – exists in any coherent fashion.

Along with a sense of schizoid fragmentation, what seems to pervade the Scottish novel of the 1980s is the self-conscious attempt to subvert tradition and challenge conventions, in the attempt to find new, more authentic ways to express the Scottish experience: 'Let Glasgow Flourish by Telling the Truth' reads the motto in the Book One title-page illustration of Gray's *Lanark*. The novel self-consciously embarks on this task, as reflected, for instance, in this well-known passage from the novel:

> [T]hink of Florence, Paris, London, New York. Nobody visiting them for the first time is a stranger because he's already visited them in painting, novels, history books and films. But if a city hasn't been used by an artist not even the inhabitants live there imaginatively. What is Glasgow to most of us? A house, the place we work, a football park or a golf course, some pubs connecting streets. That's all. No, I'm wrong, there's also the cinema and library. And when our imagination needs exercise we use these to visit London, Paris, Rome under the Caesars, the American West at the turn of the century, anywhere but here and now. Imaginatively Glasgow exists as a music-hall song and a few bad novels. That's all we've given to the world outside. It's all we've given to ourselves. (243)

Duncan Thaw – like Gray, significantly, a visual artist – laments the lack of a solid Scottish imagination, which he links to economic depression and the sectarian character of the city. A nation's aesthetic and cultural distinctiveness cannot flourish without political and economic independence: freedom of expression is strongly rooted in all other kinds of freedom, which the main characters in the novel strive to obtain. Battles for emancipation are made useless, however, by the lack of cohesion and short-sightedness of the oppressed. As Thaw puts matters, 'it is easier to fight your neighbours than fight a bad government' (244). That Gray's novel, which took over two decades in the making, is representative of the complex political climate leading up to the referendum is also made clear by the Book Three title-page illustration, in the foreground of which is a reclining sleeping figure: beside the caption, 'Oblivio', is the year 1979.

As Alison Lee points out: '*Lanark*'s primary concern is with structures of power, from familial, governmental, and corporate control, to the manipulation of the reader and the character' (100). Authority, and, in particular, the sovereign power of the state, is a major preoccupation throughout *Lanark*. Significantly, Gray's critical investigation of political power invests the narrative on all levels. While

Thaw's problematic relationships with the various authority figures – including his father – seemingly lead to his demise, Lanark, too, faces many challenges with the power structures around him: be they Unthank, the Institute or the Council, Sludden, Professor Ozenfant and Lord Monboddo are reincarnations of the repressive modes of control with which Lanark struggles. When he introduces himself to Rima at the Institute, Lanark says, 'I've never wanted anything long. Except freedom' (74). Imprisonment within both worlds is metaphorically expressed by the main characters' physical ailments: Thaw, like Gray, suffers from asthma, while Lanark suffers from a condition called 'dragonhide', a hardening of the skin (and a mirroring of Thaw's eczema), which, in some cases, can grow to encase the entire body. As well as indicating the insular solipsism of the characters' experience, both conditions are suggestive of their entrapment within the unfair mechanisms of a profit-driven capitalist world. The use made of the bodies of sick people to create energy for the hospital supports the paradoxical foundations of capitalist economy exposed in the novel: in order to survive, the hospital needs incurable patients who can be converted into energy.

Whilst exposing the impact of the politics of capitalism on individual freedom, simultaneously the novel's narrative structure and textuality destabilize any notions of linearity and cohesion, raising questions of authorial control: the novel is split into four books, but starts off with Book Three, which is followed by a Prologue, Book One, Interlude, Book Two, and finally Book Four, which is in turn interrupted by the Epilogue, before the end. Such self-conscious disruption of linear chronology is also reflected in the content of the parallel stories of Duncan Thaw in Books One and Two and of Lanark in Books Three and Four. In the realist strand, Thaw's narrative fails to move forward, because what should develop as a *Bildungsroman* becomes, instead, the story of Thaw's failure to achieve any kind of emotional and professional fulfilment, leading instead to his apparent suicide at the end of Book Two:

> He wallows under, gasping and tumbling over and over in salt sting, knowing nothing, but the need not to breathe. A humming drumming fills his brain, in panic he opens his eyes and glimpses green glimmers through salt sting. And when at last, like fingernails losing clutch on too narrow a ledge, he, tumbling, yells out last dregs of breath and has to breathe, there flows in upon him, not pain, but annihilating sweetness. (354)

Evoking Craig's view of the history of Scotland, Thaw's life story is a series of erasures, ultimately culminating in self-annihilation. Temporality and progression are also deeply problematic in the fantastic strand of the novel.

The time spent inside the Institute stretches indefinitely: 'It seemed many days since he had been there, though the clock showed it was not three hours' (76). Later, having escaped captivity within the Institute, Lanark and Rima travel through the Intercalendrical Zone, which means, Council Chamberlain Hector Munro explains, travel time is 'unpredictable': 'The light in this zone travels at different speeds, so all sizes and distances are deceptive' (373–374). Unthank itself becomes subject to the timely incoherence of the Intercalendrical Zone, speeding up the ageing process of Lanark's son, Sandy. It becomes apparent, however, that time has in fact become the new currency: talking about the creature, the nebulous conspiracy behind the dystopian world of Unthank, is a group of 'owners and manipulators', who 'pay themselves with time: time to think and plan, time to examine necessity from a distance' (410). In essence, the creature is the reincarnation of the paradoxical logic of capitalism already exposed by Aldous Huxley and George Orwell in their respective dystopian visions, both featuring in the intertextual palimpsest of Gray's narrative. In Chapter Twenty-Three, there is an allusion to *Brave New World*, 'a world with too little in it to believe or enjoy' (254). Equally the 'smell of boiled cabbage' draws a suggestive reference to *1984* (335), while, as Gray acknowledges in the Index of Plagiarisms, '[t]he poster slogans and the social stability centre are Dipflags of the Ingsoc posters and Ministry of Love in *1984*' (495). And wasting time and energy is, it transpires, the main business of the creature in *Lanark*:

> [T]he creature has invented peaceful ways of taking our time and energy. It employs us to make essential things badly, so they decay fast and have to be replaced. It bribes the council to destroy cheap things which don't bring it to a profit and replaces them with new expensive things which do. It pays us to make useless things and employs scientists, doctors and artists to persuade us that these are essential. (412)

Against the perpetual time control held by the creature, significantly, Lanark's return to Unthank also exposes subversive forms of time manipulation. A more human perception of time, based on the individual heartbeat, for example, replaces the traditional ways of measuring time. To Lanark's question about timekeeping, Grant's reply is simply 'I've a pulse' (408). But it is the birth of Alexander, his son, that brings this newly acquired notion of time home to Lanark, for whom 'the universe seemed to go silent and slow' (421), when the baby is born. That the birth of a new life is marked, at least at the level of human perception, with a universal hold on the increasingly fast pace of life seems to suggest a counter-cultural resistance to the creature's politics of speed and mass production.

The apparent textual anarchy of the novel self-consciously addresses questions of authorial control. The incongruous structure invites the novel 'to be read in one order' – as the author figure, Nastler, suggests in the Epilogue – 'and thought of in another' (483). The author would therefore be deprived of any absolute power, his authority over his text diminished in favour of the reader's increased freedom. The author's originality, too, is defied by the so-called 'Index of Plagiarisms', a list of the texts that have somehow contributed to the making of Gray's novel, and occupying the margins of pages 485–499 of the Epilogue. One such text is Thomas Hobbes's *Leviathan* (1651), one of the most influential and recurrent references: with the exception of Book Two – where it is seemingly replaced by Death – the Leviathan, as gigantic monster or whale, appears in all title pages of the four books in *Lanark*. As Gray admits in the Index (490), one particular illustration of the title page of Hobbes's work is plagiarized by Gray in the title page of Book Four: here, as in the original illustration, the sovereign state is represented as a giant, whose body is made of the bodies of its citizens; their features are, however, indistinct. The state's identity is instead dominant, as is the pose and the posture – the giant wears a crown and holds a sword in his right hand and a sceptre in his left hand – indicating absolute religious and political powers. Thomas Hobbes's famous theory '*Homo homini lupus est*', 'man is wolf to fellow man', is replaced by the novel's refrain 'Man is the pie that bakes and eats itself' (411), which exposes the weak logic of individualistic politics: in the attempt to feed off each other, men end up eating themselves. It is division and sectarianism that alienates the individual and breaks down the possibility of community. The cannibalistic tendencies of human society are exposed by Gray in both narrative strands: the 'real' world of Duncan Thaw, Glasgow and the imaginary places his alter ego, Lanark, travels to and between, the Institute, the Council, Unthank and Provan (allegorical representations of Glasgow and Edinburgh, respectively) are representative of the parasitical opportunism of human relationships on one hand, and dystopian bureaucracy on the other. Though the book may certainly be seen to address universal considerations about mankind in its allegorical commentary of notions of social contract, it is also about Scotland. There is a sense in which although history has not done Scotland any favours, the Scots should stop being complacent with each other and act against their disunion.

Although the end of the novel depicts the character awaiting what could be an apocalyptic catastrophe – or, perhaps, just the beginning of a new world – the last passage is suggestive of hope symbolized by the light, the holy grail of Lanark's quest: 'Lanark... propped his chin on his hands and sat a long time watching the moving clouds. He was a slightly worried, ordinary old man but glad to see the light in the sky' (560). The passage is followed by one final epigraph, in bold capital letters, drawing attention, one final time, to the important subtext of time – and history – in the making of a place:

> I STARTED MAKING MAPS WHEN I WAS SMALL SHOWING PLACE, RESOURCES, WHERE THE ENEMY AND WHERE LOVE LAY. I DID NOT KNOW TIME ADDS TO LAND. EVENTS DRIFT CONTINUALLY DOWN, EFFACING LANDMARKS, RAISING THE LEVEL, LIKE SNOW.
> I HAVE GROWN UP. MY MAPS ARE OUT OF DATE.
> THE LAND LIES OVER ME NOW.
> I CANNOT MOVE. IT IS TIME TO GO. (560)

The novel's ending lends itself to multiple readings. On a metafictional level, it serves the purpose of bidding the reader farewell, more explicitly expressed by the large-print '**GOODBYE**' on the next and final page of the text. Most importantly, it leaves the reader with a notion of time as the fourth spatial dimension, hinting to a psycho-geographical reading of Scotland, as a place shaped by the geological strata of its historical past, which Gray's epic novel, partially, attempts to unveil. Whichever future space the nation is to occupy will depend on its ability to lay solid foundations in its present politics.

Mistrust in – and subversion of – authority feature strongly in Banks's *The Wasp Factory*, the strange story of Frank Cauldhame, according to Punter 'a seventeen-year old monster, living on an island with his eccentric father' (168). The self-confessed murderer of three children (his younger brother Paul and cousins Blyth and Esmerelda), Frank is the first-person narrator of a story of methodical madness and apparently gratuitous violence. But concealed behind the killing of humans and rabbits is the desire to authenticate the self, through a regimental set of strategies to control the environment of the island. Ironically, while Frank attempts to control, he is also, unknowingly, being controlled. The reader, and Frank, become fully aware of the manipulative relationship between Frank and his father, only at the end of the novel, when it is revealed that Frank is a biological woman, whose body has been 'constructed' as male/masculine through hormonal therapy and psychological conditioning. Viewed retrospectively, therefore, Frank's strange games become symptomatic manifestations of repressed trauma: 'Frank proceeds not only to invent himself as a male', Victor Sage argues, 'but also a whole religion and cosmology which will explain and justify the microcosmic barbarian world he imagines himself to be the centre of' (25).

'Potential schisms in the individual ... are constantly present in Banks's fiction', comments Thom Nairn, in an essay looking at Banks's prolific and eclectic career (129). Rather than presenting Frank as the singular occurrence of abnormal deviancy, the novel proposes the thesis that in her alienated condition, Frank may in fact be representative of an endemic sense of psychological instability. Madness runs in the family: Frank's brother, Eric, becomes insane as a result of an incident – perhaps the most unpleasant image in the novel – at the hospital where he is training to become a doctor. This is the catalyst for Eric's subsequent misdeeds – which includes the burning of stray dogs – but also, according to Frank, a projection of Eric's subconscious awareness of her own condition:

> What Eric saw when he lifted that plate up, what he saw with all that weight of human suffering above, with all that mighty spread of closed-in, heat-struck darkened city all around, what he saw with his own skull splitting, was a slowly writhing nest of fat maggots, swimming in their combined digestive juices as they consumed the brain of the child. (142)

That prior to the incident Eric has been suffering from severe migraines is in itself suggestive of the predicament he shares with the child whose brain is literally being eaten away. Rather then a physical split, however, an intense sense of psychological division pervades the novel, as exemplified by another image conjured up by Frank, whose voice is here reminiscent of the sinner's schizoid narrative in James Hogg's *The Private Memoirs and Confessions of a Justified Sinner* (1824):

> Often I've thought of myself as a state; a country or, at the very least, a city. It used to seem to me that the different ways I felt sometimes about ideas, courses of action and so on were like the differing political moods that countries go through. It has always seemed to me that people vote in a new government not because they actually agree with their politics but just because they want a change. Somehow they think that things will be better under the new lot. Well, people are stupid, but it all seems to have more to do with mood, caprice and atmosphere than carefully thought-out arguments. I can feel the same sort of thing going on in my head. Sometimes the thoughts and feelings I had didn't really agree with each other, so I decided I must be lots of different people inside my brain. (62)

While Frank's (sick) mind is, by her admission, at war with itself, the analogy also reinforces the idea of a collective malaise, an endemic kind of fragmentation. In Frank's conception, the nation state is not the unified – albeit under the absolute power of the sovereign ruler – political body found in *Lanark*, a novel that Banks would 'rewrite' in *The Bridge* (1986). The fragmented social structure and the consequent unpredictability of its electorate – both echoes of the failed devolution referendum and the Conservative victory in 1979 – are compared to Frank's sick mind. Conversely, Frank's schizoid behaviour is reflected on the nation in a state of dissolution, which Scotland represents to Frank's eyes. Frank unveils her thoughts about the problematic lack of cohesion in Scottish political history, in her humorous discussion of the etymology of Union Street:

> I thought the 'union'... delineated an association of working people, and it did seem to me at the time to be quite a socialist thing for the town fathers to call a street; it struck me that all was not yet lost as regards the prospects for a possible peace or at the very least a cease-fire in the class war if such acknowledgements of the worth of trade unions could find their way on to such a venerable and important thoroughfare's sign, but... my father informed me that it was the then recently confirmed union of the English and Scottish parliaments the local worthies – in common with hundreds of other town councils throughout what had until that point been an independent realm – were celebrating with such solemnity and permanence, doubtless with a view to the opportunities for profit which this early form of takeover bid offered. (81)

Embodying the spirit of the second Renaissance, whilst producing a critical reading of the nation's self-complacency, the novel's form shows the signs of cultural rebirth necessary to subvert political apathy; Nairn has suggested that the humour in the novel is distinctly Scottish, highlighting, in the failure of English reviewers to recognize it, 'intrinsic differences in outlook between Scottish and English society' (128). Yet here, as in *Lanark*, Frank shares with Thaw a disillusioned view of the sectarianism of Scottish politics: opportunistic and short-sighted, what Union Street stands for, in the topography of Scottish towns, is in fact an admission to Scotland's disunion. There is also another ironic layer – one that the reader can only be aware of afterwards; as in *Lanark*, *The Wasp Factory* presents a problematic relationship with the father, whose Law, in *Lanark* at least, is frequently challenged. Neither the psychologically unstable Frank nor her father is a reliable source of authoritative voice: the present is corrupt because the past cannot be relied upon. History does not produce any kind of positive lesson and the Law of the Father may be challenged for the sake of sadistic pleasure:

> I've always had a rather ambivalent attitude towards something happening to my father, and it persists. *A death is always something exciting*, always *makes you realise how alive you are, how vulnerable but so-far-lucky*; but the death of somebody close gives you a good excuse to go a bit crazy for a while and do things that would otherwise be inexcusable. What *delight* to behave really badly and still get loads of sympathy! (41, emphases added)

Frank's subconscious desire to subvert her father's authority and replace it with her own is behind the primitive ritualism of her solitary games, which include the bizarre invention of the 'wasp factory'. A device created to predict the future, it serves the purpose of proving Frank's (masculine) authority. Unsurprisingly, behind such an urge to control the environment lie Frank's deepest fears and insecurities, which she reveals earlier on in the novel:

> My *greatest enemies* are Women and the Sea. These are the things I hate. Women because they are weak and stupid and live in the shadow of men and are nothing compared to them, and the Sea because it has always frustrated me, *destroying* what I have built, washing away what I have left, wiping clean the marks that I have made. And I'm not all that sure the Wind is blameless either.
>
> The Sea is a sort of mythological enemy, and I make what you might call sacrifices to it in my soul, *fearing it a little, respecting it* as you are supposed to, but in many ways treating it as an equal. It does things to the world, and so do I; we should both be feared. Women... well, *women are a bit too close for comfort as far as I'm concerned*. (43; emphases added)

The ominous and, in hindsight, ironic tone of the opening paragraph in Chapter Three hints at the psychosexual subtext of Frank's anxieties. With the 'island' representing the epicentre of most of her power-enforcing militaristic activities, the Sea comes as a natural enemy – the fear of which she sublimates through her dam-building fantasies. More problematic is Frank's misogyny, which violates the self/other boundaries, producing echoes of Julia Kristeva's theory of abjection: 'One of those violent, dark revolts of being, directed against a threat that seems to emanate from an exorbitant outside or inside, ejected beyond the scope of the possible, the tolerable, the thinkable' (1). Frank's apparent misogyny not only reveals a problematic sexuality, but is the closest she gets to the unutterable truth which emerges at the end of the novel: Frank, the self-fashioned misogynist and pseudo-castrated murderer, is, in fact, a woman.

Whilst seeking legitimization against the female other, as with Frankenstein's monster, Sage suggests, Frank's identity is also shaped by a problematic relationship with the Maker/Father (24). As well as in Frank's obsession with 'naming', in itself an act of patriarchal mimicry, the Oedipal competition for power becomes particularly manifest in the characters' territorial attitudes towards space. Outdoors, determined to claim her 'territory' on the island, the narrator is involved in activities that clearly enact archetypal forms of control over the surrounding (hostile) environment. Indoors, father and daughter also define their mutually exclusive spaces, articulating, through their spatial antagonism, the classic Gothic question of patriarchal authority: while Frank's loft, 'the home of the Wasp Factory', represents the narrator's inner sanctum – 'the loft is my domain' – the study becomes the Father's uncanny workshop: 'I think there's a secret in the study' (16). With no official status in the world, Frank has not attended school and has had to rely on her father for any information about the outside world until old enough to visit the public library. As Berthold Schoene-Harwood suggests, *The Wasp Factory* simultaneously illustrates the paradoxical enforcement and subversion of patriarchal authority, by illustrating Frank's paradigm of masculine identity through the unveiling of its deceitful foundations:

> The neo-gothic design of Banks's novel, its macabre celebration of violence, horror and death, is not an end in itself but aims to unmask the fraudulence of the old order and, ultimately, to demolish the Law of the Father by probing the subliminal turmoil that both upholds and potentially subverts it. ('Dams Burst' 132)

With the novel cast within the Gothic genre, the father's study becomes the forbidden room, the one containing the secret core of any Gothic story (think, for example, of Bluebeard's or Dracula's fortresses). Most significant, in this case, is the association with another important Victorian Gothic dark spot: Dr Jekyll's laboratory in Robert Louis Stevenson's *Strange Case of Dr Jekyll and Mr Hyde* (1886). Arguably, it is this connection that Frank – and any reader familiar with the Scottish text – is subliminally aware of. Her first reaction, having seen the male hormones and tampons lying around her father's study, is that Angus is Agnes, her long-estranged mother: 'I thought of that delicate face, those lightly haired arms...The secret. It couldn't be...Angus. Agnes. I only had his word for anything that had happened' (173). The notion that her father/mother could have been performing experiments upon her own sex is strongly influenced by a possible reference to Jekyll/Hyde: as in Stevenson's novel, the climax of the story revolves around the unsettling question of double identities. The truth about Frank's biological sex does not in fact change who the father is, as much as what the father represents in relation to the parameters behind the construction of Frank's gender identity: patriarchal rule and symbolic order.

While fooling the readers into the plot of lies and red herrings woven by the father/author, the text not only claims the social – rather than biological – 'essence' of gender identity, 'But I *am* still me; I *am* the same person, with the same memories and the same deeds done, the same (small) achievements, the same (appalling) crimes to *my* name' (182), but also questions, more broadly, all fixed paradigms of identity and *telos*. Looking ahead to her new future as a woman, Frank does not conceal her anxieties:

> I am a woman. Scarred thighs, outer labia a bit chewed up, and I'll never be attractive, but according to Dad a normal female, capable of intercourse and giving birth (I shiver at the thought of either). (182)

The novel's epiphanic revelation – and the implicit acknowledgement of one's lack of power in relation to one's destiny – is paradoxically a liberating experience. As with *Lanark*, Banks's novel ends on a note of (positive) uncertainty, an oxymoron perhaps, but also an assertive statement against the constraints of determinism: 'Our destination is the same in the end, but out journey – part chosen, part determined – is different for us all, and changes even as we live and grow' (184).

A more positive – if perhaps doomed – father–son relationship occurs in James Kelman's *The Busconductor Hines*, a novel that juxtaposes the public and private lives of Rab Hines, opening a progressively wider gap between the two. Rab's situation is defined as unavoidable and unchangeable. The novel's episodic structure defeats linearity, resisting the possibility of progression. By choosing to focus on the marginal, hopeless working-class Scot, however, Kelman enacts the first stage of a self-conscious literary revolution. Significantly, at the end of the decade in which he had published three other novels – *A Chancer* (1985), *Greyhound for Breakfast* (1987) and *A Disaffection* (1989) – in 'The East End Writers' Kelman still lamented the peripheral status of working-class narratives:

> Ninety per cent of the literature in Great Britain concerns people who never have to worry about money at all. We always seem to be watching or reading about emotional crises among folk who live in a world of great fortune both in matters of money and luck. (21)

In *The Busconductor Hines*, Rab's social paralysis is mirrored in the narrative immobility of a plot-less story. Much of the novel is instead occupied by Rab's own musings, which simultaneously support Kelman's intention to give the working-class subject a deeper psychological dimension than previously allowed, and enhance the sense of estrangement from the alienating work environment Rab's life is bound by. In the following passage, Rab projects his inner fantasies onto a future time, a prospect which, he hopes, will be better for his son:

> Into the libraries you shall go. And he'll dig out the stuff, the real mccoy but son the real mccoy, then the art galleries and museums son the palaces of the people, the subways and the graveyards and the fucking necropolises, the football parks then the barrows on Sunday morning you'll be digging out the old books and clothes and that and not forgetting the paddy's by Christ for a slab of last year's tablet son plus the second-hand pair of false teeth right enough, aye, very useful indeed though it's a pity about the ferries of course cause he would've liked to take you on one before they shut down son and it's too late now though you'd have thought it was good son the carry on backwards and forwards from one shore to the other ... (90)

Rab's considerations about his son's future unveil the regenerative cultural potential of the city of Glasgow: the passage can be read in direct response to the earlier one from *Lanark*; not only can Glasgow be 'imagined', but the specific aesthetic response Kelman introduces is distinctive because the marginal has finally reached the centre, at least in literature. The form of the novel endorses this act of social recognition: whilst drawing attention to the ostracized, Kelman's use of free indirect discourse and stream of consciousness arguably erases the barriers between high and low culture, literary and colloquial language. As Craig suggests in *Out of History*: 'The vitality of Kelman's prose comes precisely from his refusal to accept any standard for the narrative voice in his novels: narrator, character, language – all explore what happens when you cease to accept fixed positions in a structure but move restlessly between them' (195). The coexistence of different linguistic registers reflects the heterogeneous character of Scottish culture, and of the plurality of its languages, pointing to a different reading of the national imagination, one which, as Craig would have it, relies on concepts of polyphony and heteroglossia. Drawing from Bakhtin, Craig suggests in *The Modern Scottish Novel* that the only way to understand the patterns in which tradition and modernity interact within the boundaries of Scottish culture is precisely this notion of 'dialogue between opposing forces':

> The national imagination is not some transcendental identity which either survives or is erased: it is a space in which a dialogue is in process between the various pressures and inheritances that constitute the particularity of human experience in a territory whose boundaries might have been otherwise, but whose borders define the limits within which certain voices, both past and present, with all their centripetal and centrifugal implications, are listened for, and others resisted, no matter how loud they may be. (31)

Kelman's polyphonic text does not, however, produce an entirely optimistic picture; although the narrative succeeds in rendering Rab's point of view effectively, his experience of life in Glasgow in the late 1970s is far from positive. Kelman's stagnant plot is influenced by his reading of Franz Kafka and his concern with the poignant absurdity of modern life (McGlynn 51–54). Rab Hines fights against the hostile environment the city represents: the cold, the rain, the darkness hinder the negotiation of his position. Whilst giving a voice to its marginal characters, Kelman's novel also exposes the urban milieu as the stagnant repository of hopelessness, despair and hindrance to individual self-development:

> These fucking scary closes! Some of them are really evil. Strange dripping noises. Is it a burst pipe or what. A broken gutter. Just a tap with a faulty washer. And the concrete all cracked and treacherous for folks' feet. The auld yins there, having

to tread with great caution, the lights in the close dim or not working except in periodic blinks; and that dogshit in dark corners – the floor just swept too and suddenly littered with a mysterious black matter which is picked up for inspection, O my it's awful soft this whatever it is: Shite! Help ma boab right enough. No wonder they auld yins crack up. Half a lifetime spent scrubbing and whiteclaying the concrete only to have to finally admit the uncontrollable stuff going on behind their stooped backs. It is a pity. (158)

As the city appears to be subject to the capricious force of an entropic design, there is no hope of self-improvement. In spite of individual and collective efforts, there is a sense in which the space is haunted – an implicit kind of Gothic discourse is at play in passages such as the one quoted earlier – by the malignant spirit of the city, which seeps into the walls of its council houses, pavements and closes, slowly eroding its own structure.

There are no memorable experiences or iconic sights accounted for in Rab's daily trips around the city. As a conductor, Rab travels everyday, though, ironically, such journeys lead nowhere. 'The passive aspect of working on the buses has obvious metaphorical connotations for Hines' life more generally', Simon Kövesi explains, 'he has no control, no agency, no determined direction' (46). Yet Rab wants to move up – mainly to have better wages and avoid shift work – and away: like other characters in Kelman's novels, he frequently fantasizes of a better life elsewhere. But the fantasy clashes with the harsh reality in which he seems enmeshed: the city mice keep threatening to intrude even the cramped one-bedroom flat he shares with his wife and young son. Kelman does not idealize the Scottish experience; it is little wonder that Rab – entrapped in a vicious circle which does not allow him to be either happy or free – dreams about destroying Glasgow and its history:

> Glasgow's a big city, all the life etc. The scraggy mongrels, they go moseying along near the inside of the pavement then to the outside and maybe off across the street to sniff other pastures. Hereabouts the district is a melter of sniffs. A myriad of things at your nostrils. The decayed this and the decayed that. A patch of tenements set for the chop ... Better off razing the lot to the ground. And renting a team of steamrollers to flatten the dump properly, compressing the earth and what is upon and within, crushing every last pore to squeeze out the remaining gaseous elements until at last that one rectangular mass is appearing, all set for sowing. The past century is due burial; it is always being forgotten. (167–168)

Rab's vision is evocative of the notion of erasure mentioned earlier in relation to Scottish history. The difference here is that, at least in his thoughts which

Kelman's narrative accommodates, Rab is empowered and in control of the urban environment, which, in real life, wrecks his search for emancipation and autonomy.

The passing of time, in this respect, is another signifier of the lack of social mobility. Time is Rab's worst enemy. As a shift worker, his life is theoretically ruled by a rigid – and in many ways, dehumanizing – schedule. Juxtaposed to the rigid structure of shift work, Rab's private time appears to move at a different pace:

> Things passed sluggishly. All kinds of items. He was fancying a similarity between it and what was supposed to happen to people that instant prior to death. What a fucking jumble and yet also quite coherent. The idea of laughing aloud occurred, and made him smile. The clock. He raised himself to see the time: apparently 20 minutes had elapsed since the alarm clock sounded. It seemed like 20 seconds. Too late now to make any breakfast, not even time for a coffee, and coffee would have been delicious. (112)

His lack of punctuality, therefore, becomes an act of subconscious disobedience, foreshadowing later confrontations with the management. As Kövesi observes:

> Time is to be controlled, the future managed better than the past, the past not to seep into the future; these are temporal aspirations Hines has. Along with and in relation to architectural shapes and forms, time is the other major system by which he constructs and conceptualises his life. (48)

It is by opposing resistance to the given structure of time that Rab poses a challenge to the hierarchical order that pushes his existence to the cultural and geographical peripheries of society. Like the Little Tramp in Charlie Chaplin's *Modern Times* (1936), Rab's apparent inadequacy is the symptom of a wider and systematic set of dysfunctional social conditions.

As in *Lanark* and *The Wasp Factory*, *The Busconductor Hines* exposes the problematic sectarianism and the lack of class consciousness, which would strengthen Rab's position. As Craig suggests in 'Resting Arrest':

> Kelman's depiction is not of a working-class community so much as of a working-class world which has become atomised, fragmented, and in which individuals are isolated from one another – a world in which political hope has been severed and only economic deprivation remains. (101)

Such lack of social cohesion manifests itself in different ways in the novel. Rab has a distant relationship with his family, who remain in Drumchapel, the West Glasgow suburb used as part of the 1950s overspill building campaign. His relationship with his wife, Sandra, too, is haunted by the lack of prospects to move out of their current flat, while his hopes of ever becoming a driver are flattened by his inability to keep his shifts. Nevertheless, as with Duncan and Frank in the previous novels, Rab displays an assertive attitude against those in power, as revealed in the climactic episode, towards the end of the novel, when Rab is forced to return to the workplace outside his working hours:

> He said to the superintendent: I think I should remind you, I've been in the garage since half 11 this morning. I'm not getting paid for it: I'm here on my own time. And something else – I'm supposed to be looking after the wean; he's sitting up the stair with a bunch of bloody strangers. I think it's a disgrace to be honest. (210)

Rab's logic leaves the superintendent almost speechless, and Rab deserts the station with dignity, having resigned on a point of pride. In the end, however, the narrative reveals a circular structure, or, we should say, a vicious circle, with Rab back at work, trapped within the enclosed environment of the bus cabin: 'Hines shifted his position, he wiped the condensation from the back window and looked out' (237). While Lanark looks up towards the sun, Rab looks out, past the thick film of condensation that separates him from the world outside. Though still enslaved by the alienating shift work, his perspective still matters. What the rules of society deny him – autonomy, dignity, fulfilment – the new rule of Kelman's fiction allows to exist.

As with Lanark's and Thaw's stories in Gray's novel, Joy Stone, the protagonist of Galloway's *The Trick Is to Keep Breathing*, presents her story as one of post-traumatic distress; her name, as Glenda Norquay has suggested, conceals an oxymoron, suggestive of her 'ambiguous identity' and impossible existence (132). Like Frank Cauldhame, she represents an unreliable, unstable point of view; like Rab, she struggles to cope in the hostile environment of Boot Hill, the council estate in the overspill suburb she moves into whilst and after having an affair with Michael, a married man, who accidentally drowns before the novel begins. Before moving into Michael's council house, Joy's cottage shows the symptoms of sickness that the homes described earlier also share:

> Dry rot... It was more sinister than the name. The house was being eaten from the inside by the thing. The spores could pass through concrete and plaster and multiplied by the thousand thousand as we slept. They could take over the whole structure if they wanted. (65)

As with the mice threatening to invade the domestic space of Kelman's novel and, to an extent, the wasps Frank obsessively annihilates, the spores represent the enemy within, the alien, invisible presence, which malignantly threatens identity and autonomy. That the living environments in these novels present shared symptoms of disease is a clear indicator of the social malaise that is behind the social housing system, or, worse, as is the case with *The Wasp Factory*, the family home.

Indeed, as previously seen in Banks's novel, Galloway presents family as untrustworthy. Personal history is – just like national history – subject to fabrication and manipulation; whereas in Frank's case the problem is with paternal authority, in Joy's case it is to do with mothers, since Joy has an ambiguous relationship with her sister/mother, Myra:

> She and my mother/her mother were pregnant at the same time. She could have been my mother. I think about that if I feel hard done by, making myself grateful for small mercies. Myra's baby died. I didn't. Maybe that was why she hit me so much. I didn't know. Hands like shovels. (59)

As Craig has suggested in *The Modern Scottish Novel*, Joy's elliptic narrative seems to suggest that 'Myra, the apparent sister, is the real mother whose physical violence leaves the marks that erase the marks of both identities' (198). The possibility emerges strongly in the context of Myra's visit, after their/her mother's death: 'Just couldn't get my mouth round sister' (72). Origins and roots are, as seen previously, deeply problematic. Such dubious genealogical patterns represent, in a sense, a continuation of the duality central to the Scottish literary tradition, and as Craig notes: 'instead of a "doubled" identity what we get are characters whose ambiguous position between alternative genealogies and alternative cultures is experienced as displacement, absence, void' (198). Whilst pointing to the vacuum of Joy's existence, simultaneously, however, the text self-consciously addresses the problematic psychological and social voids Joy embodies. As with Kelman's fiction, Galloway's concern is with the marginal, which her narratives successfully push into the centre of the representation.

This is perhaps the novel in which trauma and sickness emerge in the rawest terms. Following Michael's death, Joy suffers a nervous breakdown. Her liminal status, as the mistress of a dead man, underpins the sense of vacuity that her self occupies. In a sense, by telling Joy's story, at a macro level, Galloway is pointing to a more universal discourse of female marginalization. As Margery Metzstein argues:

> Galloway uses the process of moving through grief as a means of foregrounding certain conditions of daily life which can be the norm for women who, although not suffering from a nervous breakdown, can be said to be in grief. (138)

Joy's doubly marginal status is thus linked to the normative ideology of patriarchal oppression, which forces women into neat categories of existence, ostracizing those who deviate from the norm. Significantly, following her breakdown, Joy becomes involved in a parody of normality, playing the role of the perfect housewife whenever the Health Visitor is due for a visit:

> She likes biscuits. I get different ones each time hoping they are something else she will enjoy. I can't choose in a hurry. I can't be trusted with custard creams so deliberately don't get them. Chocolate digestives are too expensive. I wait for too long in the queue while a confused little kid tries to bargain for his father's cigarettes with the wrong money, so I have to run back clutching fig rolls and iced coffees and nearly drop the milk. (20)

Joy's performance fights against the neurosis that makes her behaviour compulsive and obsessive at the same time. Yet her attempt to conform reveals simultaneously her inadequacy – 'I can't be trusted' – and willingness to please. Both facets of her personality expose a profound sense of instability and progressive alienation from her 'real' self. Moreover, as Mary M. McGlynn observes, '[h]er efforts, including the preparation of food she never eats and the sewing of clothes, reveal how deeply the notion of home is intertwined with ideas of female domesticity, a model Joy resists and yet enacts throughout the novel' (139). The home, however, is no longer a stronghold of safety for the female subject who has strayed away from the patriarchal structure the domestic world is defined by.

As with the other characters discussed in this chapter, it is on Joy's body that symptoms of dysfunctionality erupt. Such symptoms are also strictly connected to the notion of consumption. The four novels present similar patterns of abnormal consumption and/or addiction: the consumption of food, throughout *Lanark*, is linked with the mechanisms of capitalist exploitation; in Kelman's novel, Sandra's addiction to American doughnuts and Rab's nicotine dependency display, in different ways, the characters' unfulfilled selves and their desire to escape; you could say TV has, at least on Sandra, the same anaesthetizing function; in *The Wasp Factory*, food is the main weapon used by Frank's father to manipulate the hormonal balance in his daughter's body. In Galloway's novel, food consumption is equally problematic. While Joy becomes increasingly obsessed with the performance of conventional femininity involving food provision, her only way to control things is in fact by not eating. Joy's eating disorder becomes paradoxically the only form of structure that her chaotic story and amnesiac mind – Joy claims not to remember anything about Michael's accident – can handle. Starvation does not leave Joy's body unmarked; her teeth begin to rot and she stops menstruating, which leads to a scan, to detect whether Joy is pregnant:

> I tried to see what he saw. The green cave was me. I make light on the screen therefore I am. I tried to lie back and see my insides objectively while the gynaecologist rubbed infinity signs over and over again on my belly ... We might be doing more than discovering I exist: someone else might exist in there too ...
> I looked. I was still there. A black hole among the green stars. Empty space. I had nothing inside me. (N.pag.)

Joy's ambiguous response to the pelvic scan – and the male gaze of the doctor the machine mediates – suggests the search for self-authenticating strategies; the existence of her self may be proved by the visual representation offered by the ultrasound scan. Simultaneously, however, this leads to the disappointing realization that her uterus does not carry anything; her femininity lacks meaning. Joy's amenorrhoea is, to the extent that she chooses not to eat, self-induced. However, rather than infusing a sense of self-control, the dysfunction of her reproductive system, whilst linking Joy to previous generations of hysterics, exposes the alienating impact of biological essentialism on feminine subjectivity. Her absent pregnancy leads Joy to feel like '[a] black hole among the green stars', blank like the bottom of the page, left unnumbered.

While it has been argued by Craig in *The Modern Scottish Novel* that 'the elision of page numbers becomes symbolic of Joy's refusal of the world in which she is trapped' (196), such disregard for order and conventions also indicates Joy's own disintegration and alienation from the organized society she wants to, at least in part, belong to. The lack of page numbers is only one aspect of Galloway's creative use of typographic conventions. The pages of *The Trick Is to Keep Breathing* look deliberately messy: paragraphs may be misaligned, italics are used to tell the flashback story of Michael's death, doodles and speech bubbles are used to support Joy's narrative, which becomes a pastiche of different genres: scriptwriting, diary entries, lists and catalogues alternate with no apparent overarching structure throughout the text. Yet the chaotic anarchy of Galloway's text represents the ultimate attempt to take control; by filling the margins, and disrupting conventional typography, the text becomes the evidence of Joy's presence. As Craig notes: 'Absence has been replaced by presence; the "nobody" of the self which "needs to know" and which needs to deny its knowledge, can know itself again as the "I" which speaks in ownership of its voice and of its body' (197). As in *Lanark*, the subversion of typographic rules underpins other kinds of subversive behaviour, a pattern that recurs throughout Joy's story and her dealings with doctors, managers and vicars. Her disrupted text counterbalances the sacrificial nature of her eating disorder, and while her body loses weight, the body of her text increases in size and weight, occupying the unauthorized spaces of the text and simultaneously drawing attention to what used to be blank and no longer is. As McGlynn indicates: 'The disruptions of standard prose on the page – ... the words that evoke Joy's own blood by bleeding into the margins – these assert the physical body, the space, of the text...' (149).

Whatever signs of regeneration may be seen in a novel in which despair features as the normal emotional state come indeed from the anarchic form of the narrative itself. If there is any hope for Joy to get through, this lies in the incoherent margins of her disjointed memoir, which, whilst accounting for her psychological disintegration and, as Carole Jones has pointed out, 'psychic homelessness' (212), also denote the embracing of disorder as a positive form of self-assertion. As Norquay says: '[i]ronically what leads her towards such recovery is an acceptance of randomness, an absence of order, brought out by her Christmas horoscope which says "Submit to chaos for once"' (133). Joy may not see *the light*, like Lanark, but settles for the more mundane Christmas lights, a small step – 'Cheap. Little fairy lights with glitter frost' – towards self-recovery: 'I check the price and think what the hell' (N.pag.).

In the aftermath of the 1979 devolution referendum, Scotland witnessed the rise of a literary ferment that produced the most distinctive output of the nation's cultural tradition since the first Scottish Renaissance of the early twentieth century. It is undeniable that the four novels discussed in this chapter share an acute sense of loss, political instability and self-alienation; simultaneously, the four main characters are driven by a strong desire to control their destinies, something which is also self-consciously addressed in the textual dimension of these texts. Identities are broken; places are unknowable and difficult to negotiate; homes are unsafe; bodies are corrupt and addicted. The narratives resist self-complacency in order to react – even if without much hope to succeed – to the dissatisfying present and look ahead. A new world, or at least a new way of imagining the world, all novels seem to suggest, may after all rise from death and decay. In Lanark's words to Rima: 'This fungus is a form of life, like you and me' (384).

Works cited

Banks, Iain. *The Wasp Factory*. London: Abacus, 1997 [1984].
Brown, Ian and Alan Riach (eds). *The Edinburgh Companion to Twentieth-Century Scottish Literature*. Edinburgh: Edinburgh University Press, 2009.
Craig, Cairns. 'Resting Arrest: James Kelman.' *The Scottish Novel since the Seventies: New Visions, Old Dreams*. Ed. Gavin Wallace and Randall Stevenson. Edinburgh: Edinburgh University Press, 1993, 99–114.
——. *Out of History: Narrative Paradigms in Scottish and British Culture*. Edinburgh: Polygon, 1996.
——. *The Modern Scottish Novel: Narrative and the National Imagination*. Edinburgh: Edinburgh University Press, 1999.
Galloway, Janice. *The Trick Is to Keep Breathing* [1989]. London: Minerva, 1991.
Gardiner, Michael. 'Arcades – The 1980s and 1990s.' *The Edinburgh Companion to Twentieth-Century Scottish Literature*. Ed. Ian Brown and Alan Riach. Edinburgh: Edinburgh University Press, 2009, 181–192.
Germanà, Monica. *Scottish Women's Gothic and Fantastic Writing: Fiction since 1978*. Edinburgh: Edinburgh University Press, 2010.
Gifford, Douglas. 'Imagining Scotlands: The Return to Mythology in Modern Scottish Fiction.' *Studies in Scottish Fiction: 1945 to the Present*. Ed. Susanne Hageman. Frankfurt: Peter Lang, 1996, 17–49.
Gray, Alasdair. *Lanark: A Life in Four Books*. London: Picador, 1994 [1981].
Hageman, Susanne. *Studies in Scottish Fiction: 1945 to the Present*. Frankfurt: Peter Lang, 1996.
Jones, Carole. 'Burying the Man That Was: Janice Galloway and Gender Disorientation.' *The Edinburgh Companion to Contemporary Scottish Literature*. Ed. Berthold Schoene. Edinburgh: Edinburgh University Press, 2007.
Kelman, James. 'The East End Writers' Anthology, 1988.' *Channels of Communication: Papers from the Higher Education Teachers of English Conference held at Glasgow University*. Ed. Philip Hobsbaum, Paddy Lyons and JimMcGhee. Glasgow: HETE, 1992.
——. *The Busconductor Hines*. London: Phoenix, 1997 [1984].
Kövesi, Simon. *James Kelman*. Manchester: Manchester University Press, 2007.
Kristeva, Julia. *Powers of Horror: An Essay on Abjection*. New York: Columbia University, 1982.
Lee, Alison. *Realism and Power: Postmodern British Fiction*. London: Routledge, 1990.
Massie, Alan. 'Introduction'. *Scott and Scotland: The Predicament of the Scottish Writer*. Ed. Edwin Muir. Edinburgh: Polygon, 1982.
McGlynn, Mary M. *Narratives of Class in New Irish and Scottish Literature: From Joyce to Kelman, Doyle, Galloway, and McNamee*. Basingstoke: Palgrave, 2008.

Metzstein, Margery. 'Of Myths and Men: Aspects of Gender in the Fiction of Janice Galloway.' *The Scottish Novel since the Seventies: New Visions, Old Dreams*. Ed. Gavin Wallace and Randall Stevenson. Edinburgh: Edinburgh University Press, 1993, 136–146.

Nairn, Thom. 'Iain Banks and the Fiction Factory.' *The Scottish Novel since the Seventies: New Visions, Old Dreams*. Ed. Gavin Wallace and Randall Stevenson. Edinburgh: Edinburgh University Press, 1993, 127–135.

Norquay, Glenda. 'Janice Galloway's Novels: Fraudulent Mooching.' *Contemporary Scottish Women Writers*. Ed. Aileen Christianson and Alison Lumsden. Edinburgh: Edinburgh University Press, 2001, 131–143.

Punter, David. *The Literature of Terror: A History of Gothic Fictions from 1765 to the Present Day*, vol. 2. London: Longman, 1999 [1996].

Sage, Victor. 'The Politics of Petrifaction: Culture, Religion, History in the Fiction of Iain Banks and John Banville.' *Modern Gothic: A Reader*. Ed. Victor Sage and Allan Lloyd Smith. Manchester: Manchester University Press, 1996, 20–37.

Schoene, Berthold (ed.). *The Edinburgh Companion to Contemporary Scottish Literature*. Edinburgh: Edinburgh University Press, 2007.

———. 'Going Cosmopolitan: Reconstituting "Scottishness" in Post-devolution Criticism.' *The Edinburgh Companion to Contemporary Scottish Literature*. Ed. Berthold Schoene. Edinburgh: Edinburgh University Press, 2007.

Schoene-Harwood, Berthold. 'Dams Burst: Devolving Gender in Iain Banks's *The Wasp Factory*.' *ARIEL: A Review of International English Literature* 30(1) (1999): 131–48.

Stevenson, Robert Louis. *Strange Case of Dr Jekyll and Mr Hyde*. London: Norton, 2003 [1886].

Wallace, Gavin and Randall Stevenson (eds). *The Scottish Novel since the Seventies: New Visions, Old Dreams*. Edinburgh: Edinburgh University Press, 1993.

3

Special Topic 2
The Art of Bad Government: Thatcherism and British Fiction

Joseph Brooker

Thatcherism is not the only fact about the 1980s, even within a perspective limited to Britain. Yet it is a pivotal one. One could consider the period in terms of numerous issues and practices – such as broadcasting, shopping or war – which have their own lengthy histories stretching far beyond the 1980s. Yet in Britain in the 1980s, such practices were also affected by the story of Thatcherism. The Conservative governments of the decade appear as not just one fact among many, but a determining one, shaping and warping other stories. This sense of a political dispensation affecting a whole culture and society is itself a notable fact about Thatcherism.

The relations between Thatcherism and fiction, though, might still be relatively indirect. Literature was able to turn from the political exigencies of the present to a thousand other stories. Its low running costs – pen, paper, typewriter, Amstrad word processor – also made it relatively economically autonomous compared, for instance, with the always embattled British film industry. In any case, a vast proportion of fiction at any time is ostensibly unconcerned with the political present in which it is made. Novelists in the 1980s had many other concerns to express. The market for politically engaged writing is uncertain. And the novel – unlike the press report or now the weblog – is a form with a relatively long lead time, from conception through writing and redrafting to editing and publication. The novelist may chase the news, but by the same token risks built-in obsolescence. It is also finally true that the shape of a political era can appear clearer with hindsight. In 1984, any writer could only guess how long Thatcher's premiership would last. Its ultimate impact – or the state of debate over that impact, the range of retrospective perceptions that currently seem evident to us in the early twenty-first century – was by definition unknown.

With these caveats logged, we can consider what positive connections do exist. First, the fiction industry itself, the world of publishing, was ineluctably affected by the economic and cultural climate. This will be considered below. Second, when British fiction did aim to comment on its own time, it described a world being altered by Thatcherism. Tropes, types, landscapes that we associate with the term can be found in prominent roles: sometimes to the point where we can venture that a story is 'about' Thatcherism even though the premier herself plays no direct part in it. Third, fiction can address the political less directly: through fantasy, allegory or historical parallel, for instance. Jeanette Winterson would come to describe her novel *The Passion* (1987) in this way. The present chapter will say less about this category, which is discussed extensively elsewhere in this volume: in connection with historical fiction and heritage culture, for instance, as in Kazuo Ishiguro's *The Remains of the Day* (1989). But we shall consider examples from a fourth category: those texts that directly, unabashedly treat of the political, in some cases even zeroing in on Margaret Thatcher herself.

Do any such novels offer a sympathetic portrait of the premier and her works? Could we find an even spread of literary depictions from the satirical to the supportive? We could not. Michael Johnston (2009) has surveyed the field with the specific, heuristic aim of identifying pro-Thatcher fiction, and found largely an absence. The literary and artistic world of the 1980s and after, he suggests, displayed an in-built scepticism towards Thatcher, which made it less likely for pro-Conservative works to be published and acclaimed. Jonathan Coe (2009) states that anti-Thatcherism was 'the default position for probably 90% of writers' in the 1980s. This is an instance of a very long-range tendency, perhaps originating with Romanticism, for artists in the modern world to assume a position of marginality and social dissidence rather than celebrating the given order. In the 1980s, a majority of those artists and writers would locate themselves as liberals or leftists, and thus be still less likely to support a Conservative government. Compounding this, Margaret Thatcher herself was often viewed as philistine, or as favouring art which would didactically promote her own values, such as British patriotism. We should not, then, expect a survey of the fiction of Thatcherism to disclose an amiably even-handed view of the period. Such fiction, to a large extent, has been implicitly *critical* of political actuality. Johnston adds, however, that 'The bluest tinge that some novels of the period reveal, or rather fail to conceal, is a certain vicarious pleasure in having their protagonists deeply involved in so-called Thatcherite pursuits' (8). This points to another significant dimension. If Thatcherism indeed amounted to large-scale change and social drama, then one might find writers feeding off it and channelling its energies, even as they sought to criticize many of its effects.

Aspects of Thatcherism

What, meanwhile, do we mean by Thatcherism? It may be defined as a political movement, a body of ideas and a process of economic and social change: these alternatives being complementary, not contradictory. Debate about its very existence was audible in the 1980s. One conservative view characteristically wanted to disavow any label or theory (Utley 146–147) – articulated precepts having been suspect, for conservative thought, since the French Revolution. Others simply doubted that Thatcher's programme had the coherence worthy of an 'ism'. We have fewer such doubts now. It is customary to see in the 1980s a real process of abiding change, though complex in its effects and sometimes producing unintended consequences.

Thatcherism was the British wing of a transatlantic movement known as the New Right. Thatcher's governance from 1979 to 1990 was roughly paralleled in the United States by the tenure of President Ronald Reagan and his successor George H. W. Bush between 1980 and 1992. More locally, it was nurtured by right-wing think tanks like the Centre for Policy Studies, and thinkers like Keith Joseph and Alfred Sherman. Their programme sought a break with the administration of Britain in previous decades. It was among other things an attack on the 'post-war consensus' among Labour and Conservative parties. The consensus implied that it was desirable for government to intervene in the market, and to extend the public realm of state provision and citizenship, as well as aiming to increase social and economic equality. Thatcher herself was in no doubt about her opposition to the hitherto-prevailing consensus – or to any consensus. At the 1981 Conservative Party conference, she declared:

> To me consensus seems to be the process of abandoning all beliefs, principles, values and policies in search of something in which no one believes, but to which no one objects... [It is] the process of avoiding the very issues that have to be solved, merely because you cannot get agreement on the way ahead. What great cause would have been fought and won under the banner 'I stand for consensus'? (Campbell 122–123)

What concrete proposals paved the path beyond consensus? The era's flagship policies included the sale of council houses; the encouragement of a boom in property sales and of attendant refurbishment and redevelopment; and extensive cuts in tax for high earners, moving towards a less progressive scheme of taxation. Traditional industries were run down, with a concomitant sequence of confrontations with organized labour: most centrally and painfully in the miners' strike of 1984–85. Major utilities (gas, telephones, water and many more) were privatized, while market principles were encouraged in public services, notably health (like railway privatization, this process gathered pace in the 1990s, but reflected an enduring Thatcherite logic). All of this contributed to an emphasis on individualism, and a de-emphasizing of collective life. Margaret Thatcher's own pronouncements drove the point home: never more emphatically than in a famous interview she gave to *Woman's Own* in October 1987:

> I think we've been through a period where too many people have been given to understand that if they have a problem, it's the government's job to cope with it. 'I have a problem, I'll get a grant.' 'I'm homeless, the government must house me.' They're casting their problem on society. And, you know, there is no such thing as society. There are individual men and women, and there are families. And no government can do anything except through people, and people must look to themselves first. It's our duty to look after ourselves and then, also, to look after our neighbour. People have got the entitlements too much in mind, without the obligations. There's no such thing as entitlement, unless someone has first met an obligation. (Keay 10)

'There is no such thing as society' has become the phrase which defines Thatcherism. The prime minister succinctly voiced the suspicion of the collective and public, and the promotion of the individual and private, that ran through much of the policy of the decade, and strongly affected British culture. In practice, her government did not achieve a total ideological or social transformation by the end of the 1980s. But her 1987 statement gave an insight into the ideal state towards which her actual governance strove. The aspects of Thatcherism that we have just scanned left their mark in writing and art. Individualism, the dissolution of community, the sense of living in a different climate: all these can be seen in fiction issuing from the period, not to mention in poetry, drama and film.

Thatcherism offered other moods and motifs too. The government and its tabloid allies cultivated nationalistic imagery, most notably for the Falklands conflict of 1982, when a British task force reclaimed the islands in the South Atlantic from Argentinian invaders. Film and television would reflect on the Falklands, when permitted to by state censors. In fiction, David Mitchell's *Black*

Swan Green (2006) would look back on the conflict almost a quarter-century later. Communism was to be staunchly resisted by following the United States' policy of a nuclear deterrent. The presence of American missiles on British soil spurred protest and critique, most notably from the women's peace camp at Greenham Common. In the theatre, David Edgar's *Maydays* and Sarah Daniels's *The Devil's Gateway* (both 1983) both celebrated this campaign that joined the causes of peace and feminism. The cause was taken up by comic books (Raymond Briggs's *When the Wind Blows* [1982], Alan Moore's *Watchmen* [1986-87]) and music (Ian McEwan's oratorio *Or Shall We Die?* [1983] was followed in a different vein by Frankie Goes to Hollywood's 1984 number one single 'Two Tribes' among numerous others). The novelist Martin Amis joined the debate with *Einstein's Monsters* (1987), a collection of stories and introductory essay in which he took his own characteristically individual stance on the anti-nuclear side. While the government paraded a militaristic stance in foreign policy, a domestic law-and-order agenda was enforced and the police strengthened, and arguably politicized (Leys 67–68). As early as 1978, the social theorist Stuart Hall identified 'the key themes of the radical right' as 'law and order, the need for social discipline and authority in the face of a conspiracy by the enemies of the state, the onset of social anarchy, the "enemy within"' (44). The value and importance of family, discipline, morality and nation were reiterated, with a strong accompanying sense that they were under threat.

This aspect of Thatcherism was exemplified not only by soldiers and riot squads but by the controversial Clause (later Section) 28, a piece of legislation introduced in the late 1980s that aimed to ban local authorities from the 'promotion' of homosexuality. The policy seemed to query the legitimacy of a whole section of British society. It gave legal status to an illiberalism which had been evident in the government's rhetoric. In more shadowy fashion, this tendency was also perceptible in the government's tendency to use the police and intelligence services against perceived internal enemies and traitors. Examples of this include the centralized mass mobilization of regional police forces against NUM pickets in 1984–85; spying on trade unions and infiltrating their offices with moles; breaking into the homes of peace campaigners; the vain bid to suppress the former MI5 operative Peter Wright's memoir *Spycatcher* in 1987; and the prosecution of Ministry of Defence whistle-blowers like Clive Ponting and Sarah Tisdall. All the above may be considered under Thatcherism's authoritarian aspect. Of a piece with this is the distaste shown by Margaret Thatcher herself, and by several of her lieutenants, for the liberalizing 1960s. Thatcher thought more fondly of another earlier period. After 'no such thing as society', one of her most celebrated verbal motifs was the celebration of 'Victorian values', which she claimed to have learned while growing up in twentieth-century Grantham.

Yet much in the social landscape was developing in another direction. The government encouraged enterprise, financial services and what Peter York (138–150) called the 'voodoo arts' of PR, advertising and presentation. The characteristic architecture of the 1980s involved modern apartment buildings, converted warehouses, gleaming blocks. It was exemplified by the redevelopment of London's Docklands into a Manhattan-on-Thames, whose shining towers were serviced by warrens of apartments like Piers Gough's riverside Cascades development (York 80–89). This was a quintessentially Thatcherite environment. But one can hardly imagine Margaret Thatcher herself wanting to live in it. The people to whom such a landscape appealed were of an altogether different generation and temperament from the prime minister herself. They were the young upwardly mobile professionals of the City and media. The generally derisive word 'yuppie', borrowed from the United States, was widely applied (Wright 288). These were the most visible beneficiaries of Chancellor Nigel Lawson's 1983–87 boom, the period in which Thatcher began to speak of 'popular capitalism' (Campbell 231). The effects were widespread. John Campbell recalls 'cultural change at all levels of the economy, from the City of London to every provincial high street': from the deregulation of the stock exchange in 1986 to a proliferation of jobs in the service sector. Here is what Jeanette Winterson (1996) perceived as a 'clock-race' of those who 'never count the cost', or what the pop group Depeche Mode satirized as a 'competitive world' in which 'everything counts/in large amounts'. Peter York would become a prime narrator of this shifting landscape, in which every high street gained a branch of Next, and chain store ties were made from silk rather than polyester (63). Literature's most consistent chronicler of such change was the novelist Michael Bracewell. In *The Crypto-Amnesia Club* (1988), *Divine Concepts of Physical Beauty* (1989) and *The Conclave* (1992), Bracewell rendered the fashionable world of the late 1980s in immense detail, recording brand names and measuring hemlines, but retaining the quizzical eye of an enigmatically detached aesthete.

Transfer fees

Literature faced its own processes of restructuring. Richard Todd sees the British book industry as changing significantly since the late 1970s, along Thatcherite lines. The end of the Net Book Agreement in 1997 would allow booksellers to determine their own prices, and contributed to retailers' ascendancy over authors or publishers as the most powerful interest in the book industry. Todd presents this as 'a theoretical terminus of Thatcherite thinking', which might not have occurred 'had British politics taken a different direction in 1979' (20–21). Exemplary of changes in bookselling was the Waterstone's chain. Founded in 1982, its large stores became a dominant force in British bookselling. Proprietor Tim Waterstone (107) noted the benefits of extra consumer services: gift wrapping, delivery, local branch promotions, community initiatives with schools. Signings, tours and meet-the-author events proliferated.

In literary publishing, too, corporate conglomeration was a major theme of the 1980s. Publishing witnessed a dizzying series of key mergers and takeovers. Prestigious British houses ended the decade as jewels in the crown of multinational corporations. Mergers may have been made for the sake of survival: Randall Stevenson sees publishers 'huddling closer together to resist the economic chill' (146). But the climate of the late 1980s also produced extravagance. Reflecting on increased advances paid to established authors, Todd records that 'The caution of the early 1980s had been transformed, within the space of three or four years, to confidence leading almost to hubris'. He perceives a paradox: that 'authors, agents and publishers of serious literary fiction, many of whom might have been expected to have been hostile to the political and financial climate engendering the Lawson boom of the later 1980s, were swept along in its wake'; the buoyancy 'oddly reflected the new assurance of the Thatcherite meritocracy' (111–112). Nicci Gerrard described the new era of corporate 'transfer fees' as 'fantasy land, separating the majority of writers from the money-spinning stars'. Publishing, she judged in 1989, was following broader trends: 'Some writers are wealthier than ever before, others poorer, usually in relative, but sometimes in actual, terms. In a neat reflection of British life, the gulf between them is growing wider and more divisive' (25–26).

Publicity could adumbrate canon formation. *Granta*'s editor Bill Buford recalled that the Book Marketing Council was 'created in the characteristically eighties' belief that books should be treated like any other commodity, and that just as there was a Meat Marketing Council, urging everyone to go out and eat a British cow, so it followed there should be a comparable institution urging everyone to buy good, honest British novels' (10). The council's most successful campaign was in 1983: a list of 20 Best of Young British Novelists, all under 40 years of age. A *Granta* special issue featured work from all 20. Buford remembers how the campaign 'became, despite itself, a serious statement about British literary culture' (11). It also became a statement about *Granta*: as English and Frow note, this is 'perhaps what *Granta* is best known for' (47), with new lists following at ten year intervals.

A still more public intervention was now being made each year by the Booker Prize. This had been awarded annually since 1969. From 1981, the ceremony was broadcast live on television, making literary judgement into public spectacle (Todd 73–74). The Booker became the most prominent literary event in Britain. Numerous other prizes were initiated or enhanced in its wake. The culture of awards with substantial sums of money can be aligned with the Granta top 20 as one of the 1980s' major contributions to the 'literary value industry' (English and Frow 2006). Todd proposes that the Booker Prize is 'the best-known of the awards whose prominence during the 1980s is associated in the public mind with the entrepreneurship that characterized the Thatcher decade', and that during this decade the prize became a significant 'consumer guide to serious literary fiction' (61). The new prominence of prize culture, in its emphasis on competition, its cultivation of publicity and media attention and its channelling of money to winners, can be aligned with the spirit of enterprise whose promotion by government was a signature refrain of the decade.

In these respects, Thatcherism and British fiction would already be entangled even if no novelist had penned a word pertinent to the politics of the 1980s. But let us now consider certain British novels more directly as a commentary on the period. While mentioning other writers and texts in passing, I want to treat five texts as exemplary responses to Thatcherism. They are by Alasdair Gray, Martin Amis, Pat Barker, Emma Tennant and Ian McEwan.

Security business

Jonathan Coe's *What a Carve Up!* (1994) has been celebrated as one of the most thoroughgoing fictional anatomies of Thatcherism. Accordingly, Coe himself has often been asked for his views of the period and its literature. He repeatedly points to one earlier novel as exemplary: *1982 Janine* (1984) by the Glaswegian artist and writer Alasdair Gray.

Gray's protagonist, Jock McLeish, is a tippler of late-night whisky, who spends his life in hotel rooms while on professional trips to provincial Scottish towns. The novel consists of his monologue over one such night in Greenock. We soon gather that he habitually dreams up worlds of sadistic sexual fantasy, to which the reader is treated at length. The fantasies reflect McLeish's history with women, his mixture of guilt and resentment: he is gaining an imaginative revenge. But McLeish is also a socially specific figure. He installs and inspects security systems around Scotland's businesses and institutions, wiring businesses against intrusion and protecting managerial profits. The barbed-wire fences and impenetrable installations in which his imagined heroines are trapped are cruel projections from his own professional life.

McLeish secretly considers himself a political Conservative. At various points in the first half of the book, he justifies this allegiance – not least on the page marked 'WHY I'M A TORY': 'Every intelligent Tory knows that politics is a matter of people with a lot of money combining to manage people with very little, though of course they must deny it in public to mislead the opposition ... I'm not going to join a gang of losers' (61–62). The implication is that Conservatism is a thoroughly reactive, negative formation: a series of consciously cruel negations, somewhat analogous to his sexual fantasies. Like that fantasy world, Conservatism here is a defence mechanism, and the geopolitical meaning of 'defence' is also brought into play, as McLeish orates on the nuclear state of modern Scotland. Scotland, he reflects, is 'wired for war'; the British government has cynically placed all its nuclear weapons and potential targets as far from London as possible, and banked on the loss of Clydeside in the event of a tactical strike (134–136).

With reflections like this, we might seem to be in the territory of the political Left to which Alasdair Gray belongs. But McLeish reverts to the fact that 'Scotland has been fucked and I am one of the fuckers who fucked her and I REFUSE TO FEEL BITTER OR GUILTY ABOUT THIS' (137). 'The militarization and depression of Scotland', he insists, 'has been good for the security business'. He also manages to find deeply cynical reasons to celebrate cuts in health and education, greater unemployment and rising crime. 'A smart Tory', he insists, 'does not believe this is, or can be, a pleasant world for most folk' (137). One virtuoso passage, particularly acclaimed by Coe, offers a social panorama:

> We have become Falstaffian, our colourful past has returned, we display as rich a pageant of contrasts as in the days of Lizzie Tudor, Merry Charlie Stewart and the Queen Empress Victoria. Our own royal millionaire weds in Westminster Abbey and departs in a luxury cruiser to the cheers of the nation while unemployed children loot shops and battle with the police in the slums where ignorant armies clash by night. The Sunday papers bloom with Technicolor adverts for expensive sexy clothes, luxury furniture, tropical holidays. Beggars have returned to the

city streets... Gambling casinos and massage-parlour prostitution flourishes where wealth accumulates and men decay and every winter roofless vagrants die of exposure in greater numbers. (138)

McLeish insists 'I DON'T CARE' about such conditions. But he protests too much. Gray constructs an elaborate defence of political Conservatism in order ultimately to dismantle it and send his character, and the reader, in search of alternatives.

As the night proceeds McLeish despairs about his life and attempts suicide. After the attempt fails, he seeks a new way forward by recounting the past. The book's very long 12th chapter is an account of the few months in 1953 when he thinks the course of his life was set. Here we see that McLeish's habitual dependence on sadistic sexual fantasy is a response to the plight he now describes to us. We are invited to ask what went wrong, not only in McLeish's own life, but in broader historical terms: with Scotland, Britain and the world. The point is wryly clarified on 'Gray's Table of Contents', in which McLeish's lengthy personal narrative is logged as 'FROM THE CAGE TO THE TRAP: or: *How I Reached and Lost Three Crowded Months of Glorious Life*: or: *How I Became Perfect, Married Two Wives Then Embraced Cowardice*: or: *Scotland 1952–1982*' (9).

McLeish's tale locates the immediate post-war period as one that could still harbour social, as well as personal, hope. Though the precise virtues of Clement Attlee's Labour government are debated by two leftist characters, Gray's portrait of the post-war era suggests a deep nostalgia for a moment of as-yet-undefeated virtue. When in summer 1953 McLeish and his theatrical friends travel from Glasgow to Edinburgh to stage a play, Gray unleashes a litany of the not yet happened. Events like 'the coming of the motorways, the dismantling of the rail system, the ringroads slicing up the cities' and 'the discovery that North Sea oil benefited hardly anyone in Britain but the shareholders': 'all this', reflects McLeish, 'though partly conceivable, had not been conceived' (230). He further reflects that the public realm was a sparer, clearer place with 'no commercial radio or television, no shopping centres, leisure centres, arts centres; nothing but the B.B.C. and shops and public baths and theatres... We had come through a war, built a welfare state, had full employment' (231). The critic Liam McIlvanney comments that for Gray, post-war Britain has remained an ideal. His fiction meditates on the fall between 'the Britain of full employment and free school milk and the Britain of Thatcher and Polaris' (199). This decline parallels, and in part has shaped, the smaller fate of Jock McLeish.

In his protagonist's long night's journey into day, Gray created an extraordinary vision of corruption and redemption, which is at once personal and political.

After the catharsis of a failed suicide attempt, McLeish rhetorically throws in his lot with the ordinary and downtrodden: 'the Famous Few have no power now but the power to threaten and destroy and history is what we all make, everywhere, each moment of our lives' (340). Gray would become a godfather to new generations of creativity, including writers describing contemporary Britain. Janice Galloway's debut novel *The Trick Is to Keep Breathing* (1989), for instance, is comparable to Gray's work. It centres on a depressed, isolated schoolteacher whose suicidal monologue on a broken-down Glasgow housing estate and in drab surgeries and waiting rooms is conveyed through typographical fragmentation reminiscent of Gray's. Coe's *What a Carve Up!* (1994) bears the dedication *1994, Janine*, in tribute to Gray's example as well as Coe's partner. Coe's novel picks up and reworks Gray's story to present a solitary male whose relationship with the world has become mediated through television, and his relationship with the opposite sex onanistic. Even Coe's much later work *The Terrible Privacy of Maxwell Sim* (2010), another portrait of a man made solitary in part by the social atomization associated with neo-liberalism, would bear a quotation from *1982 Janine* at its outset.

We're here to stay

Gray's novel is notable in bidding to stage its critique of Thatcherism from the inside. This sense of complicity, of exploring a new social and ideological era through one of its representatives, is also vividly present in the most famously exemplary literary text of the British 1980s, Martin Amis's *Money* (1984). Amis's novel is narrated by the director of advertisements John Self, who shuttles between London and New York as he tries to make his first feature film. Self declares his membership of a new socio-economic vanguard: the moneyed and uncultured, those who have seized power without needing to go through the class rituals of an older elite. Amis's parvenu is grabbing what he has been too long denied, and he will not be refused. His defining trait is his capacity for consumption. In cheerfully ludicrous passages, Amis has him eat numerous burgers and hot dogs for breakfast, along with a six-pack of beer; order multiple pots of coffee from room service; and frantically splash cash on new suits and lurid fancy goods.

An unusually insistent homology suggests itself between the central character, the novel's world and the real world refracted by the book. *Money*'s temporal location is specific. Amis has spoken (Tredell 61) of his deliberate decision to place the action in 1981, at the time of riots in Brixton and Liverpool, on one hand, and the Royal Wedding of Charles and Diana, on the other: an emblematic contrast between rich and poor, violence and pomp, that was unmistakable at the time. John Self contextualizes London's young and violent:

> The dole queue starts at the exit to the playground. Riots are their rumpus-room, sombre London their jungle-gym. Life is hoarded elsewhere by others. Money is so near you can almost touch it, but it is all on the other side – you can only press your face up against the glass. In my day, if you wanted, you could just drop out. You can't drop out any more. Money has seen to that. (153)

Self points quite precisely to the moment of the novel, naming a new social situation. Critics have found the work emblematic of a historically specific mood. Elaine Showalter reckons *Money* 'the most paradigmatic British novel of the fast-track greedy 1980s' (66), and Nicolas Tredell avers that John Self 'could be seen to embody the acquisitiveness of the 1980s in the era of Thatcher and Reagan, the desire, above all, for money' (55).

Among the novel's most telling descriptions of social change in Britain is Self's description of his film production company, Carburton, Linex & Self. The partners are besuited thugs, new rich rather than old school. They explicitly represent a class fraction which has just claimed its fortune. Commandeering an elderly man's table in a restaurant, they launch into yobbish behaviour and 'a few choruses of "We Are The Champions"' (81–82). Self's analysis, as he considers the middle-aged couple at the next table, is telling: 'No, the rest of the meal isn't going to be much fun for those two, I'm afraid. I suppose it must have been cool for people like them in places like this before people like us started coming here also. But we're here to stay. *You* try getting us out' (82). The point is broadly generational and social, as Self elsewhere makes clear in addressing an implied middle-class reader: '[Y]ou hate me, don't you ... Because I'm the new kind, the kind who has money but can never use it for anything but ugliness ... You never let us in, not really ... You just gave us some money' (58).

Money hurtles past on the force of the style that Self borrows from his author. In this sense, a new social content is not merely described, but expressed through an adventure in literary form. The novel's voice is repetitive, relentless, deadpan, lyrical, ironic, bathetic. It is aptly enough named by a fictional book mentioned within the novel, *The Ironic High Style* (59). Its careering force carries and reflects the motion of its protagonist, in his lust not just for flesh and sexual gratification, but for junk food, alcohol, possessions.

This motion is signalled also by the symbolic train that rumbles through the book, figuring Self's headlong life:

> Sometimes I feel that life is passing me by, not slowly either, but with ropes of steam and spark-spattered wheels and a hoarse roar of power or terror. It's passing, yet I'm the one who is doing all the moving. I'm not the station, I'm not the stop: I'm the train. I'm the train. (112)

In a late passage the image and atmosphere are reprised one more time: 'I am that fleeing train that goes steaming past you in the night. Though travelling nowhere I have hurtled with blind purpose to the very end of my time. I have lived headlong at a desperate rhythm' (311–312).

John Self might seem an unpleasant figure, and *Money* a cautionary tale. But the novel itself runs on Self's heavy fuel and partakes of the 'desperate rhythm' described. Arguably, it is not so much a critique of its time (as can reliably be said about 1982 *Janine*) as an exemplification, a wild ride on the new social currents. In Johnston's terms quoted earlier, the novel plainly takes a 'vicarious pleasure' in Self's progress. This sense of complicity in a new culture, and the ambivalent responses that it produces, have contributed to the novel's exemplary historical status.

In this respect Amis's novel can be productively compared, and somewhat contrasted, with Alasdair Gray's. The two books in fact share an uncanny amount. Both are the first-person narratives of onanistic drunks with pornographic imaginations. Both narrators sense that their lives are in crisis, and make failed suicide bids. Both have doubts over their parentage, and both converse with versions of their creator (Martin Amis, and God). *Money*'s status as a novel of the decade is echoed by Coe's claims for *1982 Janine*. Yet Gray and Amis are also profoundly different writers, and the contrast is historically suggestive. It can be seen stylistically, in the distinction between the disarming directness of Gray's prose and the baroque brilliance of Amis's – though Gray's winning plainness is heavily compensated for by an extraordinary typographical manipulation of the printed page itself, a reflection of his craft as a visual artist. A political difference can also be discerned. Amis in the 1980s was still considered to belong loosely on the political Left – almost by default, as a former literary editor of the *New Statesman* and associate of Christopher Hitchens, James Fenton and Salman Rushdie. But Amis's politics had a relative rootlessness that contrasts strongly with Gray's tenacious attachment to Clydeside socialism. The older man (Gray, born in 1934, is 15 years older than Amis) is the passionate progressive, tied to locality and radical tradition, publishing as often with Scottish presses as London houses, and keen to promote and support working-class friends like James Kelman and Agnes Owens. The younger writer is a more coolly detached observer, ready to subject almost anything to satirical levelling – to the point where the very notion of satire, with its implication of stable value, seems an inadequate generic description.

This is also to say, in a sense, that Amis was more at home in the 1980s than Gray. Central to the literary generation that emerged from the *New Review* and *New Statesman* in the late 1970s, he featured on *Granta*'s first list of 20 writers: indeed, by virtue of Amis's alphabetical primacy, a draft of the opening of *Money* itself led off that issue. Amis, above all his contemporaries, would come to be seen as the era's emblematic writer. This was in part because he wrote so vividly about it while not clearly allying himself with any established political critique of the times. It was in part also because if any major writer essayed the role of 'celebrity author', it was he. It was not incongruous that it was Amis, in the mid-1990s, who most boldly exemplified the 'transfer fee' era of literature, with his reported £500,000 advance from a new publisher. Nor is it uncharacteristic that when Alasdair Gray received a £500 literary prize in 1984, he gave the entire sum to the striking miners.

It needs a war

Pat Barker (born in 1943) also featured in *Granta*'s top 20. But in terms of the publishing industry that we surveyed earlier, she was at least as close to Gray as to Amis: becoming a published novelist late after raising her children, and entering the literary world through the feminist publisher Virago rather than a more established and affluent London publishing house. In the present context, she will exemplify another strand of the literary response to Thatcherism, essentially that located in the de-industrializing North. The tone and milieu of Barker's early fiction are comparable to the poetry of Sean O'Brien and Tony Harrison, or to Alan Bleasdale's television drama *Boys from the Blackstuff* (1982). Barker's novel *Liza's England* (1986, first published as *The Century's Daughter*) is a good place to consider this mood in the novel form.

The book alternates scenes from 1984 with tableaux from the life of Liza, who was born as the century began. It mixes a historical drama with a regular focus on the here and now. The novel's vision of the present is bleak. Teeside's urban environment is fraying. Stephen, a gay social worker who befriends Liza, is the protagonist through whom most of the present-day action is experienced. When he seeks a public telephone, he finds a box in which 'the phone had been ripped out altogether'; a functioning box 'stank of urine' (107). The physical landscape is being torn up: Stephen's official task is to persuade Liza to vacate the house where she has lived for decades, and the novel closes with a crowd watching a wrecking ball knocking down local buildings (282–283).

The battered physical landscape supports a social world shaped by mass unemployment. Visiting his aged parents, Stephen detects a 'Sunday-morning feeling' in the area: 'It was Thursday, but very few people on this estate worked' (104). In a pub Stephen watches young men and considers their generational place in the story of industrial decline: 'Dole-queue wallahs built like their steel-making and ship-building fathers, resembling them in this, if in nothing else' (71). Youths go for their fortnightly carousal on 'Benefit day' (15). One of them, Brian Jackson, wryly tells Stephen: 'I get pissed off with people helping the unemployed and getting paid for it. It's the only growth industry there is... Time we had our cut' (14). In an era of de-industrialization, Brian suggests, benefits and social work have become a kind of parasitical industry in themselves. Later, Brian shows Stephen the bomb shelter where he used to play as a child. As the pair look out to sea, Brian announces:

> It needs a war... That's the only way they'll ever sort this lot out. That's how they did last time, isn't it?... You lot think, because of the Bomb, it can't happen, but it can. Look at the Falklands. The lads round here lapped it up. Why else do you think they voted for Thatcher? They loved every minute. It was the only *real* thing that'd ever happened to them. (196)

Stephen protests that it wasn't that real: 'They watched it on the telly!' (196). But he finds it '[u]seless to argue' with Brian's bread-and-circuses logic, in which war seems the best way out of the lethargy of the dole. Stephen's dying father Walter also gives witness to the deadening experience of unemployment: 'You don't kill time, it kills you... Some afternoons I used to look at the clock, and I swear it didn't move' (117). The ailing patriarch has been stricken by the loss of his role. '[I]t isn't his death that hurts', Stephen decides: 'It's the way he was made to feel *useless* for so long before he died. I don't forgive this country for that' (168). The main characters' view of the government of the day is a given, summed up when Liza scornfully remembers a doctor who came to test her mental faculties: 'He asked such bloody stupid questions: who was the prime minister. I told him I was trying to forget' (19).

It remains ambiguous, in this novel, how far the working-class past is a moral resource that is being decimated by the Thatcherite present, and how far it presents merely a history of hardship. Liza recalls a day in the 1960s when she met a friend who had become a Labour activist. Looking around a new shopping centre, she recalls, 'it was like a different world': 'It was all *money*. You'd have thought we had nowt else to offer. But we *did*. We had a way of life, a way of treating people' (218). But Barker's book allows no easy contrast between the failing present and a wholesome past. The history in which Liza grew up is shown to be ridden with class distinction and deference. Stephen's father has been 'bonded into silence' by his society (122). The proletarian past, here, has been one of denial and constriction. This is truer still for those who have lived through and died in the two world wars: among them Liza's husband Frank, traumatized by the first war and seeing death around him on his return to peacetime life (84).

With its landscape of scarred ground, wastelands, abandoned steelworks and houses facing demolition, *Liza's England* shows the modern nation as a melancholy place of social and physical ruin. The vision was shared by texts like *New Socialist*'s polemical survey *Thatcher's Britain: A Guide to the Ruins* (1983), or later by Patrick Wright's idiosyncratic London inquiry *A Journey through Ruins* (1991). Raphael Samuel observed that the 'journey through ruins' had become the major genre of Northern travel writing in the 1980s (160). A similar vista can be seen in the passage late in Barker's novel where Stephen takes Liza for a last day out:

> High, barbed-wire fences enclosed work yards that would never work again. The wires throbbed and hummed as the wind blew through them...
>
> 'There's nothing left', she said, and, although she'd known that it must be so, her voice was raw with loss.
>
> Tansy, dog-daisies, rose bay willow herb grew and flourished where the houses had been. Here and there, half-hidden in the grass, was the kerb of a forgotten road.
>
> The wind keened across the brown land, and it seemed to Liza that it lamented vanished communities, scattered families, extinguished fires...
>
> Silence. Silence from hearth and road, from pub and church, from foundry and factory yard. (216)

Barker's scene may well have been influenced by the tour of the dead Liverpool docks at the climax of *Boys from the Blackstuff*. Unlike the dying patriarch of the labour movement in Bleasdale's script, Barker's characters offer no particular political conviction. 'Silence' is a keynote of her novel. It ends amid the physical destruction of the urban fabric, with a sense that most things are going wrong. Yet the length of its historical vision makes it impossible to see simple decline.

Looking back, Liza insists: 'You're bound to think them days were better, aren't you? But I try not to slip into that, I try to remember what it was really like. Women wore out by the time they were thirty' (218). Barker's novel appears to show Britain in decline in the Thatcher years. But its historical double focus also compels it to question this ready assumption.

Black market

Barker is a feminist writer, whose evident concern with socio-economic division is intricately combined with her determination to describe the experience and struggles of women. Other feminist writers also responded to the politics of the era: among them the maverick Angela Carter, the young Jeanette Winterson and the journalist Joan Smith, who produced a series of academic crime fiction alongside the analysis of contemporary sexual politics offered by her *Misogynies* (1989). To this list, in still another literary flavour, can be added Emma Tennant. Tennant's novella *Two Women of London* (1989) appeared as Thatcher's decade neared its close. Unlike the Amis of *Money*, for instance, she was thus able to reflect explicitly on a process of social change that had been named and identified.

Her book is a replay of Robert Louis Stevenson's *The Strange Case of Dr Jekyll and Mr Hyde* (1886), a seminal piece of late Victorian Gothic whose name has become shorthand for the idea of a split personality or drastically two-sided phenomenon. Stevenson's duo is transformed into Tennant's Eliza Jekyll, an attractive middle-class woman, and Mrs Hyde, her poor and slovenly neighbour in West London. As in the original, a transformation between the two is effected by chemical means. It ultimately transpires that the weary and weathered Eliza Jekyll has found that she can metamorphose into a glamorous alter ego by taking the drug Ecstasy, and her original self is renamed as Mrs Hyde. As Jekyll, she takes a job at a prestigious art gallery and purchases the flat above Hyde's run-down basement. Mentally confused, Hyde kills a wealthy neighbour whom she has compounded with a local serial rapist and with other men she resents. The novella purports to be composed by an investigator who assembles a range of textual evidence. It is populated primarily by the women who live in the housing development around a communal garden, and by the prim Fife lawyer Jean Hastie, whose own encounters with Jekyll and Hyde drive much of the story.

The novella is intertextually dense. Jean Hastie suggests both Stevenson's equally rationalist Dr Hastie Lanyon and another Edinburgh icon Muriel Spark's Miss Jean Brodie (who in turn shares a surname with the real-life inspiration for Stevenson's tale, Deacon William Brodie). Eliza Jekyll's servant Grace Poole derives her name both from an equivalent character in Stevenson and from a servant who in Charlotte Bronte's *Jane Eyre* has responsibility for the deranged secret wife of Mr Rochester. Tennant also repurposes textual traits prevalent in the Victorian Gothic narrative. Her intricate series of paratexts – opening vignette, 'Editor's Introduction', cast of characters and diary entries – recall the complex framings associated with Gothic. At times Tennant's prose also gladly takes on the lurid colourings licensed by the genre.

Her novella resembles David Lodge's *Nice Work* (1988) in being at once highly intertextual and determinedly contemporary. Lodge's novel explicitly reworks the mid-Victorian industrial novel for an era of de-industrialization. Tennant's novella, for all its late-Victorian provenance, is also a topical portrait of London in 1988. The use of Ecstasy as an improbable plot device – 'the most destructive and, as yet, largely unknown in its long-term effects, substance on the black market' (252) – is the most strikingly up-to-date detail. The drug's notoriety indeed centred around 1988, dance music's so-called 'Second Summer of Love'. The book's social gatherings carry traces of zeitgeist, as women debate the value of post-feminism and Russian art. In this respect, the novella recalls Margaret Drabble's novel *The Radiant Way* (1987), which attempts a social panorama of the 1980s via the fortunes of three middle-class women: in that book, too, conversation ranges from the latest political themes to the frightening activities of a local serial killer.

Tennant offers a particular view of London. As in Pat Barker's fiction, the urban fabric is strained: Jean Hastie reports that 'London Transport has certainly worsened considerably since I was last here' (203). She travels from central London streets 'where orange shop windows beckoned with displays...like arms a-glitter with bangles and rings', to a stretch of Notting Hill where 'a mean wind wafted nothing more satisfying than paper bags and Smartie cartons to the sleeping homeless by the entrance to the Tube' (209). This contrast between wealth and poverty, which we have already seen in Gray and Amis, is a recurrent note. On Harrow Road, 'a blur of TV shops and takeaways', Jean Hastie watches Mrs Hyde using a cheap butcher's and a betting shop – while by the canal nearby, she finds 'a great red-brick warehouse, with words lit up in a neon glare...CANALOT STUDIOS'. The warehouse, used by 'a group of polo-necked young men', is an instance of gentrification, the repurposing of old buildings by a bohemian middle class. Jean Hastie reflects on the contrast, seeing 'a street as rough and garish and abandoned to the poor as that great warehouse behind her is a haven for creativity and wealth' (210).

This sense of division and contrast is the book's keynote. The extremes of the contemporary city map onto the divided self of Jekyll and Hyde. At the launch of the Shade Gallery, the feminist film-maker Mara records an eclectic 'Heritage' environment: 'you could unclip that fireplace off the wall and stick it up in the hallway in any of the new "period" developments: it's a sort of instant respectability' (182). Again, the gentrifying art world is adjacent to a less 'respectable' one. The whole chic gallery is 'not two hundred yards from the most nefarious drugs den in all London, as well as the no-go area of All Saints Road, where the police have been clamping down on the blacks since anyone can remember' (181). Jekyll and Hyde, then, are only the vivid central figures for a wider pattern of doubles and contrasts, which extends into the city and the whole society. It is in this respect that the novel stands as a literary response to Thatcherism. Its Jekyll and Hyde are literal instances of rich and poor. Mrs Hyde is a single mother on Social Security: 'ground down by life', she bears 'the reality of life's hard writing on her that makes her, seen through the eyes of guilt, so alien'. 'Aren't there', the narrator rhetorically demands, 'a vast number like her – persecuted by a hostile state? And facing hostility and fear from the public too?' (259).

Two Women of London centres around women, most of them feminists. Even Jean Hastie, considered conservative by other characters, is writing 'a work of gynocriticism' which interrogates 'the roots of the phallocracy in which women have been forced to live' (199). Yet the book's interest in feminist politics, like Pat Barker's, is entwined with a concern for class and socio-economic inequality. The 'editor' roundly declares at the outset:

> We are surrounded daily by evidence of violence, poverty and misery in this city. The media leave us in no doubt that rapaciousness and a 'loadsamoney' economy have come to represent the highest values in the land. Crime and unrest are on the increase – as, so it seems, are fear and insecurity, which go hand in hand with great wealth and its companion, deprivation. (176)

'Loadsamoney', like Ecstasy, is a remarkably contemporary reference: it derives from a TV comedy character played by Harry Enfield and prominent through 1988. Enfield's grasping plasterer became the most conveniently cartoonish embodiment of vulgar new wealth and irresponsible greed. Tennant could hardly be more explicit about her social and political theme, in an era when Jean Hastie acknowledges 'a cutting back of Government support for those unable or unwilling to help themselves', replaced by 'a self-help ethos' (202). Tennant's final stroke clarifies her project, as Eliza Jekyll is described as a 'tragic victim of our new Victorian values' (268). The Victorian values hailed by the prime minister have been reframed by a return to Victorian Gothic. Alasdair Gray's narrator perceives a 'pageant of contrasts' reminiscent of the days of 'the Queen Empress Victoria' (138). Likewise, for Tennant, Stevenson's uncanny story is a way of considering 'what England has now become – a "quick-change artist"... meaning that everything this country had once represented is liable overnight to be turned into its opposite' (236).

The nation's parent

Ian McEwan had his own Gothic roots. He had become celebrated by the end of the 1970s for his slender fictions exploring often gruesome and disturbing scenarios. His novel *The Child in Time* (1987) was another matter. His longest work to date, it echoed McEwan's avowal of the importance of feminism in demonstrating a strong interest in models of nurturing and reconciliation between the sexes. The novel tells of the children's author Stephen Lewis and his wife Julie in the melancholy aftermath of the abduction of their young child. Through Stephen's physicist friend Thelma, it also introduces challenging scientific theories of time, which are perhaps actualized by the novel's own narrative as Stephen unwittingly travels into the past to ensure his own birth. This rangy, varied novel does not always seem especially concerned with the condition of England. Yet it also has a strong political frame. The fear and loathing previously associated with McEwan are transferred from the eccentric, troubled psyche to the realm of public policy.

The book is set in the future: specifically, Adam Mars-Jones has judged, in 1996 (142). The novel's opening pages casually describe a world which has altered, yet along lines that might be recognizable from the present of the mid-1980s. The book commences: 'Subsidising public transport had long been associated in the minds of both Government and the majority of its public with the denial of individual liberty. The various services collapsed twice a day at rush hour...' (7). The second sentence is arguably meant as an exaggerated extrapolation, even if many London commuters might claim to recognize it as fact. The first sentence, as the opening note of the entire novel, is more daring. It takes an existing tendency – individualism, the relative demotion of public services and progressive taxation – and turns it into something at once extreme and matter-of-fact. That the association 'had long been' held makes it appear taken for granted, a familiar piece of the ideological landscape. We are at once startled by the extremity of the formulation – a kind of *reductio ad absurdum* of New Right thinking – and further troubled by the uncontroversial, settled way in which it is announced. Arguably, what all this amounts to is a piece of satire.

It could also be called a form of science fiction. Like much vital writing in that mode, it extrapolates a near future from present tendencies; its imaginative projections are therefore commentaries on the actual. Pete Davies's political dystopia *The Last Election* (1986) was another case of this mode, envisaging a Britain in 1996 governed by the Money Party via hedonism, media distraction and life-shortening drugs. Stating that the novel was in part inspired by the Thatcher government's apparent threat to the NHS, Davies outlined the uses of science fiction: 'I had to set it in the future because I felt people wouldn't accept it as a picture of the present, but as far as I'm concerned these things are already happening. You might say I'm exaggerating, but I'd say I'm picking out and highlighting' (Sinclair 'Pete Davies'). McEwan's novel is less flagrantly satirical than Davies's, but still, in his London, the police routinely carry guns (20) and the private cars that have displaced public transport form a vast traffic jam: 'double and treble files of trapped, throbbing cars, each with its solitary driver' (7). We might be on the edge of Philip K. Dick here, or with the immediate appearance of 'licensed beggars' at Parliament Square. This extrapolates from the new visibility of homeless people on London's streets in the second half of the 1980s, a phenomenon also noted by Gray and Tennant. Faced with a beggar, McEwan's protagonist feels 'the usual ambivalence': 'To give money ensured the success of the Government programme. Not to give involved some determined facing away from private distress. There was no way out. The art of bad government was to sever the line between public policy and intimate feeling, the instinct for what was right' (8–9). McEwan's language is brisk, as is the summary judgement that strikingly opens this last sentence. 'The *art* of bad government' implies that damage is being done consciously and deliberately, even artfully.

Ecological crisis seems on hand in McEwan's future. In a long hot summer, 'Restrictions on water use had reduced the front gardens of suburban West London to dust' (85). When extreme rain and gales follow, 'weather experts' explain the disappearance of autumn and debate climatological causes (123). The ecological undercurrent is of a piece with McEwan's conviction of the need for a newly harmonious relation with nature. He had explained this in the introduction to his oratorio *Or Shall We Die?* (1983), whose primary concern was the threat of nuclear destruction. This menace too haunts *The Child in Time*. A spat between Russian and American athletes at the Olympic Games brings the world close to doomsday: McEwan brings the impending disaster home with a vivid passing image as 'missiles bristled in the hot shrubbery of rural Oxfordshire' (35). In its twin imagined disasters, climatic and nuclear, the novel prefigures Martin Amis's *London Fields* (1989): another satirical projection from the present, this time to an apocalyptic 1999. Amis's book, though, shows much less interest in the detail of politics, or of human character, than McEwan's. Detail is certainly not lacking from one of McEwan's main subplots, in which Stephen Lewis serves on the government's Official Commission on Childcare. Through these scenes McEwan offers a close-up depiction of the workings of the state. Ultimately, it appears that the committee has been merely a charade, trumped by the publication of a book from the prime minister's office which unilaterally urges a conservative line on childcare. Each chapter of McEwan's novel is in fact prefaced by a quotation from this imaginary document. A civil servant who leaks it to Stephen notes the importance of the issue to the government: 'how the nation is to be regenerated by reformed childcare practice' (162). In Parliament the prime minister is assailed for duplicity, but responds with a stentorian statement of conservative values:

> It had been shown that there was deep concern among parents and educators about falling standards of behaviour and lack of civic responsibility among many elements of society, particularly the young. Upbringing clearly played an important part in this, and there was no doubt that parents in the past had been led astray by foolish and fashionable theories about childcare. There was a call for a return to commonsense, and the Government was being asked to take a lead. (181)

McEwan reproduces here a stock of familiar political emphases from the Conservatism of the 1980s. His 'bad government' appears to have an interest in the ideological management of the population from an early age. In a novel much preoccupied with childhood, the family appears as a site of moulding and indoctrination. Politics includes something like what Michel Foucault called 'bio-politics', the manipulation of demographics, family and sexuality in the name of order.

The prime minister speaks in '[t]he familiar voice, pitched somewhere between a tenor's and an alto's' (180). A large element in the novel's elaboration of the political future is the sense that Margaret Thatcher remains prime minister into the mid-1990s. Equally striking is the novel's refusal to spell this out unequivocally. What we see and hear of the prime minister often suggests Thatcher. Stephen sees 'a neat, stooped, sixty-five-year-old' (a glitch for the dating of the novel's action: Thatcher was 65 in 1990, the year she resigned) who is also 'the nation's parent ... a repository of collective fantasy' (83). When the character also confesses to a romantic obsession with a former minister, Stephen's friend Charles Darke, we are perhaps supposed to think of Thatcher's own Cabinet favourites like Cecil Parkinson (188). But McEwan plays an elaborate game in withholding any reference to the prime minister's name or sex, paralleling what he describes as a civil service convention (82). We thus read scenes in which the premier appears in person, but is never cited as 'he' or 'she', as McEwan passes what he calls a 'test of verbal dexterity' (82).

This makes for a very distinctive way of discussing Margaret Thatcher. On one hand we sense the implication that Thatcher has gone 'on and on', as she claimed to intend in 1987 (Campbell 520). This in itself is unsettling. The sheer political longevity that it implies is sufficiently rare as to make Thatcher seem unnatural, unbeholden to normal laws: a creature of science fiction, perhaps. It also corresponds to a real sense among her dismayed opponents that she was indomitable. Yet McEwan's refusal to name Thatcher outright leaves us uncertain. This is fiction, after all. The premier's occluded name could be anything. Most striking, though, is the reticence around the figure's sex. It implies that this figure is Margaret Thatcher, the only woman prime minister in British history: for only a woman in the role would seem to explain the elaborate convention of not mentioning her gender, which 'undoubtedly had its origins in insult' (82). It also leaves this implication incomplete and uncertified. Further, the very absence of any reference to gender arguably heightens the reader's sense of gender as an issue. To adapt a phrase from Julian Critchley, it becomes the great she-elephant in the room (Campbell 471). By featuring a prime minister of unknown gender, McEwan prompts reflection on Thatcher's femaleness in a way that a more straightforward portrait of her would not do. The reader may well think of what some observers considered Thatcher's ambiguous gender identity: the 'hard-faced femininity' described by her biographer, or (Denis Healey's image) 'Florence Nightingale with a blowtorch' (Campbell 472–476).

In any case, McEwan's was an original contribution to a sub-genre of the literature of Thatcherism: fictions that depicted not just social processes but the premier herself. In Salman Rushdie's *Satanic Verses*, the immigrant community delights 'at least three times a week' in burning a waxwork effigy of Thatcher, complete with 'Her permawaved coiffure, her pearls, her suit of blue' (293). Elsewhere in the novel the vulgar businessman Hal Valance reveres her 'revolution' while also apparently denigrating her as 'Mrs Torture', 'Maggie the bitch' (266, 269). The sadistic overtones of Rushdie's renaming echo the 'powerful sexual ambivalence' that John Campbell finds in numerous responses to her (472). Rushdie, at this point identified with the political Left, takes a form of mental revenge on Thatcher. But his depiction of her disciple Valance is artlessly crude next to the thoroughgoing portrayals of Thatcherite consciousness and its discontents previously offered by Gray and Amis. Mark Lawson's *Bloody Margaret* (1991) and Philip Hensher's *Kitchen Venom* (1996) would centre on the later days of her reign. Iain Sinclair's caricatured portrait of the premier as 'The Widow' in *Downriver* (1991) resembles McEwan's in not naming Thatcher directly, and in apparently distending her political lifespan. Sinclair's Widow is 'the longest serving politico-spiritual Papa Boss not yet given the wax treatment'; she wears a wig of golden curls and is artificially sustained by chemicals (219–220). This leader is 'a couple of years into her fifth term in what was now effectively a one-party state and a one-woman party' (220). Here as in McEwan's near future we can see the terrible grandeur that Thatcher came to have for her detractors, the difficulty of imagining a plausible end to her tenure. Yet by the time Sinclair's book was published, she had resigned. In a response to Angela Carter's review of the novel, Sinclair – always happy to dabble in the idiom of magic – insisted that his book had functioned as prophecy, a performative 'invocation' hastening Thatcher's political end (Carter 126).

The representation of Margaret Thatcher has been a notable strand within the fiction of Thatcherism, but as we have seen, it does not exhaust it. Let us review the brief survey essayed above. In Alasdair Gray we find a critique which attempts to work at the ideology of Conservatism from the inside. In Martin Amis we find a brilliantly histrionic rendition of the turbulent energies of a new era. Like Gray he presents a Thatcherite protagonist from the inside, but his fictional form does not claim any definitively detached political judgement. Pat Barker, juxtaposing past and present, partakes in a mood of elegy widespread among writers who portrayed the increasingly post-industrial North. Emma Tennant mischievously redeploys literary history in a Gothic allegory of the divisive tendencies she sees at work. Ian McEwan offers a projection of current politics into a menacing future, and in the manner of science fiction is thus somewhat able to estrange the present and suggest that it contains the seeds of worse to come.

What *was* to come, in fiction and society, will be the subject of other volumes in this series. Thatcher hoped to go on and on, and her legacy has done so. But literature may yet outlast it. In the meantime, it can help us to remember and understand the era that Thatcher made her own.

Works cited

Amis, Martin. *Money: A Suicide Note*. London: Jonathan Cape, 1984.
———. *Einstein's Monsters*. London: Cape, 1987.
Barker, Pat. *Liza's England*, first published as *The Century's Daughter* (1986). London: Virago, 1986.
Bracewell, Michael. *The Crypto-Amnesia Club*. London: Serpant's Tail, 1988.
———. *Divine Concepts of Physical Beauty*. New York: Alfred A. Knopf, 1989.
———. *The Conclave*. London: Martin Secker and Warburg, 1992.
Briggs, Raymond. *When the Wind Blows*. London: Penguin, 1986 [1982].
Buford, Bill. 'Editorial.' *Granta 43: Best of Young British Novelists* 2 (Spring 1993): 9–16.
Campbell, John. *Margaret Thatcher. Volume Two: The Iron Lady*. London: Jonathan Cape, 2003.
Carter, Angela. *Expletives Deleted*. London: Chatto & Windus, 1992.
Coe, Jonathan. *What a Carve Up!* New York: Viking, 1994.
———. *The Terrible Privacy of Maxwell Sim*. New York: Viking, 2004.
———. 'Jonathan Coe Recalls the 1980s.' *Guardian* (26 May 2007), Weekend: 43.
———. 'Aiming at a Beast Called "Thatcherism."' *Guardian* (14 April 2009), Review: 15.
Daniels, Sarah. *Plays 1*. York: Methuen, 1991.
Davies, Pete. *The Last Election*. London: Andre Deutsch, 1986.
Drabble, Margaret. *The Radiant Way*. New York: Knopf, 1987.
Edgar, David. *Maydays*. York: Methuen, 1983.
English, James F. and John Frow. 'Literary Authorship and Celebrity Culture.' *A Concise Companion to Contemporary British Fiction*. Ed. James F. English. Oxford: Blackwell, 2006, 39–57.
Galloway, Janice. *The Trick Is to Keep Breathing*. Edinburgh: Polygon, 1989.
Gerrard, Nicci. *Into the Mainstream: How Feminism Has Changed Women's Writing*. London: Pandora, 1989.
Gray, Alasdair. *1982 Janine*. Harmondsworth: Penguin, 1984.
Hall, Stuart. *The Hard Road to Renewal: Thatcherism and the Crisis of the Left*. London: Verso, 1988.
Hensher, Philip. *Kitchen Venom*. London: Hamish Hamilton, 1996.
Hutchinson, Colin. *Reaganism, Thatcherism and the Social Novel*. Basingstoke: Palgrave, 2008.
Ishiguro, Kazuo. *The Remains of the Day*. London: Faber and Faber, 1989.
Johnston, Michael. 'The Blue River of Truth: Following the Course of Margaret Thatcher across the Firm Ground of Fiction. A Study of the Impact on Contemporary Fiction of Britain's First Woman Prime Minister.' MA Dissertation, September 2009, http://www.akanos.co.uk/ma_dissertation.html.
Keay, Douglas. 'Aids, Education and the Year 2,000!' *Woman's Own* (31 October 1987): 8–10.

Keys, David, Graham Allen and Adam Sharples. *Thatcher's Britain: A Guide to the Ruins*. London: Pluto Press and New Socialist, 1983.
Lawson, Mark. *Bloody Margaret: Three Political Fantasies*. London: Pan, 1991.
Leys, Colin. 'The Rise of the Authoritarian State.' *The Future of the Left*. Ed. James Curran. Cambridge: Polity Press and New Socialist, 1984, 58–73.
Lodge, David. *Nice Work*. London: Martin Secker and Warburg, 1988.
Mars-Jones, Adam. *Blind Bitter Happiness*. London: Chatto & Windus, 1997.
McEwan, Ian with Michael Berkeley. *Or Shall We Die?* London: Jonathan Cape, 1983.
———. *The Child in Time*. London: Jonathan Cape, 1987.
McIlvanney, Liam. 'The Politics of Narrative in the Post-War Scottish Novel.' *On Modern British Fiction*. Ed. Zachary Leader. Oxford: Oxford University Press, 2002, 181–208.
Mitchell, David. *Black Swan Green*. London: Random House, 2006.
Moore, Alan. *Watchmen*. New York: DC Comics, 1986–1987.
Rushdie, Salman. *The Satanic Verses*. London: Viking, 1988.
Samuel, Raphael. *Island Stories – Unravelling Britain: Theatres of Memory, Volume II*. London: Verso, 1998.
Showalter, Elaine. 'Ladlit.' *On Modern British Fiction*. Ed. Zachary Leader. Oxford: Oxford University Press, 2002, 60–76.
Sinclair, Iain. *Downriver*. London: Paladin, 1991.
Sinclair, Mick. 'Pete Davies.' *The Mick Sinclair Archive*, first published February 1986, http://micksinclair.com/nme/davies.html.
Smith, Joan. *Misogynies*. London: Faber and Faber, 1989.
Stevenson, Randall. *The Last of England? The Oxford English Literary History, Volume 12: 1960–2000*. Oxford: Oxford University Press, 2004.
Tennant, Emma. *The Bad Sister: An Emma Tennant Omnibus*. Edinburgh: Canongate, 2000.
Todd, Richard. *Consuming Fictions: The Booker Prize and Fiction in Britain Today*. London: Bloomsbury, 1996.
Tredell, Nicolas (ed.). *The Fiction of Martin Amis: A Reader's Guide to Essential Criticism*. Cambridge: Icon, 2000.
Utley, T. E. 'Thatcherism: A Monstrous Invention.' *Britain in the Eighties: The Spectator's View of the Thatcher Decade*. Ed. Philip Marsden-Smedley. London: Paladin, 1991, 146–149.
Waterstone, Tim. 'The Other Side: Bookselling in Britain and the United States.' *Publishing Now*. Ed. Peter Owen. London: Peter Owen, 1993, 101–110.
Winterson, Jeanette. *The Passion*. London: Vintage, 1996, first published London: Bloomsbury, 1987.
Wright, Patrick. *A Journey through Ruins: A Keyhole Portrait of British Postwar Life and Culture*. London: Radius, 1991.
Wright, Peter. *Spycatcher*. New York: Viking. 1987.
York, Peter and Charles Jennings. *Peter York's Eighties*. London: BBC, 1995.

4

Postcolonial and Diasporic Voices
'Black' British Women's Fiction and Literary Institutions in the 1980s

Susan Alice Fischer

Introduction

An African and Asian presence in British literature dates back to at least the 1700s, as C. L. Innes (2002), Gretchen Gerzina (1995) and others have shown, and women have been part of this history. However, British women's fiction by authors of African, Caribbean and Asian descent has only recently entered a mainstream reading public's consciousness with the turn-of-the-millennium successes of Zadie Smith, Monica Ali and Andrea Levy. These contemporary writers have been able to emerge in large part because of their predecessors of 1980s and because of the way that Black feminist politics and culture emerged at the time. Indeed, Black women's writing blossomed during the decade, largely as a cultural response to the pressing social conditions that led to the women's and other human rights movements.

Despite the significance of Black British women's fiction from the 1980s, few of the authors discussed below have garnered the critical attention they deserve. An artistic expression of individual lives, their work can also be seen as reflecting a larger Black feminist political and theoretical discourse rooted in an understanding of the intertwining categories of gender, ethnicity, sexuality and class – a consciousness that still underpins the work of more recent Black women writers (see Shields; Fischer, 'Familiar Hearts' 176). In examining the conditions under which Black British women's fiction emerged, this chapter traces a thematic trajectory which moves from 'unbelonging' to hybridity and a redefinition of British identity.

Black feminist culture and politics overlaps with other projects in the 1980s. The extreme fertility of the period stems from a 'concatenation of extraordinary events – cultural, literary and political' which produced new voices contesting the social and political realities (Arana 231). These included responses to such issues as increasingly restrictive immigration policies aimed specifically at Black and Asian communities, culminating in the British Nationality Act of 1981 (Dixon 162), the rise of the National Front, repressive and violent policing bolstered by the draconian stop and search ('sus') laws aimed especially at Black people and widespread inequitable practices in housing, employment, education, the provision of social services and the dispensation of law, despite the passage of the Race Relations Act of 1976. Moreover, even though the Equal Pay Act was passed in 1970, overt discrimination against women was still largely an accepted cultural norm, and women's campaigns included action around work, sexual harassment and reproductive rights. Black and Asian women's groups took 'up issues of discrimination against class, race and gender at once – in the face of harassments which, under the new Tory regimen, went deep into community life, into households, into children's welfare' (Sivanandan 147). Groups included the Organization of Women of African and Asian Descent (OWAAD), the Southall Black Sisters, founded in 1979, the Brixton Black Women's Group and the Black Lesbian Group Birmingham ('SBS Timeline'; Bogle 132–135; Brixton Black Women's Group; King 127–128; and Sivanandan 147).

In *The Internationalization of English Literature*, Bruce King notes some of the decade's key literary and cultural products emanating from Black Britain. (I am using the term 'Black' in the specific 1980s sense of an inclusive political designation highlighting the shared struggles of people of African and Asian descent, whether they were born in Britain or came from Africa, Asia, the Caribbean or elsewhere (see Arana 239, n. 1; Ward 985).) This cultural work includes such important texts as Peter Fryer's *Staying Power* (1984), Paul Gilroy's *There Ain't No Black in the Union Jack: The Cultural Politics of Race and Nation* (1987) and Hanif Kureishi's films, such as *My Beautiful Laundrette* (1985). Black women brought their experiences to the fore in Beverley Bryan, Stella Dadzie and Suzanne Scafe's *Heart of the Race* (1985) and in the novels and cultural projects discussed below. This period of struggle for rights and recognition would eventually begin to change the very notion of national identity as Black people continued to, as Arana suggests, 'assert their Englishness, their demands for equal and just treatment as English citizens' (232). This redefinition of national identity continues to have repercussions today: 'Post-1980s British literature in general portrays the new England, the new Scotland, and the new Wales as *still* English, Scottish, and Welsh, respectively, though culturally *modified* and updated' to be inclusive, regardless of ethnic or national origin (232). Redefining what it means to be not only British – a category often related to citizenship – but more particularly English, Scottish or Welsh is one of the major contributions of the political and cultural projects of the 1980s, as can be seen in the continuation of this discussion around a revamped sense of national identity in the novel from the 1990s to the present.

The struggle against racial inequality and injustice resonates in Black fiction of the 1980s, and women writers also address the specifically gendered nature of such experiences. This is not to suggest that the literature is a form of social realism, and much can be said about the formal aspects of this literature, some of which experiments with the forms of prose fiction, as will be seen below. Nonetheless, these experiences permeate the themes in fiction by women of African, Caribbean and Asian descent in this period and shape their attempts to gain access to and recognition in the literary institutions.

Black women and 1980s literary institutions

Like Black male authors, Black female writers came up against the unwillingness of mainstream publishing houses and distribution outlets to see a readership for African, Caribbean and Asian British work. In addition, they shared with other women the experience of a resistance from the mainstream to publishing women's texts, particularly 'feminist' or other 'radical' forms of writing. The shape of the industry was one reason. As Nick Garnham and Ken Worpole remarked about the book trade in 1985, 'The key problem ... is no longer cultural production but distribution' (51). The majority of books were distributed by powerful companies, such as Bookwise, Menzies and WHSmith, which placed a limited number of titles in retail outlets and overlooked less mainstream readerships. This also affected publication, as Worpole notes when quoting a marketing director from Fontana, who said that when thinking of bidding on a book he would 'put in a couple of calls – one to Smiths, another to Bookwise – to see if *they* thought it promotable' (Worpole 24).

Another factor in the difficulty that Black writers – male or female – had in getting their work out simply had to do with a refusal on the part of the mainstream to see Black literature or other cultural production as art. For instance, Kwesi Owusu notes that Naseem Khan's 1976 report entitled *The Arts Britain Ignores* describes an incredibly rich and varied arts scene in a variety of 'minority' communities, but that '[w]hen the report came out it barely made the headlines, and media reception was one of apparent disinterest' (49). Moreover, artists noted the ways in which they were marginalized as 'ethnic minority' artists, something that John Agard lampoons in his poem 'Palm Tree King' (cited in Owusu 52–53). Owusu maintains that this 'refusal' to 'accept' Black artists was still as 'relevant' in the mid-1980s (60), and his data from the Arts Council of Great Britain show how few resources, a sizeable portion of which was set aside for literature, made it to any of the Black arts projects, even in London with its diverse population (61).

The situation for feminist publishing was similar. As Alice Hennegan, editor of The Women's Press Bookclub, said in 1985, the 'demand' for feminist books simply wasn't 'being met', and many mainstream publishers were unaware of the 'specialist' readership that had developed around feminist books. She argued that the cultural production existed, as more work was making it into print, but that 'it sometimes seems as though the very belief in a feminist market which presumably persuaded the publisher to undertake a particular book in the first place dwindles as production progresses. Even giant houses will fix tiny print runs... and then be astounded to find they've exhausted the entire edition in pre-publication sales' (28). Hennegan also maintained that 'a book dubbed "minority" in one part of the trade might prove "popular" in paperback format, differently marketed' (29).

To overcome these circumstances, Black women writers forged alliances with both Black and women's alternative publishing and distribution enterprises and also developed their own. In the autumn 1984 issue of *Feminist Review* – a special issue dedicated to Black women, entitled 'Many Voices, One Chant: Black Feminist Perspectives' – editors Valerie Amos, Gail Lewis, Amina Mama and Pratibha Parmar hoped that the issue would not just be a 'token exercise', but rather 'that in the future *Feminist Review* will include writings by and for Black women'. They noted the 'ongoing need for white women to take note of and act upon Black feminist critiques of the content and form of British feminism' (1).

While the literary field is still not level today, it is perhaps easy to forget in the light of some recent successes just how much more dire things were in the 1980s for writers who were Black, female, working class and/or lesbian. Few mainstream publishers were willing to take on Black women writers, and the bookshops were unlikely to stock their work, thus perpetuating a self-fulfilling prophecy that there wasn't a readership. Not only was access to publication cut off, but some Black women writers were concerned about the limited ways in which their work was deemed acceptable. In an article appearing in the feminist magazine *Spare Rib*, author Barbara Burford said that publishers 'tell me what they think the market requires. At the moment from Black women writers it seems to require what Dorothea Smartt in a review in the *New Statesman* calls "... the pathologizing of the Blackwoman's condition," or, as Grace Nichols puts it in her wonderful poem: "... a little black pain undressed"' (37).

Thus venues for publishing and distributing books by Black women writers were necessary both for getting their work out and also for representing the variety of perspectives in their communities. Despite how hard it was for Black women to make their voices heard, little work from the 1980s would have seen the light of day had it not been for the vibrant alternative publishing ventures and other literary projects. Indeed, Andrea Levy, who came of age in that period, has said of feminist literary production of those years: 'Certainly, feminist publishing was how I got into reading. All those presses, Virago, The Women's Press – those were my books; they were my people. That's where I started on the journey. Those were books that spoke of what I was going through at that time' ('Andrea Levy in Conversation with Susan Alice Fischer' 361; see also Smith 'What Does Soulful Mean?'). King notes that '[t]he First International Fair of Radical, Black and Third World Books was held in North London in 1982' (134). The fair 'brought the increasing number of black publishers to the attention of potential readers and ... the Book Fair was also a cultural convention of lectures and public discussions' (135). As King argues, alternative bookshops were important, such as the Bogle L'Ouverture Bookshop and New Beacon Books on Stroud Green Road, in Finsbury Park, which has been selling books since 1966. Small presses emphasizing Caribbean writing included Peepal Tree, founded in 1986, and celebrating its 25th anniversary in 2011, which published the poetry of Dorothea Smartt, and Karia Press, which published Merle Collins's *Because the Dawn Breaks* in 1985. The journal *Wasafiri*, now put out by Routledge, began in 1984, and Prabhu Guptara issued a bibliography of Black British literature in 1986 (133–134).

Black women writers also looked to specifically feminist projects to support their work. By the early 1980s, a number of feminist presses had been established. Among these, Virago Press was founded in 1972, Onlywomen Press in 1974, The Women's Press in 1977, Sheba Feminist Publishers in 1980 and Black Womantalk in 1983. Like the mainstream publishing industry, feminist and alternative publishing and bookshops were predominantly centred in London, but also existed in other parts of the country.

Feminist publishing had arisen because the mainstream book trade was unreceptive, if not hostile, to the cultural output of the women's movement of the 1970s. By the early 1980s, however, it was clear that feminist publishing was not as responsive as it should have been to the writing of Black women, and Black women addressed the limited number of books by Black women that Virago and The Women's Press – the two largest feminist publishers – had put out. While these publishers did produce a number of African American books, and brought the work of writers such as Alice Walker to a British audience, these books were likely to be more lucrative as these authors were already established in the US. The presses often failed to recognize the work by Black British women. As the Black Woman Talk Collective put it in Valerie Amos et al., 'Such publishers are not only reluctant to hear the voices of Black women in Britain but there is little concern about including Black women in the publishing industry in a way which gives them any decision-making powers at all levels' (100). No doubt in response to criticism, The Women's Press began to publish more original books and rely less heavily on reprints from abroad, and they issued a separate catalogue geared to a Black British readership. After various other formations, Sheba Feminist Publishers emerged as a racially mixed collective which privileged the writing of Black women, as well as that of working-class women, lesbians and new writers. Given Virago's focus at the time on the project of recovering earlier women's writing and The Women's Press's centring on making American imports available in the UK, Sheba saw the need for a predominantly contemporary British list. Another small Black collective, Black Womantalk, was set up to create 'the space and the means for our voices to be heard' (Black Womantalk 7). Like many projects at the time, the aim was not only to publish books, but also to encourage writers, and they held workshops and other events.

Another important venue for increasing discussion around Black women's literature was the First International Feminist Book Fair, held in Covent Garden in 1984. In addition to leading to several biannual fairs in various other cities around the world and to the annual Feminist Book Fortnight which promoted books throughout bookshops in the UK – and this represented a major breakthrough into chains such as WHSmith, which had not recognized the readership until this point – the Book Fair events also gave Black women a venue at which to raise their concerns about marginalization within the feminist book trade. Although the Book Fair and its weeklong series of events was in many ways a great success, the African American writer Audre Lorde, who was at the Fair, criticized the exclusion of Black British women in favour of showcasing the work of Black women from abroad. She dubbed the Book Fair 'a monstrosity of racism' which 'distorted, and deflected much of what was good and creative, almost visionary about having such a fair' (quoted in Parmar and Kay 123–125).

After the Fair, feminist publishers began to publish more books by Black writers from Britain and elsewhere. Even so, at the Second International Feminist Book Fair held in Oslo, Norway, in 1986, Black British author Barbara Burford was quoted as saying that 'publishers issue "reprint after reprint after reprint" of the books by black American women who are now popular with radically chic, white readers there, while ignoring the works by black women living and writing in Britain today'. Burford added, 'What we have to do as writers is stay put with the publishers who have the politics... They don't have the distribution, but they'll never get it until they have the writers people want to read.' Burford stressed the importance of demanding feminist books from mainstream bookshops 'to create our own mass market' (quoted in Kaufmann 13–14).

During the 1980s, there was an urgency to political organizing and related cultural projects, and Black, feminist, working-class, gay and lesbian and 'alternative' projects were numerous in and beyond the capital. In London, these projects were often supported by small grants by the Greater London Council (GLC) until 1986, when the Thatcher government abolished it for supporting what the tabloid press dubbed the 'loony left'. Projects like Sheba Feminist Publishers, which were founded as political and cultural projects rather than business enterprises and operated as collectives, began to have greater difficulties after 1986. As Linda Hunt stated, the elimination of the GLC Women's Committee axed 'the largest single source of funds for women ever established in Britain' (44). Public funding through such projects as the London Borough Grants Scheme cut off women's projects such as the Feminist Library, Asian Women's Action Group and Asian Women's Resource Centre (see Wise). Not all projects from those years survived, and Sheba went under in the early 1990s. Groups committed to equal access and opportunity for lesbians were further threatened by Section 28 of the Local Government Act of 1988, which forbade the so-called 'promotion of homosexuality' by any entity receiving local funding, including schools and libraries. This affected Black lesbian groups, as well as Black women's groups that included lesbian projects, which most feminist projects did at the time.

Black women's books from the feminist publishers

Even though Black women did not have an easy time getting their work out, their voices managed to be among the most significant of the period, and gradually some headway was made. As early as 1978, Virago published Amrit Wilson's pioneering work about Asian women's lives in Britain, *Finding a Voice: Asian Women in Britain*. This book told the story of Asian women's lives in the areas of family, work, immigration, education and so on, and included information on Asian women's organizations. Going through several editions, the book included a postscript on 'Developments in the Eighties' in the 1985 edition to address some of the changes that had occurred with the rise of Thatcherism. In 1985, Virago published an important work similarly detailing the lives of women of African Caribbean background: Beverley Bryan, Stella Dadzie and Suzanne Scafe's *The Heart of the Race: Black Women's Lives in Britain*. Like *Finding a Voice*, the volume provided a historical background to relations with Britain, including slavery and colonialism. Both books underlined the need for these groups of women to express their own realities, recognizing that white feminists – and men of their own ethnic backgrounds – however well-intentioned – were unable to tell their stories. Margaret Busby pointed out in her 1988 review of *Let It Be Told: Essays by Black Women Writers in Britain* (Virago) and *Charting the Journey* (Sheba 1988) that 'Britain has lagged far beyond the USA in nurturing and publishing Black women writers' (1374). But she saw the publication of these books – as well as the appearance of Greater Access to Publishing (GAP), an organization which aimed at greater inclusion of Black women in the industry, and of two new presses, Black Womantalk and Zora – as signs of better things to come. At the beginning of the next decade, Busby would publish the monumental volume she edited, *Daughters of Africa: An International Anthology of Words and Writings by Women of African Descent: From the Ancient Egyptian to the Present* (1992), which was instrumental in raising the awareness of Black women's writing in Britain and elsewhere.

By the end of the 1980s, The Women Press's catalogue contained about 40 fiction and 20 non-fiction titles by Black women from different parts of the world, over a third of which were original publications, rather than reprints from abroad. In 1988, the London-based Asian Women's Writers' Workshop published its first book with The Women's Press. The Women's Press also published *The Conversations of Cow* by Suniti Namjoshi (1985), *Birthday Deathday and Other Stories* by Padma Perera (1985), *Amritvela* by Leena Dhingra (1988) and *Jesus Is Indian and Other Stories* by Agnes Sam (1989) (see Paranjape 72). In 1984, Sheba issued a collection of short stories called *Everyday Matters 2*, this time including the works of writers such as Jackie Kay, Barbara Burford and Rashida Khan. In 1985, Sheba published a poetry collection entitled *A Dangerous Knowing: Four Black Women Poets*, which included poems by Barbara Burford, Gabriela Pearse, Grace Nichols and Jackie Kay, all based in Britain. In 1988, they put out the anthology *Charting the Journey: Writings by Black and Third World Women*, edited by Shabnam Grewal, Jackie Kay, Liliane Landor, Gail Lewis and Pratibha Parmar. Organized thematically, the collection included poems, stories, essays and interviews from women in Britain and around the world. While Sheba was responsible for bringing African American writers such as Audre Lorde, bell hooks and Jewelle Gomez to a British audience, they also published the works of Suniti Namjoshi (*Feminist Fables*, 1981; *Aditi and the One-Eyed Monkey*, 1986) and Meling Jin (*Gifts from My Grandmother: Poems*, 1985) and *Our Own Freedom* (1981), a book of photographs of women in Africa by Maggie Murray, with text by Buchi Emecheta. The British Library catalogue shows that Sheba published only 39 books during its years of operation from 1980 to 1992, but its impact was vital to emerging Black women's voices.

Black Womantalk began in 1983 as a collective made up of women of Asian and African descent. As a voluntary group reliant on funding that was rapidly diminishing under Thatcherism, they managed to publish two collections edited by Da Choong, Olivette Cole Wilson, Bernadine Evaristo, Syvia Parker and Gabriela Pearse – one of poetry, *Black Women Talk Poetry* (1987), and one of short stories, *Don't Ask Me Why: An Anthology of Short Stories by Black Women* (1991). Yet, like many of the other feminist publishing projects, their impact exceeded the number of books they published, and they remained active for a number of years by doing readings and workshops. Their poetry collection included the work of 20 poets, some of whom are well known today, such as Jackie Kay, Bernadine Evaristo and Dorothea Smartt. This again underlines the importance of even such a small-scale collective in developing Black women's literature for the new millennium.

By the end of the decade, a new generation of Black women were 'speaking out', as can be seen in Audrey Osler's 1989 *Speaking Out: Black Girls in Britain*, published by Virago, which drew on the experiences of schoolgirls of African and Asian descent. Indeed, while Ruth Petrie of Virago recognized that claims of racism had validity in the past, she felt that Virago were eager to publish Black British women's writing (Young 4). Some claimed that by the end of the decade, 'Books by and about women of color are now a major trend in feminist publishing' (4). However, 'groups like Sheba sometimes felt that larger presses took on such manuscripts only because, in Barbara Burford's words, they were the "flavour of the month"' (4). This points to how difficult it has been – and in many respects continues today to be, despite some obvious exceptions – for Black women writers to establish themselves and maintain visibility in the marketplace. Sheba collective member Menika van der Poorten raised some of these concerns by saying, 'While other feminist publishers, and mainstream publishers of women's books have lots of Black American writers, and now one or two British black women, I still feel they market for a white audience' (cited in Young 4). Marsha Prescod underlined the precarious position of Black women writers when she said, 'Black people in Britain have been writing for as long as we've been here... As we're not in control of the publishing scene, the appearance of our work is subject to fashion, and whether we're in fashion or not. So I don't believe there's any new explosion, as such, just that the door has opened a little' (quoted in Busby 1375).

The 'unbelonging': Buchi Emecheta and Joan Riley

Black women's experiences in the publishing industry and in society at large resonate in the themes that the authors of the period explore through their fiction. The 1980s were still very much a time when many Black British writers had been born outside of Britain, though younger, British-born Black people experienced 'unbelonging' as well. Indeed, as Buchi Emecheta notes, in 1985, 'a new survey... show[ed] that a great number of black children born here do not regard themselves [as] British' (*Head above Water* 139).

Buchi Emecheta was born in 1944 near Lagos, Nigeria, and migrated to Britain in the 1960s (Fischer, 'Buchi Emecheta' 1058). Emecheta began denouncing the multiple sense of exclusion and exploitation of migrant Black women as early as the 1970s with her novels *In the Ditch* (1972) and *Second Class Citizen* (1974). Emecheta was not published by the feminist presses – *New Statesman* serialized what would become her first novel (published by Barrie and Jenkins) – although she and her son founded their own press, Ogwugwu Afor, after a publisher cut a substantial portion of one of her books (1059). Some of Emecheta's themes continued to be explored by other migrant writers in the 1980s, such as Joan Riley, who names the experience of Black women's marginalization 'the unbelonging' in her 1985 novel of that name.

In the 1980s, Emecheta continued to examine Black women's realities in Britain with such titles as her autobiographical *Head above Water*, first published in 1986 by Ogwugwu Afor, and her novel *Gwendolyn* (1989). During the period, she located most of her narratives in her native Nigeria, where she examined the injustices that women face in that culture as well, naming the oppression of Black women the 'double yoke', as can be seen in her 1982 novel of that title. Part of her writing concerns understanding what it is to be a 'doubly culturally-enslaved woman' (*Head above Water*, 4).

Throughout her work, Emecheta connects her experience to the larger issues of colonialism in Africa as well as racism in Britain and sexism in both places. In her first two novels and in *Head above Water*, Emecheta denounces the racism that she and her husband encountered upon arrival in London, and she writes that 'Twenty-three years later, I am still suffering from that shock!' (*Head above Water* 27). Just as importantly, she focuses on the sexism she experiences within her own culture and especially at the hands of her husband, who eventually becomes abusive towards her, as he turns his own frustration against her: 'My husband always quoted this early shock we had at human nature as the strongest contributory factor to the break-up of our family. Maybe so... but he began to settle for second best. I could have followed him, but for the sake of the kids... I was prepared... to keep surviving with my head just above water' (29). When she leaves him, she is a mother of five children, trying to obtain housing, hold down a job and continue her education. Her story, also recounted in her early fiction, is remarkable for her tenacity and her refusal to give in to the expectations society places upon her as a Black woman. As she says, her survival is miraculous, something she attributes to staying true to her *chi*, or personal spirit, as well as to the camaraderie she develops with other women in similar predicaments on her housing estate in Camden and to remaining connected to her African culture. To understand the 'miracle' of survival that Emecheta refers to is to understand the role of writing as a fundamental tool of survival for Black women writing at a time when their voices were beginning to be heard in a new way (see also Ezenwa-Ohaeto).

Emecheta defines herself as a feminist with a small 'f', in that, like many other Black women, she distances herself from white Western feminism which often ignores or makes ethnocentric assumptions about the lives of Black women and overlooks diverse forms of women's resistance to patriarchy ('Feminism with a Small "F"!'). In *Head above Water*, Emecheta recounts her experiences with the International Women's Year of 1975, when she first heard the word 'feminism' and white women talking about 'women's emancipation, birth control in the Third World and how the Third World women were suffering'. She 'hated' this sort of discussion as 'one simply becomes fed up with seeing oneself as a problem' and she told 'them to mind their own business and leave us Third World women alone' (177). Throughout her extensive body of work, Emecheta traces her indoctrination under colonial rule to the ideology of British superiority, her realization upon arrival in Britain that this was a myth, her relegation to a second-class status based on 'race' and sex and her determination to struggle against 'what they told me' by giving voice to her story and, in the process, creating herself anew.

At the end of the decade, Emecheta would return to a British location, with *Gwendolyn*, a story of a Caribbean family and abuse, which Omar Sougou has rightly linked to Joan Riley's *The Unbelonging* (Fischer, 'Buchi Emecheta' 1060). By the 1990s, Emecheta's novels suggest a coming together of her Nigerian and British identities. Her novel *Kehinde* (1994) is about a woman coming to terms with being a Nigerian in London, and in her novel of 2000, *The New Tribe*, Emecheta looks at the relationship that younger Black people have to Africa and to Britain. The trajectory of Emecheta's long career thus moves from condemning the experiences of 'unbelonging' to claiming and redefining British identity.

While Emecheta's work focuses on the ways that Black women can claim their voice and survive in a hostile world, the Jamaican-born author Joan Riley, who moved to London in 1976, looks at how these same pressures can result in silence and destruction (Fischer, 'Joan Riley' 1316). In 1985, The Women's Press published her novel *The Unbelonging*, the title naming the triple marginalization based on race, class and gender that many Black British women faced. *The Unbelonging* focuses on the experiences of a young girl, Hyacinth, who has been summoned to Britain from Jamaica by her father. Leaving all she knows behind her, she lives in his house with his current 'woman', who mistreats her. At school she is teased mercilessly by her peers and horribly mistreated by her teachers. Worst of all, her father abuses her sexually. At night she dreams of her secret, safe space in Jamaica and wonders, 'Why did it have to be a dream?...She had been so sure she was back home, so sure that this time it was the real thing' (11). Removed from her father and put into care, Hyacinth has, in the end, no place to go but to escape through her imagination to the 'secret place' in Jamaica where she used to go before she came to England. Hyacinth imagines herself elsewhere and safe, far from the 'rejection and all the uncertainty' she experiences in England (144). In all of her novels, Riley underlines the dire effects of racism, classism and sexism on Black women's lives in England.

In *Waiting in the Twilight* (1987), also from The Women's Press, Riley continues this exploration of multiple marginalization by showing the journey of Adella Johnson, whose life becomes progressively more challenging the further she moves from her family home in the Jamaican countryside. But she maintains an inner strength which brings her to Britain, where she marries a man who is, like Hyacinth's father and the husband in Emecheta's work, worn down by the experiences of racism he encounters, and these lead him to treat her brutally. At first, Adella perseveres. Although at work she 'braced herself for the talk down ways she had come to expect from white people' and the way 'the English look down on foreigners...she was determined to get on, to become a success. She was determined to build a better life for the children' (15). She buys a house, gets a job and raises her children, but her personal life and the various institutions of the state grind her down to such an extent that she is left with virtually nothing. As her friend Lisa says to her, 'Adella, dis country killing yu' (47). She loses her job, her home and her husband, who abandons her for a younger woman; she is also mugged and suffers a stroke which leaves her disabled, her paralysis symbolizing her inability to move ahead in life despite all her effort. Finally, towards the end of her life, she escapes – like Hyacinth before her – into an imaginary world made up of the sunshine of Jamaica and an idealized version of her husband. *Waiting in the Twilight* shows this intense sense of loss and dislocation through its narrative strategies of shifting times and places (see Fischer, 'Joan Riley' 1316; Fischer, 'Women Writers, Global Migration and the City').

Retreat into fantasy also appears in Riley's last novel of the decade, *Romance* (1988), which, however, points to the necessity of opening one's eyes to reality. One of the two sisters at the centre of the novel, Verona, who enters the world of romance novels to escape the memory of childhood sexual abuse as well as racism, comes to feel that '[s]he should have known there was no romance in reality' (219). The rise of the National Front, police brutality and the Brixton uprising form part of the novel's backdrop, and Verona also contends with everyday hostility at work. Her sister Desiree is apparently more connected to reality and struggles in the face of her husband's traditional views of marital roles and her unfulfilled desire to return to education. Yet Verona and Desiree ultimately have more agency than Riley's earlier protagonists, Hyacinth and Adella, who can escape only into madness, and *Romance* also offers a more nuanced portrayal of male characters than Riley's earlier works.

While Black women writers have at times been criticized for portraying Black men in negative ways and thus perpetuating stereotypes about them because of the wider context in which their stories are told, here Riley chooses to show Verona's unredeemable white lover against both Verona's Black abuser and Desiree's ultimately caring Black husband. By the end of the novel, Verona realizes that bad men can be Black or white, and she recognizes 'the mistake she made was thinking [abusive men] only came in black skins' (225). Verona also perceives the lies in the romance novels she used to read and 'couldn't even lose herself in romance any more' (200). Instead, she finds a place for herself – 'the first time she had somewhere that really belonged to her' (228) – and Desiree goes to college and works with her husband to develop a better relationship.

In writing about 'unbelonging', Emecheta and Riley focus on displacement and loss of 'home', as well as on the devastation wreaked by racism, classism and sexism. Each author explores the struggle for survival through significant social institutions, such as housing, employment, education, health care and marriage, each of which marginalizes or oppresses the protagonist. Emecheta's work focuses on the ways to survive this economic and social system. In her first two novels, Riley's protagonists have few outlets beyond madness and death; however, her third novel opens up other possibilities and shows the support sisters – and other women generally – can offer each other.

Collective identities: Ravinder Randhawa and Barbara Burford

Other writers in the 1980s continue to explore the effects of migration, racism, classism and sexism, yet also look at collective politicized responses to these experiences. In 1987, The Women's Press published *A Wicked Old Woman*, whose author, Ravinder Randhawa, was born in India in 1952 and moved to Britain in 1959 (see Reichl, 'Jumbling Up Punjabi'). Mallott calls the novel 'an important early example of feminist British Asian fiction' (300), while Susheila Nasta hails it 'the first explicitly Asian British novel' (quoted in Hussain). In *Home Truths*, Nasta attributes the novel's limited critical notice to the fact that the book was by an Asian woman and published by a feminist press (183, 186). Even so, as Reichl notes, Randhawa's influence exceeds her own work because she was a founder of the London-based Asian Women Writers' Group (later Collective), which began in 1984 (Ravinder Randhawa; see also Nasta 186). Indeed, in 1988, The Women's Press published the Asian Women Writers' Workshop's *Right of Way*. The group deliberately decided to describe themselves as 'Asian', rather than Black, to create a space in which they could address their specific cultural contexts and encourage other the Asian women to join, even as they continued to collaborate with other Black women (see 'Introduction').

The novel's protagonist, the middle-aged Kulwant (or Kuli) Singh, masquerades as 'a feisty, independent, and strong-willed old woman – hence "wicked" by all patriarchal standards' (Paranjape 72). Kulwant takes on the persona of a much older and more down-and-out woman than she is by wearing second-hand clothing, tapping her way around with a cane and planning to add glasses to her disguise – all symbolic of the sense of homelessness and disorientation brought on by migration. Mallott suggests that her 'masquerade ... invites her to explore the unstable nature of identities more broadly' (300), as it allows her to try on different identities and to deconstruct people's assumptions based on the way she looks and dresses.

At first sight, Kulwant seems to be slightly mad – and in this respect initially seems similar to Riley's Adella. In both cases, madness is a metaphor for the extreme sense of dislocation brought on by the traumas of sexism, racism and migration to a hostile environment. Another metaphor which runs through Randhawa's novel is that of homelessness in its multiple permutations – the racist arson attack on an Asian family's house, domestic abuse, squatting, the ways immigration rules divide families. However, it becomes clear that, unlike Riley's novel, Randhawa's is less concerned with the loss of home and the recuperation of an idealized past and much more focused on understanding the past through the present and advocating communal action as the way forward. Eventually, as she integrates past and presents lives, Kulwant throws off her disguise and re-engages in an activist agenda which combats racism, sexism and classism.

The narration goes beyond straightforward realist conventions in so far as it shifts back and forth between past and present as Kulwant re-examines earlier parts of her life. The novel also shifts amongst several points of view without the clear-cut narratorial markers one might expect. John J. Su claims that 'postcolonial' writers of the 1970s, such as Emecheta, were less interested in stylistic experimentation than their white counterparts in part because of 'the expectations of a reading public that saw the fiction of postcolonial authors as a kind of sociological testimony' (296). Whether one accepts this assessment, by the 1980s at least, authors such as Ravinder Randhawa – and to some extent Barbara Burford and Joan Riley – do experiment with form. As seen earlier, in *Waiting for the Twilight*, Riley warps time and space in such a way as to mirror her protagonist's state of mind, and, as will be seen later, some of Barbara Burford's work draws upon speculative fiction and magical realism. And certainly, *A Wicked Old Woman* is 'informed with considerable stylistic and narratorial elan' (Paranjape 72). Nasta suggests that Randhawa deliberately obfuscates exact times and locations: 'what becomes crucial in *A Wicked Old Woman* is a process of psychic reorientation, the creation of differently conceived imaginative spaces, through the slow accretion and inscription of a number of previously unheard stories about women's lives' (206).

As Kulwant moves through space, the stories of other lives she has interacted with throughout the years emerge. We learn of Kulwant's youthful desire to experience Western mores behind her parents' backs until her white boyfriend Michael frightens her by proposing marriage. Their ensuing break-up sends

Kulwant and Michael running in opposite directions. Afraid of losing her culture, she gives up education and Western 'choice' in favour of a marriage she begs her parents to arrange, while throughout his life Michael projects the wrath he feels at his rejection onto other Asian women. As Kulwant's mother says about her daughter's confusion, 'this country has put you in one of its mixers and whirled you around till you can't tell your inside from your outside, your duty from your rights, your needs from your responsibilities' (54). Randhawa seems to be suggesting that the encounter between India and England has resulted in entrenched positions at the imperial centre: the white male power structure fears its loss of privilege and 'superiority', resulting in racial hatred, while the female migrant, defined by European preconceptions and by patriarchal notions in both European and Indian cultures, has no place to run (see also Paranjape).

Kulwant's search for identity is common to many of the women in the novel: Maya, whose research about Asian people is co-opted by whites; Kurshid, who lives with Kulwant's husband; and Big Sister who 'scorns' marriage altogether and for whom 'marriage was the same as the clothes, food, household articles that they never could afford' (68–69). She opts for 'a job in the union' where she could 'talk... politics and workers' exploitation' (70). Big Sister champions the causes of Asian workers, Asian women writers and the women at Greenham Common. This exploration of diverse women's stories points to the novel's underlying feminism.

The connection Kulwant comes to feel with other Asian women is highlighted through Rani's story. Rani, also known as Rosalind, is a younger woman who, by leaving her family, makes a different choice than the young Kulwant. Despite their opposite paths in attempting to navigate Indian and English expectations of Asian women, Kulwant and Rani find no peace and no place until they come together with a multi-generational group of other Asian women – 'each struggling to come to terms with hybridity, prejudice, and intergenerational conflict' (Mallott 300) – and connect through activism. Towards the end of the novel, the female characters unite not only to defend Rani, who killed a man as she fought off a sexual attack, but also to organize around other issues, such as 'a demonstration in support of eight young Asians, accused of various charges by the police' (Randhawa 189).

Finally, Kulwant comes to realize that she has worn her disguise 'to cover up her disintegrating world' (190), but this is no longer useful. She throws off her masquerade and joins in the action to 'help Rani all they could' (205). The novel ends with a demonstration in support of Rani, in which the various women that have appeared throughout the novel participate. Kulwant feels herself 'coming back to life', and the director who is capturing the event on film shouts 'ACTION!' – significantly the last word of the novel, and the rallying cry for a collective response to Asian women's issues (206, 207).

Another writer who explores the need to develop collective communities in response to the alienation that Black women experience in Britain in the 1980s is Barbara Burford. Her collection *The Threshing Floor and Other Stories* addresses lesbian sexuality in Black British women's lives. According to Eileen Worrow, the late Barbara Burford (1944–2010) was born in Jamaica and came with her family to Dalston in 1955. During the 1980s, she was active in Black arts projects, putting on her play *Patterns* in 1984 at the Drill Hall Arts Centre in central London and publishing her work with Sheba Feminist Publishers. That same year, her poetry appeared in Sheba's *A Dangerous Knowing: Four Black Women Poets*, and two years later Sheba published *The Threshing Floor*, which includes a novella of the same title and several short stories. Burford also co-edited an anthology of women's love poems, entitled *Dancing the Tightrope*, for The Women's Press in 1987.

The stories in *The Threshing Floor* reflect imaginatively and often humorously on the experiences of being Black, female and lesbian in Britain during the 1980s. R. Victoria Arana says her stories are 'mirrors held up to historical social realities' (238), yet they also use a range of forms. The opening story, 'Dreaming the Sky Down', follows the liberating night-time excursions of an overweight and overburdened Black schoolgirl, Donna, who grows up in a happy family, but who is bitterly under fire from her teacher who despises her size and colour. However, in the fantastical world of the story, Donna is able to experience her body as elegant, weightless and agile as she floats up first to the ceiling of her room and eventually out of her window into the night sky. Gradually, her extraordinary powers come to her during the daytime and at school where she is able to amaze her teacher with her physical prowess, despite usually being the butt of all jokes about clumsiness, fatness and not conforming to the stereotypes about 'elegant Black athletes' (1).

'The Pinstripe Summer' also deals with the loneliness of being Black in a white environment, this time the corporate world, where one's talents are exploited, but not recognized when it comes to advancement. Dorothy, the middle-aged and highly capable secretary, has rarely had anything for herself. At work, she has assisted the white men climb the corporate ladder, and she has been at the beck and call of her late mother. She has one place for herself, in the space between work and home, that she glimpses through the train window, a valley which she names Risse, and which beckons her like a female lover: 'And there was Risse: Dorothy turned in a slow circle; Risse to give and to respond to the enormous reservoir of love damned up inside her. This one place, midway between work and home, had reached out to her as not even distant childhood memories of a sun-drenched island could' (24). She shares this secret only with a young, Black, female consultant, Willoughby, who comes to computerize the company's files. Like Dorothy, Willoughby longs for something just out of reach – perhaps Dorothy herself. As in the previous story, what stands out is the bodily expression of desire which is at odds with the oppressive institutions these women inhabit, where being Black, female, fat or lesbian is seen as being less. In this story, the pinstripe summer is the combination of the oppressive straitjacketing of these women's lives in the buttoned-up corporate world and the summer which holds out the promise of freedom. As Jewelle Gomez writes of these two stories, here Burford 'uses fantasy that creates a magic that allows women to recognize their Blackness and femaleness' (954).

In the title novella – 'The Threshing Floor' – Burford focuses less directly on the experience of marginalization and more on the experiences of a Black lesbian glass-maker who has recently lost her long-time white lover to cancer. Hannah comes to terms with the fact that her white mother put her into care as a child, which undermined her sense of self: 'It had taken many years for Hannah to come to love and admire herself' (107). She remains connected to the African Caribbean world in London, but continues to make her home in Kent, where she is often reminded of her 'difference', but where she is at peace. Thus overt racism gives way to a more subtle experience of one's reality not being fully understood in the mixed environment in which the protagonist, Hannah, lives and works. She wonders, 'Why did others have to judge her actions out of *their* reality?' (96). This question cuts across both her ethnicity and her sexuality as she mourns her late lover, Jenny, who 'had been insistently brave enough to ask that [her family and her village] not only accept her reality, but the reality of the Black woman whom she loved' (109).

When she returns to the glass works after Jenny's death, she finds the collective in disarray and herself at odds with some of her friends, most significantly the only other Black member, Caro. This is compounded when Caro's friend, Marah, a Black woman artist who is recovering from a bad divorce, meets Hannah, resulting in an immediate attraction. Protective of Marah, Caro tries to warn Hannah off, but ultimately comes to accept their relationship, and the friendship amongst the three deepens. While at the beginning of the novella Hannah focuses on the fact that people do not see or acknowledge her realities, particularly as a Black woman, by the end, she has worked through how her personal traumas of abandonment and loss have contributed to this experience. She has also realized that Marah needs to 'mak[e] sure that Hannah understood *her* reality' (155). The metaphor of the 'threshing floor' symbolizes both Hannah's artistic work and the project of creating herself anew as she mourns one relationship and begins another. 'The Threshing Floor' ends with a vision of Black women joining together and communicating more deeply than is possible within the multiracial collective as a whole. Hannah 'find[s] herself met and answered, mirrored and surprised, at every dip and curve of this new and different beginning' (210). Still, she remains committed to the collective of women artisans at the glass workshop and to a Black, feminist and lesbian politics, and in this regard the novel reflects some of the discourses of the 1980s.

Hybrid identities and the legacy of the 1980s

At the end of the decade, Beryl Gilroy published *Boy-Sandwich* (1989), not with a feminist or Black press, but with Heinemann's Caribbean series. Becky Ayebia Clarke, former long-time editor of Heinemann's African & Caribbean Writers Series, has said, 'It is...no exaggeration to claim that African literature could not have attained its present form without the pioneering role that Heinemann played' ('Becky Ayebia Clarke: AW Interview'). However, Heinemann did not focus on Black *British* writing, despite publishing Gilroy's novels, reprinting some of Emecheta's work and publishing first editions of some of her later novels.

Born in 1924, Beryl Gilroy came to Britain from Guyana in 1951 (Macedo 1105). Her memoir *Black Teacher* (1976) focuses on her experiences of teaching in London schools, where she became the first Black head teacher despite experiencing extensive discrimination (1105). It is perhaps also worth noting that she is Paul Gilroy's mother. In *Boy-Sandwich* (1989), her protagonist Tyrone's family come from an unnamed Caribbean island, and he will journey to the island only to realize that he belongs in Britain. Gilroy's novel moves the focus away from the experiences of first-generation migrants to the experiences of their British-born offspring, who were caught between cultures – hence the 'boy-sandwich' of the title.

Here, partly because the protagonist and narrator is male, the focus seems to be less on issues of sexism and more on questions of race and class. The novel evokes the 'sus' laws and the New Cross fire of 1981, which claimed numerous lives and was believed to have been started deliberately by National Front sympathizers. As a young Black man, Tyrone is often viewed with suspicion by white people: 'I am just a London black, dreadlocked, feckless and looking for trouble, and "should be sent back with my spliffs to God knows where"' (18). In fact, Tyrone is about to go to Cambridge University.

Throughout the novel, Tyrone looks back to his grandparents' and parents' experiences of coming to Britain, ultimately comparing them to his own. He wonders whether he is 'facing the same difficulties' as the previous generations and how his response to the situation differs (75). When he witnesses a fire started by racists that almost kills his girlfriend Adijah, some questions remain the same:

> I ask myself again and again, why, nearly forty years after the coming of my grandparents to this land that was the source of their beliefs about life and civilised living, people burn others, deny others' capacity to feel and applaud their terror and their deaths. (76)

Despite having worked hard in Britain for years, Tyrone's parents' and grandparents' place is still tenuous and they return to the 'island' for good, while Tyrone and Adijah accompany them. It is significant that Adijah goes after being attacked, as a return to the ancestral home in African Caribbean writing often signifies a moment of healing, what Lynne Macedo calls 'the therapeutic effect of returning to the Caribbean' (1106). Ultimately, however, Tyrone returns to London, understanding his duality of 'belonging' and 'not belonging' (110). While he enjoys his time in Picktown, he also feels trapped by the culture's expectations. Instead, he revels in the experiences of hybridity that his life in London affords him, even with all the hostility he still encounters. At the end of the novel, he says, 'I am British and believe it. ... I want to call myself British for the first time in my life' (115).

As the 1980s drew to a close and the projects that sustained the literary output were increasingly threatened, Black women's writing clearly had an audience. While some of the writers explored here focus on identifying and naming the experiences of Black women in Britain in the 1980s – particularly with Emecheta's 'double yoke' and Riley's 'unbelonging' – the fiction of Randhawa and Burford underlines collective agency and action. By the end of decade, racism was still prevalent, as Gilroy's novel shows, but what emerges is an exploration of the hybrid nature of identity and a need to reconnect with places of familial origin while still claiming and redefining British identity, a theme that will become central to second-generation writing in the 1990s and 2000s. In developing these themes – and in creating a readership for their work – Black women writing in the 1980s paved the way for Black women's writing in the next 20 years.

Works cited

Amos, Valerie, Gail Lewis, Amina Mama and Pratibha Parmar. 'Many Voices, One Chant: Black Feminist Perspectives.' *Feminist Review* 17 (Autumn 1984), 1–118.
'Andrea Levy in Conversation with Susan Alice Fischer.' *Changing English* 12(3) (2005): 361–371.
Arana, R. Victoria. 'The 1980s: Retheorising and Refashioning British Identity.' *Write Black, Write British: From Post Colonial to Black British Literature*. Ed. K. Sesay. Hertford: Hansib, 2005, 230–240.
Asian Women Writers' Workshop. *Right of Way: Prose and Poetry from the Asian Women Writers' Workshop*. London: The Women's Press, 1988.
'Becky Ayebia Clarke: AW Interview.' *African Writing Online: Many Literatures, One Voice* (October–November 2007), http://www.african-writing.com/ayebia.htm. Web. 16 Oct. 2011.
Black Womantalk. *Black Women Talk Poetry*. London: Black Womantalk, 1987.
Bogle, Marlene T. 'Brixton Black Women's Centre: Organizing on Child Sexual Abuse.' *Feminist Review* 28 (Spring 1988): 132–135.
Brixton Black Women's Group. 'Black Women Organizing.' *Feminist Review* 17 (Autumn 1984): 84–89.
Bryan, Beverley, Stella Dadzie and Suzanne Scafe. *The Heart of the Race: Black Women's Lives in Britain*. London: Virago, 1985.
Burford, Barbara. *The Threshing Floor and Other Stories*. London: Sheba Feminist Publishers, 1986.
——. 'The Landscapes Painted on the Inside of My Skin.' *Spare Rib* (June 1987): 36–39.
——. Gabriela Pearse, Grace Nichols, and Jackie Kay. *A Dangerous Knowing: Four Black Women Poets*. London: Sheba Feminist Publishers, 1984.
——. Lindsay MacRae, and Sylvia Paskin. Eds. *Dancing the Tightrope: New Love Poems*. London: The Women's Press, 1987.
Busby, Margaret. 'Defiant Creativity.' *Third World Quarterly* 10(3) (July 1988): 1374–1376.
Dixon, David. 'Thatcher's People: The British Nationality Act 1981.' *Journal of Law and Society* 10(2) (Winter 1983): 161–180.
Emecheta, Buchi. *In the Ditch*. London: Barrie and Jenkins, 1972.
——. *Second-Class Citizen*. London: Allison and Busby, 1974.
——. *Double Yoke*. London: Ogwugwu Afor, 1982.
——. 'Feminism with a Small "F"!' *Criticism and Ideology: Second African Writers' Conference, Stockholm, 1986, Seminar Proceedings No 20*. Ed. K.H. Peterson. Uppsala: Scandinavian Institute of African Studies, 1988, 173–185.
——. *Gwendolen*. London: Collins, 1989.
——. *Head above Water: An Autobiography*. Oxford: Heinemann Educational, 1994.
——. *Kehinde*. Oxford: Heinemann Educational, 1994.
——. *The New Tribe*. Oxford: Heinemann Educational, 2000.

Ezenwa-Ohaeto. 'Tropes of Survival: Protest and Affirmation in Buchi Emecheta's Autobiography, *Head above Water*.' *Emerging Perspectives on Buchi Emecheta*. Ed. M.A. Umeh. Trenton, NJ: Africa World Press, 1996.

Fischer, Susan Alice. 'Women Writers, Global Migration, and the City: Joan Riley's *Waiting in the Twilight* and Hanan Al-Shaykh's *Only in London*.' *Tulsa Studies in Women's Literature* 23(1) (2004): 107–120.

——. '"Familiar Hearts": Metaphor and the Ethics of Intersectionality in Contemporary Women's Fiction.' *Literature and Ethics: From the Green Knight to the Dark Knight*. Ed. Stephen Brie and William Rossiter. Newcastle upon Tyne: Cambridge Scholars Publishing, 2010, 175–189.

——. 'Buchi Emecheta.' *The Encyclopedia of Twentieth-Century Fiction. Vol. 3: World Fiction*. Gen. Ed. Brian W. Shaffer. Ed. John Clement Ball. Oxford: Wiley-Blackwell, 2011, 1058–1061.

——. 'Joan Riley.' *The Encyclopedia of Twentieth-Century Fiction. Vol. 3: World Fiction*. Gen. Ed. Brian W. Shaffer. Ed. John Clement Ball. Oxford: Wiley-Blackwell, 2011, 1316–1317.

Garnham, Nick and Ken Worpole. 'The Book Industry. Greater London Council.' *The State of the Art or the Art of the State? Strategies for the Cultural Industries in London*. Ed. Greater London Council. London: Industry and Employment Branch Department for Recreation and the Arts Greater London Council, 1985, 51–68.

Gerzina, Gretchen. *Black London: Life before Emancipation*. London: John Murray, 1995.

Gilroy, Beryl. *Boy-Sandwich*. Oxford: Heinemann, 1989.

——. *Black Teacher*. London: Bogle-L'Ouverture, 1994.

Gomez, Jewelle. 'Speculative Fiction and Black Lesbians.' *Signs: Journal of Women in Culture and Society* 18(4) (Summer 1993): 948–956.

Hennegan, Alison. 'A Demand that is not Being Met.' *New Statesman* (26 July 1986): 28–29.

Hunt, Linda. *The GLC Women's Committee 1982–6: A Record of Change and Achievement for Women in London*. London: GLC Public Information Branch, 1986.

Hussain, Ahmede. 'In Conversation with Ravinder Randhawa.' *Black and Gray* 3 (April 2007), http://ahmedehussain.blogspot.com/2007/04/in-conversation-with-ravinder-randhawa.html. Web. 8 May 2011.

Innes, C. L. *A History of Black and Asian Writing in Britain, 1700 – 2000*. Cambridge: Cambridge University Press, 2002.

Kaufmann, K. 'A World of Writers.' *The Women's Review of Books* 4(1) (October 1986): 13–14.

King, Bruce. *The Internationalization of English Literature* (*The Oxford English Literary History*, vol. 13: 1948–2000). Oxford: Oxford University Press, 2004.

Macedo, Lynne. 'Beryl Gilroy.' *The Encyclopedia of Twentieth-Century Fiction. Vol. 3: World Fiction*. Gen. Ed. Brian W. Shaffer. Ed. John Clement Ball. Oxford: Wiley-Blackwell, 2011, 1105–1106.

Mallott, J. Edward. 'Postcolonial Fiction of the British South Asian Diaspora.' *The Encyclopedia of Twentieth-Century Fiction. Vol. 1: Twentieth-Century British and*

Irish Fiction. Gen. Ed. Brian W. Shaffer. Ed. Brian W. Shaffer. Oxford: Wiley-Blackwell, 2011, 298–303.

Nasta, Susheila. *Home Truths: Fictions of the South Asian Diaspora in Britain*. Gordonsville, VA: Palgrave Macmillan, 2002.

Owusu, Kwesi. *The Struggle for Black Arts in Britain: What We Can Consider Better than Freedom*. London: Comedia, 1986.

Paranjape, Makarand. 'Distinguishing Themselves: New Fiction by Expatriate Indian Women.' *World Literature Today* 65(1) (1991): 72–74.

Parmar, Pratibha and Jackie Kay. 'Frontiers.' *Charting the Journey: Writings by Black and Third World Women*. Ed. Shabnam Grewal, Jackie Kay, Liliane Landor, Gail Lewis, and Pratibha Parmar. London: Sheba Feminist Publishers, 1988.

Randhawa, Ravinder. *A Wicked Old Woman*. London: The Women's Press, 1987.

Reichl, Susanne. '"Jumbling Up Punjabi, English, Urdu, and Any Other Lingo-bingo": Transculturality and Different Readers in Ravinder Randhawa's Hari-jan.' *Cultures in the Contact Zone: Ethnic Semiosis in Black British Literature*. Ed. A. Nünning and V. Nünning. Trier: Wissenschaftlicher, 2002, 146–159.

———. 'Ravinder Randhawa. Twenty-first-century "Black" British Writers.' *Dictionary of Literary Biography*, vol. 347. Ed. R. Victoria Arana. Detroit: Gale, 2009. Literature Resource Center. Web. 8 May 2011.

Riley, Joan. *The Unbelonging*. London: The Women's Press, 1985.

———. *Waiting in the Twilight*. London: The Women's Press, 1987.

———. *Romance*. London: The Women's Press, 1988.

'SBS Timeline'. *Southall Black Sisters*, 2012, http://www.southallblacksisters.org.uk/sbs-timeline/. Web. 29 Apr. 2012.

Shields, S. 'Gender: An Intersectionality Perspective.' *Sex Roles* 59(5/6) (2008): 301–311.

Sivanandan, A. 'From Resistance to Rebellion: Asian and Afro-Caribbean Struggles in Britain.' *Race and Class* 23 (1981): 111–152, http://rac.sagepub.com/content/23/2-3/111.citation.

Smith, Zadie. 'What Does Soulful Mean?' *The Guardian* (1 September 2007). Web. 2 Sept. 2007.

Sougou, Omar. *Writing across Cultures: Gender Politics and Difference in the Fiction of Buchi Emecheta*. Amsterdam: Rodopi, 2002.

Su, John J. 'Postcolonial Fiction of the African Diaspora.' *The Encyclopedia of Twentieth-Century Fiction. Vol. I: Twentieth-Century British and Irish Fiction*. Gen. Ed. Brian W. Shaffer. Ed. Brian W. Shaffer. Oxford: Wiley-Blackwell, 2011, 294–298.

Ward, Abigail. 'Black British Fiction.' *The Encyclopedia of Twentieth-Century Fiction. Vol. 3: World Fiction*. Gen. Ed. Brian W. Shaffer. Ed. John Clement Ball. Oxford: Wiley-Blackwell, 2011, 985–986.

Wilson, Amrit. *Finding a Voice: Asian Women in Britain*. London: Virago, 1985.

Wise, V. 'Goodbye to All This?' *Women's Review* (January 1986): 4–5.

Worpole, Ken. *Reading by Numbers: Contemporary Publishing and Popular Fiction*. London: Comedia, 1984.
Worrow, E. 'Barbara Burford Obituary: She Fought for Equality in the Public Sector.' *The Guardian* (26 May 2010). Web. 1 May 2011.
Young, E. 'The Business of Feminism: Issues in London Feminist Publishing.' *Frontiers: A Journal of Women Studies* 10(3) (1989): 1–5.

5

Historical Representations
The Heritage Industry and Historiographic Metafiction: Historical Representation in the 1980s

Alex Murray

In the autumn of 2010 it seemed as though history was repeating. Austerity breeds escapism, and the dramatic success of ITV's *Downton Abbey* was generally accepted as providing a 'heritage'-fuelled escape from the 'financial crisis' and the drastic cuts in public funding that followed the election of the Conservative-Liberal Democrat government. As Mark Lawson put it in the *Guardian*:

> With uncanny regularity, costume drama on British TV has flourished while Tory governments are managing a recession: Thatcher and Lawson in 1981 had *Brideshead Revisited*, Major and Clarke in 1995 got the wet-shirted Colin Firth in *Pride and Prejudice* and now Cameron and Osborne cut public spending to the backdrop of the Granthams and Crawleys. The reason, presumably, is that, in times of financial pain, viewers crave escapism.

Historical representation is then never neutral or produced in a vacuum, and the success of *Brideshead Revisited* in the 1980s is just one particular instance in which the familiar nexus of conservative politics, lavish production and national history all came together to capture the national zeitgeist. Yet then, as now, it is vital that we remain aware of the strange lure of saccharine versions of the past, not as escapism but as a very active and engaged dialogue with our own contemporary moment.

In the 1980s, the broader question of historical representation was clustered around a curious friction. On the one hand, it saw the rise of 'historiographic metafiction', that self-conscious literary form that rejected all stable meta-narratives regarding the past, placing history on the same 'level' of veracity as fiction. On the other hand, it saw the emergence of a modern heritage industry and the rise of TV heritage culture. The relationship between these two areas, the experimental and the popular, will be my focus in this chapter. There is, of course, a whole continuum of historical representations that lie in between, yet in what follows I will argue that we must read the two symbiotically in order to understand the politics of historical representation in the period. I will begin with a broad survey of the rise of the heritage industry, focusing on the attempt by Thatcher's governments to manipulate the nation's past, both near and far, in order to both justify their policies in the present and draw the production of that past into the enterprise culture that lay at the heart of Thatcherism. The majority of the chapter will then be given over to an examination of historical fictions of the period, focusing on three case studies: Jeanette Winterson's *Sexing the Cherry* (1987), Kazuo Ishiguro's *Remains of the Day* (1989) and Michael Moorcock's *Mother London* (1988). I will present these texts as representative of an experimental and political continuum of historical fiction that can allow for a clearer sense of the subtle techniques employed in challenging the broader heritage turn in British culture in the 1980s and the problems, both political and aesthetic, they raise.

The rise of the heritage industry in Thatcher's Britain

One must be careful not to suggest that the 1980s invented the heritage industry which still dominates our popular relationship to the past. Any genealogy of the modern heritage industry must take into account the Victorian conservationism of William Morris and others inspired by Ruskin's important re-articulation of architecture and material remains in the national imaginary. As Ben Cowell notes, heritage is such a multifaceted term that one should be both precise and wide ranging in order to understand and articulate the 'complex matrix of cultural ideas that bind together the past, the present and the future' (11). Just as importantly one should be wary of heritage's distortion of all relationships to the past. While, as David Lowenthal points out, it is not the same as history, the ascendancy of heritage in the twentieth century has led to it becoming the dominant mode of our engagement with the past, turning the epistemological practices of an academic discipline into a belief: 'The world rejoices in a newly popular faith: the cult of heritage' (1). Yet within the rise of this 'faith' in the cultural presentation and celebration of the past, the period of Margaret Thatcher's Conservative governments (1979–90) witnessed some specific shifts in heritage culture that can allow us to provide a more stable definition of heritage for the 1980s. It is these particular political and cultural contexts that can then help us to grasp the politics of the fiction that would emerge in response to it.

While many accounts of the Thatcherite abuse of the past emphasize her manipulation of national history, it is arguably the legislative changes ushered in by her first government that had the most lasting effects. The 31st of March 1980 saw the passing of an act that was to transform Britain's relationship to the past. The National Heritage Act was created to

> establish a National Heritage Memorial Fund for providing financial assistance for the acquisition, maintenance and preservation of land, buildings and objects of outstanding historic and other interest; to make new provision in relation to the arrangements for accepting property in satisfaction of capital transfer tax and estate duty; to provide for payments out of public funds in respect of the loss of or damage to objects loaned to or displayed in local museums and other institutions; and for purposes connected with those matters. (National Heritage Act, Chapter 17)

It sounds, on the surface, like a rather benevolent piece of legislation, but its effect was anything but innocuous. It transformed the ways in which museums and stately homes were funded, creating a range of incentives to encourage the establishment of private, for-profit museums in order to reduce their reliance on the state. In doing so, heritage opened itself up to Thatcherite entrepreneurialism. As the advertisement for the Enterprise Allowance in the 1980s read, 'inside every unemployed person there's a self-employed one', and the start-up allowances for small businesses were part of the movement from state to individual, of which the new heritage industry was exemplary. For many in the 1980s, it was unthinkable that heritage could provide a true spur to rejuvenate the national economy. As Patrick Wright has recently reflected: 'I remember being astonished when I first heard government figures proclaim that heritage and tourism would be developed as an economic alternative to heavy industries like steel-manufacture or coal mining' (xiv). Yet the rise of heritage theme parks, private museums and, in 1983, English Heritage demonstrated that economic recovery would be led by transforming the economic infrastructure of many areas of the UK. English Heritage is a public body, outside of any government department, set up to manage buildings and ancient monuments across England. It replaced previous arrangements under various state departments and now manages some 400 sites and properties, including Stonehenge and Dover Castle.

The shift towards a new heritage culture was not simply limited to museums and television programmes. As Howard Malchow has explored, the seemingly worthless material history of the past was altered drastically in this new environment as the world of antiques was transformed from the elite to the quotidian: 'the most ordinary domestic objects – horse brasses and blue-glass medicine bottles, toasting forks and pot-lids – apparently became talismanic objects of desire by their "heritage" associations' (196). Here, material history becomes imbued with an almost supernatural power, an aura that is largely oblivious to the mass-produced and insignificant nature of these items and radically alters their relationship to the period in which they were produced. Malchow argues that the movement towards a heritage industry based upon the commodification and presentation of material history can drastically alter our understanding of the past, rendering it as ideologically entrapped as any other form of institutionalized history: 'it is a history fixed as *things*, shorn of dynamic processes, ready to be picked over for illustrating heritage myths and heritage morality. This is history seen from the antiques marketplace, where the past is its physical detritus – commodities stripped of social relations in their production or use' (202). Raphael Samuel also observed this 'retro' movement but saw in it positive possibilities for the democratization of history. While many were willing to condemn the government's appropriation of heritage, he wanted to focus on 'the legions of bargain-hunters who through the medium of the flea market and the car-boot sale have created a whole new everyday'. It was the creation of a new everyday that would lead Samuel to suggest that we live 'in an expanding historical culture, in which the work of inquiry and retrieval is being progressively extended into all kinds of spheres that would have been thought unworthy of notice in the past' (*Theatres of Memory*, vol. I, 27, 25). It is important to remember Samuel's voice in the debates around heritage and the opening up of history in the 1980s and 1990s, particularly as we think about the radical attempts to rewrite history in the fiction of the period.

The rise of a 'new' form of heritage was apparent to many in the 1980s, but to none more than Robert Hewison, whose scathing 1987 study *The Heritage Industry* typified the anger and cynicism of many intellectuals towards heritage. Along with Patrick Wright, Neal Ascherson and others, Hewison argued that the shift in the infrastructure of heritage was accompanied by a movement in politics: 'we have a heritage politics as well as a heritage culture; their mutual influence on our economic situation is such that all three can be seen as the products of the same deep social convulsion caused by the twin disruptions of modernisation and recession' (10). The political stakes of heritage were made abundantly clear in two famous statements made by Margaret Thatcher during the course of the 1980s. Her overt politicization of the nation's past in her 'victory speech' following the Falklands War and her endorsement of 'Victorian values' were, in many ways, confirmations of the importance that history had taken on in the nation's psyche. The collapse of the post-war consensus and faith in the rebuilding of the country had led to a permanently retrogressive tone that seeped into all levels of political discourse. As Stuart Hall pointed out at the time, the rhetoric of nationalism was as important as any shift in economic policy: 'questions about moral conduct ... about cultural and national identity ... are as central to Thatcherism's hegemonic project as the privatisation programme or the assault on local democracy' (8). To understand the language of politicized nostalgia, it is necessary to examine Thatcher's famous statements in some detail.

Thatcher's idea of 'Victorian values' was given its fullest articulation in a radio interview with Peter Allen for *The Decision Makers* in 1983. Thatcher's responses are a classic exercise in historical revisionism and deserve to be quoted at length:

> Well, there is no great mystery about those. I was brought up by a Victorian grandmother. You were taught to work jolly hard, you were taught to improve yourself, you were taught self-reliance, you were taught to live within your income, you were taught that cleanliness was next to godliness. You were taught self-respect, you were taught always to give a hand to your neighbour, you were taught tremendous pride in your country, you were taught to be a good member of your community. All of these things are Victorian values ...
>
> There are some values which are eternal and in fact you found a tremendous improvement in conditions during Victorian times because people were brought up with a sense of duty. I was brought up with a very strong sense of duty. And part of the sense of duty was if you were getting on better, you turned yourself to help others; that as you did better yourself so you had a duty to your community to turn to help others. And so, as you got an increasing prosperity during Victorian times and as you got an immense national pride during Victorian times, so you had a duty voluntarily to help others. (Thatcher 1983)

Thatcher's view of the Victorian period was deeply suspicious, as Allen tried to show in the interview. Thatcher's attempt to narrate her own past alongside that of the Victorians was a powerful means of making the past seem both immediate and deeply personal. The deeply personal nature of this recounting of the past was particularly effective at smoothing over the inequalities of the present. It is within this movement between autobiographical and national historical narratives that we can locate a vital element of Thatcherite historical representation. As Samuel asserts:

> if short on legislative pay-offs, the metaphor of Victorian Values was a rich political source of psychic satisfactions. It confirmed misanthropists in the belief that the country was going to the dogs, while rallying traditionalists to the defence of 'standards'.

For Samuel, this 'traditionalism allowed her to act as an innovator – arguably the most ruthless of our twentieth-century prime ministers – while yet sounding like she were a voice from the past' (*Theatres of Memory*, vol. II, 341–343). This attempt to sound like a voice from the past was precisely what spurred on many writers, such as Iain Sinclair, to attempt radical historical revisionism in their own fiction to counteract Thatcher. For Sinclair, Thatcher was a voice from the past, but also a ghoul from beyond England. As he stated in an interview: 'Thatcher introduced occultism into British political life … I can't look at it in any other way but as actual demonic possession. She opened herself up to the darkest demons of world politics, and therefore writers were obliged to counter this by equally extraordinary projects' (*The Verbals* 72). As Sinclair notes, Thatcher's 'occultism' was only ever really a product of the present, of an attempt to transform the fabric of the present through a misuse of the past. Yet it is often forgotten that Thatcher's attempts to manipulate 'Victorian values', or Britain's military history, were coupled with her attempt to denigrate the values of the more recent past.

If 1979 marked the beginning of the Thatcher period, it also marked the end of the 'cultural revolution' of the 1960s and, in effect, the post-war consensus. The cultural legacy of the 1960s was debated widely throughout the 1980s. For many young people, the seismic social changes of the 1960s had been far more powerful than World War II had been for the generation before. The ways in which we understand that period and represent it are, however, vexed issues. As Arthur Marwick asserts: 'what happened between the late fifties and early seventies has been subject to political polemic, nostalgic mythologizing, and downright misrepresentation' (3). This misrepresentation was intensified in the immediate period after Thatcher's election as it became clear that her election would mark a great divide in the post-war period. According to Jonathan Green: 'on 3 May the party came so abruptly to its end and the last diehard, desperate celebrants, puffing on the last roaches, downing the very dregs of long-emptied bottles, were finally turfed out into the unwelcoming dawn of a very different day' (xii–xiii). The dawning of this 'very different day' was signalled by the conservative counter-revolution against the liberal attitudes and dependence on the state that had characterized the 1960s. As Thatcher stated in a speech to the Conservative Central Council in March 1982:

> over these past two decades and more, you and I have watched all these standards steadily and deliberately vilified, ridiculed and scorned. And for years there was no riposte, and no reply … We are reaping what was sown in the sixties. The fashionable theories and permissive claptrap set the scene for a society in which the old virtues of discipline and self-restraint were denigrated.

Bruce Robertson's 1986 cult film *Withnail & I* stands as an attempt to capture the *fin-de-siècle* air of the 1980s when looking back to the radical, recent past. The story of two out-of-work actors living in Camden Town in 1969, the film is based upon Robertson's experiences as a student in the 1960s. Made at the height of Thatcherism, the film is his paean to the 1960s that can be seen as a reflection on the loss of cultural vibrancy under Thatcherism. As Will Self commented of the film: 'In Marwood and Withnail, Robinson has created an apotheosis of the idea of romantic, artistic youth as countercultural rebel. I feel sure that part of the film's enduring popularity is the sense contemporary youth have that the 60s were the last time when rebellion like this was valid' (35). The melancholia of the film and its repeated references to Thatcher ('we can't go on like this' – a phrase repeated by Thatcher before the 1979 election and throughout her premiership in relation to issues of fiscal management and immigration and, perhaps unsurprisingly, used in 2010 by David Cameron) underscore the 1980s as a historical terminus, the brave new world in which the very idea of society had been announced to have come to an end.

Historiographic metafiction and *Sexing the Cherry*

Thatcherism's complex attempt to posit itself as both radical break and gentle continuity raised the ire of many cultural commentators. Yet many of the literary representations of the past produced during the period appeared to be more academic, removed from their immediate political context. The historical fiction of the decade has, largely, been seen as an exemplary body of what the literary theorist Linda Hutcheon dubbed 'historiographic metafiction'. The conjunction of radical historiography and literary experimentation inspired by post-structuralism was central for a large number of critics during the 1980s and 1990s, including Hayden White. In *A Poetics of Postmodernism* (1988), Hutcheon framed the formal experimentation of writers such as Rushdie, E.L. Doctorow, Thomas Pynchon and others as part of a broader postmodern challenge to historiography, concluding that the business of history was the construction of stories that had manufactured an authority that privileged their accounts of the past. To this end, Hutcheon asserts that 'the meaning and shape are not *in the events*, but in the systems which make those past "events" into present historical "facts"' (89). For both fiction and historical discourses share certain traits in their construction and, subsequently, so should their analysis: the two discourses are no longer part of a binary that would privilege historical 'truth' over literary fiction. As Hutcheon explains: 'they have both been seen to derive their force more from verisimilitude than any objective truth; they are both identified as linguistic constructs, highly conventionalised in their narrative forms, and not at all transparent either in terms of language or structure; and they appear to be equally intertextual, deploying the texts of the past within their own complex textuality' (105). This formulation leads to fiction becoming equally viable in presenting a historiographical questioning of dominant historical narratives. But this is precisely a questioning, not an oppositional challenge. To posit historical fiction, and for that matter historiography, as counter-discourse would be to privilege a binary that would reinstate a hierarchy of interpretation. Instead, she asserts that historiographical metafiction 'keeps distinct its formal auto-representation and its historical context, and in so doing problematizes the very possibility of historical knowledge, because there is no reconciliation, no dialectic here – just unresolved contradiction' (106). This idea of history as unresolved contradiction is in many ways attractive as it provides an automatic politics for a relativistic approach to history. The main dilemma with unresolved contradiction is that it does not necessarily overcome the authority of dominant narratives of the past. The subtle, unresolved histories of the metafictional have hardly been seen to usher in a radicalized historiography beyond the academy. The ambiguity and open-endedness of contradiction increasingly appeared as political apathy and ideological cynicism covered in the clothes of textual radicalism. If the 1980s produced both the literature and the theorization of radical historical fiction, then that fiction now needs a more contextual, historicized reading in order to bring its politics to the surface.

The unresolved contradictions of these fictions can be seen in any number of novels from the 1980s. Many of them were the product of university-educated young writers who had encountered the radical ideas of post-structuralism and literary theory in the late 1970s and used them as the basis for their take on historical fiction. Graham Swift's 1983 novel *Waterland* is exemplary as a fictional challenge to the dominant idea of history. Swift's narrator, Tom Crick, presents us with an idea of counter-history as fluid, non-eventual and in essence about the telling of stories. This is in opposition to our dominant idea of the past, the idea of 'reality'. For this battle Swift uses the metaphor of land reclamation as it takes place in the Fens in East Anglia: 'So forget indeed, your revolutions, your turning points, your grand metamorphoses of history. Consider, instead, the slow and arduous process, the interminable and ambiguous process – the process of human siltation – of land reclamation' (8). The repetitious, fluid nature of the relationship between past, present and future works to disrupt the narrative time of linear history. It also works to call into question any narrative that pits itself as a form of progress, as Emily Horton explores in Chapter 1.

This sense of the fluidity between past and present is presented with varying degrees of experimentation and fantasy, as Rick Holmes details in Chapter 6. The fluidity is captured in Angela Carter's *Nights at the Circus* (1984), where Lizzie's house is described as 'an old-fashioned house, so much so that, in those years, it had a way of seeming almost too modern for its own good, as the past so often does when it outruns the present' (26). For Salman Rushdie, in *Midnight's Children* (1981), the same sense of time as elastic and unpredictable was at play: 'Reality is a question of perspective; the further you get from the past, the more concrete and plausible it seems – but as you approach the present, it inevitably seems more and more incredible' (229). For Rushdie there is a comfort to the past that is created by distance, with the result that we can no longer grasp the complexity of the present. This fluid, complex interplay between past, present and future in these novels resulted in many cases in a relativism in which there were no longer any stable means of examining the past. This relativism often turned into a cynical nihilism, modelled in exemplary fashion by Flint, the literary biographer in Peter Ackroyd's 1987 novel *Chatterton*: 'everything is instantly forgotten. There is no history any more. There is no memory. There are no standards to encourage permanence – only novelty, and the whole endless cycle of new objects. And books are simply objects – consumer items picked up and laid aside' (149–150). Yet the material production of the past need not always result in an emptiness of meaning, with a writer like Iain Sinclair presenting a model of subjective engagement with the past as a form of deliverance. As the narrator of Sinclair's 1987 novel *White Chappell, Scarlet Tracings*, states: 'So it's all there in the breath of the stones. There is a geology of time! We can take the bricks in our hands: as we grasp them, we enter it. The dead moment only exists as we live it now' (112). Sinclair's redemptive model of historiography is one that works within the parameters of historiographic fiction yet also works to call them into question. It is a position that is analogous with that of Jeanette Winterson.

The beginning and the end of Winterson's *Sexing the Cherry* (1989) see references to the Hopi tribe's approach to time, with a language that is 'as sophisticated as ours, but no tenses for past, present and future. The division does not exist' (8). The Hopi's lack of tenses provides Winterson with a philosophical position for challenging a whole raft of models of historical representation. Winterson's novel revolves around a central narrative – of the Dog-Woman and her adopted son Jordan in the period 1630–67. Within this central narrative there are a series of sub-narratives, such as the story of the 12 dancing princesses, and then in the later section of the novel a contemporary narrative featuring two characters who appear to be modern reincarnations of Jordan and the Dog-Woman. The reincarnations and the repetition of action (both the Renaissance Dog-Woman and her contemporary incarnation advocate arson as a form of cleansing) underscore Winterson's fluid approach to questions of temporality.

The opening of the novel foregrounds the unreliability of what is to follow. Jordan, our narrator in those sections marked with a whole pineapple, informs us that the journeys he will record are 'not the ones I made, but the ones I might have made, or perhaps did make in some other place or time' (10). This other place and time, Winterson makes clear, is the imagination, which she chooses to celebrate in opposition to the 'seasons and the clock' (89). Hers is then a narrative time that exists, like Hopi time, out of our idea of tense. It is fluid and infinite, unrestrained by any existing ideas of time. Winterson then asks her reader to suspend belief in the rational, yet not in the idea of reality. Her novel can be read as a form of magical realism, a suspension rather than an erosion of the divide between the rational and the fantastical. It is in this moment of suspension that Winterson is able to draw her reader into the problems of the contemporary, revealing that the narrative of Jordan and the Dog-Woman has only ever been a reflection on and interrogation of the 1980s.

So where exactly does Winterson's interrogation of the 1980s lie? Whereas other novels, such as those of Ishiguro and Moorcock, will make an explicit or implicit attack on the heritage culture of 1980s Britain, Winterson's engagement with her contemporary moment is more diffuse. The introduction, in the final section, of the environmental campaigner confirms the importance of gender and ecology as the key points of critique. These have been foregrounded in the main narrative: the ambivalent gender of the Dog-Woman, who exhibits many masculine characteristics alongside a monstrous femininity, is mirrored, in part, by Jordan, who, although not of ambivalent gender, is certainly constructed as sensitive and understanding, and is aligned with the 12 dancing sisters and of course with Fortunata, with whom he falls in love. The ecological concerns are ushered in through the figure of John Tradescant, the royal gardener. The arrival of the banana and the pineapple in England signal the beginning of a global approach to environment and ecology, whereby the rest of the world becomes a resource to exploit, and the consequences of that exploitation can be always expropriated.

The contemporary narrative places us in Thatcher's Britain, most clearly through the character of Jack, Nicholas Jordan's City stock analyst friend, who launches a tirade against the environmentalism of the modern-day Dog-Woman: 'stupid woman's camping by some river in the middle of nowhere and moaning about the mercury levels. What does she want? Does she think industry can just pack up and go home? They've got to put it somewhere. It's not as though they're chucking it in the Thames' (137). It is this voice, the voice of the market, that seems Winterson's most explicit political target in the novel. The machismo of the monetarist policies of Thatcherism becomes a strange reawakening of the Puritanism of the novel's earlier historical narrative. The challenge to this attitude comes from a bodily femininity and from the imagination, a position that appears to have significant parallels with the work of second-wave French feminism. Winterson's novel, however, remains ultimately ambivalent in its political and ethical message. So much of the novel has worked to undo the relationship between the past and the present that we struggle to reconcile the action of the novel with any 'reality' from which to ground decisions. This is, undoubtedly, part of Winterson's textual tactic, yet it raises the question of the efficacy of a critique which cannot tangibly connect to the realities of historical representation in the 1980s, specifically the lived, material effects they produce. The closing paragraph of the novel highlights the separation this radical historiographic position offers, but also the costs of deconstructing the hierarchy between representation and experience. The final section is narrated from a perspective that seems to be the contemporary Nicholas Jordan aboard the HMS *Gauntlet*. Yet the whole pineapple that heads this final section suggests an amalgamation with the modern-day female protestor, an overcoming of self and a unity that works against the divisions of history: 'the future and the present and the pasts only exist in our minds... even the most solid of things and the most real, the best-loved and the well-known, are only hand shadows on a wall. Empty space and points of light' (144). That historical categories and our idea of time are culturally constructed is unquestionable. Yet reducing the experience of the world to pure representation, 'hand shadows on a wall', is to potentially obviate the material violence that is done in the name of that representation. In the 1980s, the representation of the past was used to cloak the suffering of many thousands of the most deprived as government policy destroyed 'the most solid of things' – homes, communities, livelihoods – suffering that should never be flattened out as it has the potential to be in the radical historiographic fiction of the period.

Pastiche and the paradoxes of critique in *Remains of the Day*

One of the most enduring images of the past in the 1980s was the 1981 Granada television adaptation of Evelyn Waugh's *Brideshead Revisited*. The lavish visual qualities of the film were taken up and repeated in other successful television series and films of the decade including *A Jewel in the Crown* (1982), *A Passage to India* (1984) and *A Room with a View* (1986). The popularity of these productions was an essential part of the heritage turn that I explored above. Here was a manufactured past for a malcontent present, a world in which the lives of the aristocracy in the heyday of empire was the perfect cinema and televisual entertainment in a period of decline. As Andrew Higson argues, the past here is displayed as 'visually spectacular pastiche, inviting a nostalgic gaze that resists the ironies and social critiques so often suggested narratively by these films' (109; see also Wollen). Higson identifies a problem that pertains right across representation, not simply film: how do we separate the 'pleasures' of the medium from the politics of the narrative? It is a problem that faces the reader of Kazuo Ishiguro's 1989 novel *Remains of the Day*, one of the most famous historical novels of the decade, whose popularity with readers has continued long into the twenty-first century. The novel won the Booker Prize in 1989, but it arguably become most firmly lodged in the public imagination as a period piece – all country houses, immaculate clothes and cut-glass accents – when it was turned into a Merchant Ivory film in 1993, starring Anthony Hopkins as the anachronistic butler Stevens and Emma Thompson as Miss Kenton. Yet the novel is clearly a self-conscious exploration of a mythical England that never existed, drawing attention to the constructed mythologies of English nationalism. As Ishiguro stated in an interview in 1990:

> Now, at the moment, particularly in Britain, there is an enormous nostalgia industry going on with coffee table books, television programmes, and even some tourist agencies who are trying to recapture this kind of old England. The mythical landscape of this sort of England, to a large degree, is a nostalgia for a time that didn't exist. The other side of this, however, is that it is used as a political tool – much as the American Western myth is used. It's used as a way of bashing anyone who tries to spoil this 'Garden of Eden'. This can be brought out by the left and the right, but usually it is the political right who say that England was this beautiful place before the trade unions tried to make it more egalitarian or before the immigrants came and ruined everything. I actually think it is one of the important jobs of the novelist to actually tackle and rework myths... *The Remains of the Day* is a kind of parable. (*Mississippi Review* 139–140)

So if we take Ishiguro at his word, then the parable is that mindless mythic nationalism is a bad thing as it attempts to reinforce difference for political ends by deploying narratives of continuity and therefore the illusion of essentialism. In the same interview, when asked about his stylistic nods to Evelyn Waugh, G. K. Chesterton and others, Ishiguro claimed that he was creating a pastiche, a parody of the mythic nationalisms and nostalgic air of those authors (even though he also admitted to not having read them). It is a pastiche that he undertakes with such a thin thread of parody that it has little comic force. I doubt many people laugh when reading the novel, except at Stevens's rather stilted attempts to humour his new American master or to explain sex to young Mr Cardinal. Contemporary reviews, plastered across the cover of the paperback, described it as 'moving', 'heartbreaking' and a 'convincing portrait of human life'. Some did pick up on the novel's attempt to tackle myths of nationalism, but on the whole it was consumed as part, rather than a critique, of the heritage industry. This subtlety can be usefully interrogated by turning to Fredric Jameson's definition of pastiche as blank parody:

> Pastiche is, like parody, the imitation of a peculiar or unique idiosyncratic style, the wearing of a linguistic mask, speech in a dead language. But it is a neutral practice of such mimicry, without any of parody's ulterior motive, amputated of satiric impulse, devoid of laughter and of any conviction that alongside the abnormal tongue that you have momentarily borrowed, some healthy, linguistic normality still exists. Pastiche is thus blank parody, a statue with blind eyeballs. (17)

It may seem unfair to suggest that Ishiguro's novel is devoid of irony, but it certainly lacks 'bite' when it comes to critiquing the heritage industry under Thatcherism. Stevens is rendered in a relatively sympathetic light, a man brought up in the late Victorian and Edwardian period attempting to accept a changing world. In the novel, the changes that most dramatically affect the world that Stevens has known are the rise of America as a new global power, represented through the arrival of Mr Farraday as his new master, and the technological transformations of the domestic sphere. As Stevens tells us: 'now naturally, like most of us, I have a reluctance to change too much of the old ways. But there is no virtue at all in clinging to tradition merely for its own sake. In this age of electricity and modern heating systems there is no need to employ the sorts of numbers necessary even a generation ago' (7). Recognizing the need to 'move with the times', Stevens begins a modest attempt at altering the traditions to which he is so beholden. His attempts to dismiss the formality of the master/servant relationship, with him allowing an entire village to think he is an aristocrat, are evidence of the shifting social barriers in the post-war world. As he says of being forced to alter his approach to Mr Farraday: 'It is essential, then, to keep one's attention focussed on the present; to guard against any complacency creeping in on account of what we may have achieved in the past' (139). Yet at the same time he is forced to defend his disgraced former master, Lord Darlington, insisting that he was a man who stood up for what he believed in, values he considers timeless. Yet the figure of Lord Darlington represents a paradoxical relationship to the future and innovation. Ishiguro has painted Darlington as the misled peer who couldn't see the potential abuses of power lurking behind the 'modernization' of fascism: 'Exactly, Stevens. We are, quite frankly, behind the times in this country' (198). Ishiguro thus presents the desire to overcome being 'behind the times' as just as dangerous as being indebted to the past. Stevens is attempting to develop a series of timeless values to exonerate Lord Darlington, and himself, from any association with the ideologies of fascism. He is faced with a fear of the future and of the past, which forces him into the construction of a mythic nationalism.

It is, then, the timeless values of Stevens, and the mythic nationalism that he represents, that is Ishiguro's target here. Stevens's place within this discourse of nationalism is signalled at various points throughout the novel, but perhaps most symbolically in the guides he uses to undertake his journey through the West Country: 'perusing also the relevant volumes of Mrs Jane Symons's *The Wonder of England*...I heartily recommend them. They were written during the thirties, but much of it would still be up to date' (11). This series is a fiction of Ishiguro's own making, but it is clearly meant to stand in for the explosion of road travel books in the 1920s and 1930s. The most famous of these was Henry Vollam Morton's *In Search of England* (1927). The travel writing of Morton and others represents an important moment in the construction of modern national identity in Britain. Whereas nationalism had previously been aligned to the state and the crown, the 1920s saw the attempt to identify a national 'spirit' in the rural life of England. As C. R. Perry has argued, Morton 'faced the task of trying to convert his mass audience of readers to social, ecological, and aesthetic positions that not only cut against the grain of the nation's general historical and economic development since the early nineteenth century, but which also rejected much of the specific underpinning of his readers' daily existence' (436). His rejection of consumerist culture, suburbia and standardized education therefore presented an England almost pre-industrial, developing in his readers a desire for a world at odds with their own. Ishiguro's gesture towards writing such as Morton then suggests that Stevens is trapped in an escapist fantasy that, even in the 1920s, was anachronistic and ideologically dubious, a nostalgia for an impossible past.

Ishiguro, by exposing the nostalgia of and for the English class system in Stevens, implies that those values should be rejected in favour of a new, egalitarian model of social organization. John J. Su has argued that the novel posits a celebration of working-class stoicism and pragmatism against the immovable traditions of the aristocracy. In Su's reading, the movement from elite aristocratic to popular, working- and middle-class culture is captured in the cultural cartography of the novel which 'ultimately associates the British ethos with the pier at Weymouth rather than the estate' (556). The end of the novel also presents the retired butler whom Stevens encounters on Weymouth pier as a model for escaping from the constraints of the past. He offers the following sage advice: 'Don't keep looking back all the time, you're bound to get depressed... Look at me. Been happy as a lark since the day I retired. Alright, so neither of us are exactly in our first flush of youth, but you've got to keep looking forward' (243). But the problem, of course, is that to not look back risks historical amnesia, a loss of an active engagement with the past and the reliance on what Pierre Nora calls 'sites of memory', those representations and commemorations of the past that preserve it for us. For Nora the transformation of memory into memory-history sees the ossification of the past into the archive and the memorial, which are 'fundamentally vestiges, the ultimate embodiments of a commemorative consciousness that survives in a history which, having renounced memory, cries out for it. The notion has emerged because the society has banished ritual' (6). So for Nora a loss of active, communal memory doesn't lead to a freeing from the past, but a new form of enslavement to its representation. And it is perhaps this paradox that lies in the background to Ishiguro's novel and to the question of historical representation in the 1980s more generally. It cannot simply be a matter of rejecting or deconstructing the dominant mythic representations of the past. Instead, it is necessary to move beyond blank parody and a critical interrogation of the past into the production of new counter-myths by which to live.

Myth and counter-myth in *Mother London*

If Ishiguro's novel attempts to call into question the mythic national identities that circulated in and after World War II, Michael Moorcock's *Mother London* occupies similar territory. Here, it is the great myth of a stoic nationalism that emerged during the Blitz that Moorcock takes as his target. Yet Moorcock's novel, tracing the decline of London from the Blitz to Thatcherism, offers a radical historical fiction that is far more engaged with the politics of historical representation in the 1980s. Moorcock's challenge to the myth of the Blitz sees the possibility for a counter-myth of community and memory in London that can work to rebuild forms of working-class belonging and identity that were eroded under Thatcher, who, famously, in an interview in *Woman's Own* in 1987, would declare the primacy of the individual and the family as she declared there to be no such thing as society.

From Churchill's attempt to develop a lineage between Britain's darkest hour and those naval and military battles at the height of Britain's imperial power, the war was the theatre in which a national ideology was both deployed and created. Within the war, the Blitz is undoubtedly one of the most dramatic and effective symbols of British national identity. 'The Blitz' refers to the aerial bombardment of London (although many other cities were targeted in the same period) from August 1940 to March 1945 by the German *Luftwaffe*, in which 29,890 citizens were reported killed and large sections of the city destroyed. Beyond these facts, the Blitz, and representations of it, descends into manipulation, becoming an ideological battlefield. The Blitz is remembered as being a time in which the city and its citizens showed an incredible resolve, maintaining their lifestyles with good humour, showing the rest of England, along with the rest of the world, that the city would not be beaten into submission as soon as many had thought (see White 38). In this process, the experience of the city became the experience of the country, symbolizing 'British' characteristics and qualities.

This relationship between the Blitz and nationalism is a complex one, which has seen the Blitz become a formative element in the narrative of British identity. This process is far from organic, with both wartime propaganda and post-war mythologizing creating a myth of identity from the event. During the war itself, the British population was subject to a massive propaganda campaign at the hands of its Ministry of Information. In an attempt to galvanize public morale, the government instituted a series of both overt and covert manipulatory measures. These included sending spies into workplaces to gauge levels of public support/criticism of the war effort, encouraging people to spy on workmates/ neighbours/friends and to report any dissent to the government and massive advertising campaigns attempting to dissuade public gossip on the progress of the war, while simultaneously carrying out a widespread campaign of controlled misinformation through the BBC. As part of this wartime propaganda, the Ministry of Information created a new national unity. As Freedman suggests: 'British propagandists depended heavily upon the weapons of intellect and persuasion. Unity was secured by the careful creation of an ideology that stressed support for the war-effort' (22). This ideology actively set about creating a mythological essence of London and Londoners in the 'spirit', summed up in the phrase 'London can take it!' The Ministry of Information made two films during the war entitled *London Can Take It* and *Ordinary People: London Carries On*. These films celebrated the resilience of Londoners, utilizing them as a model for a national response to the hardships of war, turning a potentially divisive show of regionalism into a new collective national identity, one that has set the model for the displays of nationalism that later flourished under Thatcherism and into the New Labour period.

Examples of this wartime mythologization of the Blitz can be found in post-war historical representation, too. As Lucy Noakes's study of the Imperial War Museum and the Winston Churchill at War Theme Museum suggests, the Blitz has become a symbol of national unity, a sanitized picture of a nation at war. Both museums create a Blitz 'experience' in which the visitor interacts with a presentation of a past. Noakes asserts: 'Because these themed museum "experiences" begin with the choice of a period, event or lifestyle as particularly significant and worthy of commemoration rather than beginning with the discovery or acquisition of artefacts, they have the ability to tell us more about current preoccupations with the past... rather than preserving the past, they create it' (94). For Noakes, current preoccupations reveal the need for palatable versions of a past, with the experience of a minority represented as a unified majority. This version of history ignores the unsanitary living conditions in bomb shelters and the tragedies at Bethnal Green and Balham Tube stations (where residents using the station platforms as bomb shelters were killed during Luftwaffe attacks), and as a model of representation it precludes any interrogation of the way in which the blitz-as-mythology is constructed. Not only do these presentations ignore the constructed nature of the Blitz within the national past, but they perpetuate contemporary conservative ideological practice. As Noakes, supporting the contention of critics such as Stuart Hall, suggests: 'Oppositional or problematic images of the Blitz are overwhelmed by more positive images; images which serve to support the New Right's construction of British national identity as something natural and unchanging, untouched by "modern" impositions such as gender, race or class' (101). While the Blitz may be liable to ideological manipulation, Alan Sinfield suggests in *Literature, Politics and Culture in Postwar Britain* (1989) that it marked a possibility for radical change that, writing in the 1980s, had never materialized. Reflecting on a letter that Queen Elizabeth, the wife of George VI, wrote to his mother in 1940, in which she suggests the people 'deserve a better world', Sinfield states, 'they didn't really get it, and our current predicament is a consequence of that' (7). It is a sentiment with which Moorcock would undoubtedly concur.

Of the three novels explored in this chapter, Moorcock's *Mother London* (1988) stands out as the least well known and, to some extent, the least representative of the 'literary' historical fiction produced in the 1980s. Moorcock is known, primarily, as a fantasy and science fiction novelist, having published over 60 novels since the 1960s. Moorcock's background and readership are then markedly different from Ishiguro's and Winterson's, and his novels stand, to a large extent, outside the literary fashions of the 1980s.

Michael Moorcock's *Mother London* (1988) is, if nothing else, a scathing critique of Margaret Thatcher. As Iain Sinclair has asserted:

> *Mother London* pivoted on the Blitz, on psychic damage, small urban miracles worked by human affection, a woman walking out of the fire with a newborn baby in her arms. The novel's trajectory of hurt runs from Thatcher's denial of the concept of society, the unappeased demons of the free-market, to the communality of war and the shaky utopianism of Old Labour's green lungs, swimming pools and bright new housing projects. ('Crowning Glory')

Sinclair's summary outlines the novel's position as a genealogy of post-war failure, an indictment of the failed utopian dreams that turned into a Thatcherite nightmare. Moorcock's novel then is a deconstruction of the myth of the Blitz, but also, and this separates his novel from Ishiguro's, a positive attempt to create a new, oppositional myth based around the culture of working-class London.

Mother London's narrative is centred upon the lives of three mentally unstable Londoners – Mary Gasalee, Josef Kiss and David Mummery – and attempts to trace through them both the failure of national government and an oppositional myth of the city, using the Blitz as the foundation of both tasks. Josef Kiss's rumination on the Blitz is a condensed account of how he believes it should be remembered:

> It was the first time I fully understood how detached governments became from ordinary people... expecting London to collapse, the authorities made no real provision for defence. The ordinary people pulled the city through... It wasn't Churchill or the King of bloody England who kept up our morale. It was men and women whose homes and families were bombed to bits discovering their own resources. (386)

For Moorcock, the government failed London during the Blitz, yet what resulted from that failure – the resistance of the citizens of London – was then re-incorporated back into the nationalist ideology that was the foundation of government. So for Moorcock it is about reclaiming the event from nationalist ideology by attempting to dramatize the 'true' relationship between London and government. As Kiss asserts:

> I hated the Germans, but I hated our leaders far more. I wasn't alone in that. People weren't allowed to report how we felt. We were depicted as valiant, chirpy Cockneys, taking our hats off to His Majesty. They didn't say how they were too scared to let any aristocrat go into the East End for fear they'd get torn to pieces, how Churchill's life was in danger from the salt of the earth. They were all the same to us. They hardly got bombed at all and any concern they displayed was a fraud. (387)

Moorcock's attempt to document the 'fraud' of right-wing mythologization is coupled with a counter-history of the Blitz, one that is multifaceted and refuses to become monolithic and ideological. Moorcock achieves this primarily through the italicized lines of text that intersperse the narrative. These, initially, have a defamiliarizing effect as the reader attempts to read them as an intrinsic part of the central narrative. Yet after a while it becomes clear that they are the voices of the city, its nameless citizens whose narratives are lost within the larger framing narratives of history. Many of these function as 'flashbacks' to the Blitz, for example: '*One V-Bomb landed on the common. No one realised it would be followed so closely by another. By mine*' (15). One of the most powerful effects of these italicized transmissions, for want of a better word, from the city itself is our temptation to skip them in order to focus on the central narrative. In this way, we, as readers, produce a form of forgetting, realizing our desire to be given a coherent narrative at the expense of a multi-valent and multi-vocal past. The counter-myth that Moorcock provides, then, refuses to allow itself to become static and single, recalling the Blitz in a way that evokes the trauma it caused for individuals, whose experiences must be allowed to echo as a cacophony, rather than an imposed, mythic harmony.

While the plurality of voices interject throughout the novel, creating a fragmented record of the Blitz, Moorcock's novel focuses on the three central characters in the novel, Josef Kiss, Mary Gasalee and David Mummery, for whom it was a foundational and transformative moment. Gasalee's house was bombed during the Blitz, leaving her husband dead and her in a 15-year coma. The Blitz is a simultaneous death and rebirth. For Mummery it was his first childhood memory, and playing in the ruined landscapes of the city was vital in his personal development. For Kiss the Blitz was the moment where he first realized his own insanity, but also how his insanity or 'gift' could be utilized to help those around him. The Blitz also represents the possibility for rebuilding the city and the nation anew. This vision is equated with Blake's *Jerusalem*. As Mary Gasalee sings the hymn adapted from Blake's poem at the funeral of a friend, 'she could see with Blake that vision of a perfect London, where slums and misery were abolished and God's perfection touched every building, every park, every spinney. It was how others visualised heaven: it was what many had hoped to see after the bombing' (122). Yet that chance of salvation, this opportunity to create London as a New Jerusalem, was, according to Moorcock, destroyed by the failure of successive post-war governments.

For Kiss this failure is embodied in the great council estates that litter London. The years of post-war rebuilding were, for Moorcock, dominated by the blight of Modernism. The Modern Movement, inspired by the works of Le Corbusier, was an attempt to create architecture and urban design that promoted a more egalitarian society, in which an ordered and clean environment could create the space in which their inhabitants could create their own futures. In the novel, a sense of the failure of this vision is conveyed as Mummery's friend Joe Houghton casts his gaze over a housing estate:

> Behind him a neat grass bank dotted with daisies and late daffodils sloped down from the new brick of the council flats, a fragment of that postwar dream that he himself had once shared, of a landscaped urban paradise, of airy dreams and good housing alive with light, where people lived in security and dignity. That dream's singular failure still astonished him. (129)

In contemporary theorizations of urban development, that same disillusionment with the Modern Movement is widespread. As Lafaivre asserts, it 'became synonymous with inhumanity, desolation and devastation' (quoted in Ellin 44). For Josef Kiss that disillusionment is made all the more powerful by the effects of later post-war development, which made the immediate post-war rebuilding of London look like the last opportunity to significantly alter the city's direction: 'The mist still refused to lift. It married with the Portland facings of the steel-framed sixteen decked blocks and here and there appeared to take concrete shape, to form a giant beside other giants: Tombstones to a vanished future, our single chance at Grace, thought Josef Kiss' (60). While the death knell of the Modern Movement's egalitarian housing in England was effectively sounded on 16 May 1968 when a gas explosion at the Ronan Point Tower Block in Canning Town led to major structural damage and the death of four residents, the skyline and housing of London had already been forever transformed, with 68,500 flats existing in tower blocks ten or more stories high (White 55).

The advent of Thatcherism represents the definitive termination of this future. The failure of Thatcherism is represented as an invasion of the city, a contagion that is seeking to stifle London's identity by means of gentrification. As Josef Kiss states: 'Those scoundrels from the Thatcher belt Dandy! Thatching this, Thatching that. Its rural blight, old lad. Arcadian spread. It's hideous. They've no right to be throwing their weight about in London. Give them Westminster as a free zone, but draw the line there' (378–379). The invasion of gentrification and the rise of enterprise culture consumerism that I documented earlier are confirmed in the novel when Kiss's friend Dandy Banaji opens up a themed chop-house to cater for the tourist market. For Kiss this represents the final nail in London's coffin, with its citizens attempting to crassly package its culture in accordance with the rise of privately funded museums and history theme parks under Thatcher's government. This commodification of the city and its past is, however, counteracted by the ways in which Moorcock's three central characters exist in opposition to the rise of economic rationalism and the destruction of London. As Josef Kiss asserts to his gathered friends in 1980: 'we survive. We are all veterans of the psychic wars, I think' (395). Their survival in this war is built around the myth of the city, and their role as both its celebrants and conduits.

Moorcock attempts to develop an organic myth of the city, one that is based in the remarkable yet quotidian lives of its citizens. Here we see the three central characters of the novel as all having the ability to internalize the psychic energy of London, to hear the voices of its past and present in their heightened consciousness. As Moorcock states in the novel:

> Mummery's theory was that their mutual condition was a product of what he called urban evolution: as a Brazilian native of the rain forest was able instinctively to use all his senses to build up a complex picture of his particular world, so could a city dweller read his own relevant signs, just as unconsciously, to form an equally sophisticated picture. (30)

Yet this sense of awareness is framed not as a form of critique but as a heightened means of reception, a sensitivity to the timeless rhythms of London. As David Mummery asserts of their power: 'unable easily to block the wealth of information provided by a great city, he, she and Josef Kiss were like powerful wireless receivers' (30). This sense of perception is then equated with a neo-Romantic celebration of the experiential as the foundation of a higher consciousness. David Mummery asserts: 'I live in this world of colour, of sound, of touch and sexuality so much more vivid than your own that sometimes it seems my body can hardly contain it all' (171). This expression of a certain non-rational engagement with the world is then part of the ability to access the myth, yet this notion of accessing a mythical essence of the city raises a series of questions regarding the construction of an alternate mythology.

Moorcock's interrogation of historical representation in the 1980s demonstrates, as I hope I have shown, a far more explicit engagement with the politics of the period. The ludic textuality of Winterson and subtle pastiche of Ishiguro may seem somewhat apolitical alongside Moorcock, but that isn't to suggest that Moorcock's representation of the past is unproblematic. Moorcock's form of mythology is, arguably, imbued with a sense of deep nostalgia for a disappearing London of tow paths, the working-class inner city and the public house. Moorcock therefore places a new counter-myth squarely within his Londoners and their rituals: it is their ability to access this disappearing world that will be integral to the psychic survival of London and Londoners. The final lines of the book attempt to underscore this sense of a precarious London myth in the marginal character Nonny. Her engagement with the spatiality of London is guided by an awareness of the city's past:

> the paths Non follows grew out of singular tensions, eccentric decisions, whimsical habit, old forgotten purposes, so that she appears to move at random when actually she travels ancient and well used arteries, though most would not recognise her signposts since she steers by association, by an instinct as profound as any jungle hunter's, and will say her skill is nothing more than common sense. (495)

This past is then the past of myth that cannot be contained in official narratives of the city, but is equated with the nexus between place, ritual and oral culture. Nonny is able to 'tell the old tales of Brutus, Boadicea and Dick Turpin with the same vivid relish as she recounts the newer legends of the Blitz' (495–496). Moorcock is unequivocal about the need for this storytelling, or mythic feature of London life, asserting in the salutary closing lines of the novel: 'such stories are common amongst all ordinary Londoners, though few are ever noted by the press. By means of our myths and legends we maintain a sense of what we are and who we are. Without them we should undoubtedly go mad' (496). Yet this attempt to revert to a form of community based on a culture of myth and legend is strikingly anachronistic. It also repeats many of the constricting functions perpetuated by the national ideology of myth that Moorcock is attempting to challenge. The danger here is of legitimizing a form of authenticity, that of the 'real Londoner', that works to exclude and alienate those new to the city, which is no less exclusionary than any other form of collective identity.

Conclusion: History repeating?

History, it seems, was everywhere in the 1980s. From mainstream television to national politics, there was no escaping the fact that a retrogressive, postmodern gaze had made the past the ground on which the politics of the present was fought, and the future forgotten. These multiple uses and abuses of the past should, I have argued, be the context through which we read the fiction of the period. Moorcock, Ishiguro and Winterson reflect three very different means of challenging dominant ideas of time and history in the 1980s, whether they be the meta-narratives of modernity or the myths of nationalism. These challenges offer, I have suggested, their own problems, as well as partial solutions, to the pitfalls inherent in any representation of the past, including those we face in a period which many commentators have suggested is a form of Thatcherism redux.

The historical representations I have examined in this chapter seem to us both uncannily close and very far away. The radical, ludic historiographical narratives of Winterson and others are a long way from the more conventional historical fictions of, for instance, Hilary Mantel's *Wolf Hall* (2009) or the seemingly endless stream of historical novels set in the Tudor or Elizabethan period by Philippa Gregory, Vanora Bennett or Christie Dickason. Yet strangely enough the 1980s have now become a serious location for historiographical fictions of our own time. From Alan Hollinghurst's *The Line of Beauty* (2004) to Philip Hensher's *The Northern Clemency* (2008), the 1980s continue to be interrogated with a sustained sense of that decade as a profound historical moment. While the fictions of the 1980s may have eschewed the idea of historical moments in general, a novel such as David Peace's *GB84* (2004) is unforgiving in its anatomization of Thatcher's assault on Britain's past, present and future. It is perhaps to these fictions that we should turn our attention, instead of the saccharine images of a national past that grace our television screens, another legacy of historical representation in the 1980s.

Works cited

Ackroyd, P. *Chatterton*. London: Abacus, 1988.
Carter, A. *Nights at the Circus*. London: Vintage, 2006.
Cowell, B. *The Heritage Obsession: The Battle for England's Past*. Chalford: Tempus Publishing, 2008.

Ellin, N. *Architecture of Fear*. New York: Princeton Architectural Press, 1997.
Freedman, J. *Whistling in the Dark: Memory and Culture in Wartime London*. Lexington: The University Press of Kentucky, 1999.
Green, J. *All Dressed Up: The Sixties and the Counterculture*. London: Pimlico, 1999.
Hall, S. *The Hard Road to Renewal: Thatcherism and the Crisis of the Left*. London: Verso, 1988.
Hewison, R. *The Heritage Industry: Britain in a Climate of Decline*. London: Methuen, 1987.
Higson, A. 'Re-presenting the National Past: Nostalgia and Pastiche in the Heritage Film.' *Fires Were Started: British Cinema and Thatcherism*. Ed. Lester Friedman. Minneapolis, MN: University of Minnesota Press, 1993, 109–129.
Hutcheon, L. *A Poetics of Postmodernism: History, Theory, Fiction*. London: Routledge, 1988.
Ishiguro, K. *The Remains of the Day*. London: Faber, 1989.
———. 'An Interview with Kazuo Ishiguro.' By Alan Vorda and Kim Herzinger. *Mississippi Review* 20 (1991/1992): 131–154.
Jameson, F. *Postmodernism, or, the Cultural Logic of Late Capitalism*. Durham: Duke University Press, 1991.
Lawson, M. 'Downton Abbey Triumphs as Toff Television Takes Orff, Again.' *Guardian* (8 November 2010). Web. 10 Feb. 2011.
Lowenthal, D. *The Heritage Crusade and the Spoils of History*. Cambridge: Cambridge University Press, 1998.
Malchow, H. 'Nostalgia, "Heritage," and the London Antiques Trade: Selling the Past in Thatcher's Britain.' *Singular Continuities: Tradition, Nostalgia and Heritage in Modern British Culture*. Ed. George Behlmer and Fred Leventhal. Stanford: Stanford University Press, 2000.
Marwick, A. *The Sixties: Cultural Revolution in Britain, France, Italy and the United States, c. 1958–1974*. Oxford: Oxford University Press, 1988.
Moorcock, M. *Mother London*. London: Scribner, 1988.
National Heritage Act. 1980, http://www.legislation.gov.uk/ukpga/1980/17
Noakes, L. 'Making Histories: Experiencing the Blitz in London's Museums in the 1990s.' *War and Memory in the Twentieth Century*. Ed. Martin Evans and Ken Lunn. Oxford: Berg, 1997.
Nora, P. *Realms of Memory: Rethinking the French Past*, trans. Arthur Goldhammer, vol. 1, *Conflicts and Divisions*. New York: Columbia University Press, 1996.
Perry C. R. 'In Search of H.V. Morton: Travel Writing and Cultural Values in the First Age of British Democracy'. *Twentieth Century British History* 10(4) (1999): 431–456.
Rushdie, S. *Midnight's Children*. London: Vintage, 2008.
Samuel, R. *Theatres of Memory, Volume I: Past and Present in Contemporary Culture*. London: Verso, 1994.
———. *Theatres of Memory, Volume II: Island Stories: Unravelling Britain*. London: Verso, 1998.

Self, W. 'Play Things.' *Sight and Sound* 5 (November 1995): 11.
Sinclair, I. *White Chappell, Scarlet Tracings*. London: Palladin, 1988.
———. 'Crowning Glory: Michael Moorcock's London.' *Guardian Unlimited Books*. Web. 25 Mar. 2011. First published in *The London Review of Books*, 25 November 2000.
———. *The Verbals: Iain Sinclair in Conversation with Kevin Jackson*. London: Worple Press, 2003.
Sinfield, A. *Literature, Politics and Culture in Postwar Britain*. Oxford: Basil Blackwell, 1989.
Su, J. J. 'Refiguring National Character: The Remains of the British Estate Novel.' *MFS: Modern Fiction Studies* 48(3) (2002): 552–580.
Swift, G. *Waterland*. London: Picador, 1985.
Thatcher, M. (1982) 'Speech to Conservative Central Council,' http://www.margaretthatcher.org/document/104905. Web. 30 Mar. 2011.
———. (1983) *Radio Interview for IRN Programme the Decision Makers (with Peter Allen)*, http://www.margaretthatcher.org/document/105291. Web. 30 Mar. 2011.
———. (1987) *Interview for Woman's Own*, http://www.margaretthatcher.org/document/106689. Web. 30 Mar. 2011.
White, J. *London in the Twentieth Century*. London: Penguin, 2001.
Winterson, J. *Sexing the Cherry*. London: Vintage, 1999.
Wollen, T. 'Over Our Shoulders: Nostalgic Screen Fictions for the 1980s.' *Enterprise and Heritage: Crosscurrents of National Culture*. Ed. J. Corner and S. Harvey. London: Routledge, 1991.
Wright, P. *On Living in an Old Country: The National Past in Contemporary Britain*. Oxford: Oxford University Press, 2009.

6

Generic Discontinuities and Variations
Crises of Authority and Innovations in Form and Technique in British Fiction of the 1980s

Frederick M. Holmes

Experiments with novelistic form and technique began early on in the twentieth century with the modernist revolution, and in one fashion or another they have continued up to the present day. Although books written in the 1980s by novelists such as Maggie Gee, J. G. Ballard, James Kelman and Alasdair Gray were notably innovative, the bulk of the fiction published in Britain during the decade was not experimental in ways that deeply challenged readers and jeopardized sales. Summarizing Richard Bradford's argument (47–48), Joseph Brooker concludes that many ostensibly radical novelists actually exemplified the period's entrepreneurial ethos in 'craft[ing] intellectually playful novels for a mass Waterstone's public' (53).

However easy of access and entertaining such novels might be, many of them actually do feature significant generic modifications of traditional narrative techniques and structures, and in thematic terms they are often bitterly critical of the direction of British society during the Thatcher decade. Although bestselling novelists were beneficiaries of the capitalist economy, many nevertheless lamented the growing inequalities that resulted from the dismantling of the social security network that had been established following World War II. They were appalled by a society that commodified human relations to a degree unprecedented in their lifetimes. In her Introduction (first published in 2009) to *Restoration* (1989), for example, in which the decadent court of King Charles II serves as an analogue of Britain in the 1980s, Rose Tremain identifies her novel as 'my fictional response to the climate of selfishness and material greed that began to prevail in our society during the Thatcher years, from which we have never recovered and for which we are beginning to pay a terrifying price' (xi). Many writers, particularly immigrants such as Salman Rushdie from former colonies, resisted the then prime minister's nostalgia for the glory days of the Empire and her narrow conception of a national identity that seemed to exclude visible minorities, who were too often the victims of racial prejudice. Novelists who had been vitalized by the cultural ferment of the 1960s balked at both the authoritarianism and the repressiveness that were associated with both Thatcher's persona and her politics. As Nick Bentley states, she was anathema to feminist writers because she disagreed with many of their key ideas about the place of women in society, even though she herself became 'an unlikely icon ... of feminism' as 'a visible example of the way in which women could achieve top positions of power in the 1980s' (13). Even though they are set in the historical past, novels written by Angela Carter and Jeanette Winterson during the decade expose and attack the patriarchal, hetero-normative foundation of the 'family values' glorified by Thatcher; these books explore new ways of conceiving of and expressing gender and sexuality.

Despite their emphasis on order and traditionalism, the Conservatives effected a revolution that caused various kinds of social turmoil and unrest. For example, economic change produced widespread confusion about class affiliations and identities, and this is manifested in novels such as Martin Amis's *Money* (1984) and *London Fields* (1989). Dominic Head writes of the creation of a new, dispossessed underclass (73), and he adds that the middle class suffered 'a crisis of identity no less problematic than that which surrounds working class experience' (75). Brian Finney is right to say that beginning in the 1980s, the problematic nature of identity became a central topic in the fiction of Britain, 'a country undergoing rapid change, during a period when identities of all kinds were being radically questioned and undermined' (*English Fiction* 8). Against the international backdrop of the Cold War, with its constant threat of nuclear annihilation, these social dislocations had traumatizing psychological effects that were reflected in novels of the period, such as Graham Swift's *Waterland* (1983), Julian Barnes's *A History of the World in 10½ Chapters* (1989) and Amis's *London Fields*. According to Malcolm Bradbury, 'the apocalyptic note became a familiar feature of Eighties fiction in which the culture was random and "junk," time frequently dislocated, and oppressive hints of disaster and crisis seemed universal' (410).

Novels, then, were frequently animated by a dark energy that seemed connected to millennial forebodings about the perilous state of both British society and the planet at large, but these anxieties marked and shaped the texts in a variety of different ways. The fictional scene was characterized by diversity and an absence of clear direction or authority. As Bradbury states, the

1980s were ... historically confusing, culturally various, and aesthetically plural, a time when fiction took on a much greater variety of voices and a wider spread of styles and manners. Postmodern ways increasingly entered British fiction, which grew far more open to the fantastic, the Gothic and the grotesque. So did the postmodern problem, which is an acceptance of the catholicity of all styles, along with a doubt and indeterminacy about their use and authority. (448)

There was a symbiotic relationship during the 1980s between cultural manifestations of postmodernism in literature, architecture, films and advertising, on the one hand, and, on the other, a growing body of theory in academe designed to explain and justify it. In its anti-foundationalism, this theory overlapped with deconstruction, which also gained ascendancy in universities during this period and influenced some of the fiction written. As Bradford says, 'one cannot treat as accidental the parallels between post-structuralism/deconstruction ... and literary writing which seems intent upon eschewing logic and defying interpretation' (65). These intellectual strains contributed to a pervasive crisis of authority within the fiction of the 1980s, which revealed itself not only in content and themes but also in generic instability and plurality. In this chapter, I shall analyse in detail six novels that manifest this crisis: D. M. Thomas's *The White Hotel*, Julian Barnes's *A History of the World in 10½ Chapters*, Martin Amis's *London Fields*, Angela Carter's *Nights at the Circus*, Jeanette Winterson's *The Passion* and Salman Rushdie's *The Satanic Verses*. Before I do so, however, I shall need to address some broader concerns relating to the nature of literary genres.

Contemporary narrative theorists would argue that those novels of the 1980s that exhibit themselves as impure and unstable merely disclose the real, but frequently effaced, nature of all literary genres (and especially of the novel form in particular). Fiction of the decade that shows the influence of postmodernism tends to flaunt its own lack of generic integrity, and this propensity received intellectual support from genre theorists of that period, who treated the very concept with deconstructionist scepticism. In an essay published in 1988, Ralph Cohen explains that, because of 'the claim that postmodern writing blurs genres, transgresses them, or unfixes boundaries that conceal domination or authority', some critics have even concluded that '"genre" is an anachronistic term and concept' (11). Cohen, however, goes on to show that there are ways of thinking about genre 'that are perfectly compatible with multiple discourses, with narratives of discontinuity, with transgressed boundaries' (11). A central figure in the evolution of these new ideas about genre was Mikhail Bakhtin, who rose to prominence in the English-speaking world in the 1980s, possibly because his theories of dialogism and the carnivalesque, which overlap in some respects with post-structuralism, seem less deterministic in that they allow for human agency. Cohen (11), in company with John Frow (30) and Heta Pyrhönen (113), emphasizes Bakhtin's importance in differentiating between primary speech genres and secondary, mainly written ones that incorporate primary genres. A genre such as the novel is thus not a unitary form, since it embeds within itself many unwritten genres of everyday life and many written ones as well, such as the confession, the memoir, the personal letter, the history and the travel narrative. Genres are not fixed, natural forms, as classical and neoclassical theory held them to be. Frow argues that genres are dynamic, open-ended frames and also that texts do not belong to genres but, rather, perform them; texts, says Frow, 'refer not to "a" genre but to a field or economy of genres, and their complexity derives from the complexity of that relation' (2). Any individual text, therefore, is always multi-generic, although this is more obvious with some texts than others, since only some of them self-consciously exhibit their hybrid forms in the way that the novels to be discussed in this chapter do.

Pyrhönen claims that genres are in constant flux because of 'their intimate link with society, for they are social institutions that always stand in some relation to dominant ideology' (113). Genre, then, is not simply an aesthetic or stylistic concern. As Frow says, 'genre matters [because] it is central to human meaning-making and to the social struggle over meanings' (10). He goes on to state that 'a central implication of the concept of genre is ... that the realities in and amongst which we live are not transparently conveyed to us but are mediated by systems of representation' (18–19). Sometimes obliquely and sometimes more directly, the multiplicity of genres in evidence in the six novels that I have selected mediates disturbing social and psychological realities, and it also communicates imagined alternatives to these realities. For example, the Gothic and grotesque modalities mentioned above by Bradbury can be used to express revulsion and horror at the debased state of society, which these forms and techniques exaggerate and therefore emphasize. This phenomenon is apparent in *London Fields*, for instance, in which Amis creates a dystopian, even apocalyptic, fantasy of life in London. Set in the near future, the novel actually speaks to the depraved state of the city and the world at large in the late 1980s, although the darkly comical mode of representation that Amis employs mitigates the bleakness of his vision, at least to a degree. One might make a similar claim for *The Satanic Verses*, where some of Rushdie's whimsical, magic realist narratives feature grotesque details that convey the intolerable conditions of life for immigrants of colour. In both *Nights at the Circus* and *The Passion*, Gothic character types and narrative incidents testify to the power of misogyny to terrify and brutalize women, and although both novels are set in the historical past, it is easy to infer that they are meant to signify a contemporary social reality. In the same texts, however, relationships between characters and plot patterns derived from romance create alternative, utopian spaces of freedom and fulfilled desire.

What Bradbury calls the 'postmodern problem' manifested itself very early in the 1980s with the appearance of *The White Hotel*, a fragmentary text that refuses to privilege any particular kind of writing as authoritative. Lacking narrative unity or a consistent perspective from which readers can understand the female protagonist, this novel treats the subject of psychological and historical trauma by comprising several distinctly different kinds of documents, including erotic poetry, Freudian case study, holocaust narrative and utopian fantasy of the afterlife. The critical commentary of Linda Hutcheon, one of the decade's leading academic theorists of postmodernism, helped to establish Thomas's novel as an exemplary fictional excursion into this slippery, self-conscious terrain. She observes that the book's form not only displays but also mimics its content, the breakdown of its female protagonist's subjectivity, which is fractured and dispersed across several different kinds of texts narrated from different points of view, both first and third person (*Poetics* 166). The subject positions that she inhabits are gendered and produced in part by patriarchal ideology – especially as it is embodied in the iconic figure of Sigmund Freud. As Hutcheon states, '[i]t is the presence of "Freud" as a character in the novel that underlines the specifically male inscriptions of subjectivity by psychoanalysis' (166). She notes that the novel dramatizes issues that were of central concern to feminists in the 1980s: the objectification of woman as spectacle and the construction of female identity through male texts such as Freud's case history (166).

The White Hotel is postmodernist in what Hutcheon calls its 'metafictional stress on reading, writing, and interpreting' (166). Readers are constantly aware that Lisa's identity cannot be encountered directly but only indirectly through highly ambiguous narratives, poetic images and metaphors that she has inscribed in Don Giovanni and the Gastein Journal; through her correspondence with Freud and his case study; and through the subsequent sections presided over by an anonymous, undramatized narrator. Thomas's Freud teaches readers to distrust surface details and to seek for foundational truths hidden beneath them. Such interpretations, however, lead to other texts and more interpretations, not to unambiguous truths about human identity. *The White Hotel* is a dialogic echo chamber of other authors besides D.M. Thomas. In addition to his notorious reliance on Anatoly Kuznetsov's *Babi Yar* for 'The Sleeping Carriage' section, which lead to charges of plagiarism being levelled against him in the *TLS* (Nicol 2–3), Thomas ventriloquizes Freud's case histories and books such as *Beyond the Pleasure Principle*. Hutcheon adds the operas *Don Giovanni* and *Eugene Onegin* to the intertextual list, and Brian Nicol quotes Thomas as acknowledging Turgenev's writing as a model for 'The Health Resort' (36).

At the beginning of the novel, readers are given the misleading impression that the heroic figure of Freud will anchor the text to reality, that his theories will serve as explanatory models with the power to solve the mysteries of Lisa's psyche. As Hana Wirth-Nesher says, in comprising letters written by Freud and other members of his psychoanalytic circle, the 'Prologue' that follows the 'Author's Note' works 'as a framing device that links the fictional novel to documented reality' (18). The 'Prologue' further solidifies the reader's belief that Freudian theory will provide the interpretive key to the novel. The sections written by Lisa that follow directly after the 'Prologue' seem to validate a clinical orientation inasmuch as they are seeded with dreamlike imagery that all but demands a Freudian reading; as Wirth-Nesher states, in Lisa's writings, where 'wombs and breast fly through the air ... Freud's paradigm [even] seems to have replaced the laws of physics' (19). With calm rationality, in magisterially assured prose, Thomas's Freud then develops his case study so as to gradually lay bare the root causes of Lisa's psychosis in her childhood. '[T]he unconscious', he tells us, 'is a precise and even pedantic symbolist' (99), and his methodology seems to be perfectly devised to decode this symbolism.

What undermines the case study as a definitive explanation of Lisa's psychological difficulties is its placement in the middle of Thomas's text instead of at the end. Since it is not the final section, it cannot supply closure, and since numerous details in the sections that follow it subvert Freud's analysis, the case study seems seriously flawed rather than scientifically accurate. In fact, Thomas appears to have designed the structure of *The White Hotel* specifically to disclose general weaknesses in psychoanalysis as a master plot. Both Wirth-Nesher (22) and Nicol (32) point out that the novel as a whole invites readers to understand Lisa's symptoms as premonitions of her death as a Jew at the hands of the Nazis, not primarily as a consequence of traumatic experiences related to her upbringing. The limitations of Freud's approach stem from the ahistorical, restricted nature of his focus, from what Wirth-Nesher refers to as his 'ingenious singlemindedness, his unwillingness to consider evidence extraneous to the nuclear family drama' (21). While Lisa does acknowledge in the section following the case study that Freud deepened her self-understanding immeasurably, she informs him in a letter that during her analysis she was 'incapable of telling the truth, or facing it' (182) and that she lied to him repeatedly, distorting much of the information that was crucial to his diagnosis of her condition. That Thomas's Freud is willing to proceed with the publication of her case study even after he receives her letter destroys any credibility that he might have had as a man of science. He is apparently more concerned with the dramatic shape and rhetorical power of his narrative than he is with its empirical soundness.

In being generically distinct from one another, the three last sections of *The White Hotel* compete with each other to impose very different conceptions of life upon the novel. 'The Health Resort' not only undercuts the Freudian case study that precedes it but also provides a coherent view of Lisa as a middle-aged woman who has won a hard-fought victory over her psychological afflictions and earned a belated, autumnal happiness as the wife of the opera singer Victor Berenstein. Near the end of this section, in a passage suggestive of both Wordsworth and Proust, she has an epiphany, brought on by the scent of a pine tree, in which she discovers a continuous, core identity that links her past and future in the present moment:

> That knowledge flooded her with happiness... For as she looked back through the clear space to her childhood, there was no blank wall, only an endless extent, like an avenue, in which she was still herself, Lisa... And when she looked in the opposite direction, towards the unknown future, death, the endless extent beyond death, she was there still. It all came from the scent of a pine tree. (214)

This section, then, builds to a comic ending, but it proves ephemeral rather than enduring when, in the next section, readers are plunged into the tragic world of the Babi Yar massacre and the badly wounded Lisa is killed in horrific fashion when she is raped with a bayonet. Feeling that he needed 'to re-assert the life principle' rather than to end the novel with the Freudian death drive in the ascendant, Thomas composed what he called a 'spiritual fantasy' (quoted in Nicol 41–42), a much more hopeful vision of life after death that seems in part modelled on the Christian idea of Purgatory (Nicol 42). This final section's redemptive power would seem to extend retrospectively to the novel as a whole, but at the same time 'The Camp's' obvious status as a fantasy undermines its authority. In describing this ambiguity, Hutcheon coins the oxymoron 'anti-closure closure' to capture the paradoxical effect that this section has as *The White Hotel's* conclusion (*Poetics* 176). Giving with one hand what he takes away with the other, Thomas creates a sort of postmodernist aporia, thus subverting the capacity of his text to embody a single, consistent vision of reality.

Julian Barnes's *A History of the World in 10½ Chapters* is like *The White Hotel* in responding to destructive historical forces by splintering into a variety of sometimes incommensurable genres written from many different perspectives in a number of stylistic registers. In fact, although the dust jacket identifies the book as a novel, it more closely resembles a collection of short fictions linked by common themes and motifs. Barnes's announced topic is world history, which he conceives to be uncontrollably violent and anarchic, without inherent pattern or purpose. Hence, he presents not one unified, universal history of the world, but numerous stories, not ordered chronologically, which are set in a variety of different eras. The effect is one of jarring discontinuity. Jackie Buxton observes that Barnes's inclusion of a half-chapter even destroys the sense of completeness conventionally associated with the number ten (56). His fictions violate ontological boundaries without establishing a stabilizing hierarchy of meanings. In 'The Stowaway', for example, he inverts the positions of humans and animals, bestowing literacy, reason and a higher morality on the woodworm that serves as narrator and presenting the prophet Noah as a debauched, murderous beast. The biblical Noah, who drinks himself into a stupor, is hardly perfect, but Barnes's woodworm characterizes him as 'a monster, a puffed up patriarch who spent half his day grovelling to his God and the other half taking it out on us [animals]' (12).

'The Stowaway's' parody of Genesis exemplifies how Barnes incorporates mythical narratives along with historically documented ones, such as that describing the sinking in 1816 of the French frigate *Medusa*. As Claudia Kotte states (108), the novel's blend of the factual and the fabulous overturns the convention that historiography exclude the latter category. But Barnes doubts that fictional events can be neatly separated from actual ones. In 'Three Simple Stories', his narrator comments on a nineteenth-century report of an incident very like the biblical story of Jonah and the whale by saying '[m]yth will become reality, however sceptical we might be' (181). And, conversely, in its representations, the empirical reality of history will become adulterated with myth and fiction, which in the half-chapter 'Parenthesis' Barnes refers to as fabulation: 'We make up a story to cover the facts we don't know or can't accept; we keep a few true facts and spin a new story round them. Our panic and our pain are only eased by soothing fabulation; we call it history' (240).

Many different kinds of discourses make up *A History of the World in 10½ Chapters*, but all lack foundational status. Rather than being grand metanarratives, most are personalized accounts of particular events, some of which have no obvious bearing on world history. In this respect, the novel illustrates 'the incredulity toward metanarratives' that for Jean-François Lyotard defines the postmodern condition (xxiv). By his own account, Barnes has read very little critical theory (Freiburg 52–53), but postmodernism and post-structuralism, which were in the cultural air that he breathed during the 1980s, obviously influenced him. He has said, for example, that he finds the idea that language constitutes our reality, rather than merely describing it, 'quite attractive' (McGrath 23), and many of his books are responsive to deconstructionist and Bakhtinian readings. *A History of the World in 10½ Chapters* is such a polyphonic babble of different discourses that even Barnes himself, when he appears in his own person as the narrator of the essayistic 'Parenthesis', must compete for attention and supremacy with the voices of the characters in the other chapters. He allots them much more space than the single half-chapter that he occupies. 'Parenthesis' and the other chapters that are written in the first person are obviously highly subjective in character, but even the third-person narratives that seem to be the most authoritative are without obvious sanction or full objectivity. For example, the genre of the third chapter, 'The Wars of Religion', is that of the legal transcript, which would seem to have considerable weight as a document, inasmuch as it is backed by the power of the state. In the 'Author's Note', Barnes tells us that he drew on actual sixteenth-century French transcripts of trials in which animals were prosecuted for breaking human laws. What undermines the universality of Barnes's chapter as a discourse is its laughably anachronistic nature. By contemporary Western standards it is self-evidently absurd to try animals for violating laws that they could not possibly understand or to base legal arguments exclusively on Scripture, as the story's lawyers do.

One positive feature of the dialogic welter of voices in Barnes's text is that it permits usually silenced voices from society's margins to be heard. This facilitates the telling of revisionist accounts of history that expose injustices that are normally covered up. For instance, the woodworm's unauthorized version of the story of the Flood in Genesis uncovers the self-serving, anthropomorphic bias of the Judeo-Christian tradition and introduces the theme of animal rights. That theme is picked up again in 'The Survivor', in which the narrator, Kath Ferris, adds feminist and environmentalist concerns to her critique of the globe's predominantly male power structure. She overturns orthodox ways of representing the past, emphatically rejecting the familiar 'Great Man' paradigm of historiography: 'There was a battle here, a war there, a king was deposed, famous men – always famous men, I'm sick of famous men – made events happen ... I look at the history of the world, which they don't seem to realize is coming to an end, and I don't see what they see' (97).

It is important to recognize, however, that the narratives of victims such as Kath have no more claim to authority than those of the victors. In the history of the world according to Julian Barnes, relativity prevails. Kath's story is rendered doubtful by hints in 'The Survivor' that she might be hallucinating her tale of fleeing in a boat from nuclear catastrophe. Lacking any perspective on events that is not restricted or compromised in some way, *A History of the World in 10½ Chapters* concludes in a way that denies readers a comforting sense that it has served a teleological purpose by arriving at a transcendent destination. As does Thomas, Barnes ends his novel by depicting the afterlife. But whereas Thomas presents a dignified vision of holocaust victims being healed in a setting that resembles a sanitized post-war Palestine, one without armed conflict between Jews and Arabs, Barnes's final chapter is an obvious travesty: an anonymous narrator's dream of a bourgeois Heaven in which shopping, hobnobbing with celebrities and playing golf are the main activities. Barnes's God is an avuncular old gent whose idea of the Last Judgement is to tell the narrator, 'You're OK' (292). Not surprisingly, the narrator learns that out of boredom everyone who inhabits this banal afterlife eventually chooses extinction over immortality. Like the ending of *The White Hotel*, that of Barnes's novel undermines the sense of closure that it seems to provide, thereby weakening rather than strengthening the authority of the text as a whole.

Like *A History of the World in 10½ Chapters*, Martin Amis's *London Fields* also expresses widespread fears of nuclear apocalypse, environmental degradation, cultural debasement and social chaos, but rather than reflecting these dilemmas by fragmenting into a discontinuous collection of micro-narratives, *London Fields* takes the form of an intricately plotted, self-reflexive, parodic murder mystery. As Peter Childs says, the novel also has elements of the condition-of-England novel and of the love story, although in this case one that is inverted, 'an anti-love story' (46). Amis shares Barnes's proclivity for irony, parody, satire and black comedy. He has said that

> comedy is the only form left. The reason why comedy looks so odd is that tragedy doesn't exist anymore, it doesn't resonate – no one's going to believe in it anymore. So comedy is having to take on all the real ills, the refugees from other genres. The original butts of comedy used to be buffoonery, pretension, pedantry, but now they have to include murder and child abuse, the decay of society. (Wachtel 53)

Amis's darkly comic mode in *London Fields* can produce discomfort in readers, since it invites us to laugh at a world rife with cruelty, violence, racism, class prejudice and misogyny. The novel creates ambiguity about whether Amis is lamenting and satirizing a society deformed by Thatcherite greed, social inequality and the spectre of nuclear annihilation or whether he is participating in that society and sharing its cultural sickness. *London Fields* thus exhibits the postmodern condition in being unable to separate itself from what it attacks. As Linda Hutcheon succinctly states, '[c]omplicity always attends [postmodernism's] critique' (*Politics* 99).

London Fields is a metafiction that lays bare the artifices behind the mimetic illusion of realism. Although its narrator, the American Samson Young, denies having the capacity for invention and claims to be either recording events directly from life or copying from Nicola Six's diary, his running stream of comments about the process of writing the book have the contradictory effect of exposing its fabricated character. Our attention is frequently focused on the medium by the fact that all of the major characters are authors of one sort or another. Guy Clinch has written high-toned, unpublished short stories, and even the semi-illiterate Keith Talent struggles heroically with words to compose his unintentionally risible darter's diary. Nick Bentley shrewdly asks why Samson's narrative, if it is non-fictional, comes to us in the form of recognizable literary genres, such as the murder story, the 'really snappy little thriller' that he brags at the onset of the novel about being able to concoct (Amis 3). If, as Bentley asks (36), Samson's characters are real people, why does he use literary stereotypes to identify them: the murderer, the murderee and the foil? We might also ask why they all have such outlandish names and behave like one-dimensional caricatures. Clearly, Amis has not designed a text that activates the conventions of Jamesian realism. This does not mean, however, that *London Fields* is not representational. To call the plot of the novel artificial or mechanical, says Luc Sante, 'would be to belabour the obvious. It *is* a mechanism, the way a Tom and Jerry escapade is a mechanism, only in this case every pratfall is informed by rich sociological context. It is a panoramic cartoon that takes in a whole world of culture and custom and speech' (46). In other words, although Amis's novel exaggerates to achieve comical and grotesque effects, it nonetheless reflects a shallow postmodern society in which reality is culturally constructed and electronically mediated and in which people frequently behave like decentred automatons. Paradoxically, Amis has rejected the protocols of traditional social realism because he thinks that they no longer correspond to social reality: 'I ... feel', he says, 'that the old nineteenth-century views about motivation have exhausted themselves. Motivation is now nothing more than literary convention; I don't think people in the real world are coherently motivated' (Wachtel 53).

Malcolm Bradbury discusses how postmodernist novels such as *London Fields* can be seen as 'elaborate combinatorial games playing with the fictional elements – author, character, progression, outcome, narrative time – and the ways they can be manipulated and made metaphorical' (428). Another element that could be added to his list is the reader. 'I'm all for this intense relationship with the reader', says Amis. 'I really want the reader in there' (Fuller 75). The metafictional dimension of London Fields seems designed to impel the involvement and complicity of readers in its unsavoury events. Sam confides in us directly about the difficulties involved in writing the novel, some of which are ethical. After all, the plot spun by Nicola involves enlisting Sam's aid and then deceiving two other men, Keith and Guy, in order to engineer her own murder. If Thomas's character Lisa, who suffers from periodic hallucinations of apocalypse, is in the clutches of Thanatos, the heavily symbolic Nicola *is* Thanatos personified. She requires that her death attain an inverted, nihilistic significance by incorporating the death of love. Consequently, she must first inspire Guy's love for her before betraying him and humiliating Keith badly enough to make him want to kill her. In the end, it is Sam who takes responsibility for completing the design of his own novel by standing in for the other two and murdering Nicola himself. Even before crossing an ethical divide to commit this act, he warns us about the tainted character of his work in progress: 'I want to give it up', he says. 'It's a wicked book. It's a wicked thing I'm doing' (435).

But who is ultimately morally responsible for the novel? As a ludic, postmodern text, London Fields creates ambiguity about who manipulates its events. As I have just said, Sam is an active participant in the action, not just a passive scribe, but in the end he is just another of Nicola's male dupes, not the one in control. 'The plot of the narrative', observes Brian Finney, 'is ostensibly being concocted by Nicola. She, not Sam, is in control of the *fabula* (story), although the *syuzhet* (plot) is necessarily in the hands of the story's narrator' ('Narrative' 10). But, like Sam, Nicola is finally just another fictional character, not the creative genius of the text that she seems to be. And while Sam is indeed the narrator, has he actually had the power to shape the narrative, as Finney claims? That task, as Bentley states (37), might have been accomplished by Mark Asprey, who, presumably, found the manuscript that was left for him and might have edited it after Sam's death. As Mick Imlah states (1051), there are even hints that Asprey, who never appears in the text 'in the flesh' and who shares the initials M.A. with Martin Amis, might be on a higher ontological plane than that of the dramatized characters. 'You didn't set me up. Did you?' (468), asks Sam in the suicide letter that he leaves for Asprey. But behind this surrogate for the author is the actual creator of the world of London Fields, Amis himself, whose metafictional sleights of hand are intended to enmesh readers not just in the moral quagmire that the novel depicts, but also in his own actions as a novelist. As Finney points out, '[w]hoever narrates a story both creates and annihilates characters' ('Narrative' 3). The author, he goes on to say, 'in mercilessly manipulating his characters to suit his purposes, ... vicariously participate[s] in the viciousness of the age in which he lives ... By inserting the writer's substitute self, the narrator, into the action, he is inviting his readers to share with him his unease at the role he is asked to play as novelist' ('Narrative' 4). Amis is, effectively, working to corrupt us, to engineer our fall into experience, and this intention is disconcerting in that it upsets one traditional justification for literature: the moral improvement of readers.

Genre and gender are linked in Angela Carter's *Nights at the Circus* so as to present an interesting contrast with *London Fields*. Whereas Amis is seemingly unable to use a postmodernist narrative form in order to unequivocally repudiate socially harmful forces such as racism or sexism, Carter's metafictional experiments are fashioned to advance the cause of women's liberation from the constraints of patriarchy. Although Nicola is fully aware that human subjectivity is made up of fabricated, socially produced narratives and stereotypes, as a proxy for her author, she is unwilling to create scenarios that let her play the traditional female roles of virgin and whore in ways that do not lead to her own victimization. But Carter's protagonist, Fevvers, also a *bricoleur* who mimics her creator by trafficking in received fictions, manages to manipulate the Madonna/whore binary so as to avoid captivity and death while winning fame, wealth and love. She escapes from deadly oppressors such as Madame Schreck, Christian Rosencreutz and the Grand Duke, and as the New Woman poised to enter a new century, she unites with the American journalist Jack Walser only after his experiences in Siberia have shorn him of his patriarchal attitudes and expectations.

It is not surprising that several commentators on *Nights at the Circus* have invoked Bakhtin's ideas about the carnivalesque and grotesque realism, for, as Beth Boehm states (38), it is a thoroughly carnivalized text that resists firm generic classification. Carter was very well versed in 1980s critical theory, including Bakhtin, although she claimed not to have read his work until after she wrote *Nights at the Circus* (Sage 'Angela Carter' 188). In any event, her novel plays with, parodies and revamps the conventions of many forms and modes, including historical fiction, magic realism, fairy and folk tales, myths, comedy, romance, Gothic fiction, the *Bildungsroman* and the picaresque narrative. Carter acknowledged in an interview with John Haffenden that she drew on the eighteenth-century tradition of the picaresque (87), and Fevvers resembles the grasping, sly *picaro* figure in both her greed and her need to use her wits to survive in a hardscrabble environment. As a sort of female rogue's tale, her account of growing up in a brothel recalls Defoe's *Moll Flanders*.

Fevvers's episodic adventures also have many of the trappings of the quest romance, but one redesigned to grant her agency rather than to confine her to a passive role, secondary to that of the male hero. The novel, which concludes with Fevvers's raucous laughter ringing out over the Siberian wilderness, has the festive ending typical of romances in that it celebrates the union of Fevvers and Walser. Carter stated explicitly of the book that 'it is a comedy and has to end happily' (Haffenden 90). To view comedy in this way might seem to be an act of bad faith, in the sense that it presupposes that genre is a fixed, unchanging category. In contrast, we have seen that Amis adapted the conventions of comedy to fit his understanding of contemporary social conditions. It needs to be recognized, though, that Carter actually has modified the stock festive ending in order to advance a feminist theme. Fevvers's laughter proclaims her victory over Walser, whom she had fooled into believing that she was a virgin, not her submission to him as a wife cast in the traditional mould. She prizes him not primarily as a lover but as her helpmeet in the coming political struggle to advance the cause of women. She tells Lizzie to think of Walser 'as... the amanuensis of... those women who would otherwise go down nameless and forgotten' (285). Walser, then, who undergoes a succession of humiliating misadventures in the book's second and third parts, is not the stock hero of the romance. As Boehm observes (41), when Fevvers is held captive, she briefly casts herself in the role of a damsel in distress, crying out that '[m]y young man will come and save us!' (241). But she quickly reasserts her own independence, declaring instead that '[w]e shall set boldly forth and rescue ourselves' (244).

There are several other respects in which Carter's book draws on the romance genre. According to Northrop Frye (59) and Gillian Beer (2), romances often recycle stories and motifs that have been used previously, and the highly self-conscious *Nights at the Circus* reverberates with echoes from other texts. Carter said that she tended to use the literature of the West 'as though it were a kind of folklore' (Haffenden 82). Her novel ostentatiously borrows from writers such as Shakespeare, Swift and Yeats, but, as Boehm says, 'instead of using literary allusions to shore up the male tradition of great literature, Carter often alludes to works of the past parodically, thereby challenging the unacknowledged politics of aesthetic representation, particularly the representations of femininity' (43). In this regard, Lorna Sage astutely notes that in creating Fevvers, Carter has overturned a symbol, the winged woman, that has 'served throughout the centuries as a carrier of men's meanings' (*Angela Carter* 47). Fevvers, as Sage goes on to say, 'is a symbol come to life *as a character*, who makes meanings on her own account, and evades the symbol-hunters who try to murder, vitrify, petrify, and pin her down' (48).

Carter, then, paradoxically, employs the fantasy characteristic of romance in her role as a demythologizer. 'Myth', she says in *The Sadeian Woman*, 'deals in false universals, to dull the pain of particular circumstances. In no area is this more true than in that of relations between the sexes' (5–6). She debunks and de-familiarizes not only by altering myths but also by exposing the specific historical contexts that they must suppress in order to appear timeless. In this connection, Heather Johnson is right to say of *Nights at the Circus* that 'however remote [its] imaginary worlds may seem,... the novel never entirely leaves a recognizable frame of reference' (77). Its magic, in other words, is grounded realistically through references to actual places, historical events and personages, such as Alfred Jarry, who is said to have proposed marriage to Fevvers in Paris.

Nights at the Circus also resembles numerous romances in its dilatory narrative strategy, its tendency to proliferate and interlace stories rather than to move in a linear fashion to a climax and denouement. After the novel's first part, which is focalized through Walser, the point of view is disrupted and relativized, which violates the aesthetic norm of coherence but compensates by creating a rich polyphony of voices. In this respect, Carter's text is like Barnes's: it allows those who have no access to society's official discourses to be heard. As Boehm states, in giving us the life stories of characters such as Mignon, Buffo the clown and the Russian women imprisoned in a panopticon, Carter 'give[s] voice to eccentrics, those who exist on the margins of dominant culture and dominant literary structures' (44).

In multiplying tales as profusely as it does, *Nights at the Circus* not only makes room for the disenfranchised but also resists closure, which is another tendency of romance. Frye accounts for this propensity by arguing that because quest romances give expression to the wanderings of insatiable human desire, the wanderings of their protagonists are endless (30). Although Carter's novel, as I have said, does seem to provide the finality of a comic resolution, she said that she thought of the ending as open in the sense that it is an invitation to readers to use their imaginations to fabricate alternative stories about the book's characters. According to Carter, Fevvers's exclamation to Walser at the end of the book, '[t]o think I really fooled you!' (295), refers to the narrative act as well as to the business of Fevvers's virginity (Haffenden 90). Ending on that line, said Carter, challenges readers to perform their own confidence tricks by 'inventing other fictions, things that might have happened – as though the people were really real, with real lives' (Haffenden 90–91). Fevvers's metafictional double entendre, then, is meant to sustain and extend fictional illusion, not to dispel it.

The similarities between Carter's narrative methods and those of Jeanette Winterson in *The Passion* are many. One obvious point of connection is their common use of fabulist or magic realist effects as a way of undermining existing social codes governing sexuality and the performance of gender roles. Whereas Carter endows her female protagonist with wings that enable her to fly, Winterson's Villanelle has the webbed feet of a waterbird. In both cases, the techniques of formal realism anchor and naturalize such marvellous details in historically specific contexts, individualizing touches and particularizing details. For example, Winterson not only literalizes the common poetic trope of the stolen heart, as Paulina Palmer states (107), but also locates Villanelle's lost, still beating heart within the Queen of Spades' densely cluttered walk-in closet, hidden in 'an indigo jar' wrapped in a silk shift (*The Passion* 120). *The Passion* is also like *Nights at the Circus* in exhibiting the following postmodernist attributes, itemized here by Lynn Pykett: 'parody, irony, pastiche, self-reflexivity, and playfulness, a sense of multiplicity, fragmentation, instability of meaning, and an apparent distrust of grand narratives' (54). Like Carter's, Winterson's novel is multi-generic in its intertextuality. Judith Seaboyer notes that '*The Passion* gathers a heterogeneous mixture of stories within two intertwined narratives, and this together with an expressed bias toward literary sleight of hand results in a narrative ground that from the reader's perspective is unstable' (495). As a carnivalized text, *The Passion*, like *Nights at the Circus*, invites Bakhtinian readings that highlight the subversive effects of grotesque realism, masquerade and the inversion of social hierarchies. Palmer, for example, links Bakhtin's concept of the grotesque body to the depiction of Villanelle, through the webbed feet that symbolize her sexual difference, as a character displaying 'the lesbian as a figure of "excess," in that her sexuality exceeds the image of woman as commodity and object of exchange perpetuated by patriarchal culture' (110). By turns farcical and serious, comical and tragic, Winterson's novel incorporates elements of historical fiction, Gothic horror (such as the scene in which Henri stabs the Cook to death with a knife in the Venetian gloom and then cuts out his heart), fairy tales and myths (Seaboyer observes that the Cook materializes before Villanelle and Henri like the Minotaur in the centre of the labyrinth that is Venice [502]), the personal diary, the *Bildungsroman* and the quest romance.

In view of the many similarities outlined above between these two novels by Carter and Winterson, it is easy to assent to Pykett's contention that Carter's fiction has been an important influence on Winterson's, one that she has not adequately acknowledged (59–60). But, as the very title of her novel would suggest, Winterson is also quite different from Carter in her romantic privileging of the essential importance of passion in human life. Villanelle is her creator's spokesperson in declaring that '[p]assion is not so much an emotion as a destiny' (62). Palmer persuasively argues that Winterson tends to deploy the techniques of magic realism so as to accentuate the importance of passion by suggesting that it has the power to turn the banality of life into something marvellous (107–108). Seaboyer notices that *The Passion* is set in the heyday of High Romanticism (483), and like Coleridge and other writers of that era Winterson glorifies the creative imagination. As Pykett says, this is something that qualifies Winterson's postmodernism: 'despite the fact that it disrupts all sorts of foundationalist assumptions Winterson's early fiction is nevertheless very affirmative, especially of such universals as art, the imagination, and romantic love' (56). In *Art Objects*, Winterson declares that 'the original role of the artist as visionary is the correct one' (133), and with her stark, laconic writing style in *The Passion*, she crafts a poetic prose that sometimes attains visionary intensity. In contrast, Carter's verbose, exuberant style, which she herself labels 'mannerist' (Haffenden 91), is often deliberately prosaic and deflationary rather than poetic.

Winterson is like Carter, though, in adopting the form of the romance only to transform its codes so as to equip her heroine with more agency and freedom than the genre traditionally allows female characters. Since the characters in romances are typically stereotyped according to gender, Winterson's flouting of convention in this regard is readily apparent. As Palmer points out (104), it is ironic that Henri, despite his quest to fulfil himself through the quintessentially male pursuits of war and hero worship, is feminized, whereas Villanelle, with her cross-dressing, audacity and aggressiveness, displays 'masculine' traits in her pursuit of the Queen of Spades. It is she, not the more passive, sexually timid Henri, who possesses the symbolic phallus, the webbed feet that are a marker of male sexual identity within the society of Venetian boatmen.

Yet Villanelle and Henri both fail in attaining the goals of their romance quests and satisfying their desires. Bitterly disappointed by Napoleon and the horrific reality of the Russian campaign, Henri transfers his allegiance to Villanelle, but he is bereft by her refusal to reciprocate his love, just as she has been devastated by the loss of her heart to the Queen of Spades. As Seaboyer states, the romance quest that the novel narrates and embodies formally is dark and destructive; it is 'a romance trial by landscape that inexorably leads to the monster at the heart of the labyrinth; a Romantic *voyage intérieur* whose unrecognized goal proves equally monstrous' (488). Venice not only hides an implacable, bestial enemy who must be overcome with violence; it also symbolizes the un-chartable landscape of the psyche, the chaotic perils of which destroy Henri, who descends, after killing the Cook, into a madness from which he is unable to recover. As Philip Tew says, 'it is the lack of fixity, the irrationality, the mystery of things that finally defeats Henri, his refusal to live among the contingent magnitude and eventfulness of the historical present' (121). In contrast, Villanelle has the resilience and equipoise to ride the chaos and retain her sanity, perhaps because her experience as a bisexual has taught her that all of the roles that we play and categories that we use to structure life are malleable and provisional.

Like *London Fields*, Salman Rushdie's *The Satanic Verses* expresses horror at the social dislocation, economic disparities, violence and chaos of Thatcher's Britain, and like both *Nights at the Circus* and *The Passion*, Rushdie's novel uses magic realism in order to disrupt and challenge prevailing ideologies. Whereas Carter and Winterson target social codes and stereotypes that construct gender roles and regulate sexual relationships, Rushdie combines fabulation with realism to render the phantasmagoric nature of the migrant experience and to expose and condemn the racism that non-whites encounter in England. Perhaps the most widely discussed example of magic realism is Saladin Chamcha's metamorphosis into a demonic figure (complete with horns, hooves, sulphurous breath and a huge, erect penis) while he is being transported in a police van. Gregory Rubinson astutely links this episode with Gregor Samsa's transformation into a gigantic insect in Kafka's *The Metamorphosis*: both make literal unbearable experiences of being dehumanized by racial hatred (49). Chamcha's metamorphosis, then, shows what it feels like to be 'demonized' as a member of a visible minority. He is forced to recognize that, despite his apparently successful career as a voice-over actor and his marriage to an English woman with a pedigree, he has always been reviled and feared in British society as the Other. The meaning of Rushdie's psychological fable here is obvious: if immigrants are habitually characterized by the majority as sub-human, they may begin to internalize this identity. As the manticore, also an immigrant from India, explains to Chamcha in the sanatorium in which they have both been incarcerated, '[t]hey have the power of description, and we succumb to the pictures they construct' (168). One of the hallmarks of magic realism is the normalization or matter-of-fact acceptance of fabulous or supernatural events or personages, and Rubinson observes that in the case of Chamcha's transformation,

> [t]hose things that appear most fantastic to him are actually the most 'real' to the experience of immigrants ..., which helps to explain why no one except for himself finds the actual fact of his transformation particularly shocking. For the

racist policemen, he is exactly what they expect him to be; for Jumpy Joshi and the Sufyans, his appearance merely confirms British society's extreme racism. (51)

Paradoxically, then, for Rushdie magic realism is a mode that facilitates a more capacious and complex representation of sometimes bizarre, multi-form social and psychological realities than the conventions of formal realism alone would permit.

The Satanic Verses is like the bulk of the novels discussed in this chapter in being generically mixed and thoroughly intertextual. Because multiple narratives and points of view jostle for ascendancy within Rushdie's text, as well as numerous, sometimes incompatible genres from both the West and the East, none can become totalizing. He adapts the conventions of many of the same genres that Carter and Winterson draw on. *The Satanic Verses* is a hotchpotch of various forms: the oral narrative and tall tale, myth, fairy tale, fable, the *Bildungsroman*, the picaresque narrative, historical fiction, the novel of ideas, satire, comedy and farce, and tragedy (or, if not tragedy, then, in the novel's reprise of *Othello*, with Gibreel Farishta, Alleluia Cone and Saladin Chamcha in the roles of Othello, Desdemona and Iago, respectively, what the narrator refers to as 'the echo of tragedy...[a] burlesque for our degraded, imitative times, in which clowns re-enact what was first done by heroes and kings' [424]). Rushdie makes use not only of recognized literary genres but also of 'low' cultural forms, such as advertisements, some of which are drawn from television, the cinema and other media. Peter Nazareth, who states that the novel 'is dominated by references to, and forms from, movies, T.V., comics, and so on' (170), notices that several episodes resemble scenes from particular movies (171), and Steven Connor even argues that the scene depicting the filming of a musical version of Dickens's *Our Mutual Friend* opens up 'a particularly rich seam of self-reflexivity'; here, he says, 'the novel mirrors something of its own procedure' (124).

In moving towards a multimedia method of novel writing and in making both of his protagonists actors who work in films and television, Rushdie sensitizes us to the centrality of electronic simulation in postmodernist culture and links it with the fragmenting and decentring of the subject. 'O the conflicting selves jostling and jogging within these bags of skin', thinks Chamcha as he flies from London to Bombay in order to reclaim his Indian heritage and reconcile with his dying father. 'No wonder we are unable to remain focused on anything for very long; no wonder we invent remote-control channel hopping devices. If we turned these instruments upon ourselves we'd discover more channels than a cable or satellite mogul ever dreamed of' (519). Rushdie is like Amis in decrying one of television's chief effects: the flattening or deadening of culture, which takes on a one-dimensional quality. '[W]hat a leveller this remote control gizmo was', thinks Chamcha, 'a Procrustean bed for the twentieth century; it chopped out the heavyweights and stretched out the slight until all the set's emissions, commercials, murders, game-shows, the thousand and one varying joys and terrors of the real and the imagined, acquired an equal weight' (405).

The Satanic Verses, then, resembles *London Fields* in focusing on the mediated quality of people's lives in contemporary societies and in critiquing the role that global capitalism plays in this dislocating process. Rushdie's novel is also like Amis's – and like the other books that I have discussed – in its prominent metafictional dimension. Rushdie not only creates an identically named proxy for himself as novelist within the fictional world – Salman the Persian, who transcribes and secretly alters the mystically inspired utterances of the Prophet, Mahound – but Rushdie himself also briefly appears as a dramatized character within the text. Like John Fowles in *The French Lieutenant's Woman*, Rushdie presents himself as an ironic, distinctly dubious god, one who has created the fictional world of the novel, with its overlapping levels of reality and conflicting characters and ideas, but who, paradoxically, refuses to exercise his omnipotence by intervening to 'fix the fights' (408). (Rushdie even borrows this metaphor from *The French Lieutenant's Woman* [Fowles 406].) The narrator of *The Satanic Verses* adds a disconcerting twist to the author-as-god topos when he refuses to deny Farishta's suspicion that he might be the 'Guy from Underneath' rather than the 'Fellow Upstairs' (319). This ambiguity is consistent with the paradoxical, Blakean idea explored in *The Satanic Verses* that what is conventionally understood as evil is actually good, and vice versa.

Because they flaunt its papery, made-up status, the text's self-reflexive qualities have the effect of promoting the Lyotardian 'incredulity toward metanarratives' that characterize the postmodern condition. As is widely known on account of the infamous fatwa issued against Rushdie in 1989 by Iran's Ayatollah Khomeini, the most important meta-narrative that *The Satanic Verses* undermines is the Koran, which, Rushdie insinuates, is no more sacrosanct or objectively true than his own fabricated characters and stories. As Rubinson says, Rushdie's exaltation of himself as a god, however ironic it might be, is a 'desacrilization of religious ideals: he equates the authorship of the Koran with the authorship of fiction, again suggesting that there should be no genres of writing or individual texts privileged above others' (61). Rubinson makes a useful connection between what Rushdie does in retelling the story of the founding of Islam and what Barnes does in revising the Old Testament (53). Both writers subvert the monologic authority not only of religious texts but also of dominant secular ideologies. As Rushdie himself says in an essay, *The Satanic Verses* 'dissents... from imposed orthodoxies *of all types*, from the view that the world is quite clearly This and not That. It dissents from the end of debate, of dispute, of dissent' (*Imaginary Homelands* 396). In embracing relativity, both Rushdie and Barnes create possibilities for characters on the margins to contest the discourses of the centre. In order to participate in politically meaningful debates, members of minorities need to be able to appropriate the language of power and use it to shape their own narratives, as can one of the Shaandaar Café's habitués, the barrister Hanif Johnson, who 'was in perfect control of the languages that mattered: sociological, socialistic, black-radical, anti-anti-anti-racist, demagogic, oratorical, feministic' (281). The novel implies that only through such debates will a more flexible and inclusive national identity be forged.

What I hope to have demonstrated in this chapter about the experiments in genre and technique that I have discussed is that they have not resulted in texts that are self-reflexively and narcissistically closed off from the world. On the contrary, lexical playfulness, magic realist inventions and other kinds of formal deviations from conventional realism are the means by which these novelists involve readers imaginatively in explorations of social and political concerns. Sometimes the issues are topical in character. Finney points out, for example, that the London riots presented as a nightmarish fantasy late in *The Satanic Verses* directly parallel the Brixton riots of 1981 (*English Fiction* 118). The novel's anti-Thatcherite stance is quite overt; one of its characters even refers to the former prime minister as 'Mrs Torture' (266). Novels set in the historical past, however, such as *The White Hotel, Nights at the Circus, The Passion* and parts of *A History of the World in 10½ Chapters*, address contemporary issues more indirectly, but, as I have tried to show in this chapter, they do focus on the politics of gender, sexuality, race and social class. All six of the novels display apocalyptic currents of feeling that seem to relate to the troubled condition of British society during the decade in which they were written. Ideas derived from postmodernism, deconstruction and other academic theories then current certainly inform all of the novels and influence the extreme generic instability that they all self-consciously display. The flair and inventiveness with which they do so become a paradoxical source of fictional authority. Even as the writers undermine the ontological solidity and totalizing power of their own discourses, they establish their own artistic credentials as postmodernists.

Works cited

Amis, Martin. *Money*. London: Jonathan Cape, 1984.
——. *London Fields*. London: Penguin, 1989.
Barnes, Julian. *A History of the World in 10½ Chapters*. New York: Knopf, 1989.
Beer, Gillian. *The Romance (The Critical Idiom 10)*. London: Methuen, 1970.
Bentley, Nick. *Contemporary British Fiction*. Edinburgh: University of Edinburgh Press, 2008.
Boehm, Beth A. 'Feminist Metafiction and Androcentric Reading Strategies: Angela Carter's Reconstructed Reader in *Nights at the Circus*.' *Critique* 37(1) (1995): 35–49.
Bradbury, Malcolm. *The Modern British Novel*. 1993. London: Penguin, 1994.
Bradford, Richard. *The Novel Now: Contemporary British Fiction*. Oxford: Blackwell, 2007.
Brooker, Joseph. *Literature of the 1980s: After the Watershed (The Edinburgh History of Twentieth-Century Literature in Britain*, vol. 9). Edinburgh: University of Edinburgh Press, 2010.
Buxton, Jackie. 'Julian Barnes's Theses on History (in 10½ Chapters).' *Contemporary Literature* 41(1) (2000): 56–86.
Carter, Angela. *Nights at the Circus*. London: Penguin, 1984.
——. *The Sadeian Woman*. 1979. London: Penguin, 2001.
Childs, Peter. *Contemporary Novelists: British Fiction since 1970*. Basingstoke: Palgrave Macmillan, 2005.
Cohen, Ralph. 'Do Postmodern Genres Exist?' *Postmodern Genres*. Ed. Marjorie Perloff. Norman and London: University of Oklahoma Press, 1989, 11–27.
Connor, Steven. *The English Novel in History, 1950–1995*. London: Routledge, 1996.
Finney, Brian. 'Narrative and Narrated Homicides in Martin Amis's *Other People* and *London Fields*.' *Critique* 37(1) (1995): 3–15.
——. *English Fiction since 1984: Narrating a Nation*. Basingstoke: Palgrave Macmillan, 2006.
Fowles, John. *The French Lieutenant's Woman*. 1969. London: Back Bay-Little, Brown, 1998.
Freiburg, Rudolph. 'Julian Barnes.' *Do you Consider Yourself a Postmodern Author? Interviews with Contemporary English Writers*. Ed. Rudolph Freiburg and Jan Schnitker. Munster: Lit Verlag, 1999, 41–66.
Frow, John. *Genre (The New Critical Idiom)*. London: Routledge, 2005.
Frye, Northrop. *The Secular Scripture: A Study of the Structure of Romance*. Cambridge: Harvard University Press, 1976.
Fuller, Graham. 'Murder he Wrote: Martin Amis's Killing Fields.' *Village Voice* (24 April 1990): 75.
Haffenden, John. *Novelists in Interview*. London: Methuen, 1985.
Head, Dominic. *The Cambridge Introduction to Modern British Fiction, 1950–2000*. Cambridge: Cambridge University Press, 2002.

Hutcheon, Linda. *A Poetics of Postmodernism: History, Theory, Fiction*. London: Routledge, 1988.
———. *The Politics of Postmodernism* (*New Accents*). London and New York: Routledge, 1989.
Imlah, Mick. 'A Dart in the Heart.' Rev. of *London Fields*. *Times Literary Supplement* (29 September 1989): 1051–1052.
Johnson, Heather. 'Metafiction, Magical Realism and Myth.' *Angela Carter's Nights at the Circus*. Ed. Helen Stoddart. London and New York: Routledge, 2007, 70–81.
Kotte, Claudia. 'Random Patterns? Orderly Disorder in Julian Barnes's *A History of the World in 10½ Chapters*.' *Arbeitenaus Anglistik und Amerikanistic* 22 (1997): 107–128.
Lyotard, Jean-François. *The Postmodern Condition: A Report on Knowledge*, trans. Geoff Bennington and Brian Massumi (*Theory and History of Literature 10*). Minneapolis: University of Minnesota Press, 1984.
McGrath, Patrick. 'Julian Barnes.' *Bomb* 21 (1987): 20–23.
Nazareth, Peter. 'Rushdie's Wo/Manichean Novel.' *Iowa Review* 20(1) (1990): 168–174.
Nicol, Brian. *D.M. Thomas* (*Writers and Their Work*). Horndon: Northcote, 2004.
Palmer, Paulina. '*The Passion*: Storytelling, Fantasy, Desire.' *'I'm Telling You Stories': Jeanette Winterson and the Politics of Reading*. Ed. Helena Grice and Tim Woods. Amsterdam and Atlanta: Rodopi, 1998, 103–115.
Pykett, Lynn. 'A New Way with Words? Jeanette Winterson's Post-Modernism.' *'I'm Telling You Stories': Jeanette Winterson and the Politics of Reading*. Ed. Helena Grice and Tim Woods. Amsterdam and Atlanta: Rodopi, 1998, 53–60.
Pyrhönen, Heta. 'Genre.' *The Cambridge Companion to Narrative*. Ed. David Herman. Cambridge: Cambridge University Press, 2007, 109–123.
Rubinson, Gregory. *The Fiction of Rushdie, Barnes, Winterson, and Carter: Breaking Cultural and Literary Boundaries in the Work of Four Postmodernists*. London: McFarland, 2005.
Rushdie, Salman. *Imaginary Homelands: Essays and Criticism 1981–1991*. London: Granta in association with Penguin, 1991.
———. *The Satanic Verses*. 1988. Dover and Delaware: The Consortium, 1992.
Sage, Lorna. 'Angela Carter Interviewed by Lorna Sage.' *New Writing*. Ed. Malcolm Bradbury and Judith Cooke. London: Minerva, 1992, 185–192.
———. *Angela Carter* (*Writers and Their Work*). Plymouth: Northcote, 1994.
Sante, Luc. 'Cheat's Tale.' Rev. of *London Fields*. *New Republic* (30 April 1990): 45–46.
Seaboyer, Judith. 'Second Death in Venice: Romanticism and the Compulsion to Repeat in Jeanette Winterson's *The Passion*.' *Contemporary Literature* 38(3) (1997): 483–509.
Swift, Graham. *Waterland*. London: William Heinemann, 1983.
Tew, Philip. 'Wintersonian Masculinities.' *Jeanette Winterson: A Contemporary Critical Guide*. Ed. Sonya Andermahr. London and New York: Continuum, 2007, 114–129.
Thomas, D. M. *The White Hotel*. London: Penguin, 1981.
Tremain, Rose. *Restoration*. 1989. London: Vintage-Random House, 2009.

Wachtel, Eleanor. 'Eleanor Wachtel with Martin Amis: Interview.' *Malahat Review* 114 (1996): 43–58.

Winterson, Jeanette. *The Passion*. 1987. London: Penguin, 1988.

———. *Art Objects: Essays on Ecstasy and Effrontery*. 1995. Toronto: Vintage Canada-Random House, 1996.

Wirth-Nesher, Hana. 'The Ethics of Narration in D.M. Thomas's *The White Hotel*.' *Journal of Narrative Technique* 15(1) (1985): 15–28.

7

International Contexts (North America)
The American Reception of British Fiction in the 1980s

Brian Finney

Following the accession to power of Margaret Thatcher in 1979 and Ronald Reagan in 1980, neo-liberalism rapidly emerged as the dominant ideology of the Anglo-American world. A belief that free markets are the most efficient way of harnessing and managing a country's resources resulted in crucial political and social consequences. A triumphant New Right insisted on deregulation and privatization; they redistributed national wealth to the benefit of the richest sectors of society and removed social safety nets that were designed to protect the less privileged. The liberal left, including many novelists, reviewers and critics, were notably ambivalent about such changes, finding the prescription of individualism and competition unpalatable. The New Right of the 1980s abandoned earlier notions of consensus and social cohesion. Despite their opposition, most British novelists, while rejecting the damage inflicted on communities, individuals and the environment by rampant consumerism, were themselves compromised by the effects of globalization on the book publishing world. After the advent of the Booker Prize, many found themselves in competition for the new large advances offered to star names. Colin Hutchinson argues, 'Ambivalence is the distinguishing feature of the contemporary white male left-liberal', torn between individualism and collectivism (3). Such ambivalence is featured in many Anglo-American novels of the period.

Correspondingly many writers' attitudes towards postmodern culture were deeply ambivalent. In the 1960s, postmodernism was considered the obverse of realism, with influential American novelists such as John Barth, Donald Barthelme, William Gaddis, Thomas Pynchon and Kurt Vonnegut experimenting playfully with representations of time and history, reconsidering notions of subjectivity and toying humorously with language as a determinant of meaning. Malcolm

Bradbury has argued that from the mid-1970s this ludic propensity gave way to various other forms of linguistic and technical playfulness employing strategies constituting what might be considered a tenuous neo-realism. Such a renewed interest is what in *The Modern American Novel* he labels 'an elusive and ironic realism' within history (268). In *The Modern British Novel*, he argues that British fiction shared with American fiction its preference for 'grotesque, experimental, heightened realism' (411). In both countries a sense of impending apocalypse resulted in 'Gothic violence, the uncanny, the fantastic and the grotesque' (411). These shared assumptions brought American reviewers, critics and readers closer to British fiction than had been the case in the 1960s. Nevertheless, continuing differences in length, cultural assumptions and style remained, many of which largely prevented British fiction from rivalling its American counterparts in terms of popularity and sales in the much larger American market, resulting perhaps in a renewed parochialism. In fact, Colin Hutchinson claims additionally that a clear distinction between the fictions produced in each of the two countries can be made based on their different perceptions of class. American writers invested social resistance primarily in the rights of ethnic and other minorities, and in the individual; British writers sought strength in the collective realm, especially in terms of class. So the decade is characterized simultaneously on the one hand by a growing coincidence of socio-political dynamics and fictional styles (partly the consequence of British novelists being drawn to American fictional models), and on the other by a continuing difference in cultural attitudes and formal literary traditions, all part of yet another ambivalent aesthetic dynamic in the British literary scene.

Despite subtle aesthetic changes, by 1980 a consensus had been reached in Britain and abroad that British fiction was mired in mediocrity and insularity. As early as 1970, Bernard Bergonzi was complaining in *The Situation of the Novel* that the British novel 'is truly no longer novel' (23). In *Notes for a New Culture* (published in 1976, but written in 1973 when he was Mellon Fellow at Yale), Peter Ackroyd denounced English fiction for being 'insulated' in 'a false context of realism' (147). Bill Buford quotes Gore Vidal's remark at the Edinburgh Festival of 1979 that in Britain writers produced in the main 'middle class novels for middle class readers with middle class problems' (Buford 1). Buford was a young American writer who had moved to Cambridge as a Marshall scholar, becoming in 1979 editor of the reinvigorated literary magazine *Granta*. As Americans, both Buford and Vidal took for granted the necessity for innovation, diversity and inclusiveness. As Buford saw matters, '[t]he American writer's sense of experiment is largely the consequence of participating in an international dialogue' (5). He goes on to cite such American novelists as John Barth and Gilbert Sorrentino, William Gass, William Gaddis and John Hawkes.

This criticism of British fiction might seem surprising given that Britain had generated its own movement of anti-realist novelists in the 1960s and 1970s, with figures such as B. S. Johnson, Christine Brooke-Rose and Ann Quin, all rejecting literary realism and radicalizing the novel form. Other novelists later associated with 1980s fiction and praised for their break with the older traditions actually made their initial breakthroughs in the 1970s. Angela Carter had published seven novels and two collections of stories before 1980. Ian McEwan published two collections of short stories and his first novel in the late 1970s, just as Martin Amis brought out his first three novels between 1973 and 1978. Why this critical divide generationally? The explanation probably lies in the fact that the vast majority of British fiction published and admired before 1980 was broadly realist, confined largely to British settings and concerns, and the experimentalists were seen as a radical fringe. The rupture with this earlier realist conservatism was not adopted as a perceptible movement until the 1980s, when it was embraced as the new norm by the literary establishment, even though in fact the majority of fiction reviewed during this decade could still loosely be described as realist.

Perhaps significantly Buford's observations appeared in an article published in the third issue of *Granta* (1980) entitled 'The End of the English Novel'. Employing an outsider's insight, he attributes much of the problem afflicting British fiction to the old-fashioned practices of the major British publishers suffering the worst slump for 50 years, blaming them for the insularity of British novels of the 1970s, and pointing out that in 1977 only 486 literary works were translated in Britain, compared to 1186 in France and 3389 in Germany. He insisted that there was no dearth of good writing in Britain. He saw the country 'moving into a different period of creative prose':

> it is characterized by a writing which, freed from the middle-class monologue, is experimentation in the real sense, exploiting traditions and not being wasted by them. The writer today is managing to reassert the act of narration – the telling not simply of fictions but stories – not in deference to the referential workings of bourgeois realism but as an instance of the human imagination. (19)

The focus is no longer on the mimetic substance of the narrative, but rather is on the act of narration itself 'where telling is at the centre of our consciousness' (19). Three years later, issue 7 of *Granta* featured work from the Book Marketing Council's remarkably prescient list of 'Best Twenty Young British Novelists' to watch out for in the future. Buford distinguished these younger novelists from an older generation associated with the previous decade who subscribed to what he called 'that post-war, pre-modern variety of the middle-class monologue, with C. P. Snow on one side and perhaps Margaret Drabble and Melvyn Bragg on the other' (4).

The same year Michiko Kakutani, the new lead critic of the *New York Times*, who was to become the most respected and influential book reviewer in the States, published an article titled 'Novelists Are News Again'. And discerning a new resurgence of British fiction, she announced, 'a new generation of novelists is emerging' (3). That the new novelists being promoted by the British Book Marketing Council were such a disparate group was, she claimed, part of their identity. And these newcomers drew their inspiration from a wide variety of foreign novelists – Nabokov, Bellow, Borges, Gabriel García Márquez, Günter Grass and others. What had changed, she claimed quoting John Gross, was the way publishing in Britain had 'become a mirror image of what you have in America' (22). In particular, she pointed out, 'a measure of American-style hype has ... become attached to the Booker Prize' (3). Worth £10,000 in the 1980s, the Booker Prize became an annual occasion for newspaper celebrity controversy and guaranteed vastly increased sales for the winner of Britain's most valuable fiction prize. At the same time, because the British book market was a quarter the size of that in America, Kakutani argued, 'English authors are really dependent on sales in the States' (22). Her assertion may represent a certain distortion, resulting from her perspective across the Atlantic, but this mention of 'American-style hype' does draw attention to the fact that during the 1980s the pressure on authors to justify publishers' investments in their work became a significant factor in the kind of fiction they produced. In part, such demands may well account for the way many British novelists in the 1980s avoided such extreme avant-garde experimentation that characterized Johnson and Brooke-Rose's generation in favour of various forms of playful, self-conscious neo-realism, as well as widening the focus of their novels to appeal to an international readership. British authors such as the new younger generation of novelists who according to Kakutani (with little evidence presented) 'take on large issues and employ modern experimental techniques ... [do] far better in the States' (22).

Nevertheless, despite the dynamics outlined above, in Britain new novelists spent the 1980s competing for attention with their established predecessors and their breakthroughs were only occasional. The list of Booker Prize winners during this decade features just two of the Book Marketing Council's list of 20 novelists (Rushdie and Ishiguro). More often the prize was awarded to such traditional realist novelists as Penelope Lively for her fiction of memory, *Moon*

Tiger; Anita Brookner for *Hotel du Lac*, a novel of brooding introspection in the realist tradition of Jane Austen; and Kingsley Amis for *The Old Devils*, a comic novel featuring a group of ageing Welsh drinking friends that was likely to have a hard time with American readers, according to *Publishers Weekly*. In America, none of the Booker Prize winners in the 1980s became best-sellers. If you look at the *New York Times Book Review*'s best-seller lists for the 1980s, virtually the only British fiction writers who qualify are the authors of spy novels (especially John Le Carré) and thrillers (Len Deighton, Frederick Forsyth, Jack Higgins). The exception is Salman Rushdie's *The Satanic Verses*, which came sixth among hardback fiction best-sellers for 1989 according to *Publishers Weekly*. While Le Carré's success in the States can be largely attributed to his dramatization of the Cold War, *The Satanic Verses* was given unintended international press coverage following riots in the Muslim world and the fatwa (death sentence) issued by Iran's Spiritual Leader Ayatollah Khomeini. Yet in the US among the best-sellers in hardback fiction for the decade one can find such classic American novels as John Irving's *The Hotel New Hampshire* (second in 1981), Gore Vidal's *Lincoln* (fourth in 1984) and Tom Wolfe's *The Bonfire of the Vanities* (second in 1988). Despite the move towards a more global perspective and admiration for American fiction among the newer British novelists, most of them were not competing for the great (American) novel, the British continuing to write novels of only 200–300 pages.

***

One British novel acts as a marker for the start of the new decade, incorporating some of the new directions that British novelists of the 1980s would take. This is Salman Rushdie's *Midnight's Children*, which was published in early March 1981 in the States and later in Britain in April 1981 due to a dock workers' strike. In the *New York Times* review section, John Leonard announced, 'We have an epic on our hands... Mr. Rushdie gives us history, politics, myth, food, magic, wit and dung' (21). For a start the text has many of the features characteristically associated with the American literary novel, being over 500 pages long and equally ambitious in scope, international in its subject matter, linguistically inventive and overtly political. Concerning the last feature, Rushdie claimed at the time, as quoted in Kakutani, that 'In England, there's a sense that literature is diminished by politics, or at least that's been true' (23). It is interesting that another *New York Times* reviewer of the novel, Towers, found that it 'suggests John Barth's *Letters* (though it has none of the emotional aridity which... impairs that prodigious work)' (30). Here is concrete evidence for Malcolm Bradbury's assertion that the experimental, anti-realist novels of the 1970s were superseded by the more accessible neo-realist novels of the 1980s. In an interview Rushdie justified his neo-realist stance to Wajsbrot by asserting, 'realism can no longer express or account for the absurd reality of the world we live in' (22). Sales in Britain and America were slow at first. After winning that year's Booker Prize, however, sales climbed to over 20,000 hardback copies in Britain and 7,000 in the US, both still small change by American standards. The novel went on to win the Booker of Bookers Prize in 1993 (for the best book in 25 years) and again in 2008 (for the best book in 40 years), and, according to Ion Trewin in a letter in *The Bookseller*, by 2010 Rushdie's book had sold over a million copies, illustrating the growing influence this novel had over time.

What is it about *Midnight's Children* that made many US reviewers instantly acclaim it as an important new departure? For a start, it is written from the perspective of a migrant writer, one who feels he is 'both inside and outside' two cultures, Indian and British. His ability to combine the British literary sensibility with that (so different) of the Indian subcontinent gave him what he calls 'stereoscopic vision' in an interview with Reder (5). Rushdie has written that, writing as a migrant, his novel comes closer to the American tradition of fiction which he describes in *Imaginary Homelands*:

> America, a nation of immigrants, has created a great literature out of the phenomenon of cultural transplantation ... it may be that by discovering what we have in common with those who preceded us into this country, we can begin to do the same. (20)

Rushdie's global viewpoint, as Frank explains, 'is one reason why the novel has come to represent a new phenomenon in literary history and to foretell the destabilization, or maybe even the decreasing relevance, of the concept of national literature' (190). Among American reviewers, Chaudhuri called it 'a novel of international importance' (533), and Towers 'one of the most important [novels] to come out of the English-speaking world in this generation' (28). Rushdie told *Publishers Weekly* in an interview with Amanda Smith that the high praise given to the novel by American critics, who unusually had a first shot at reviewing the novel, helped produce a similarly favourable reaction in the British press, which had recently rubbished another neo-realist novel, D. M. Thomas's *The White Hotel*, only to be contradicted by near-universal approval from American reviewers (49). Rushdie's work is not simply another British novel about a foreign country, but one in which, as Saleem, the novel's protagonist, says, 'Europe repeats itself in India, as farce' (212). Rushdie has described the novel to Reder as a 'comic epic', complete with a visit to the underworld (37). But it is so many other things as well. It is a *Bildungsroman* that undoes itself by revealing after 130 pages that Saleem is not the son of the family whose history has been the exclusive subject of the book to that point. It is also encyclopaedic in its indebtedness to such other genres as the magic realist novel, the picaresque, science fiction, the family saga and the historical novel combined with satire, to mention the most obvious.

Its dazzling combination of Eastern and Western narratives offered a model of a new direction in which the British novel could travel. American critics and reviewers repeatedly cited Günter Grass's *The Tin Drum* and Gabriel García Márquez's *One Hundred Years of Solitude* as significant intertexts, while cautioning, as did the *New York Times* book reviewer Blaise, 'This is a book to accept on its own terms, and an author to welcome into world company' (1). Rushdie countered by pointing to the *Mahabharata* and *One Thousand and One Nights* as equally important literary predecessors. The ways in which the latter two books are organized and narrated owe much to the tradition of oral narrative, one already cultivated by some African American writers and one to which Rushdie has expressed an explicit debt. While Rushdie's immediate debt is to the oral tradition in Indian and Arabic literature, Americans' growing appreciation of the African American oral tradition being successfully employed at this time by Alice Walker and Toni Morrison among others made them particularly receptive to *Midnight's Children*. To Reder, Rushdie has said that it is a very eclectic form, not at all linear: 'it goes in great loops and circles back on itself, repeats earlier things, digresses... It seems formless' (76). But it is not. Thousands of years old, the oral tradition is determined by the need for the storyteller to hold his audience. In the same interview, Rushdie defined the structure of the oral narrative as 'a multitude of stories... through which one picked one narrative path' (37). Strangely, Rushdie explained to Reder, he found that by reverting to this ancient tradition of narration, he was simultaneously being postmodern by having his narrator enter his story and comment metafictionally on it (59).

To assist his appropriation of the oral tradition in a written narrative, Rushdie further internalized his audience in the person of Padma, Saleem's one-time nurse. Her lack of education and low social status (the name literally means *dung*) make her the ideal auditor – literal minded, easily distracted or bored, impatient to learn the outcome of the plot. At one point, Saleem states: 'But here is Padma at my elbow, bullying me back into the world of linear narrative, the universe of what-happened-next' (37). But, he continues, her very impatience tells him that she is hooked. You might say that Rushdie has incorporated the success of his oral method of narration within his narrative. In *Salman Rushdie and the Third World* (1989), Timothy Brennan, an American academic, criticized Padma's role as auditor on the grounds that she 'is, aesthetically speaking... an image of the Indian masses' gullibility – a translation of her readerly naiveté into social terms' (105). Brennan typifies the American academy's need to politicize *Midnight's Children*, to turn it into a multicultural text. As Anthony Alessandrini has pointed out, American academics have been driven by a larger agenda into treating the novel as a representation of modern India in its entirety: '*Midnight's Children* has been placed, like Saleem himself, in the position of "national representative" in spite of the fact that Rushdie's novel succeeds so magnificently in fracturing the whole idea of a single national identity'. Or, as Arun Mukherjee laments, American liberal-humanist critics have explicated it 'in terms of the time-honored East–West dualism (*Midnight's Children* as an Indian novel)' (111). While Roger Clark in *Stranger Gods* (2001) has reminded everyone that one of Padma's important roles is to persuade the novel's readers of the possibility of believing in the non-material world of omens, dreams and sorcery (78), the widespread tendency to focus exclusively on the novel's portrayal of national identity offers proof of the politicized pressures bearing down on American critics and academics.

Rushdie's resort to the oral narrative is very similar to what Leslie Fiedler called on American novelists to do in a 1975 essay, that is to return to writing novels that were 'popular, not quite reputable, a little dangerous' (349). American novelists such as Robert Stone, Kurt Vonnegut, John Irving and Richard Brautigan had already been drawing on other popular genres prior to the publication of *Midnight's Children*. India, as Rushdie has pointed out, has over 15 major languages. In the course of celebrating India's plurality of languages in the novel, Rushdie is simultaneously exposing the limitations of the unitary language of nationalism, political authoritarianism and the colonial mindset. The novel's description of the excitement as well as the confusion accompanying the birth of a nation naturally appealed to American readers, who could not help seeing parallels between the founding of India and that of the United States. *Midnight's Children* became a major postcolonial text. But it insists on adopting a complex, multiple response to India's (and Saleem's) mixed genetic inheritance. As a bastard child fathered by a representative of the British Empire, Saleem parallels the way Rushdie described Indian writing in English in a talk at Amherst College on 4 April 1997 as the 'Empire's bastard child'. Rushdie's pluralistic style constitutes another defining feature of many British novels of the 1980s.

The year after *Midnight's Children*, Rushdie published an article in the London *Times*, 'The Empire Writes Back with a Vengeance'. There he claimed, 'English, no longer an English language, now grows from many roots; and those whom it once colonized are carving out large territories within the language for themselves. The Empire is striking back' (8). Rushdie further undermines any idea that the Empire is homogeneous, like the centre against which it is rebelling. He talks of 'the new English literatures' in the plural. In offering a bewildering variety of voices, *Midnight's Children* offered a compelling model for his literary contemporaries. A decade later, an American academic critic, Samir Dayal, was citing *Midnight's Children's* 'self-reflexive and organic "english"' as a leading instance of a typical 'postcolonial gesture of reappropriation of the former colonizer's language' (433). For American academics, the novel had become a leading instance of postcolonialism's resistance to imperialist hegemony and a canonical postcolonial text in American academic syllabi.

It is his multi-voicedness that gives Rushdie's work its unique appeal, its sense of being less postcolonial than supranational or global. Seen together, Rushdie's non-linear narration, his use of fragmented episodes to lure the reader into the construction of the narrative, his use of a fallible narrator, his mixture of historical fact and fantasy, his insistence on a plurality of viewpoints and interpretations and his manipulation of the English language to embody his supranationalist, centrifugal outlook made this novel a seedbed for British fiction succeeding it during the 1980s. Nevertheless, the highly innovatory nature of *Midnight's Children* and its alien cultural context led to initially tepid sales in the United States. As one admiring reviewer of *Midnight's Children* in the *New York Review of Books*, Towers, wrote, 'I doubt that it will reach a very wide audience in this country ... it cannot be gulped down'. Yet he was prescient enough to predict, 'The book will gain ground slowly but, I believe, inevitably'.

***

In 2010, in a *New York Times* book review, Chotiner wrote that since the publication of *Midnight's Children* 'the American appetite for Indian culture has only grown' (35). He was referring to the success of novels by Vikram Seth, Arundhati Roy, Kiran Desai and Jhumpa Lahiri. But the impact of Rushdie's novel extended much further. At least one or more of its features contributed to its role as a trendsetter for important British novels appearing in the 1980s and beyond. Its embrace of a multinational perspective informs Kazuo Ishiguro's first two novels, *A Pale View of the Hills* (1982) and *An Artist of the Floating World* (1986), as well as Timothy Mo's *The Monkey King* (1980), *Sour Sweet* (1982) and

An Insular Possession (1986). Rushdie's use of magic realism to give equal status to material and imaginative worlds had already been employed by Angela Carter in her 1970s fiction and was again employed in *Nights at the Circus* (1984), which combined the fantastic with a feminist theme, just as Jeanette Winterson did in *The Passion* (1987) and *Sexing the Cherry* (1989). Rushdie's foregrounding of the overtly political in the fictional resurfaces in Martin Amis's *Money* (1984) and Ian McEwan's *The Child in Time* (1987). Finally, in a postmodern age, fragmentation (including Saleem's fissured body) and non-linear narration, such as what Rushdie employs, represent a new direction, or at least a renewed emphasis on new and differing kinds of ambivalence characteristic of younger novelists of the 1980s who in various ways reject a traditional realist aesthetics while sustaining a renewed sense of historical reality.

Angela Carter's *Nights at the Circus* clearly incorporates more than one of the above features. In her *New York Times* review, Kakutani referred to Carter's 'gift for enchantment' (magic realism) and her metafictional discussion of storytelling 'so dear to practitioners of the nouveau roman' (17). In the *Washington Post*, Carolyn Banks focused on Carter's innovative use of language, 'a luscious and gooey dessert ... doled out in sinful proportions' (1). Most American reviewers, however, initially read the book as 'an ebullient tall tale' in the *Los Angeles Times*, 'good fun' in the *San Francisco Chronicle*, 'loud, bawdy, and unabashedly sentimental' in the *New York Times* or 'a three-ring extravaganza' in *Time*. No American reviewer at the time hailed the novel as the classic it was to become. Kakutani suggested that as the novel progresses, the 'narrative gradually loses both its focus and its drive' (17). A month later, Carolyn See, also reviewing the novel for the *New York Times*, agreed that by the third section 'it's hard not to get queasy'.

In 1987, Paulina Palmer distinguished between Carter's earlier work (up to 1978), which she characterized as 'analytic' and 'demythologising', and her later work, which she described as 'celebratory and utopian' (179–180). Two years after Carter's death, Marina Warner drew a similar distinction between Carter's earlier work up to *The Bloody Chamber* (1979) and her later work from *Nights at the Circus* onwards. She discerned a palpable shift from 'a gorgeous, phantasmagoric eloquence of excess and voluptuousness, rooted in the work of the Symbolists ... to a particularly British savoury brand of bawdy' (246–247). Maybe this specifically British characteristic helps explain why initial American responses were half-hearted. Carter opens fantastically with a Cockney protagonist, Fevvers, who wasn't born but hatched out of an egg, so avoiding any known parentage. Born at the turn of the twentieth century, 'the New Age in which no woman will be bound to the ground' (25), she is raised in an all-women's society (a brothel) and grows wings during her adolescence. As such, she is representative of the new liberated woman whose wings help her to escape the nets of nineteenth-century patriarchy. Or rather, she imagines herself as such a prototype, while continuing to harbour dreams of marriage, although a marriage that entails a new equality between man and woman.

Helen Stoddart differentiates the responses of reviewers from those of critics: 'while journalistic comment...frequently accented the novel's stylistic density and excess, conversely, academic criticism drew attention to its relative lightness compared to Carter's previous work' (46). Academic critics may have stressed the novel's playfulness, but most did it in a heavy-handed fashion. Even before Carter's death, American and British academic critics had seized on the novel as exemplifying many of the characteristics of the newly fashionable theories of post-structuralism and postmodernism. In one wholly negative instance, after publishing her book on *The Sadeian Woman* in 1979, Carter had been attacked by Andrea Dworkin in America and by Susanne Kappeler in Britain for defending (as they saw it) 'Sade's pornographic assault on one particular patriarchal representation of woman – the Mother' (134). Both critics misunderstood her radical reinterpretation of the Marquis de Sade as a writer who understood the way sex had been politicized in his day. In 1991, two American critics, Robin Ann Sheets and Carol Siegel, repudiated Dworkin's charge that Carter 'verges dangerously close to pornography' by interpreting *The Bloody Chamber* and *Nights at the Circus* respectively through a closer reading of *The Sadeian Woman* (10–11).

English critics responded to Carter in the late 1980s, with Paulina Palmer's 1987 essay setting the tone. Employing a predominantly feminist approach, she privileges 'acts of resistance against patriarchy' (180), reading the protagonist Fevvers's precarious flights through the air as 'predominantly an image of liberation' (199), when they may represent, as Finney has argued, just as much an image of the precarious balancing act in the performance of narration (164). Fevvers turns out to be another teller of tall tales, like Saleem, and it is her narrative skill that enables her to capture a husband at the end of the book by narrating him into a subject position of her choosing. By 1993, the year after her death, one eminent American critic Kendrick declared confidently, 'Carter has lately joined the canon' (67).

Both British and American critics of *Nights at the Circus* share certain similar theoretical concerns, with feminine subjectivity, and with postmodern play, magic realism and the carnivalesque. However, British feminists tended at first to adopt a more Marxist approach (embodied by Lizzie in the novel), while American feminists adopted from the start a more thoroughgoing post-structuralist stance. Thus by the early 1990s one finds three American critics refining earlier interpretations by stressing various forms of post-structuralist ambivalence and semantic seepage. Sally Robinson shows how Fevvers, by turning her gaze on herself as well as on Walser, 'does not simply reverse masculine and feminine positions...; rather, [her act] also works to displace this gendered opposition' by using 'both/and logic' (123). In 1994 Joanne Gass drew on Foucault in her essay 'Panopticism at the Circus' to show how Walser attempts to adopt an all-seeing and objectifying position in the novel. But Fevvers has wings that let her escape the male gaze. The same year, American critic Magali Michael argued that *Nights at the Circus* used 'disruptive strategies' to incorporate two strands of feminism, 'an engaged Marxist feminism and a subversive utopian feminism' (493), what she later calls 'postmodern feminism' (492). Although she has difficulty reconciling the two feminisms, Michael represents the point at which both have entered a dialogue, ending any distinguishable difference between the two national responses to the novel. From the mid-1990s on, two critics – American Shirley Peterson and British Anne Fernihough, respectively – co-opt such recent approaches as queer theory and the work of Judith Butler to question whether Carter's unusual feminist stance does not 'freak out' feminists of the 1960s and 1970s, who assumed according to Peterson a form of 'normative femininity' (293). Critical reaction to the novel on both sides of the Atlantic has converged by concentrating on the various ways in which Carter has employed neo-realism to avoid the simplicities and essentialisms of first-wave feminist interpretations.

***

Carter wrote in *Shaking a Leg*, 'Like most Europeans of my generation, I have North America in my bloodstream... But it was the movies that administered America to me intravenously... Hollywood had colonized the imagination of the entire world' (607). Martin Amis, who, like Carter, spent periods of time in America (his tenth year and summers starting in 1980), and both of whose wives were from the Americas, made transatlantic experience a major theme of *Money: A Suicide Note* (1984), a novel that Ian Hamilton forecast would be 'one of the key books of the decade' (4). The novel, told in the first person by John Self, a highly fallible narrator, alternates chapters set in London and New York. Self's mother is American, his father English, and he was shipped off to America when he was 7, remaining there until he was 15. Both cities become interchangeable centres of rampant capitalist greed, epitomes of an uncompassionate Thatcherism and a deficit-spending Reaganism. When interviewed by Stout, Amis said he wrote partly out of a conviction that 'the money age we're living through now is a short-term, futureless kind of prosperity... Civility, civilization is falling apart' (36). American critic James Diedrick has called Self's narrative 'an extended hangover following the "Me" decade' (247). As Will Self remarked, with *Money* Amis 'seemed to go global' (73). Subsequently, a new generation of British novelists, among whom Amis was prominent, as Ishiguro summed up – when quoted by Wilson – no longer assumed that 'British values and British society were de facto of international importance... Somehow, British culture had become peripheral to the big themes of the time... The front line was somewhere else' (100–101). Despite favourable reviews, it took time for Amis's *Money* to become popular and sell well in the United States. But by 2005 *Money* was included by Grossman and Lacayo in *Time* magazine's '100 best English-language novels from 1923 to the present' (1).

Amis situates *Money* both politically and historically at the start of the decade in 1981, with references to the royal wedding of Charles and Diana, the inner-city riots in England that year and the Polish military action against Solidarity, all symbolic reminders of the new political climate emerging in the 1980s. Both London and New York show signs of neglect and decay. There is '[b]lasted, totalled, broken-winded, shot-faced London, doing time under sodden skies' (150), while Self reflects, 'Heat, money, sex and fever – this is it, this is New York' (51). At the root of this decline lies the triumph of money values, which Amis holds responsible for having, as he explained in an interview by Morrison, 'turned paradise into a toilet' (102). Early in his life Amis had developed a strong conviction (shared with many other writers of the time, such as Saul Bellow, whom he admired) that the modern world had taken a catastrophic turn for the worse. He has said, for instance when interviewed by Basel, that since 1945: 'we can unmake the world. Extinction is a possibility' (22). In a universe dying from our abuses, humans (and their fictional counterparts) show their connection to it by staging their own figurative deaths – and Self's is not just figurative as he plans to commit suicide.

Amis explicitly connects his negative view of global modernity to his rejection of literary realism. As 'Martin Amis', his fictional avatar in the novel explains to an uncomprehending Self, 'we're pretty much agreed that the twentieth century is an ironic age – downward-looking. Even realism, rockbottom realism, is considered a bit grand for the twentieth century' (231). Amis has stated when interviewed by Stout that he is in full flight from 'the typical English novel... 225 sanitized pages about the middle classes' (35). He shares with Rushdie and

Carter a belief that the only appropriate literary response to the West of the 1980s is a form of black, sardonic comedy. The comedy is darkened by the tragic nature of the times that are nevertheless unworthy of a tragic rendering. As Amis explained in his interview with Morrison, this is why he employs a 'sort of hung-over laughter, where it hurts' (96). His consequent rejection of traditional realism leads him to create characters that, as one American critic Hawkes has remarked, 'are extremely lifelike without being fully human' (27). This is intentional on Amis's part. He thinks that 'motivation has actually been exaggerated in, and by, the novel'. According to Haffenden, for Amis motivation 'has become a depleted, a shagged-out force in modern life' (5). 'Martin Amis' in the novel repeats this conviction, explaining: 'It hasn't got what it takes to motivate people any more' (331). For Amis's generation, lack of motivation (random violence, for instance) is the outcome of a civilization bent on its own destruction, and calls for correspondingly neo-realist narrative responses.

What effect does this have on his portrayal of subjectivity? As John Gross noted in the *New York Times*, a character like Self 'doesn't hang together' because 'he has only one foot in the real world anyway' (25). Belonging to a darkly comic fictional world, Amis's characters border on caricature, primarily serving fictional imperatives, not evoking real people. Self is, as Amis has explained to Haffenden, 'consumed by consumerism', brought up on a diet of television that he mistakes for real life (7). As Jonathan Yardley noted in the *Washington Post*, 'In the fast-track world of the late 20th century, John Self is Everyman: perpetrator and victim, exploiter and exploited, cynic and naif' (3). Almost as much American as British he is the novel's fall guy, someone who thinks he is writing his own life's script when it is being written for him by others, above all by the author.

It may be thought anomalous that this novel by Amis, himself drawn to America and heavily influenced by American novelists, should have received so much praise from American reviewers, given that it satirizes the degrading effects that American money values have on its notionally English protagonist. Norman Snider, a Canadian reviewer of *Money*, offered a credible explanation, if one is needed seeing how many American novelists themselves spent time satirizing the effects of rampant capitalism on the American psyche. Snider pointed out, 'Just as the ex-patriot American in search of European culture was a typical social type of the late nineteenth century [he mentions Henry James and Ernest Hemingway], the Brit in search of a buck in North America is characteristic of the late twentieth'. He concludes that *Money* 'represents the complete victory of the American novel over the British, after 300 years of cultural influence going the other way'. However contentious this opinion is, the reversal of cultural supremacy seems factual enough. Amis indirectly supported such a view when he told Stephanie Mansfield, a *Washington Post* staff writer, that the reason the book received better notices in the United States than in Britain was that John Self is 'the first transatlantic hero that Americans don't at all feel inferior to' (K1). As Sheppard says in a review in *Time*, Self 'is always a step behind his Yankee associates. He ... doesn't live on the sharp end.'

Self is a creature of the late twentieth century. He is both cretinized by television and pornography, and he lacks autonomy as a subject, a feature commonly found in the new fiction of the 1980s. Just as Saleem complains that he is 'the sort of person *to whom things have been done*' (272), so Self confesses: 'Sometimes I think I am controlled by someone' (305). Self similarly resembles Saleem in remaining a 'perennial victim' who 'persists in seeing himself as protagonist' (272). As such he typifies many 1980s protagonists. Fevvers too loses agency when she loses her feathers and her wings and is taken captive by Russian rebels. So does Stevens in *The Remains of the Day*, and many others. Self is fooled by Selina, his unfaithful girlfriend in England, and by Fielding Goodney, the American producer who lures Self to the States to make a film financed – unknowingly – by Self himself. Selina acts out Self's pornographic fantasies to support herself until she can find a wealthier long-term partner. Goodney resembles Shakespeare's Iago with his seemingly motiveless malignancy. He commissions a screenplay (already a staged form of reality) he knows will turn off the egocentric actors he has cast for the planned film. Amis comes closest to satire in portraying Hollywood stars whom he indicates are second-rate or has-beens. Three of them are modelled on actors whom Amis met in Los Angeles when doing rewrites for the screenplay of *Saturn 3* in 1980: Kirk Douglas, Harvey Keitel and Farah Fawcett. But Self turns the tables on Goodney by hiring the character 'Martin Amis' to rewrite the screenplay in such a way that the actors' fantasies are indulged while exposing their pretensions – the triumph of one form of representation (neo-realist) over another (realist).

Amis plays fast and loose not just with fictional character but also with plot and form. Amis in an interview with Francesca Riviere in *Paris Review* described this book as 'essentially a plotless novel. It is what I would call a *voice* novel' (N.pag.). Yet it is stylistically ebullient, and as Carlos Silva Campañón comments, 'Everything we perceive in the book, we perceive through John Self's arresting, energetic monologue' (89). And as Amis says in *The War against Cliché*, like many of his contemporaries, he has 'always believed in the indivisibility of form and content' (114). Self, who at the opening of the novel announces, 'Recently my life has taken on form' (9), ends up in the italicized final chapter as an author who has escaped his own suicidal narrative, leaving him formless. According to the interview with Haffenden, the plot of *Money*, such as it is, amounts to what Amis called 'a totally unexplained confidence trick' (6). As he told Veronica Geng, who reviewed *Money* for the *New York Times*, 'I wanted to get away from a tight structure and worries about form and proportion and let the language carry me along... What I've tried to do is create a high style to describe low things' (36). Amis chose to distinguish between the style he used when Self spoke to others (colloquial, debased) and that he employed to represent Self's inner thoughts (literate, articulate). To Haffenden, he expressed his indebtedness for this distinction to Saul Bellow, one of the two American novelists he most admired: 'I learned from Saul Bellow's *Henderson the Rain King* that you can have a great dolt of a character who says completely realistic things like, "Thanks, Prince. I wish you all kinds of luck with your rain ceremony...," after a beautifully complicated paragraph about all his warring responses and yearnings' (8). This enables Self simultaneously to say, 'I live like an animal' (257), while referring to his metamorphosis and wiggling his legs in the air (312), totally unconscious of the allusions to Kafka's story *Metamorphosis*. While a few British critics found Self's dual forms of language confusing or what Faulks labels as 'too intrusive' (15), American critics and readers, perhaps acclimatized to the convention by Bellow and Nabokov, appear not to have any difficulty with this aspect of the novel.

Self's colloquial speech earned the praise of most American reviewers, among whom Geng concluded, 'One theme of *Money* is rich and impoverished language' (36). According to Geng, Michael Billington noted in the *New York Times* that the influence of Nabokov, the other novelist of what Amis called in *Experience* his 'twin peaks' (119n), 'can be felt in the book's sheer delight in language' (36). The importance of language in the construction of subjectivity is a commonplace of post-structuralism. Amis is more articulate than many of his contemporaries about the importance of style. But his explanation in *The War against Cliché* of why it is so important offers an insight into the writings of many of these new writers of the 1980s: 'the more superbly an author throws away the crutches of verisimilitude, the more heavily he must lean on his own style and wit' (95). Style for Amis is a matter of morality: 'all writing is a campaign against cliché. Not just clichés of the pen but clichés of the mind and clichés of the heart' (xv). He concurs with Nabokov, who 'regarded cliché as the key to bad art' (245). Amis uses Nabokov's ludic playfulness, while drawing on Bellow's use of the high style in Self's inner musings. By 1993, two American critics were both characterizing *Money* as in effect neo-realist. Amy Elias argues that Amis's novels problematize reality itself, 'blurring the boundaries between the experiential "real" and media representation or recreation' (20). Catherine Bernard reaches a similar conclusion by arguing that *Money* and *London Fields* 'rely on a rhetoric of excess, on the systematization of a mode of representation the distortion of which ultimately proves to bear a new and disconcerting relevance to the real' (137).

When interviewed by McGrath, Amis has said that *Money* upends the tradition of a Pooterish Englishman who goes abroad because '(a) John Self is half American, and (b) as a consequence cannot be scandalized by America' (187). American reviewers were quick to hail a new voice that owed, as *Time*'s reviewer Sheppard wrote, 'much of its drive to contemporary American fiction'. He went on to suggest that Amis 'learned his heightened personal voice from Saul Bellow, the humorous use of inverted logic from Joseph Heller and his naughty bits from Philip Roth'. Self's unique voice, with its two registers of streetwise slang and segments of articulate self-reflection, is what holds this novel together, not plot or form. Amis's debt to especially Nabokov and Bellow helped to ensure the immediate, enthusiastic reception of this book in the States. At the same time, reviewers in Britain and America recognized Amis's style as uniquely his own, one that had already in 1980 attracted an imitator or rather plagiarist in the American novelist Jacob Epstein.

***

Malcolm Bradbury has written in *The Modern British Novel*, 'The British fiction of the Eighties felt less like the writing of a common culture than of a multiplying body of cultures...extending and varying the prevailing notion of what the British novel might be' (415). I only have time to consider briefly the way this break with the past affected one newly popularized genre – historical fiction – which can stand for the multiplicity of ways in which British fiction reached out to new cultures and new forms of representation. In America the historical novel was a popular genre for most of the century. Writing in 1995 Dean Rehberger wrote, 'Each year since 1920, several historical novels have been among the top ten best sellers, making the genre one of the most popular in America' (59). What has come to be called the 'new historical fiction' came to life after the publication of John Fowles's innovative *The French Lieutenant's Woman* (1969). This new sub-genre, according to Suzanne Keen, 'emphasizes postmodern uncertainties in experimental styles, tells stories about the past that point to multiple truths or the overturning of an old received Truth, mixes genres, and adopts a parodic or irreverently playful attitude to history over an ostensibly normative mimesis' (171). In the 1970s, Robert Coover's *The Public Burning* (1977) and E. L. Doctorow's *The Book of Daniel* (1971) and *Ragtime* (1975) adopted a similarly neo-realist attitude to history and fiction, treating both equally as forms of narrative. If one looks at the novels published by Amis's generation in the last three years of the 1980s, there is a noticeably large number of novels that deal with the past in a self-reflective and ironic manner, notably: Peter Ackroyd's *Chatterton* (1987); Jeanette Winterson's *The Passion* (1987) and *Sexing the Cherry* (1989); Salman Rushdie's *The Satanic Verses* (1988); Graham Swift's *Waterland* (1983) and *Out of This World* (1988); Julian Barnes's *Flaubert's Parrot* (1984) and *A History of the World in 10½ Chapters* (1989); William Boyd's *An Ice-Cream War* (1984) and *The New Confessions* (1988); and Kazuo Ishiguro's *The Remains of the Day* (1989).

In the following sections, I will concentrate my remarks on *A History of the World in 10½ Chapters* and *The Satanic Verses*. Both novels interrogate the accessibility of the past, the 'pastness' of the past, various narrative reshapings of the past and the power the past exerts on the present. Julian Barnes's *A History of the World in 10½ Chapters* received wide attention from American critics on its publication in 1989. Most American reviewers had difficulty understanding the ironic handling of history in what Oates called 'a gathering of prose pieces' (12), and Adams 'a novel in deep disguise'. Barnes's use of indirection and parody to debunk the positivist assertions of history left American reviewers uncomfortable, complaining either that, as Walton says, its various narratives 'just don't happen to mesh together in any exciting or memorable way' (6D), or, according to Walters, that they constitute 'not a "seeming" collage but a real one' (8). Alternatively they charged that the book couldn't be called what Adams describes as a 'good yarn', mainly because it lacks emotional charge, being written 'at a temperature not far from zero centigrade'. Perhaps Barnes's intellectual playfulness seemed to American reviewers too much like that of the 'failed' experiments of American writers of the 1960s such as Gaddis, Barth and Barthelme. Or maybe they missed the degree of irony Barnes employed. Later American critics reversed this verdict. Gregory Salyer concluded a 1991 review article of Barnes's book: 'Umberto Eco has said that it may be that the only way to speak seriously to the world today is with irony. If he is right, Julian Barnes is one of the most serious authors writing today' (32–33).

One reviewer who demonstrated his understanding of what Barnes attempts in this novel was the *New York Times*' Michiko Kakutani. Fastening on the book's definition of the history of the world as 'strange links, impertinent connections'

(240), she argues that the book's collage of various kinds of narrative is 'tangentially linked by repeated images, phrases and preoccupations' (33). The motif she pursues through the book's chapters is that of Noah's Ark, introduced in the first chapter in which a woodworm (an outcast from the Ark and from official history) offers a cynical version of the story of the Flood. Although she sees the numerous reappearances of Noah's Ark in subsequent chapters as instances of 'the cruelty of selection' (33) – of only selected pairs of animals – the truly impertinent connection lies in the recurrence of this image as a representation of the way humans seek shelter from the storms of life in a vessel that they invariably manage to turn into a prison ship for the unfortunate half. Other chapters recount the hijacking of an *Achille Lauro*-type cruise ship on which passengers are sorted into the clean and unclean (just as the animals were in Noah's Ark) and the shameful episode of the *St Louis*, where a boatful of Jewish emigrants fleeing Hitler's persecution in 1939 are subsequently refused entry by many of the world's free countries, including the United States. Kakutani comprehends Barnes's treatment of history as fabulation, the narrative of the conqueror: 'History, he suggests does not exist in itself; it is up to us to find the pattern in the carpet, the designs that give the illusion of order in a random universe' (33). Nevertheless, even Kakutani was put off by what she saw as 'a hodgepodge of non sequiturs', and concluded, 'the sum is smaller, not greater, than its parts' (33). By contrast, Salman Rushdie in his review of the book published in *Imaginary Homelands* claimed that what Barnes was attempting was 'the novel as footnote to history, as subversion of the given...fiction as critique' (241). Rushdie and Barnes share a similar distrust of history and fictionalize it accordingly.

The Satanic Verses simultaneously re-situates the origins of Islam in its historical context while undermining any claims to historical objectivity, mainly by narrating the past in the form of dreams or nightmares belonging to a psychotic Indian movie star who imagines that he is the Archangel Gabriel or Gibreel. The novel caused outrage in large segments of the Muslim community (most of whom, however, appear not to have read it), especially angering clerics who had paradoxically turned the accidents of history into a timeless origin for their religion, and a figure of history into a figure of divinity (despite Mohammad's insistence that he was simply a messenger of God's word). Rushdie, who had studied history, particularly Islamic history, as an undergraduate at Cambridge, added fuel to the fire by drawing on two disputed historical sources to recount Mohammad's supposed compromise with the polytheism of the time. Mohammad (or Mahound, as he is called derogatively in the novel) is induced first to admit three pagan female deities of the Meccans into the Muslim religion as intercessors, only to retract the verses as dictated by Satan and to substitute one in favour of unalloyed monotheism. Through Gibreel Rushdie seeks to historicize and relativize – by psychologizing – the timeless absolutism of the supposedly uncreated word of God.

Rushdie uses his second protagonist, Chamcha, an Indian voice-over actor, to expose the same absolutism in the racist policies of Margaret Thatcher, whose call for a return to Victorian values demonstrated, Rushdie wrote in *Imaginary Homelands*, that she, like the followers of Mohammad, 'had embarked upon a heroic battle against the linear passage of Time' (92). The so-called 'realist' chapters offer what D. J. Enright in the *New York Review of Books* called 'a decade's headlines' of news that concentrate in particular on a new Britain where immigrants have changed the very nature of British society. Rushdie opposes the unitary discourses of religion and imperialism with the pluralistic, competing languages of the novel. He uses history to undermine the timeless narratives of religion and politics, only to expose the fact that history is itself just another form of narrative. While the modern history of post-imperial Britain is told in the more so-called 'realist' chapters and the distant history of the founding of Islam is framed in alternating chapters recounting the hallucinatory dreams of a psychotic, half way through the novel Gibreel realizes that 'the world of dreams was leaking into that of the waking hours, that the seals dividing the two were breaking, and that at any moment the two firmaments could be joined' (304). Here, Rushdie has engineered the collapse of historical into fictional narrative.

Hardly surprisingly, *The Satanic Verses* offended those who cultivated the absolute certainties of religion and neo-colonialism. What is called the Rushdie Affair is better known than the novel itself. The reality that overtook Rushdie after the publication of *The Satanic Verses* proved almost as bizarre as the events described in the novel. In America, after the proclamation of Ayatollah Khomeini's fatwa, Walden Books, B. Dalton and Barnes & Noble book chains withdrew the book from their shelves, two Berkeley bookstores carrying the novel were firebombed, and ex-President Jimmy Carter, the Archbishop of New York and Yusuf Islam (formerly Cat Stevens) condemned the book as inflammatory. Writers hit back with public readings of Rushdie's work in Manhattan and elsewhere. The furore over the novel's publication ironically ensured it best-seller status. By May 1989, Viking had sold over 750,000 hardback copies in the States alone.

American critics compared its author to Thomas Pynchon and John Barth, as well as such internationally celebrated writers as Gabriel García Márquez,

Günter Grass and Italo Calvino (Mojtabai 3). Like these writers, Rushdie resorts to a non-realist mode of narration as the only way he can provide the reader with, as Michiko Kakutani wrote in the *New York Times*, 'a sense of just how fantastic recent history has become' (30). Kakutani offers an interesting explanation of why versions of magic realism came to be adopted by writers such as Rushdie, Carter, Roth (of *Our Gang* and *The Breast*) and other writers of this generation. '[I]n the 1960's', she writes, '– which witnessed the assassinations of the Kennedy brothers and the Rev. Martin Luther King Jr., the divisive war in Vietnam and growing unrest in the third world – novelists, both here and abroad began to experiment more freely with alternatives to naturalism'. The intermingling of the quotidian and the supernatural mirror 'a reality in which the fantastic is frequently part of everyday life'. In the case of *The Satanic Verses*, Rushdie 'has used the devices of magic realism to try to capture, metaphorically, the sweep and chaos of contemporary reality, its resemblance to a dream or nightmare' (30). Paradoxically, in his nightmares, Gibreel becomes a participant in a series of historic occurrences (suggesting that history itself is a collective dreaming about the past). Meanwhile Chamcha suffers his own daylight nightmare among London's immigrant community after he has assumed the demonic shape that Britain's racist police have projected onto him and his fellow immigrants. Yet dreams belong to the world of the imagination. As Rushdie writes in *Imaginary Homelands*, 'Unreality is the only weapon with which reality can be smashed, so that it may subsequently be reconstituted' (122).

Rushdie told a senior editor of *Harpers*, Marzorati, 'I wanted to write globe-swallowing, capacious books, ones with that sense of size, novels that expressed history, the public side of things as well as the private, the intimate'. The same editor hails *The Satanic Verses* as 'the first new novel of the new England, an England with more than two million immigrants, one in which it is no longer clear, exactly...what "being English" means' (24). It is this relatively new fictional representation by British novelists of a post-imperial Britain and British identities as part of a new global reality that attracted attention from American reviewers and critics. Most American reviewers responded to these novels with a mixture of awe and dismissal, awe at the stylistic craft and dismissal of what they saw as poor structure. After the award of the Booker Prize drove some American reviewers to belatedly notice Kazuo Ishiguro's *The Remains of the Day* (1989), the *New Yorker*'s reviewer, Rafferty, while praising Ishiguro's 'phenomenal narrative gifts', went on to assert, 'The novel holds us by technique alone' (103). Similarly, the *Washington Post*'s reviewer Yardley charged that in *The Satanic Verses* 'diverse elements never merge into a cohesive whole' (X3), just as the *New*

Yorker's reviewer Leithauser likewise faulted its structure, calling it 'a book of splendid but segmental components that do not quite cohere into a satisfying whole' (126). As has proved so often the case, it took time for American critics to reassess the reasons for and effects of such deliberately fractured forms of narrative employed by Rushdie and his fellow British novelists. By the end of the next decade, a representative American critic Baucom shows extreme sophistication in his response to *The Satanic Verses*' unifying motif of migrancy as an act of translation: 'Translation is a belated writing ... a moment ... in which beginning is posterior to the begun, in which newness emerges as a reinscription, a cross-inscription, a writing over' (215).

It is difficult to draw many generalized conclusions from a survey of American responses to British fiction during the 1980s. Clearly best-seller lists offer no satisfactory criteria for assessing the long-term evaluation or success of this category of fiction. It has been shown that many of the British novelists of this decade have testified to the powerful influence American novelists have exercised on their own writing, although this has not automatically led to immediate recognition of their work in the States. If anything, novels such as those focused on in this chapter have slowly become part of the canon taught at American universities and kept in print by US publishers. Some reasons why many American reviewers initially failed to fully recognize the stature of these British novels include a misreading of elements such as irony, comic convention and the use of British vernacular or specifically British cultural material not so well understood by American readers. Perhaps a more general explanation lies in the natural preference that American readers, students and reviewers show for works of fiction about their own country. Most of these innovative British novels took years, sometimes decades for American critics from the academy to recognize as classics. Yet it needs to be remembered that the immediate American reception of British fiction during the decade was largely positive, even if the difficulties resulting from the adoption of postmodern and metafictional techniques (among others) did lead to some incomprehension of them. What can be asserted with confidence is that novelists of both countries during the 1980s came to regularly affect one another's work and to see their writings as belonging to a wider English-speaking community. The supranational trend noted in British fiction during the decade, itself partly the result of American influence, made American novelists pay renewed attention to British fiction, after at least half a century of conscious rejection of the yet earlier ascendancy of British fiction in the United States.

Works cited

Ackroyd, Peter. *Notes for a New Culture. An Essay on Modernism*. London: Vision Press, 1976. Print.

Adams, Robert M. 'Balancing Act.' Rev. of *A History of the World in 10½ Chapters*, by Julian Barnes. *New York Review of Books* (26 Oct. 1989). N.pag. Web. 6 Jul. 2011.

Allesandrini, Anthony. 'A Creature Which Would Be Impossible If It Did Not Exist: "Midnight's Children" Turns Thirty.' *Jadaliyya* (15 Aug. 2011). N. pag. Web. 10 Sep. 2011.

Amis, Kingsley. *The Letters of Kingsley Amis*. Ed. Zachary Leader. New York: Hyperion, 2001. Print.

Amis, Martin. *Money: A Suicide Note*. New York and London: Penguin, 1986. Print.

———. 'Amis, Martin (Louis).' Interview by Marilyn K. Basel. *Contemporary Authors (New Revision Series)* 27 (1989): 19–22. Print.

———. 'Down London's Mean Streets.' Interview by Mira Stout. *New York Times Magazine* (4 Feb. 1990): 32–36, 48. Print.

———. 'The Wit and Fury of Martin Amis.' Interview by Susan Morrison. *Rolling Stone* (17 May 1990): 95–102. Print.

———. 'Martin Amis.' Interview by Patrick McGrath. *Bomb Interviews*. Ed. Betsy Sussler. San Francisco: City Lights, 1992, 187–97. Print.

———. *Experience: A Memoir*. New York: Hyperion/Talk Miramax, 2000. Print.

———. *The War against Cliché: Essays and Reviews 1971–2000*. New York: Vintage, 2002. Print.

Banks, Carolyn. 'Angela Carter's Flights of Fancy.' Rev. of *Nights at the Circus*, by Angela Carter. *Washington Post* (3 Feb. 1985). Book World 1. Print.

Barnes, Julian. *A History of the World in 10½ Chapters*. New York: Vintage/Random, 1989. Print.

Baucom, Ian. *Out of Place*. Princeton, NJ: Princeton University Press, 1999. Print.

Bergonzi, Bernard. *The Situation of the Novel*. London: Macmillan, 1970. Print.

Bernard, Catherine. 'Dismembering/Remembering Mimesis: Martin Amis, Graham Swift.' *British Postmodern Fiction*. Ed. Theo D'haen and Hans Bertens. Amsterdam and Atlanta, GA: Rodopi, 1993, 121–144. Print.

Blaise, Clark. Rev. of *Midnight's Children*, by Salman Rushdie. *New York Times Book Review* (19 Apr. 1981): 1. Print.

Bradbury, Malcolm. *The Modern American Novel*. New York: Penguin, 1994. Print.

———. *The Modern British Novel*. London & New York: Penguin, 1994. Print.

Brennan, Timothy. *Salman Rushdie and the Third World: Myths of the Nation*. New York: St Martin's, 1989. Print.

Buford, Bill. 'The End of the English Novel.' *Granta* 3 (1980): 1–19. Print.

Campañón, Carlos Silva. 'Through the Looking Glass: America in Martin Amis's *Money: A Suicide Note*.' *Atlantis* 26(2) (Dec. 2004): 87–96. Print.

Carter, Angela. *Nights at the Circus*. New York and London: Penguin, 1986. Print.

———. *Shaking a Leg: Collected Journalism and Writings*. London: Chatto & Windus, 1997. Print.

Chaudhuri, Una. Rev. of *Midnight's Children*, by Salman Rushdie. *Commonweal* 108 (25 Sep. 1981): 533. Print.

Chotiner, Isaac. 'Midnight's Other Children.' *New York Times* (3 Oct. 2010): 35. Print.

Clark, Roger Y. *Stanger Gods: Salman Rushdie's Other Worlds*. Montreal: McGill-Queen's University Press, 2001. Print.

Dayal, Samir. 'Talking Dirty: Salman Rushdie's *Midnight's Children*.' *College English* 54(4) (Apr. 1992): 431–445. Print.

Diedrick, James. 'The Fiction of Martin Amis: Patriarchy and Its Discontents.' *Contemporary British Fiction*. Ed. Richard J. Lane, Rod Mengham and Philip Tew. Cambridge: Polity, 2003, 239–255. Print.

Elias, Amy J. 'Meta-*Mimesis*? The Problem of British Postmodern Fiction.' *British Postmodern Fiction*. Ed. Theo D'haen and Hans Bertens. Amsterdam and Atlanta, GA: Rodopi, 1993, 9–31. Print.

Enright, D. J. 'So, and Not So.' Rev. of *The Satanic Verses*, by Salman Rushdie. *New York Review of Books* (2 Mar. 1989). N.pag. Web. 6 Jul. 2011.

Faulks, Sebastian. 'Butching It Out.' Rev. of *Money*, by Martin Amis. *Books & Bookmen* (Oct. 1984): 15. Print.

Fiedler, Leslie A. 'Cross the Border – Close That Gap: Post-Modernism.' *American Literature Since 1900*. Ed. Marcus Cunliffe. London: Sphere, 1975, 344–366. Print.

Finney, Brian. 'Tall Tales and Brief Lives: Angela Carter's *Nights at the Circus*.' *Journal of Narrative Technique* 28(2) (Spring 1998): 161–185. Print.

Frank, Soren. 'The Aesthetics of Elephantiasis: Rushdie's *Midnight's Children* as an Encyclopaedic Novel.' *Journal of Postcolonial Writing* 46(2) (2010): 187–198. Print.

Gass, Joanne M. 'Panopticism in *Nights at the Circus*.' *Review of Contemporary Fiction* 14(3) (Fall 1994): 71–76. Print.

Geng, Veronica. 'The Great Addiction.' Rev. of *Money*, by Martin Amis. *New York Times* (24 Mar. 1985): 7, 36. Print.

Gross, John. 'Books of the Times.' Rev. of *Money*, by Martin Amis. *New York Times* (15 Mar. 1985): C25. Print.

Grossman, Leo and Richard Lacayo. 'All Time 100 Novels.' *Time* (16 Oct. 2005). N.pag. Web. 16 Sep. 2011.

Haffenden, John. *Novelists in Interview*. London & New York: Methuen, 1985. Print.

Hamilton, Ian. 'Martin and Martina.' Rev. of *Money*, by Martin Amis. *London Review of Books* (20 Sep., 3 Oct. 1984): 3–4. Print.

Hawkes, David. 'Martin Amis.' *British Writers, Supplement IV*. Ed. G. Stade and C. Howard. New York: Scribners, 1997, 25–44. Print.

Hutchinson, Colin. *Reaganism, Thatcherism and the Social Novel*. London: Palgrave Macmillan, 2008. Print.

Kakutani, Michiko. 'Novelists Are News Again.' *New York Times Book Review* (14 Aug. 1983): 3, 22–23. Print.

———. 'Books of the Times.' Rev. of *Nights at the Circus*, by Angela Carter. *New York Times* (30 Jan. 1985). Sec. C: 17. Print.

———. 'Telling Truth through Fantasy: Rushdie's Magic Realism.' *New York Times* (24 Feb. 1989). Sec. C: 30. Print.

———. 'A Cast of Characters Afloat on History's Indifferent Sea.' Rev. of *A History of the World in 10½ Chapters*, by Julian Barnes. *New York Times* (29 Sep. 1989). Sec. C: 33. Print.

Kappeler, Susanne. *The Pornography of Representation*. Cambridge: Cambridge University Press, 1986. Print.

Keen, Suzanne. 'The Historical Turn in British Fiction.' *A Concise Companion to Contemporary British Fiction*. Ed. James F. English. Malden, MA: Blackwell, 2006, 167–187. Print.

Kendrick, Walter. 'The Real Magic of Angela Carter.' *Contemporary British Writers: Narrative Strategies*. Ed. Robert E. Hosmer. New York: St. Martin's, 1993, 66–84. Print.

Leithauser, Brad. 'Demoniasis.' Rev. of *The Satanic Verses*, by Salman Rushdie. *New Yorker* (15 May 1989): 124–128. Print.

Leonard, John. 'Books of the Times.' *New York Times* (23 Apr. 1981). Sec. C: 21. Print.

Mansfield, Stephanie. 'Martin Amis and the Stink of Money.' *Washington Post* (28 Apr. 1985): K1. Print.

Marzorati, Gerald. 'Salman Rushdie: Fiction's Embattled Infidel.' *New York Times Magazine* (29 Jan. 1989). Sec. 6: 24. Print.

Michael, Magali C. 'Angela Carter's *Nights at the Circus*: An Engaged Feminism via Subversive Postmodern Strategies.' *Contemporary Literature* 15(3) (1994): 492–521. Print.

Mojtabai, A. G. 'Magical Mystery Pilgrimage.' Rev. of *The Satanic Verses*, by Salman Rushdie. *New York Times* (29 Jan. 1989). Sec. 10: 3. Print.

Mukherjee, Arun. 'Characterization in Salman Rushdie's *Midnight's Children*: Breaking out of the Hold of Realism and Seeking the "Alienation Effect".' *The New Indian Novel in English: A Study of the 1980s*. Ed. Viney Kirpal. New Delhi: Allied Publishers, 1990, 109–119. Print.

Oates, Joyce Carol. 'But Noah Was Not a Nice Man.' Rev. of *A History of the World in 10½ Chapters*, by Julian Barnes. *New York Times* (1 Oct. 1989). Sec. 7: 12. Print.

Palmer, Paulina. 'From "Coded Mannequin" to Bird Woman: Angela Carter's Magic Flight.' *Women Reading Women's Reading*. Ed. Sue Roe. New York: St. Martin's, 1987, 179–205. Print.

Peterson, Shirley. 'Freaking Feminism: *The Lives and Loves of a She-Devil* and *Nights at the Circus* as Narrative Freak Shows.' *Freakery: Cultural Spectacles of the Extraordinary Body*. Ed. Rosemarie G. Thomson. New York: New York University Press, 1996, 291–301. Print.

Rafferty, Terrence. 'The Lesson of the Master.' Rev. of *The Remains of the Day*, by Kazuo Ishiguro. *New Yorker* (15 Jan. 1990): 102–104. Print.

Reder, Michael (ed.). *Conversations with Salman Rushdie*. Jackson, MI: University Press of Mississippi, 2000. Print.

Rehberger, Dean. 'Vulgar Fiction, Impure History: The Neglect of Historical Fiction.' *Journal of American Culture* 18(4) (1995): 59–65. Print.

Riviere, Francesca. 'Martin Amis, the Art of Fiction No. 151.' *Paris Review* 146 (Spring 1998), http://www.theparisreview.org/interviews/1156/the-art-of-fiction-no-151-martin-amis. N.pag. Web.

Robinson, Sally. *Engendering the Subject: Gender and Self-Representation in Contemporary Women's Fiction*. New York: State University of New York Press, 1991. Print.

Rushdie, Salman. 'The Empire Writes Back with a Vengeance.' *Times* (London) (3 Jul. 1982): 8. Print.

———. Interview by Cecile Wajsbrot. 'Salman Rushdie: Utiliser une technique qui permettrait à Dieu d'exister.' *La Quinzaine littéraire* 449 (16–31 Oct. 1985): 22. Print.

———. *Imaginary Homelands: Essays and Criticism 1981–1991*. New York: Granta/Viking Penguin, 1991. Print.

———. Interview by Peter Kemp. 'Magical Mystery Tour.' *Sunday Times* (London) (9 Jun. 1991). Sec. 6: 6–7. Print.

———. *Midnight's Children*. New York and London: Penguin, 1991. Print.

———. *The Satanic Verses*. New York: Holt/Picador, 1997. Print.

———. Talk, on being awarded an honorary degree. Amherst College, 4 Apr. 1997. Qtd. in Rege, Josna E. 'Victim into Protagonist? *Midnight's Children* and the Post-Rushdie Narratives of the Eighties.' *Studies in the Novel* 29(3) (1997): 342–375. Print.

Salyer, Gregory. 'Review Article: One Good Story Leads to Another: Julian Barnes' *A History of the World in 10½ Chapters*.' *Journal of Literature and Theology* 5(2) (1991): 220–233. Print.

See, Carolyn. 'Come On and See the Winged Lady.' Rev. of *Nights at the Circus*, by Angela Carter. *New York Times* (24 Feb. 1985). N.pag. Web. 13 Sep. 2011.

Self, Will. 'Something Amiss in Amis Country.' *Esquire* (British ed.) (Apr. 1993): 70–76. Print.

Sheets, Robin Ann. 'Pornography, Fairy Tales, and Feminism: Angela Carter's "The Bloody Chamber."' *Journal of the History of Sexuality* 1(4) (1991): 633–657. Print.

Sheppard, R. Z. 'Books: One More Fat Englishman.' Rev. of *Money*, by Martin Amis. *Time* (11 Mar. 1985). N.pag. Web. 30 Jun. 2011.

Siegel, Carol. 'Postmodern Women Novelists Review Victorian Male Masochism.' *Genders* 11 (Fall 1991): 1–16. Print.

Smith, Amanda. 'Salman Rushdie.' *Publishers Weekly* (11 Nov. 1983): 49–50. Print.

———. 'Martin Amis.' *Publishers Weekly* (8 Feb. 1985): 78–79. Print.

Snider, Norman. 'Trends: Brits Discover the Sun Also Rises in America.' Rev. of *Money*, by Martin Amis. *Globe and Mail* (Canada) (22 Dec. 1984). N.pag. Web. 30 Jun. 2011.

Stoddart, Helen. *Angela Carter's* Nights at the Circus. London: Routledge, Chapman & Hall, 2007. Print.
Towers, Robert. 'On the Indian World-Mountain.' Rev. of *Midnight's Children*, by Salman Rushdie. *New York Review of Books* (24 Sep. 1981): 28. Print.
Trewin, Ion. 'Letter.' *The Bookseller* (18 Jun. 2010). Print.
Walters, Colin. 'Many Loose Ends in Disordered View of World History.' Rev. of *A History of the World in 10½ Chapters*, by Julian Barnes. *Washington Times* (23 Oct. 1989). Sec. E: 8. Print.
Walton, David. 'Awash in a Voyage of Ideas: Barnes' Collection of Stories Drift from Chapter to Chapter.' Rev. of *A History of the World in 10½ Chapters*, by Julian Barnes. *St Petersburg Times* (Florida). (24 Dec. 1989). N.pag. Web. 6 Jul. 2011.
Warner, Marina. 'Angela Carter: Bottle Blonde, Double Drag.' *Flesh and the Mirror: Essays on the Art of Angela Carter*. Ed. Lorna Sage. London: Virago Press, 1994, 243–256. Print.
Wilson, Jonathan. 'A Very English Story.' *New Yorker* (6 Mar. 1995): 96–106. Print.
Yardley, Jonathan. 'The Comic Madness of Martin Amis.' Rev. of *Money*, by Martin Amis. *Washington Post* (24 Mar. 1985). Book World: 3. Print.
———. 'Wrestling with the Angel.' Rev. of *The Satanic Verses*, by Salman Rushdie. *Washington Post* (29 Jan. 1989). Book World: X3. Print.

8

International Contexts (Europe)
The Romanian Context:
Between Realism and Postmodernism

Ana-Karina Schneider

The 1980s in Romania remains in collective memory as a decade of political extremes resulting in divergent narratives about innovation in every art form. Literary history is particularly explicit about the discrepancies between the dominant discourse and dissident voices: writers referred to themselves as postmodern or as Generation Eighties in order to set themselves apart from the doctrinally controlled literature of earlier generations. Retrospectively, writer Mircea Zaciu speaks of 'the omnipotent evil of this satanic decade' in the first volume of his *Journal* (1993: 7, my trans.) and Radu Țeposu devotes an entire eponymous volume to the 'tragic and grotesque history of the dark literary decade nine' (1993, my trans.). As these negative valuations of the decade suggest, in retrospect the most audible narratives are those of the dissidents, who are now free to reveal the degree to which realism, (neo-)modernism and postmodernism were fraught categories, and appurtenance to them became a political statement. In what follows, I investigate ways in which the reception of British fiction participated in the scramble for autonomous critical expression in the 1980s Romania. The problematic of naming and narrativizing that decade plays itself out in the extent to which certain genres and certain writers were allowed to penetrate and influence the Romanian literary scene and in the rationalizations of their relevance.

There are two sources of difficulty to an undertaking such as this. One is the relative paucity of critical studies devoted to British literature during that decade. From the existing studies, it is difficult to recuperate a sense of the extent to which contemporary British novelists were read outside the academia, beyond a general, largely anecdotal sense that some of them were popular (see Deciu 7).

The other is a disjunction at the very heart of Romanian criticism: critics focus either on Romanian writing or on international writing, but almost never on both; even comparative literature tends to be world literature that seldom includes Romanian productions. Similarly, reviews of translations into Romanian tend to discuss the book strictly within its original context, with only the occasional reference to the translation itself, and almost none to the culture into which it has been received. This changed in the late 1990s – see for instance the studies of Mircea Cărtărescu, Marcel Corniş-Pope, Ion Bogdan Lefter, Carmen Muşat, Liviu Petrescu, Monica Spiridon and Mihaela Ursa, cited below – but even in these books British literature is only marginally mentioned, American literature being the more visible and influential of English-language literatures. When the study of the reception of specific British novelists in Romania is undertaken in more recent years, it typically records reviews and studies against a more or less blurred background of autochthonous contemporary critical and literary productions, but there is no sense of the British writers' impact on the receiving literature. An account of the reception of British literature in the 1980s can therefore only be reconstituted by reconciling, on the one hand, both contemporary and retrospective discussions of the Romanian literary scene during that decade and, on the other, the reviews and occasional critical studies of contemporary international productions. That British literature had an impact at all, in a culture which was otherwise effectively sealed off from most things Western, was due to the fact that a measure of formal synchronization with Western literary and artistic fashions was always allowed after 1964, when an ideological thaw took place in Romania.

These difficulties are revealing of the Romanian cultural context in the 1980s. The disjunction at the heart of criticism reflects a series of equally significant, deeply ingrained disjunctions between the private and the public, reality and language, experience and representation, etc. These had been forced upon the intellectuals of earlier decades by a regime that thrived on division and schizophrenia and which had itself contributed crucially to creating such rifts by imposing fictions of its own about reality and by preventing alternative accounts from challenging the official version (Muşat 15, 165–172). The monolithic discourse of power was, however, circumvented through a return to a modernist proclamation of the primacy of the aesthetic as soon as the post-Stalinist relaxation allowed, and then more openly challenged in the 1980s, when the emergence of postmodernism sparked what is unanimously considered the most far-reaching, most systematic and theoretically grounded debate in post-war times, involving by far the largest number of artists and theoreticians and reaching well into the following decades.

In this context, the critical reception of contemporary British productions shared the ambivalence of British criticism towards the emerging postmodernism. In a 1978 synthetic survey of the state of the British novel, Virgil Stanciu relays a view that would remain largely unchallenged until the 1990s, according to which, although not radically innovative, post-war British fiction had settled into a stately maturity that involved a knowing return to a traditional conception of the novel. This recuperation, however, was neither unimaginative nor neglectful of the innovation and experimentalism of the first three decades of the twentieth century (1978: 221). Stanciu follows Bernard Bergonzi in foregrounding the revival of genre and narrative conventions and the thematization of Englishness, and celebrates the vitality and diversity of contemporary productions. In a culture that was seeing its own way through a belated and fraught neo-modernism, this article echoed familiar predicaments. Rather than vindicate British fiction, however, this view foreshadowed its relegation to a realistic tradition to which, increasingly, a preference for postmodern polymorphism, polyphony and play was opposed in the following decade.

With hindsight, in a 1993 essay on British postmodern fiction, Amy J. Elias notes how inadequate the prevailing classifications into postmodern experimentalism and realism had been rendered by the novels of the 1980s (9) and shifts focus from the mimetism attributed to the latter to interrogating the 'ontological bases of each' (10). Her essay is included in a volume which sets out to dismantle the well-established belief that Britain had 'a staunchly anti-postmodern, because irradicably mimetic, tradition' (D'Haen and Bertens N.pag.). In 1995, Andrzej Gąsiorek devoted an entire book to proving the untenability of this simplifying dichotomy. In post-war British fiction, he argues, quoting Heath, realism is informed by an 'awareness ... of the terms of its production' (Gąsiorek 15) and of its own mediation of the reality it purports to reflect (17). This awareness is the legacy of modernism and it includes the recognition that the referentiality of realist fiction is 'irreducibly metaphoric' (16). The realism–experimentalism polarization still organized Romanian criticism in the 1990s (see Mușat 26), and Mircea Cărtărescu challenges it along similar lines (159–162), although preference, as with American postmodern fiction, tends to be given to formal experiment and the 'complete abolition of the criterion of verisimilitude' (160, my trans.).

Two of the novelists whose names recur in both British and Romanian criticism are Iris Murdoch and John Fowles. In British criticism, according to Elias, the former is listed among the representatives of realism, whereas the latter represents postmodern experimentalism (9); in Mușat they are both listed on the side of 'image-centric or anthropocentric', rather than metafictional, postmodernism (26), whereas in Cărtărescu only Fowles is mentioned, then dismissed from amongst the experimentalists (112). Written retrospectively in the 1990s, these studies reveal and organize the main critical tendencies of the previous decade, helping to clarify the appeal and impact of certain writers. In what follows, I undertake a somewhat similar project, describing first the Romanian context of the critical reception of British fiction in the 1980s and then illustrating with reference to two case studies, namely the criticism devoted to Fowles and Murdoch, respectively. While these two novelists' visibility throughout that decade was undiminished, they would not be regarded as the most representative figures nowadays. To Romanian readers in the 1980s, nonetheless, they epitomized the current realism–experimentalism dichotomy: their ambivalent situation vis-à-vis postmodernism enabled interpretations that were sites where theories of representation played themselves out and were tested.

The Romanian context

In Romania, the 1980s was a fairly clearly demarcated decade, marked by an increasingly paranoid repression of the intellectuals. The decade began with the tightening of political control over the Writers' Association and it ended dramatically with the overturn of the communist regime in December 1989. On the literary scene, the neo-modernist aestheticism, typified by 'inward-looking, metaphorical and symbolic literature', is succeeded – though not completely displaced – by what has often been referred to as Romanian postmodernism (I. B. Lefter 1995: 869). Both modes have the merit of making censorship very difficult (870) and both are essentially forms of resistance to the official discourse which promotes 'proletarian art' and ideology-driven socialist realism. Practicing novelists of that decade such as Gheorghe Crăciun write retrospectively about formal experimentalism as an assertion of 'a kind of liberty of the spirit' (in Spiridon et al. 60), a quest for 'the syntax of the freedom of saying things', to paraphrase the title of a 1973 book by Gheorghe Iova, and a refuge from the socialist realism recommended by the authorities as the supplement to history. Inevitably, the experimentalism of the Generation Eighties was attacked as a form of escapism and a refusal to acknowledge culture's complicity in social and political events and internalize the guilt, or, alternatively, a kind of serial novelty rather than a programmatic innovatorism, as Crăciun shows (in Spiridon et al. 63–64). Mușat explains that their 'sin' was to have spurned 'proletarian art' which purported to 'free art', a desideratum which they had recognized as 'an empty formula whose sole meaning remains, in fact, that it "freed" art of the "prejudice" of aesthetic value, which was considered bourgeois, elitist, reactionary and obsolete' (15, my trans.).

Critics have emphasized the idiosyncratic nature of this postmodernism that emerged not as 'the cultural logic of late capitalism' but, if anything, as the last bastion of late modernism. Mihaela Ursa points out some of the ways in which it diverged from Western postmodernism, most notably through an overemphasis on textualism, a new anthropocentrism and humanism that resisted being described in the terms of Enlightenment rationalism and a comparative neglect of hyper-reality and the media (10, 34–38). Like other commentators before her, Ursa indicates that much of the terminology, though eagerly deployed by writers and critics of the day, remained largely undefined (20–32), which made it possible for the discrepancies between the Romanian and Western variants of postmodernism to go unnoticed. Cărtărescu shows that many of the Romanian theoreticians writing in the mid-1980s remained in the main indebted to neo-modernism, which in his taxonomy includes all preoccupations with formal issues, whereas the 'true philosophical premises' of postmodern literature are 'constructive nihilism, the disappearance of metaphysics, the sense of derealization, the end of historicity, perspectivism and indeterminacy' (182, my trans.). The acknowledgement of Romanian postmodernism's indebtedness to neo-modernism and the avant-gardes is inevitable, as indeed much of the innovative critical discourse of subsequent years remains essentially form bound and humanist in purport, as will be illustrated by the case studies below.

Much of the post-1990 controversy surrounding the postmodernism of the 1980s has revolved around the apparent failure of Romanian writers to engage the issue of realism as other than a set of formal conventions. Marcel Corniș-Pope foregrounds the extent to which '[l]iterature and criticism provided for a while the only available forms of oppositional discourse', not only in Romania, but also in Czechoslovakia, East Germany and even the Soviet Union (9). Writing in the mid-1990s, he opposes those commentators who allege that the deconstructions proposed by the literature and criticism of the 1980s raised no serious challenges to the epistemology and ideology of the age (21). However, Corniș-Pope concedes, before 1989 it was practically impossible to foreground the implicit challenge posed by postmodernism to 'the ideological configurations that allowed a monologic structure of power to survive' (22). Relatedly, what he calls 'the mimetic bias' persisted in criticism: 'Romanian poeticians... preferred... to elude the term realism, compromised by the dogma of "socialist realism", or to use half-qualified versions of it ("magic realism", "dissociative realism", "textual realism")' (20). This reticence to confront the realist paradigm is a critical disparity between Romanian and Western versions of postmodernism. Like modernism, the Romanian literature and criticism of the 1980s are content to operate within the privileged – and once again autonomous! – realm of the aesthetic rather than the ontological.

Against this precarious backdrop, literary translation became professionalized, and paradoxically the majority of literary works translated into Romanian were from Western, rather than Soviet or East European, literatures. The periodization of literary reception shares the inherent time lag attendant on translation, so that some of the books available in the 1980s aesthetically and thematically belonged to earlier decades, whereas much of the fiction we associate with that decade nowadays was not read in Romania until much later. Significantly, however, according to the Romanian Academy's *Chronological Dictionary of Novels Translated into Romanian, from the Beginnings to 1989* (2005), in the very relative terms of the hundred-odd novels and fragments translated every year throughout the 1980s, many were from the English and they belonged to writers as diverse as Jane Austen, Arnold Bennett, James Clavell, Joseph Conrad, Lawrence Durrell, William Faulkner, William Golding, Graham Greene, Thomas Hardy, Ernest Hemingway, Henry James, Somerset Maugham, Iris Murdoch or Virginia Woolf, to mention a few of the most frequently translated. There is the occasional single feature from Doris Lessing and Jean Rhys and the outstandingly creative translation of James Joyce's *Ulysses* by Mircea Ivănescu in 1984, whereas from Nadine Gordimer and Salman Rushdie only the odd fragment was included in a periodical. Important contemporary British novelists such as Peter Ackroyd, John Banville, Anthony Burgess and Graham Swift only received the odd citation in a critical article, but their novels were not translated until much later, while writers such as Martin Amis, Julian Barnes, David Lodge and Ian McEwan are conspicuously absent. For all its rigorous recording of translations into Romanian, however, the *Dictionary* is not completely reliable. Noticeably, it contains no mention whatsoever of John Fowles, although the holdings of the National Library of Romania and much criticism confirm that three of his novels were translated prior to 1989.

It is important to record what books got translated into Romanian during the decade under scrutiny here, not only because private ownership of books in languages other than Romanian was officially banned, but also in that literary criticism itself was restricted to books which the censurers could read. This explains the very limited number of critical references to un-translated books listed by the *Dictionary*. The ban, however, was not as effective as might be expected, and books circulated in the original or in foreign translations through networks based on trust (Ciugureanu 49). Additionally, university libraries held a modicum of world literature in the original, which students and professors could consult for language-learning purposes. Consequently, the impact of international fiction was much stronger and more insidious than the hundred-odd yearly quota of translations might suggest.

Much of the critical function in the reception of world literature was performed by reviews, rather than monographs. In a pair of 1991 articles on post-Stalinist Romanian criticism, Ion Bogdan Lefter reveals that, being one of the genres that were revived in the mid-1960s as part of the recuperation of interwar modernism, the book review became an institution committed to promoting aesthetic excellence, but also, gradually, a declaration of autonomy from political pressures. By the late 1980s, however, the latter function had displaced the former almost completely, reviews had become largely manneristic and opaque and in their indiscriminate enthusiasm for novelty they failed to offer astute value judgements (I. B. Lefter 2002: 494–496). Nonetheless, they retained the role of introducing both local and international productions to the Romanian reading public, sometimes greeting the appearance of a book in the original before it was translated into Romanian. As such, they participated in synchronizing Romanian criticism with international responses and approaches.

The two case studies that follow will examine a fair sampling of the Romanian criticism devoted to two British novelists who in their home culture were assigned to the two categories, experimentalism and realism, with which British criticism habitually operated in the 1980s. I analyse the extent to which this taxonomy obtains in Romanian critical studies. Moreover, some of the evolutions and preoccupations of the 1980s Romanian scene may explain the particular appeal of these two writers. It will therefore be of particular relevance to see if the aesthetic controversies that animated Romanian critical theory translate into the critical reception of British fiction as well.

Case study I: Iris Murdoch

No less than six of Murdoch's novels were translated into Romanian before 1990: *Under the Net* (*Prins in mreje*, 1971), translated by Ioana Maria Nicolau, with a foreword by Mircea Ivănescu; *The Sandcastle* (*Castelul de nisip*, 1977), translated by Mihaela Bucur; *Bruno's Dream* (*Visul lui Bruno*, 1978), by Dana Crivăț; and *A Word Child* (*Vlăstarul cuvintelor*, 1981), *The Sea, the Sea* (*Marea, Marea*, 1983) and *The Philosopher's Pupil* (*Discipolul*, 1986), translated by the prolific Antoaneta Ralian. Several others have been added since 1990: *The Sacred and Profane Love Machine* (*Mașina de iubit, cea sacră și profană*, 1991), *Jackson's Dilemma* (*Dilema lui Jackson*, 1998), *The Bell* (*Clopotul*, 2002), *The Nice and the Good* (*Oameni buni și oameni de bine*, 2006), *A Severed Head* (*Capul retezat*, 2007) and *The Good Apprentice* (*Ucenicul cel bun*, 2011). A few of the earlier translations have received new editions and Nadina Vișan retranslated *The Sand Castle* in 2011. The overflow of translations invading the Romanian book market post 1990 has frequently been explained as a celebration of our exit from the earlier cultural isolation and as the response to a psychological law of compensation. But the comparison of pre-1990 and post-1990 productions tends to dwarf the former's achievement rather unjustly: given the circumstances, having six novels translated into Romanian was in fact a sign of great success with Romania's powers that be, which has been put down to Murdoch's early association with the Communist Party in Britain and comparisons of her work to that of the Angry Young Men (Cojocariu in Gilder et al. 95). Additionally, she was invited to Romania together with John Bayley in 1978, when they gave talks at the Universities of Bucharest and Cluj-Napoca and visited the Danube Delta. These events contributed to bringing her to the attention of Romanian readers.

Her popularity, however, is very relative: Marinela Cojocariu, who has studied Murdoch's reception in Romania, enumerates a mere handful of prefaces, afterwords and critical studies included in various volumes, but notes that she was a household name in the literary press between 1970 and 1989 (in Gilder et al. 108). Moreover, in 1984, Antoaneta Ralian remembers her excitement at having been able to tell Murdoch as early as 1974 that she was already well known to the Romanian readership and mentions her 'public and press success' (105, my trans.). As only *Under the Net* had been translated before Ralian's first meeting with Murdoch in London, it is difficult to ascertain how real this success was or whether she was merely paying lip service to the authorities' sanction of Murdoch's work, in whose translation she was heavily involved. At any rate, by the time Ralian was writing her account, a few more of the novels had been translated, Murdoch had visited Romania and she had corresponded regularly with Andrei Cujbă, Ralian and possibly others, and the unfailing willingness of those who met her (Brezianu, Cujbă, Ralian, Stanciu, Stoenescu, etc.) to recount the experience is reliable testimony to the impression she made both in person and as a writer. Throughout the 1980s, there is a thin but steady trickle of articles and reviews devoted to Murdoch and published in the literary press, alongside the occasional chapter in critical volumes. Moreover, Adina Ciugureanu states, her novels were included in the English studies curriculum at universities such as the ones in Iaşi and Bucharest (48), although her philosophical works did not come to the attention of Romanian readers until the late 1990s, according to Cojocariu (in Gilder et al. 105).

Reviews and studies of Murdoch's novels published in the 1980s trace an evolution of critical discourse and method, from fairly straightforward synopses of the plot, with the occasional, perfunctory praise for the translation, or the structuralist discussion of the symbolism and/or of Shakespearean influences, to increasingly more sophisticated discussions of generic instability (Galea 1983), intertextuality (V. Lefter) or the 'postmodern' quality of *The Philosopher's Pupil* (Tupan) as the decade progressed. It might be argued that, as the novels were translated in the order in which they had been written, this evolution parallels that of Murdoch's own craft, but it remains a fact that the criticism itself charts a trajectory of its own towards an increasingly more specialized discourse and terminology.

In 1981, for instance, the recently translated *Word Child* does not elicit more than a perfunctory investigation of literary predecessors in the treatment of the theme of adverse fate, who emerge to be either D. H. Lawrence (Grigorescu 1981) or Thomas Hardy (Burlui 1981). Both reviews foreground Murdoch's treatment of a rich variety of human experiences that are overdetermined by the social and natural worlds, with Grigorescu proposing also that, like *Women in Love*, the novel focuses on the individual's relationship to the world of ideas, while Burlui goes along the anthropocentric line that foregrounds the richness of personal experiences assigned to the characters. Burlui further contributes a brief commendation of Murdoch's avoidance of 'mannerisms and artifices of construction' (1981: 10, my trans.); Grigorescu adds a commendation of the translation, without however going into any details.

Criticism of *The Sea, the Sea*, whether in the form of the more elaborate study or the review, unanimously foregrounds the Shakespearean influence and the symbolism of the sea as life source. In a 1982 volume on world literature, Andrei Brezianu includes an essay on *The Sea* written in 1979, before the translation was published. Unlike many of the reviews that will appear in the wake of the translation, Brezianu shifts focus from the adaptation of *The Tempest* towards the Shakespearean conceit of the world as a stage, foregrounding the extent to which the characters are manipulated by an authorial agency that is alternately the Prospero-like Arrowby and the author herself. The critic dwells at some length on Murdoch's dramatization of *The Tempest*'s moral dilemmas in modern key and illustrates this largely by following the unfolding of the psychological theme. Towards the end, he addresses 'the refined parodic comedy' of the novel, which he also finds in Murdoch's more recent novels, and its counterbalance, her 'intellectualism', which gestures towards tragedy, although the register of the novel remains 'superficial, luminous and light' (247, my trans.). He remarks on the novelty of this syncretism which is philosophical, rather than generic, yet warm and empathetic (248, my trans.). Brezianu associates this not merely with the Shakespearean influence but rather with a kind of intellectual kinship that draws Murdoch to Shakespeare. In pointing out this kinship, he acknowledges the influence of ideas already in circulation in British reviews of the novel.

Perforce more concise, the reviews of the translation of *The Sea* note the Shakespearean intertext and single out relevant aspects of the novel. Irina Burlui avers that the Shakespearean quality of the novel does not reside in the reproduction of certain types of characters or conflicts, but rather in the 'unique imbrication of realism and magic – the capacity of presenting characters that are strongly individualized...and at the same time the strength to integrate them into a mythical pattern of broad human meanings' (1984: 7, my trans.). She then reiterates her thesis of the Hardyan fatalism infusing the 'open spaces of singular human experiences, distorted by strong feelings, tormented by acute philosophical dilemmas' (1984: 7, my trans.). All this, Burlui insists, is done with the formal instruments of realistic narrative.

Aurel Dragoș Munteanu would agree: although it approaches contemporary issues, according to him *The Sea* is a 'classic' of realist fiction, replete with factual details (1983: 7, my trans.). Unlike Burlui, however, he does not think the ending brings closure; rather, he avers, the parable-like ending comes as something of a surprise in this, 'most realistic of novels' (7, my trans.). His insistence on the typicality of the novel's realism, echoing Shklowsky's description of *Tristram Shandy* as the most typical of novels, feeds into the main thesis of his review, namely that Ralian's translation is a valuable contribution to familiarizing the Romanian public with the British novel and especially with the quintessential British genre, the so-called 'bourgeois novel', a 'form of literature at the centre of which is social man, with his more or less coherent personal determinations' (7, my trans.). His essentialism is programmatic: himself a polyglot and writer, Munteanu seeks to promote this kind of imports. His close attention to the translation, evinced by his occasionally taking issue with Ralian's choices in what however he acknowledges to be a very accurate and effective rendition, is similarly targeted.

A third review, by Livia Szász, embraces what Cărtărescu would call a neo-modernist approach to *The Sea, the Sea*, taking its cue from an interview in which Murdoch speaks to Jack I. Biles about the writer's need to break the mould in order to find the form that can contain the complexities and absurdities of modern life. *The Sea*, according to Szász, instantiates this principle: the novel is 'the product of the tension between author and her narrative material, in a fervent quest for the artistic form' (1983: 20, my trans.). The critic therefore goes on to foreground formal indeterminacies, the open ending, the interrogation of the origin and status of the novel as a genre, the tension between various narrative modes, the metafictional account of the telling of the story, etc. Although Szász lacks some of the terminology that was to become the jargon of criticism soon enough (she doesn't use terms such as metafiction or indeterminacy, for instance), her clearly formal focus complements the thematic analyses mentioned above rather nicely and instantiates that critical tendency which declared the independence of literary studies from ideological fetters.

This privileging of the primacy of formal concerns becomes evident in the reviews of *The Philosopher's Pupil*, translated a few years later. Both Nicolae Manolescu and Maria-Ana Tupan split their reviews between noting the philosophical content of the novel and grappling with Murdoch's fraught allegiances, on the one hand, and her experimentation with perspective and modes of representation, on the other. To Manolescu, the philosophical thematic is more straightforwardly existentialist, Sartre's influence being evident in the aspiration to an authenticity of being, the attendant spiritual crisis and the quest for answers to existential questions, which nonetheless yields no straightforward results. What troubles the critic is the formula of the novel, which, although that of the moral fable previously tested by Dostoyevsky and Camus, is here compromised by the intra-diegetic narrator's vacillations between partial vision and omniscience, which give the reader 'narratological *malaise*' (1986: 8). According to Tupan, Murdoch's philosophical stance is far from clear-cut: it is a '*sui generis* transcendentalism' that rejects both existentialism and positivism – both viewed here as representational modes rather than as systems of thought (1987: 20, my trans.). The novelist attempts instead to 'navigate between the Scylla of symbolism and the Charybdis of realism': although nominally paying allegiance to the great realistic tradition, her writing practice demonstrates 'the extent to which the modernist experiments have rendered impossible the unconditional return to earlier artistic techniques' (20, my trans.). After deploying the full interpretive repertoire of symbol, allegory, metaphor and subtextual irony and showing that the philosophical problematic appeals to intuition rather than speculation, the critic concludes boldly: '[t]ypologically, [the novel] belongs to postmodern prose through the baroque construction, the combination of the serious and the ludic, elaborateness and referential games' (20, my trans.). Published at the height of the discussion surrounding postmodernism, this is the first critical text to associate Murdoch with that trend in Romania.

Unlike the reviews and short essays devoted to specific novels, a third category of studies tends to be rather more comprehensive in range. In 1981, Antoaneta Ralian devotes a capacious page of the *România literară* revue to the recently published *Nuns and Soldiers*. In addition to the translation of the opening pages of the novel, Ralian includes a synopsis of Murdoch's career to date, dispelling some of the conventional classifications and emphasizing the novelist's belonging in the longevous English tradition of psychological realism and moral philosophy (1981: 21). Ralian's column has the air of being an advertisement for Murdoch's new novel, but although *Nuns and Soldiers* has not been translated to date, to many readers her lines must have served as a welcome introduction to Murdoch's fiction. Two years later, Anglist Ileana Galea tries to locate Murdoch within a generic classification drawn by the novelist herself – dividing fiction broadly into novels written in the tradition of the 'eighteenth-century allegories of reason and moralizing tales' and descendants of the 'journalistic' realism of the nineteenth century – who then dismisses it in favour of a fusion of the two (1983: 55). Galea's conclusion, based on an analysis of *Under the Net, The Flight from the Enchanter* and *Bruno's Dream*, is that Murdoch's fiction belongs to none of these categories: 'If through certain dominants of her creation Iris Murdoch belongs amongst the novelists who reflect reality metaphorically, through the theoretical system that is enveloped in this fictional mode her work might in fact be illustrative of a different category, that of the novel of ideas' (1983: 55, my trans.). The world she creates remains, nonetheless, credible and verisimilar. Galea's vacillation, as she seems well aware, reflects an emergent inadequacy of the olden categories.

Virgil Lefter approaches Murdoch's appurtenance to the republic of letters very differently: although his language is largely that of liberal humanism – he speaks of the 'odyssey of the human spirit', for instance, and of Murdoch the humanist who pleads that the classics are relevant to our modern dramas and dilemmas (1987: 55) – he also evinces an awareness of books existing in a kind of constellation reminiscent of Walter Benjamin, illuminating each other and inciting new readings and writings. As Murdoch's characters undergo their initiations, the wisdom they acquire, though originating in life itself, is always filtered through books (54–55). Lefter thus comes close to discerning the constructedness of that wisdom and the intertextuality in which all books are now said to engage. Again, the language is not quite at his disposal for conceptualizing what he finds in Murdoch, but, like Galea, he seems to have absorbed enough of the current critical discourse to be aware of the imponderable lives of books. By and large, however, Murdoch, like Fowles, resonates mostly with those rather eccentric features of Romanian postmodernism mentioned by Ursa: humanism, anthropocentrism and existentialism.

Case study II: John Fowles

In a 1983 essay on Fowles included in a volume chronicling a century of world literature and also comprising chapters on writers as diverse as Goncourt, Macaulay, Tolstoy, Caragiale, Svevo, etc., Silvian Iosifescu begins by warning against the easy classification of Fowles as a best-selling author, with all the attending connotations of facility and commercial conventionalism. That a Romanian critic engaged the best-seller phenomenon as early as 1983 is doubly significant: much of subsequent Fowles criticism was to mention his best-selling status as almost a badge attesting his appurtenance to a kind of literature that erased the boundary between high and popular. Along the same line, Iosifescu also discusses the film adaptation of *The French Lieutenant's Woman*, as well as paratextual elements such as notes, forewords and articles written by Fowles himself in clarification of his novels. Second, Iosifescu's chapter worked as a plea in favour of importing a successful English writer of whose already extensive *oeuvre* only one novel, *The French Lieutenant's Woman*, had been translated (by Adina Arsenescu, as *Iubita locotenentului francez*, in 1974). However, only two more novels were translated into Romanian in the 1980s: *Daniel Martin* (1984) and *The Magus* (*Magicianul*, 1987), both by Mariana Chițoran and Livia Deac. After 1990, several others of Fowles's books were rendered in Romanian: *The Collector* (*Colecționarul*, 1993), *The Ebony Tower* (*Turnul de abanos*, 1993), *A Maggot* (*Omida*, 1995), *Mantissa* (*Mantisa*, 1995) and *The Tree* (*Copacul*, 1999); most received second editions and *The French Lieutenant's Woman* were retranslated by Mioara Tapalagă, with an afterword by Dan Grigorescu (1994). Less prolific than Murdoch, for Fowles, too, the three pre-1990 translations signal broad acceptance, as does the more plentiful criticism.

Fowles criticism is not as uniformly enthusiastic as Murdoch studies is, nor does it follow so faithfully on the publication of translations. Rather, much of it was either triggered by the publication of his novels in Britain or retrospective and synthetic. It is also more eclectic in approach, signalling a widespread perception of Fowles's work as protean and even controversial. Thus, one of the least laudative pieces is translator Felicia Antip's 'An addition of comparatively little worth' (1983, my trans.), which she wrote for her permanent column in *România literară* called 'I've read that they're reading' and which is a brief review of the recently published *Mantissa*. Antip believes the project to be rather too demanding for Fowles's understanding of fiction and recommends a return to creating believable incidents and characters rather than proceeding along the metafictional track inaugurated by *Mantissa*. It is unclear if it is self-reflexive fiction generally that she objects to or only this particular instance of it, but given the nature of her column, one wonders how damaging this piece turned out to be.

On the laudatory side, Ileana Galea wrote an article in 1981 that is in many ways an earlier companion to her Murdoch article mentioned above. Always open to experiment, Galea remarks upon the generic instability of *The French Lieutenant's Woman* and Fowles's intrusions in his narrative, his representations of authorial dilemmas in the very process of making choices, his theorizing of novel-writing à la Fielding and Huxley, his recuperation of the Victorian tradition (particularly Dickens and Thackeray) and the good use to which he puts the innovations of Joseph Conrad and Henry James. She delights in the ambiguity of the characters' motivations, which, like the epigraphs and metafictional reflections, have the role of dispelling the Victorian illusion of verisimilitude and authenticity and of opening up unsuspected possibilities not only for interpretation, but for creation (1981: 53). In another early piece that seems meant as a guide for readers interested in contemporary British fiction, Liviu Cotrău discusses Fowles's 'collectors', that is, the protagonists of *The Collector* and *The Magus*, foregrounding in both cases the mysterious atmosphere, the uncanny coincidences, the un-decidability created by competing narratives, but also the profound morality upheld by the novels (1983: 51). His thesis originates in Lawrence Durrell's proposition that the artist must strive to render the correspondence between nature and character, environment and destiny (50). Inspired by *The Magus*, critic Manuela Tănase views Fowles's work as an instance of the god game, where the godlike author creates a situation, then withdraws from his creation, leaving the characters to work out their issues and allowing the reader to entertain the illusion of complete freedom to manipulate that world – that is, endow it with meaning. The only condition of the game is complete, unqualified involvement. Yet a few rules apply: the mystery – that is, psychological tension – is kept beyond the ending, and there is no resolution or closure to be expected; the characters must be allowed freedom of action and of choice within the limits of their identity; the reality of the game must be accepted unconditionally; there is an element of hazard, or luck (Tănase 1986: 20). This is clearly a celebration of Fowles's fiction as structuralist game rather than post-structuralist play.

More remarkably, perhaps, Fowles gets his first chapters in volumes on world literature in the early 1980s – Iosifescu is soon joined by Monica Pillat in this – despite the relative unavailability of his novels. While Iosifescu's praise is at times no more than lukewarm, by and large he appreciates Fowles's authorial gimmicks and contextualizes them interestingly with reference to his readership (215). His textual analysis, however, remains firmly within the remit of modernist criticism. Focusing largely on critical categories such as voice, perspective, enigmas, ambiguities and multilayered representations of reality, Iosifescu is concerned with the extent to which the books conform to already-established conventions of factual representation and seems ambivalent about the 'fragmentary' solutions to the moral dilemmas raised in novels and short stories. The dominant of Fowles's fiction, if Iosifescu were to use McHale's terms *avant la lettre*, is firmly epistemologic: the purport of each story is the revelation of a truth, even when the motivations of the characters remain obscure to the author himself. Tellingly, the critic finds antecedents of Fowles's multiple endings in the novels of J. B. Priestley (209) and of his authorial interventions in Richard Aldington (210); similarly, the only Romanian novel he compares Fowles's books to is the modernist Camil Petrescu's daringly experimental *Patul lui Procust* (*The Procrustean Bed*, 1933) (208). Iosifescu's effort of synthesizing Fowles's achievement is in many ways the most comprehensive and challenging discussion of the British novelist's narrative virtuosity in Romanian criticism and remains unequalled in the 1980s.

Pillat's 1985 chapter on 'fabricating the illusion' in *The Magus*, by comparison, is saturated with structuralism. She discusses the novel in terms of the initiatory quest of both the protagonist Urfe and the authorial figure Conchis, comparing it to other dramatizations of that quest such as Shakespeare's *The Tempest* and Defoe's *Robinson Crusoe* and emphasizing the extent to which the quest itself takes place in language. To her, the conflict between Conchis and Urfe is that between *écriture* and writing, between potential and the falsifying, finite, concrete instance (93). The process of signification undergone by the setting – the island – is interpreted as a competition between the Apollonian and the Dionysian, the divergent creative modes. The triumph of the Dionysian, centrifugal, demythologizing impulses of both language and form empowers the reader (103) and it enables the artist to celebrate creation as perpetual play (105). Pillat is unique in quoting a hefty theoretical bibliography, from Bakhtin and Barthes to Bachelard, Pierre Richard and Benveniste, alongside two of the fictions for which structuralist criticism showed a decided predilection, Borges's *Labyrinths* and Lewis Carroll's *Alice in Wonderland*.

Similarly theoretically minded, Gheorghița Dimitriu draws a brief yet substantial comparison between the 'Penelope' section in Joyce's *Ulysses* and chapter 13 of Fowles's *The French Lieutenant's Woman* in terms of narrative strategy. Her aim is to contrast the interior monologue as a manifestation of the modernist doctrine of the impersonality of art with the self-reflexivity of postmodern fiction along the lines of the relationship established – and challenged – between the narrator and reader through devices such as voice and the 'illusion of life' (32). Dimitriu concludes that while the two books illustrate two ages of the novel, they both hail back to Sterne's *Tristram Shandy*, a text which takes stock, early on, of the narrative potential of its genre.

Reviews of *Daniel Martin* are unanimously enthusiastic, whether they see the book as a dramatization of philosophical dilemmas (Burlui 1985: 13), of the predicament of moral man who withdraws into imagination to face his demons (I. Grigorescu 1985: 20) or of the dialectical relation between liberty and determinism (Apostolescu 1986: 47). Both Irina Burlui and Irina Grigorescu praise the novel's supremely modern, experimental, protean style and form. To Grigorescu, the prose is in no way ostentatious or arrogant, but rather an 'almost telepathic' communication between the author and the reader (1985: 20, my trans.). To Burlui, there is an iconoclastic freedom to the form of the novel, which knows no other limits than those of language: she praises the shape-shifting characters and the metafictional ironies of the text (1985: 13). Roxana Apostolescu, too, notes the preoccupation with language's tendency of veering into the general, the conventional, the ambiguous, but also the metaphoric, which the protagonist registers and resists as he strives to recuperate authentic feeling and communication (1986: 47). Both Grigorescu and Apostolescu interpret the novel as a representation of English identity, associating Englishness with social rituals, self-delusion, the wearing of masks, the sense of failure – both personal and historical – and the compensatory flights of imagination, but also, significantly, with the novelistic tradition (I. Grigorescu 20).

Two other reviews of the same novel move beyond the text at hand to draw broader conclusions. For Monica Botez, the publication of the novel in English occasions an early overview of Fowles's major novels to date. She traces an evolution from what she calls the early postmodernism of *The Collector* and *The French Lieutenant's Woman* which remains essentially formal, to the more comprehensive vision bodied forth by *The Magus*, and beyond, into a fiction that leaves behind the pretence of angst and absurdism in favour of closure and a humanist ethos in *Daniel Martin* (1982: 65–66). Unique among reviewers, Lidia Vianu, a translator and translation studies specialist, analyses the Romanian rendition of *Daniel Martin* from the perspective of the challenges it poses to the translators and of the solutions found by Deac and Chițoran. Their expertise in contemporary literature and their interest in the pedagogic addressability of fiction come to their aid, Vianu avers, emphasizing the degree to which this translation could serve as an illustration of recent tendencies in British fiction (1987: 2).

Reviews of the Romanian translation of *The Magus* focus on Fowles's programmatic challenging of our sense of tradition as a source of stability and its displacement by the realization that it is in fact a limitation (Ungureanu 1987: 12), or the way in which Fowles's prose breaks the mould and thematizes the tension between referent and representation (Szász 1988: 20), whereas a third is essentially an enthusiastic ode to the joys of reading the book despite – or perhaps precisely because of – its inconsistencies and obscurities (Manolescu 1987: 10). As with Murdoch's *The Sea, the Sea*, in her review Livia Szász is interested in the way in which 'the speculative faculty' is complemented by 'a lucid understanding of novelistic construction', emphasizing the tendency to fabulate but also to metaphorize and allegorize experience (1988: 20, my trans.). According to her, 'Fowles is perfectly in control of that radical craft of challenging forms, which turns the border between artificiality and originality, excessive symbolism and erudition, kitsch and pretentiousness into a malleable demarcation. His writing thus becomes a mannerist exercise sublimated into an abundant and vigorous narrative flux' of Victorian descent (1988: 20, my trans.). The critic's language indicates familiarity with both the features of postmodern fiction and the critical terminology to describe them.

Two constants emerge from these brief studies of Fowles: his status as a best-selling author and his propensity for formal experimentation. Neither of these features is shared to the same degree by Murdoch, although in other respects the two novelists are said to have much in common, a shared literary tradition and an interest in existential and moral quandaries in particular. As with Murdoch, there is only very sporadic discussion of the alterity of the culture in which Fowles's books were produced. The rigours of translation are only occasionally mentioned, and even then, they merely receive the approving nod for the translators' attention to cultural codes and the linguistic subtleties of Fowles's prose (Szasz 1988: 20, I. Grigorescu 1985: 20, Ungureanu 1987: 12). The social context is even more seldom described. Galea has a rather singular intervention in this sense, as she mentions Charles's and Sarah's refusal of upward social mobility and the negative valuation of Sam's emancipation through shrewd mercantilism as instances of the anti-Victorian ethos of *The French Lieutenant's Woman* (1981: 52). Iosifescu contextualizes Fowles's books only in biographical terms (192–194). Apostolescu contrasts the English and American ethos as experienced by Daniel Martin along psycho-social lines: the former relies on conservative conventions and traditions to safeguard personal emotional and moral integrity, whereas in the latter, the accumulation of objects is meant to create the illusion of stability (48). This reluctance to address social issues, which is shared by Murdoch criticism despite its frequent mention of Murdoch's realism, contravenes Gąsiorek's recommendation that realism be regarded as 'an impulse to represent the social world' (14): in 1980s Romania, most critics prefer to operate with a definition of realism as a formal strategy. The absence of historicizing details is supplemented by the frequent reference to a novelistic tradition that is largely coincidental with that mentioned in connection with Murdoch (Fielding, Sterne, Dickens, Thackeray, Hardy), to which the occasional reference to Conrad and James is added in Fowles's case. This selective obstruction of cultural alterity, whereby the literary tradition is foregrounded but socio-cultural identity is not, is strategic, resulting not merely in the importation of many an international writer but also in implicitly placing them in the category of 'valuable' – rather than the Stalinist 'relevant' – literature.

The 1980s and beyond

Looking back on the 1980s more than 20 years later, Murdoch and Fowles may not appear as the most emblematic writers of that decade. Yet, through a concatenation of circumstances that may never be completely elucidated, to the Romanian readership of that time, they represented contemporary British fiction. One wonders whether their importation to Romania confirmed the impression of British postmodernism as comparatively unadventurous and of British society as politically conservative and dominated by a firmly middle-class ethos. In a 1992 article, Stanciu briefly takes stock of the contingent biases and limits of Romanian criticism addressing contemporary British fiction, the most significant of which have to do with the geographical and cultural distance separating Romanian readers from the world described by that fiction. He concludes, however, that by and large recent novels suffer from an exhaustion and anomie which their traditional – but by now formulaic and almost caricatural – recourse to realism does little to compensate for (2004: 175–180). Nonetheless, Stanciu continued to write with variable degrees of enthusiasm about writers as diverse as Iris Murdoch, David Lodge, Julian Barnes, Ian McEwan, Martin Amis and others throughout the 1990s and beyond, many of the articles being collected in his 2004 volume.

What is more relevant perhaps than the valuations circulated in the studies in a minor key discussed above is the stress laid on particular aspects of Murdoch's and Fowles's work. The distinction realism–postmodernism plays itself out, as we have seen, not only in the classifications of writers but sometimes in criticism analysing the same writer at different times. Thus, the 'realism' discerned by critics in the works of Murdoch and Fowles is seldom associated with the surrealism and hyperrealism of the postmoderns; rather, it is a throwback to Victorian fiction, a view which the novelists themselves seemed to encourage up to a point – witness the frequent quotes from essays and prefaces that the reviewers and critics incorporate in their analyses and, in Murdoch's case, the interviews (see for instance Stanciu 2004: 290). By the late 1980s, however, Fowles becomes firmly established as a postmodernist, whereas Murdoch's fiction is acknowledged to propose a humanist alternative to postmodernism. While specific works may indeed be more amenable to one description than another, it is also the case that the critical discourse reveals the critic's allegiance to a certain exegetical persuasion. That criticism itself marks an evolution becomes obvious not only by observing the shifts taking place during that decade but also by looking into the kind of retrospectives instantiated by Andreea Deciu's 1995 'Succese de odinioară' ('Successes of yesteryear'). In this brisk review of the new translation of Fowles's *The French Lieutenant's Woman*, Deciu avers that much of Fowles's appeal may have vanished because the aura of mystery and rebellion that had once accompanied postmodernism has been explained away and postmodern fiction itself has become ever more radical, leaving behind Fowles's comparatively timid forays.

By and large, however, the approach throughout the 1980s remains primarily formalist. In a retrospective study, Bogdan Lefter concludes polemically that Romanian criticism between the 1960s and 1990s had a hard time leaving modernism behind and keeping up with the new developments in literature (2002: 503–504). In a society in which, as Mușat shows, the communist regime emptied the world of reality (189) by using means similar to those of literary utopia to create a widening gap between what people were conditioned to believe and their experience of the world (165–169), an awareness coagulated in the 1980s of the constructedness of reality and of language's constitutive role. As it was triggered not by a proliferation of discursive possibilities but by the enforcement of a unique discourse, this awareness, unlike in Western societies, is not celebrated as enabling in communist cultures; the flight from ideology, itself an ideological gesture, leads back to the safer realm of essences – whether aesthetic (form), humanist (morality) or anthropological (empirical experience). Hence the appeal of writers such as Fowles and Murdoch: as in their fiction, this is not an innocent return to a lost Arcadia; rather, it is a loop through the familiar territory of modernism in search of a way out of the dominant monolithic discourse.

The fall of the communist regime brought about such discontinuities as to suggest a change of cultural paradigm. In the early 1990s, the editorial system collapsed, book reviews lost their authority as the reviewers of earlier decades retired and the book market became ever more plentiful and diversified, and a revisionist fever began to drive and check every critical thought. Gradually, an infrastructure was set up: the publishing industry began to thrive on translations of books that had previously been inaccessible; cultural journals greeted the new diversity of publications and celebrated the newly acquired freedom of expression; foreign language departments reopened and new ones emerged where there had never been any. However, a discrepancy persisted between critical discourse and institutional infrastructure, best illustrated by literary reviews, which remained largely derivative, perfunctory and ineffective throughout the 1990s and beyond.

The need to revise discursive practices was so acutely felt that for a while it stalemated critical thinking. Much of the criticism published in the early 1990s consisted of revised editions of earlier studies, from which all remarks that could be construed as paying lip service to the former regime were carefully expurgated, such that references to social realism were even more cautious than before. Moreover, there was a generalized reluctance not only to confront the communist legacy but even to become in any way associated with Marxism or post-structuralism. This reluctance resulted in a return to a discourse of aesthetic and humanist values that was so anachronistic as to be described as the symptom of an epistemological crisis of Romanian criticism (I. B. Lefter 2002: 504). It was not until the turn of the century that these issues were confronted, and, significantly, the revaluation started by addressing the literary phenomenon of the 1980s, as against a reconsideration of Western postmodernism.

Once literary studies began to address the issue of postmodernism critically, publishing houses likewise began to commission translations from writers who had come into their own in the 1980s and are widely regarded as the British postmoderns: Kazuo Ishiguro, Graham Swift, Ian McEwan, Salman Rushdie, Julian Barnes and Peter Ackroyd received their first translations into Romanian between 1998 and 2002; J. M. Coetzee, Martin Amis and D. M. Thomas not until the mid-2000s, according to the UNESCO Index Translationum. At the same time, the increasing demand for academics triggered by the massification of higher education resulted in an increasing number of doctoral dissertations and monographs on recent British fiction. Many of the dissertations undertaken around the turn of the century focused on writers like Murdoch and Fowles who had been popular in Romania and for whose study Romanian, not only Western, criticism was available. Others, however, taking advantage of increasing mobility opportunities, approached writers hitherto unknown to the Romanian reading public, such as Ackroyd, Barnes and Rushdie. However, there is no clear evidence that developments in English studies impacted the publishing industry in any substantial way before the late 2000s, when indeed Anglists began to engage critically with the practice of literary translation. At about the same time, scholarly journals became increasingly competitive, such that they began to pose a challenge to the cultural press in terms of authoritativeness, despite their more restricted circulation.

Scholarly studies of Murdoch and Fowles have continued to appear both in cultural magazines and in academic journals. The authors of these articles have also written monographs devoted to either of the two novelists and their approaches vary widely, from psychoanalysis to pragmatic analysis of fictional discourse to comparative studies to interdisciplinary approaches involving philosophy or painting. True to her comparatist interests, Ana Olos, for instance, finds similarities between Murdoch's word-child and Kipling's man-cub (in Gilder et al. 45–66) and discerns 'Murdoch's shadow' in McEwan's novels, particularly *Amsterdam* and *Atonement* (2004 online). At the same time as the pool of translated contemporary novelists increases, the repertoire of critical approaches shows evidence of the influence of – and the intention of becoming synchronized with – current British criticism.

In the absence of effective reviews, afterwords are occasionally appended to recent translations from Murdoch and Fowles, so as to introduce the novels and their authors to the Romanian reading public. Thus, for instance, postmodernism specialists Mihaela Irimia and Dan Grigorescu wrote the afterwords for the 1995 translations of *Mantissa* and *The French Lieutenant's Woman*, respectively. Their studies evince not only a hitherto unexampled mastery of the international bibliography and the terminology of the field, but also a more secure sense of Fowles's place amongst the postmoderns. Rather than demonstrate the appurtenance of *The French Lieutenant's Woman* to postmodernism, for instance, Grigorescu challenges Patricia Waugh's definition of metafiction for not accommodating the kind of thematization of ontological speculativeness that the novel undertakes. Irimia proceeds to unravel the texture of what to Antip had seemed an insignificant book but what to her is the perfect illustration of the pervasive textu(r)ality of the world, both fictional and extratextual. Similarly, the 1998 translation of Murdoch's *Jackson's Dilemma* had an afterword by Monica Bottez, and the 2002 translation of *The Bell* had one by Ștefan Stoenescu, two other influential Romanian critics of contemporary literature. The prestige of the critics writing these studies, like the fact that neither Murdoch nor Fowles is ever out of print in Romania, testifies to the ongoing interest in their fiction, a popularity which is matched by few contemporary British novelists.

Not all recent Murdoch and Fowles criticism is equally substantial, however. Some studies are fairly straightforward retrospects of Romanian and/or Anglo-American criticism to date, with very little to contribute to the understanding of either these novelists' fiction or the contexts of their reception; others merely rehearse shopworn assessments of the novels. Most, however, make an evident effort to either participate in current international literary dialogues or recuperate a critical tradition whose pre-1990 achievements would otherwise go largely unknown. As with earlier criticism, socio-cultural phenomena are reflected by and in their turn inform critical attitudes and approaches, but the nature of those phenomena is so different now as to make the discourse of the reception of British fiction increasingly diverse and dialogic.

Conclusions

Both Murdoch and Fowles remain widely read in Romania: their bid for authenticity at the expense of extravagant experimentalism continues to appeal in the wake of the revisionist controversies that unsettled the prestige of formal postmodernism in the 1990s. They have become fixtures of the Romanian narrative of 1980s British fiction, illustrating what at the time were perceived to be two divergent tendencies, towards the mediation of moral dilemmas through realistic and allegorical representations of modern living and through formal and ontological un-decidability, respectively. My supplementary, retrospective narrative of Romanian criticism focusing on these two popular, widely reviewed British novelists, who however remain marginal in their home culture of that decade, has aimed to reveal some of the seminal tensions informing the selective reception of British fiction as well as the circuitous problematization of referentiality they enabled at a time when the concept of referentiality was ideologically fraught in Romania.

Works cited

Antip, Felicia. 'Un adaos de importanță comparativ mică.' Rev. of *Mantissa*, by John Fowles. *România literară* (7 Apr. 1983): 22.

Apostolescu, Roxana. '*Daniel Martin* între două opțiuni culturale.' Rev. of *Steaua* (Jan. 1986): 47–48.

Botez, Monica. 'John Fowles: "Daniel Martin". Teorie și practică literară.' *Analele Universității București: Limbi și Literaturi Străine* 31 (1982): 65–66.

Bottez, Monica. 'Iris Murdoch 'și universul operei ei.' Afterword to *Dilema lui Jackson*. București: Univers enciclopedic, 1998, 245–260.

Brezianu, Andrei. '*Marea* lui Iris Murdoch sau viața privită ca scenă.' *Translații*. Cluj-Napoca: Dacia, 1982, 243–248.

Burlacu, Doru, et al. *Dicționar cronologic al romanului tradus în România, de la origini până la 1989*. București: Editura Academiei Române, 2005.

Burlui, Irina. Rev. of *Vlăstarul cuvintelor*, by Iris Murdoch. *Cronica* (9 Oct. 1981): 11.

———. Rev. of *Marea, marea*, by Iris Murdoch. *Cronica* (18 May 1984): 7.

———. 'John Fowles și virtuțile proteice ale romanului.' *Cronica* (5 Apr. 1985): 13.

Călinescu, Matei. *Cele cinci fețe ale modernității: Modernism, avangardă, decadență, kitsch, postmodernism*. Trans. Tatiana Pătrulescu and Radu Țurcanu, with Mona Antohi. Iași: Polirom, (1987) 2005.

———. 'Modernism and Ideology.' *Modernism: Challenges and Perspectives*. Ed. Monique Chefdor, Ricardo Quinones and Albert Wachtel. Urbana and Chicago: University of Illinois Press, 1986, 79–93.

———. 'Romanian Literature: Dealing with the Totalitarian Legacy.' *Literature and Revolution in Eastern Europe*. Special Issue of *World Literature Today* 65(2) (Spring 1991): 244–248.

Cârneci, Magda. *Art of the 1980s in Eastern Europe*. Pitești: Paralela 45, 1999.

Cărtărescu, Mircea. *Postmodernismul românesc*. București: Humanitas, 1999.

Ciugureanu, Adina. 'English Studies Curricula and Romanian Anthologies of English Literature.' *English Studies in Romania*. Ed. Suman Gupta and Ana-Karina Schneider. Special Issue of *American, British and Canadian Studies* 14 (Jun. 2010): 43–58.

Corniș-Pope, Marcel. *The Unfinished Battles. Romanian Postmodernism before and after 1989*. Iași: Polirom, 1996.

Cotrău, Liviu. 'Colecționarii lui John Fowles.' *Steaua* (Apr. 1983): 50–51.
Deciu, Andreea. 'Succese de odinioară.' Rev. of *Iubita locotenentului francez*, by John Fowles. *România literară* (8–14 Mar. 1995): 7.
D'Haen, Theo and Hans Bertens. Series Editors' Preface. *British Postmodern Fiction*. Amsterdam and Atlanta, GA: Rodopi, 1993.
Dimitriu, Gheorghița. 'Polaritatea: monolog autonom/discursul naratorului conștient de sine.' *Analele Universității București: Limbi și Literaturi Străine* 31 (1982): 31–32.
Elias, Amy J. 'Meta-*Mimesis*? The Problem of British Postmodern Realism.' *British Postmodern Fiction*. Ed. Theo D'Haen and Hans Bertens. Amsterdam and Atlanta, GA: Rodopi, 1993, 9–31.
Galea, Ileana. 'John Fowles și experimentul romanesc.' *Steaua* (Sep. 1981): 52–53.
———. 'Iris Murdoch și metamorfozele romanului.' *Steaua* (May 1983): 6.
Gąsiorek, Andrzej. *Post-War British Fiction: Realism and After*. London: Edward Arnold, 1995.
Gilder, Eric, Ana-Karina Schneider and Ana Lița (eds). *For the Love of the Good: Meditations on the Mind and Manners of Iris Murdoch*. Special Issue of *American, British and Canadian Studies* 9 (Dec. 2007).
Grigorescu, Dan. Rev. of *Vlăstarul cuvintelor*, by Iris Murdoch. *Contemporanul* 37 (11 Sep. 1981): 11.
———. 'Postfață.' *Iubita locotenentului francez*, by John Fowles. București: Univers, 1994, 545–558.
———. 'Ce înseamnă „postmodernismul britanic"?' *Studii de literatură engleză*. București: Grai și Suflet, 2003, 539–562.
Grigorescu, Irina. Rev. of *Daniel Martin*, by John Fowles. *România literară* (28 Feb. 1985): 20.
Iosifescu, Silvian. 'John Fowles: între virtuozitate și autenticitate.' *De-a lungul unui secol*. București: Eminescu, 1983, 188–216.
Irimia, Mihaela Anghelescu. 'Postfață.' *Mantisa* by John Fowles. București: Univers, 1995, 255–263.
———. 'Aristocraticul foc.' Afterword to *Aristos* by John Fowles. București: Univers, 2002, 120–127.
Lefter, Ion Bogdan. 'Romanian Literature and the Publishing Industry since 1989: Asymmetries between History and Rhetoric.' *Canadian Review of Contemporary Literature* (Sep./Dec. 1995): 867–879.
———. *Anii '60–'90: Critica literară*. Pitești: Paralela 45, 2002.
———. *Postmodernism: Din dosarul unei „bătălii" culturale*. Pitești: Paralela 45, 2002.
Lefter, Virgil. 'Iris Murdoch și elogiul cărții.' *Steaua* (Jul. 1987): 54–55.
Manolescu, Nicolae. 'Corpul și sufletul.' Rev. of *Discipolul*, by Iris Murdoch. *Cronica* (26 Dec. 1986): 8.
———. 'Insula misterelor.' Rev. of *Magicianul*, by John Fowles. *Cronica* (8 Apr. 1988): 10.
Marino, Adrian. *Comparatism și teoria literaturii*. Trans. Mihai Ungurean. Iași: Polirom, 1998.

Mihăilescu, Clementina. *Interpersonal Relationships in Iris Murdoch's Novels via Kelly and Jung*. Sibiu: Editura Universității Lucian Blaga, 2004.
Munteanu, Aurel Dragoș. Rev. of *Marea, marea*, by Iris Murdoch. *Luceafărul* 8 (Oct. 1983): 7.
Mușat, Carmen. *Perspective asupra romanului românesc postmodern și alte ficțiuni teoretice*. Pitești: Paralela 45, 1998.
Negrici, Eugen. *Iluziile literaturii române*. București: Cartea Românească, 2008.
Olos, Ana. 'Umbra Iris-ei Murdoch la Ian McEwan.' *Observator Cultural* 207 (Febr. 2004). Web. 15 Oct. 2012.
Petrescu, Liviu. *Poetica postmodernismului*. 3rd ed. Pitești: Paralela 45, 2003.
Pillat, Monica. 'Fabricarea iluziei: John Fowles, *Magul*.' *Ieșirea din contur*. București: Eminescu, 1985, 91–105.
Postmodernismul. Special Issue of *Caiete critice* 1–2 (1986).
Ralian, Antoaneta. 'Iris Murdoch: *Călugărițe și ostași*. Prezentare și traducere de.' *România literară* (18 Jun. 1981): 21.
———. 'Iris Murdoch.' *Secolul 20* (Nov.–Dec. 1983): 105–109.
Spiridon, Monica, Ion Bogdan Lefter and Gheorghe Crăciun. *Experiment in Post-War Romanian Literature*. Trans. Della Marcus, Ruxandra-Ioana Patrichi and David Hill. Pitești: Paralela 45, 1999.
Stanciu, Virgil. 'Starea romanului.' *Secolul 20*(10–12) (1978): 219–228.
———. *Războiul gândului cu literele. Eseuri de literatură americană și engleză*. Cluj-Napoca: Editura Tribuna, 2004.
Stoenescu, Ștefan. 'Binele-i o revărsare.' Afterword to *Clopotul*, by Iris Murdoch. București: Polirom, 2002, 371–395.
Stroia, Olga. *The Literary World of John Fowles and Its Reception in Romania*. Sibiu: Alma Mater, 2004.
Szász, Livia. 'În căutarea formei.' Rev. of *Marea, marea*, by Iris Murdoch. *România literară* (29 Dec. 1983): 20.
———. Rev. of *Magicianul*, by John Fowles. *România literară* (7 Apr. 1988): 20.
Tănase, Manuela. 'Fowles și jocul creației.' *România literară* (6 Mar. 1986): 20.
Țeposu, Radu. *Istoria tragică și grotescă a întunecatului deceniu literar nouă*. 3rd ed. București: Polirom, 2006.
Tupan, Maria Ana. 'O carte cuprinzătoare ca viața.' Rev. of *Discipolul*, by Iris Murdoch. *România literară* 2 (Jul. 1987): 20.
UNESCO. *Index Translationum: World Bibliography of Translation* (26 Feb. 2003). 7 Jun. 2012. Web. 12 Jul. 2012.
Ungureanu, Traian. 'Oxford vs. Phraxos.' Rev. of *Magicianul*, by John Fowles. *Amfiteatru* (Apr. 1988): 12.
Ursa, Mihaela. *Optzecismul și promisiunile postmodernismului*. Pitești: Paralela 45, 1999.
Vianu, Lidia. 'Gustul experimentului.' Rev. of *Daniel Martin*, by John Fowles. *Ramuri* (15 Apr. 1987): 2.
Zaciu, Mircea. *Jurnal*. Vol. 1. Cluj-Napoca: Dacia, 1993.

Timeline of Works

1980

Douglas Adams *The Restaurant at the End of the Universe*
Julian Barnes *Metrolodge*
Anthony Burgess *Earthly Powers*
William Golding *Rites of Passage*
David Lodge *How Far Can You Go?*
Iris Murdoch *Nuns and Soldiers*
Graham Swift *The Sweet Shop Owner*
Alice Thomas *The Birds of the Air*
Barry Unsworth *Pascali's Island*
Michael Westlake *One Zero and the Night Controller*

1981

Martin Amis *Other People*
Alasdair Gray *Lanark*
Maurice Leitch *Silver's City*
Ian McEwan *The Comfort of Strangers*
Christopher Priest *The Affirmation*
Bernice Rubens *Birds of Passage*
Salman Rushdie *Midnight's Children*
Graham Swift *Shuttlecock*
D.M. Thomas *The White Hotel*
Rose Tremain *The Cupboard*

1982

Pat Barker *Union Street*
William Boyd *An Ice-Cream War*
Bruce Chatwin *On the Black Hill*
John Fowles *Mantissa*
Kazuo Ishiguro *A Pale View of the Hills*
Timothy Mo *Sweet Sour*
Alice Thomas *The 27th Kingdom*

Barry Unsworth *The Rage of the Vulture*
Marina Warner *The Skating Party*

1983

Peter Ackroyd *The Last Testament of Oscar Wilde*
Maureen Duffy *Londoners: An Elegy*
Maggie Gee *The Burning Book*
Howard Jacobson *Coming From Behind*
Terry Pratchett *The Colour of Magic*
Bernice Rubens *Brothers*
Salman Rushdie *Shame*
Graham Swift *Waterland*
Alice Thomas *The Other Side of the Fire*
Fay Weldon *The Lives and Loves of a She-Devil*

1984

Douglas Adams *So Long, Thanks for All the Fish*
Martin Amis *Money*
J. G. Ballard *Empire of the Sun*
Iain Banks *The Wasp Factory*
Pat Barker *Blow Your House Down*
Julian Barnes *Flaubert's Parrot*
Christine Brooke-Rose *Amalgamemnon*
Anita Brookner *Hotel du Lac*
Angela Carter *Nights at the Circus*
Kay Dick *The Shelf*
Buchi Emecheta *The Rape of Shavi*
Ellen Galford *Moll Catpurse, Her True History*
Alasdair Gray *1982, Janine*
James Kelman *The Busconductor Hines*
David Lodge *Small World: An Academic Romance*
Christopher Priest *The Glamour*
Mary Wesley *The Camomile Lawn*

1985

Peter Ackroyd *Hawksmoor*
Iain Banks *Walking on Glass*
John Fowles *A Maggot*

Maggie Gee *Light Years*
Alasdair Gray *The Fall of Kevin Walker*
James Kelman *A Chancer*
Bernice Rubens *Mr Wakefield's Crusade*
Clive Sinclair *Blood Libels*
Rose Tremain *Journey to the Volcano*
Barry Unsworth *Stone Virgin*
Jeanette Winterson *Oranges Are Not the Only Fruit*

1986

Kingsley Amis *The Old Devils*
Iain Banks *The Bridge*
Pat Barker *Liza's England*
Julian Barnes *Staring at the Sun*
Christine Brooke-Rose *Xorandor*
Pete Davies *The Last Election*
Ellen Galford *The Fires of Bride*
Kazuo Ishiguro *An Artist of the Floating World*
Timothy Mo *An Insular Possession*
Ben Okri *Incidents at the Shrine*
Caryl Phillips *A State of Independence*
Terry Pratchett *The Light Fantastic*

1987

Peter Ackroyd *Chatterton*
Martin Amis *Einstein's Monsters*
Iain Banks *Espledair Street*
Malcolm Bradbury *Cuts*
Margaret Drabble *The Radiant Way*
James Kelman *Greyhound for Breakfast*
Maurice Leitch *Chinese Whispers*
Ian McEwan *The Child in Time*
Alan Moore *Watchmen*
Iris Murdoch *The Book and the Brotherhood*
Joan Riley *Waiting in the Twilight*
Bernice Rubens *Our Father*
Iain Sinclair *White Chappell, Scarlet Tracings*
Alice Thomas *The Clothes in the Wardrobe*
Marina Warner *The Lost Father*

Michael Westlake *Imaginary Women*
Jeanette Winterson *The Passion*

1988

Iain M. Banks *The Player of Games*
Michael Bracewell *The Crypto-Amnesia Club*
Bruce Chatwin *Utz*
Maggie Gee *Grace*
Alan Hollinghurst *The Swimming Pool Library*
David Lodge *Nice Work*
Michael Moorcock *Mother London*
Ben Okri *Stars of the New Curfew*
Glenn Patterson *Burning Your Own*
Terry Pratchett *Sourcery* and *Wyrd Sisters*
Joan Riley *Romance*
Salman Rushdie *The Satanic Verses*
Graham Swift *Out of This World*
Alice Thomas *The Skeleton in the Cupboard*
Barry Unsworth *Rum and Sugar*

1989

Martin Amis *London Fields*
Julian Barnes *A History of the World in 10½ Chapters*
Michael Bracewell *Divine Concepts of Physical Beauty*
Buchi Emecheta *Gwendolyn*
Janice Galloway *The Trick Is to Keep Breathing*
Beryl Gilroy *Boy Sandwich*
Kazuo Ishiguro *The Remains of the Day*
James Kelman *A Disaffection*
Robert McLiam Wilson *Ripley Bogle*
Caryl Phillips *Higher Ground*
Ravinder Randhawa *Right of Way*
Emma Tennant *Two Women of London: The Strange Case of Ms Jekyll and Mrs Hyde*
Rose Tremain *Restoration*
Fay Weldon *The Cloning of Joanna May*
Michael Westlake *The Utopian*
Jeanette Winterson *Sexing the Cherry*

Timeline of National Events

1980

Workers at British Steel begin nationwide strike
Thatcher's 'Not for turning' speech at the Conservative Party conference in Brighton
The National Heritage Memorial Fund is established under the National Heritage Act
Zimbabwe becomes independent of the UK
The Iranian embassy siege: six armed men storm the embassy in London, taking 26 hostages; two hostages are killed
British embassy in Iraq is attacked by gunmen
Sheba Feminist Publishers founded
Britain enters recession – unemployment reaches 2 million
Strike in steel industry
Government ends postal monopoly – private providers will be allowed to carry mail
Michael Foot elected leader of the Labour Party

1981

British Nationality Act passed (effective 1983)
Wedding of Prince Charles and Lady Diana
Riots (in Brixton and Southall in London, Moss Side in Manchester, Toxteth in Liverpool, St Pauls in Bristol)
Hunger strike by IRA prisoners in the Maze Prison near Belfast ends after ten deaths
New Cross Fire
Peter Sutcliffe, known as 'The Yorkshire Ripper', murders 13 women and attempts to murder seven others
Alasdair Gray wins Saltire Society Scottish Book of the Year Award for *Lanark*
Launch of the Social Democratic Party (SDP)
Salman Rushdie's *Midnight's Children* wins the Booker Prize

1982

Argentina invades the Falklands Islands and the Falklands War begins. It lasts from April to October.
Unemployment rises to about 3 million
Channel 4 begins transmission

Greenham Common Women's Peace Camp: 30,000 women hold hands in protest at Britain's decision to allow cruise missiles on the base

The first International Fair of Radical, Black and Third World Books held in North London

Unemployment breaches 3 million during economic recession

Sinn Féin wins its first seats on the Northern Ireland Assembly

1983

Margaret Thatcher is re-elected in a landslide victory of 379 seats (a majority of 144 seats)

The British Nationality Act of 1981 comes into effect

National Heritage Act

Neil Kinnock is elected leader of the Labour Party

The Maze Prison escape: 38 IRA prisoners escape from the Maze Prison in County Antrim, Northern Ireland. One prison officer dies and another 20 are injured.

Stephen Waldorf shooting: A British policeman shoots and injures an innocent man, believing him to be escaped prisoner David Martin

The chancellor, Nigel Lawson, announces cuts to public spending of £500 million

The NHS privatizes its laundering, cleaning and catering services

The Glasgow's Miles Better campaign is launched

Black Womantalk is founded

1984

Miners strike over pit closures (lasting 12 months, 1984–85)

The Trade Union Act prohibits unions from striking without a ballot

Hurricane force winds kill six people

Youth gangs in Wolverhampton loot shops

Yvonne Fletcher is killed in the Libyan embassy siege, in St James Square, London

Assassination attempt on Thatcher and the British cabinet by the IRA at the Conservative Party conference in Brighton

Arthur Scargill is arrested on the charge of obstruction at Orgreave

Under the Sino-British Joint Declaration, the British agree to transfer sovereignty of Hong Kong to the People's Republic of China in 1997

The Oxford Circus fire traps almost 1000 passengers underground, but no one is killed

The O-level and CSE exams in the British school system are replaced the GCSE

Nearly 2.5 million buy shares in British Telecom share offer. Later British Telecom is privatized.

In response to the famine in Ethiopia, the pop music organization Band Aid is formed and records 'Do They Know It's Christmas?'

Asian Women Writers' Group (later Collective) is founded

First International Feminist Book Fair held in Covent Garden, London, which leads to the annual Feminist Book Fortnight promotion in the UK

1985

The BBC soap opera *EastEnders* goes on air
Close to 4000 miners go back to work, reducing those on strike to just over half
Riots in Brixton and Tottenham sparked by encounters with the police
Mohamed Al-Fayed buys Harrods
Manchester air disaster: British Airtours Flight 28M bursts into flames after take-off is aborted, killing 51 passengers
As a response to the Haysel Stadium disaster, the Football Association bans English football clubs from playing in Europe (lifted in 1990–91)
Virago publishes Beverley Bryan, Stella Dadzie and Suzanne Scafe's *The Heart of the Race: Black Women's Lives in Britain*

1986

Major industries are privatized, including British Gas, British Aerospace, Cable and Wireless, Britoil, the National Bus Company, British Airways, Rolls Royce, British Steel and British Telecom
The Wapping dispute: Print unions announce strike and in response News International open a new plant in Wapping. Many members of the National Union of Journalists (NUJ), who came to be known as 'refuseniks', refuse to work at this plant.
Rioting in prisons across Britain
A new £20,000 campaign organized by the British government promises to advise the public of the dangers of AIDS
On 'Big Bang Day', the London Stock Exchange becomes computerized and open to foreign companies
The Greater London Council (GLC) is abolished by Conservative government
Prince Andrew marries Sarah Ferguson
The Peepal Tree Press is founded

1987

Margaret Thatcher is re-elected for a third term, with 376 seats (a majority of 101 seats)
The Great Storm of 1987 – the strongest on record since 1703
The Hungerford massacre: Michael Robert Ryan shoots and kills 16 and wounds 15
The King's Cross fire at King's Cross St Pancras tube station kills 31
Terry Waite, the envoy to the Archbishop of Canterbury, was kidnapped in Lebanon, where he remained a hostage until 1991
The MS *Herald of Free Enterprise* capsizes shortly after leaving the Belgian Port of Zeebrugge
The Remembrance Day bombing in Enniskillen, County Fermanagh, Northern Ireland, kills 11 and injures 63

1988

Section 28 (also known as Clause 28) of the Local Government Act forbids the 'promotion of homosexuality'
The Education Reform Act is passed
Nurses in the thousands strike outside hospitals in protest of inadequate NHS funding
Thatcher's speech at Bruges ('We have not successfully rolled back the frontiers of the state in Britain')
IRA terrorists kill a British soldier at Inglis Barracks, London, and later six more soldiers near Belfast
The Lockerbie bombing: Pan Am Flight 103 is bombed and 270 people are killed
The Women's Press publish Asian Women Writers' Workshop's *Right of Way*

1989

Muslims demonstrate at Bradford against Salman Rushdie's *The Satanic Verses*
Ayatollah Ruhollah Khomeini of Iran places a fatwa on author Salman Rushdie, and later Iran breaks off diplomatic relations with Britain
The Kegworth air disaster at East Midlands Airport kills 44 people
Fifty soldiers injured after the IRA bomb the Tern Hill barracks in Shropshire. Later, one British soldier is killed by an IRA bomb in Hanover, Germany, and 11 soldiers are killed at the Deal barracks bombing at the Royal Marine School of Music in Deal.
The Hillsborough disaster: 94 football fans killed during the FA Cup semi-final between Liverpool and Nottingham Forest at the Hillsborough Stadium in Sheffield
Margaret Thatcher becomes the first British Prime Minister to complete ten years in office
Unemployment falls below 2,000,000
The *Marchioness* disaster on the Thames kills 51
The Church of England's General Assembly votes to allow the ordination of women

Timeline of International Events

1980

Reagan elected President of the United States of America
Failed US rescue attempt to save hostages in Tehran
The Iran–Iraq War starts
Zimbabwe becomes independent of the UK
Mount St Helens erupts
Ted Turner establishes CNN
John Lennon is assassinated in New York
The US boycott Olympic Games as a result of growing tensions with the USSR over Afghanistan
The arcade game 'Pac-Man' is first released

1981

Reagan wounded in assassination attempt by John Hinckley
Assassination attempt on Pope John Paul II by Mehmet Ali Ağca
Reagan fires all air traffic controllers who refused to respond to his order to return to work
First woman appointed to the US Supreme Court
The AIDS virus is identified
The launch of first space shuttle, *Columbia*
IBM introduces its first personal computer
MTV goes on the air

1982

Argentina invades the Falklands Islands and the Falklands War begins. It lasts from April to October.
Reverend Sun Myung Moon marries 2075 couples at Madison Square Garden
Michael Jackson releases *Thriller*
Vietnam Veterans Memorial is opened in Washington, DC
King Henry VIII's ship the *Mary Rose* is raised after 437 years

1983

Reagan calls the USSR 'the focus of evil in the modern world', and proposes a Strategic Defense Initiative (SDI or 'Star Wars')
The US Armed Forces, under Reagan, invade Grenada
The Infrared Astronomical Satellite is launched
A famine begins in Ethiopia and continues to 1985
Sally Ride becomes the first American woman in space
The Soviet military shoots down a Korean airliner
The US embassy in Beirut is bombed
Michico Kakutani's 'Novelists Are News Again' appears in the *New York Times*

1984

Reagan re-elected President. Congress cuts off all funding for Reagan's secret wars in Central America.
Brunei gains its independence from the United Kingdom
Indira Gandhi, India's Prime Minister, assassinated by two bodyguards
Poison gas leak in Bhopal, India
'Postmodernism, or the Cultural Logic of Late Capitalism' by Fredric Jameson is published in *New Left Review*
Publication of *Wasafiri* begins

1985

The new Soviet premier, Mikhail Gorbachev, introduces reform with the policies of *perestroika* (restructuring) and *glasnost* (openness)
A Franco-American expedition discovers the wreak of the *Titanic*
AIDS epidemic gains attention in the US
Compact discs introduced in the US
Live Aid concerts, held in London and Philadelphia, raise over £50 million in famine relief for Ethiopia
The Heysel Stadium disaster: before the start of the European Cup final between Liverpool and Juventus at Haysel Stadium in Brussels, 39 football fans die in a crush
Hole in the ozone layer discovered

1986

Soviet nuclear reactor explodes in Chernobyl
Space Shuttle Challenger explodes, killing its seven astronauts
The Iran–Contra and insider trading scandals are exposed

The US bombs Libya
The USSR launches Mir space station
The Windows program is invented by Microsoft

1987

Reagan and Gorbachev agree on limiting medium-range nuclear missiles
Black Monday: Dow Jones index drops 22.6 per cent in one day
DNA is first used to convict criminals
Klaus Barbie is sentenced to life in prison
A West German pilot lands unchallenged in Russia's Red Square

1988

George H. W. Bush is elected as President of the United States
The US shoots down an Iranian airliner
US savings and loans lose over $13 billion
Soviet troops begin final withdrawal from Afghanistan under Gorbachev

1989

Tiananmen Square massacre in Beijing
The government of Nicolae Ceauşescu, in Romania, is overthrown in the December 1989 Revolution; he and his wife are executed on public television following a two-hour court session
The fall of the Berlin Wall heralds the break-up of the USSR and the end of the Cold War
Bush invades Panama
Exxon Valdez creates largest oil spill in US history in Alaska
Ayatollah Khomeini issues fatwa against Salman Rushdie
The World Wide Web is invented by Tim Berners-Lee

Biographies of Writers

Martin Amis

Born in 1949 in Swansea, south Wales, Martin Amis is the son of the novelist Kingsley Amis. After graduating from Oxford in 1971, where he studied English, Martin Amis worked as a literary journalist until 1979. During this time he worked on his first four novels: *The Rachel Papers* (1973), *Dead Babies* (1975), *Success* (1978) and *Other People: A Mystery Story* (1981). In 1984 he published his most acclaimed novel, *Money: A Suicide Note*. After publishing a collection of essays, *The Moronic Inferno and Other Visits to America* (1986), and a collection of stories, *Einstein's Monsters* (1987), he published the second of an informal trilogy of novels, *London Fields* (1989) (the first being *Money*). His other works include *Time's Arrow* (1991), *The Information* (1995) (the third novel of his trilogy), *Night Train*, a pseudo-detective story (1997), *Yellow Dog* (2003), *House of Meetings* (2006) and *The Pregnant Widow* (2010). His other published work includes a collection of stories, *Heavy Weather and Other Stories* (1998); a highly original memoir, *Experience* (2000); a collection of his journalism, *The War against Cliché: Essays and Reviews, 1971–2000* (2001); and a political essay about Stalin's years of terror, *Koba the Dead: Laughter and the Twenty Million* (2002).

Iain Banks

Iain (Menzies) Banks was born in Fife in 1954, and studied English Literature, Philosophy and Psychology at Stirling University. He died in June 2013. He was the author of mainstream novels and science fiction, which he published under the name of Iain M. Banks. His first novel, *The Wasp Factory*, was published in 1984 after being rejected by a number of publishers. He went on to publish numerous novels, including *Walking on Glass* (1985), *The Bridge* (1986), *Espedair Street* (1987), *The Crow Road* (1992), which was adapted for television in 1996, *Complicity* (1993), which was adapted as a film (dir. Gavin Millar, 2000), *Whit* (1995), *A Song of Stone* (1997) and *Dead Air* (2002). As Iain M. Banks, he created The Culture, an interstellar anarchist and utopian civilization, and wrote ten novels in The Culture Series. He won the Hugo Award for Best Novel for his science fiction novel *The Algebraist* (2004).

Pat Barker

Pat Barker was born in Yorkshire in 1943. She studied at the London School of Economics, graduating in 1965. She began to write in her mid-twenties. Her first novel, *Union Street*, was published by Virago Press in 1982, after being rejected by many publishers as too depressing. This novel and the next two, *Blow Your House Down* (1984) and *Liza's England* (1986) (originally published as *The Century's Daughter*), depict the lives of working-class women in the north of England. *Blow Your House Down* alludes to the serial killer Peter Sutcliffe, known as the Yorkshire Ripper, who murdered 13 women around Leeds between 1975 and 1980. In the 1990s, Barker published the Regeneration Trilogy – *Regeneration* (1991), *The Eye in the Door* (1993) and *The Ghost Road* (1995) – which explores the history of World War I. The final novel in the trilogy won the Booker Prize. Other works include *Another World* (1998), *Border Crossing* (2001), *Double Vision* (2003) and *Life Class* (2007).

Julian Barnes

Born in Leicester in 1946, Julian Barnes grew up in two London suburbs, Acton and Northwood, and attended City of London School. During his degree at Oxford, Barnes spent his second year in France, which led him to become a Francophile, as is reflected in several of his books. After graduating in Modern Languages in 1968, he moved to north London and became a lexicographer for the Oxford English Dictionary Supplement. He then worked in various editorial positions from 1971 to 1979, and from 1979 to 1986 as a television critic. Barnes's first novel, *Metroland* (1980), is set in the London suburbs in which he grew up. It won the Somerset Maugham Award and was made into a film in 1998. Barnes also published *Duffy* in 1980, the first of four detective novels under the name of Dan Kavanagh. The other three are *Fiddle City* (1981), *Putting the Boot In* (1985) and *Going to the Dogs* (1987). In 1982 he published his second novel, about a man's descent into insane jealousy, *Before She Met Me*, followed by *Flaubert's Parrot* (1984). After *Staring at the Sun* (1986), a more realist novel begun before *Flaubert's Parrot*, he reverted to the innovative mode of the latter with *A History of the World in 10½ Chapters* (1989). His subsequent novels are: *Talking It Over* (1991), *The Porcupine* (1992), *England, England* (1998), *Love, Etc.* (2000), *Arthur and George* (2005) and *The Sense of an Ending* (2011), which won the Booker Prize. He has published three collections of stories and four books of non-fiction: *Letters from London* (1995), *Something to Declare* (2002), *The Pedant in the Kitchen* (2003) and *Nothing to Be Frightened Of* (2008).

Barbara Burford

Barbara Burford was born in Jamaica in 1944, and moved to London in 1955. Once in London, she was educated at Dalston County Grammar School and studied zoology at King's College London, going on to qualify as a medical laboratory scientific officer. From 1964 she worked in the National Health Service, working in electron microscopy in the 1980s. She went on to work in the civil service and in the wider public sector in the areas of diversity and equality. Burford was active in feminist politics, as well as writing plays, poetry and fiction. Her poems were included in the first black British women's poetry anthology, *A Dangerous Knowing: Four Black Women Poets* (1984), published by Sheba Feminist Press, and which included Burford's work along with that of Gabriela Pearse, Grace Nichols and Jackie Kay. Also in 1984, her play *Patterns*, commissioned by Changing Women's Theatre and examining women's labour, was performed at the Oval Theatre in London. Her *The Threshing Floor*, consisting of a novella of the same name and a number of short stories, was published in 1986. It has since often been included on school curricula. In 1987, she co-edited *Dancing the Tightrope: New Love Poems by Women*, published by the Women's Press. Barbara Burford died in 2010.

Angela Carter

Angela Carter was born in 1940. She spent the war years in Yorkshire, and after the war moved with her family to Balham in South London. Her father apprenticed her to the Croydon Advertiser, where she first acquired her journalistic skills. In 1960, she married Paul Carter, an industrial chemist, and followed him to Bristol University the next year. While studying for a degree in English, specializing in the medieval period, she wrote her first novel, *Shadow Dance* (1966) – called *Honeybuzzard* in the US – a Gothic detective novel. Her second novel, *The Magic Toyshop* (1967), won the John Llewellyn Rhys Prize, and her third novel, *Several Perceptions* (1968), won the Somerset Maugham Prize. Using the money from the prize to leave her husband, Carter spent two years in Japan. She wrote about her Japanese experiences in articles for *New Society* and in the stories collected in *Fireworks* (1974). She had published two more novels, *Heroes and Villains* (1969), a post-apocalyptic novel, and *Love* (1971). Her newfound feminism found expression in *The Infernal Desire Machines of Doctor Hoffman* (1972). This highly anti-realist novel marked a turning point in Carter's career, receiving a lukewarm reception but gaining a cult readership. After returning to London, she published *The Passion of New Eve* (1977). Her distinctive brand of feminism attracted criticism from some feminists when she brought out *The Sadeian Woman* (1978), a polemical essay defending the Marquis de Sade. In 1979, she published *The Bloody Chamber and Other Stories*, the book that made her well known in the US and resulted in several visiting professorships at universities there. The collection retells a number of European fairy stories from a feminist point of view, restoring the sexual content that had been removed by earlier writers. Her last two novels were *Nights at the Circus* (1984), which won the James Tait Black Memorial Prize, and *Wise Children* (1991). Carter died in 1992.

Buchi Emecheta

Buchi Emecheta was born in Lagos, Nigeria, in 1944. She was orphaned when only nine years old, and went the following year to be educated at the Methodist Girls' School, where she stayed until she was 16. The same year she married a student, Sylvester

Onwordi, to whom she had been engaged since she was 11. In 1962, she followed him to London, where he was studying. Emecheta and her husband had five children together, but separated in 1966. As recounted in her early novels, the marriage was an unhappy and sometimes violent one. Following the end of her marriage, Emecheta began studying at the University of London, graduating with a BSc in sociology in 1972. During this time she also worked at a library officer at the British Museum, and raised her children on her own. She went on to work as a youth worker and sociologist with the Inner London Education Authority. Emecheta's first two novels, *In The Ditch* (1972) and *Second Class Citizen* (1974), are semi-autobiographical works, based on her childhood, her marriage, her move to London and her struggles as a single mother. She published her autobiography, *Head above Water*, in 1986, and has published 11 more novels, as well as plays for television, works for children and young adults and non-fiction on women's experiences in Nigeria. In 1983, she was one of Granta's 'Best of Young British Novelists'. Emecheta's success led to numerous lectureships in the 1980s in universities in Nigeria, the US and the UK. From 1982 to 1983 Buchi Emecheta, together with her son Sylvester, ran the Ogwugwu Afor Publishing Company. She was awarded an OBE (Order of the British Empire) in 2005.

John Fowles

John Fowles was born in 1926 in Leigh-on-Sea in Essex. After completing his military service in 1947, he studied French at Oxford, where he first read Jean-Paul Sartre and Albert Camus, who were to be considerable influences on his work. He then spent a year teaching at the University of Poitiers, and then taught English in Greece until 1953. On his return to the UK, he spent the next ten years teaching English as a foreign language in London. Having already completed much of *The Magus* (1966), the first of Fowles's novels to be published was *The Collector* (1963), for which he received one of the highest advances to date for a first novel. The novel was a critical and commercial success, and Fowles stopped teaching in order to concentrate on writing. He published *The Aristos*, a collection of his writings on philosophy, in 1964, and then *The Magus*, which he revised and republished 11 years later. Fowles went on to publish five more novels: *The French Lieutenant's Woman* (1969), *The Ebony Tower* (1974), *Daniel Martin* (1977), *Mantissa* (1982) and *A Maggot* (1985). His two volumes of journals were published in 2003 and 2004. Fowles died in 2005.

Janice Galloway

Janice Galloway was born in Ayrshire in 1955. She studied Music and English at the University of Glasgow and worked as a teacher before starting her career as a writer. She was the first Scottish Arts Council writer in residence to four prisons, HMPs Cornton Vale, Dungavel, Barlinnie and Polmont YOI. Her first novel, *The Trick Is to Keep*

Breathing, was published in 1989. This won the MIND/Allan Lane Award. Her second novel, *Foreign Parts*, was published in 1994, and won the McVitie's Prize. Her third, *Clara* (2002), based on life of Clara Schumann, won the Saltire Book of the Year. She lives in Lanarkshire. Her other works include the short-story collection *Blood* (1991), the opera libretto *Monster* (2002) and 'anti-memoir' *This Is Not about Me* (2008).

Beryl Gilroy

Beryl Gilroy was born in Guyana, then British Guiana, in 1924. She did not receive a formal education until she was 12. Between 1943 and 1945 she attended a teacher training college in Georgetown. She moved to Britain in 1951 to take up a place at the University of London to study for a Diploma in Child Development. She spent a number of years in other kinds of employment, while bringing up her family, unable to find work as a teacher because of racism. In 1968 she returned to teaching, and eventually became the first black head teacher in London, writing about these experiences in her *Black Teacher* (1976). She went to work as a researcher at the University of London, and worked as a psychotherapist, mainly with black women and children. Gilroy gained a PhD in counseling psychology in 1987. In 2000, she was also awarded an honorary doctorate from the Institute of Education. Gilroy's creative writing began in childhood, as a teacher for children, and then in the 1960s when she began writing what was later published by Peepal Tree Press as *In Praise of Love and Children*. Between 1970 and 1975, she wrote the pioneering children's series *Nippers*. Her first novel was published in 1986, *Frangipani House*. *Boy Sandwich* was published in 1989, followed by *Stedman and Joanna: A Love in Bondage* (1991). Her poetry collections include *Echoes and Voices* (1991). Her last novel, *The Green Grass Tango*, was published posthumously in 2001.

Alasdair Gray

Alasdair Gray was born in Riddrie, Glasgow, in 1934. During World War II, he was evacuated with his mother and younger sister to Auchterarder, Perthshire, and then to Stonehouse, Lanarkshire. He attended Glasgow School of Art and worked as an art teacher whilst producing his own artwork, which included murals such as 'Horrors of War' (Scottish–USSR Friendship Society); 'The Seven Days of Creation' (Chancel of Greenhead Church of Scotland, Bridgeton, Glasgow) and 'The Firmament' (Belleisle Street Synagogue, Giffnock, Glasgow) (both now demolished); 'The Book of Jonah' (private flat, Hillhead, Glasgow). Gray wrote a number of plays in the 1970s, and was writer in residence at Glasgow University between 1977 and 1979. His first novel, *Lanark* (1981), written over a period of 30 years, received the David Niven and Saltire Awards. His subsequent novels are *1982 Janine* (1984), *The Fall of Kelvin Walker: A Fable of the Sixties* (1985), *McGrotty and Ludmilla* (1990), *Something Leather* (1990),

Poor Things (1992), *A History Maker* (1994), *Mavis Belfrage* (1996) and *Old Men in Love* (2007). He has published three books of poetry and his autobiography, *A Life in Pictures*, was published in 2010. He has also written on politics and particularly on Scottish independence. He lives in Glasgow.

Kazuo Ishiguro

Kazuo Ishiguro was born in 1954 in Nagasaki, Japan. His family moved to the UK in 1960. Ishiguro graduated from the University of Kent in English and Philosophy. He worked as a social worker for a while, and went on to gain an MA in Creative Writing from the University of East Anglia in 1980. He became a British citizen in 1982, the year of the publication of his first novel, *A Pale View of the Hills*. Both this novel and his second, *An Artist of the Floating World* (1986), are set in Japan, although, after his family's emigration, he did not visit Japan again until 1989. *A Pale View of the Hills* won the Winifred Holtby Memorial Prize and *Artist of the Floating World* won the Whitbread Prize. His next novel, *The Remains of the Day*, won the Booker Prize in 1989. Ishiguro was included in the Granta 'Best of Young British Novelists' in both 1983 and 1993, and was awarded an OBE in 1995. His remaining novels are *The Unconsoled* (1995), *When We Were Orphans* (2000) and *Never Let Me Go* (2005). Two of his novels have been adapted for films, *The Remains of the Day* in 1993 (dir. James Ivory) and *Never Let Me Go* in 2010 (dir. Mark Romanek). He also published a collection of short stories, entitled *Nocturnes: Five Stories of Music and Nightfall*, in 2009.

James Kelman

James Kelman was born in Glasgow in 1946. After leaving school at the age of 15, he undertook a six-year apprenticeship in the printing industry and worked as a bus driver, before beginning his writing career. In 1971 Kelman joined a creative writing evening class under the direction of Philip Hobsbaum, where he met Alasdair Gray. His work is committed to a complex and politically engaged representation of working-class life. His first novel was *The Busconductor Hines* (1984) and his second *A Chancer* (1985). He won the Cheltenham Prize for his short-story collection *Greyhound for Breakfast* (1987), and the James Tait Black Memorial Prize for his third novel, *A Disaffection* (1989) (also shortlisted for the Booker Prize). His fourth novel, *How Late It Was, How Late*, won the Booker Prize in 1994. Other works include *Translated Accounts* (2001), *You Have to Be Careful in the Land of the Free* (2004), *Kieron Smith, Boy* (2006), which won Scotland's most prestigious literary award, the Saltire Society's Book of the Year Award, and *Mo Said She Was Quirky* (2012). He has published two collections of essays and numerous short-story collections.

Ian McEwan

Ian McEwan was born in Aldershot, Hampshire, into an army family in 1948. He spent much of his childhood until he was 12 abroad. He graduated from the University of Sussex in English Literature in 1970, and went on to be one of the first students to graduate from the MA in Creative Writing at the University of East Anglia. His first collection of short stories, *First Love, Last Rites*, was published in 1976, followed by another, *In Between the Sheets*, in 1978. His first two novels, *The Cement Garden* (1978) and *The Comfort of Strangers* (1981), were both short and concerned with dark psychological states, perverse relations and violence. His next novel, *The Child in Time* (1987), marked a change in his work, the novel combining political satire with the possibility of redemption, and won the Whitbread Novel Award. McEwan's nine subsequent novels have generally alternated between historical fiction and narratives dealing with very contemporary concerns and situations. They are *The Innocent* (1990), *Black Dogs* (1992), *Enduring Love* (1997), *Amsterdam* (1998), *Atonement* (2001), *Saturday* (2005), *On Chesil Beach* (2007), *Solar* (2010) and *Sweet Tooth* (2012). McEwan has been shortlisted for the Booker Prize six times, winning in 1998 with *Amsterdam*. He has also won many other prizes and awards, has written screenplays including adaptations of his own work, an oratorio and children's fiction. He was awarded a CBE in 2000.

Michael Moorcock

Michael Moorcock was born in London in 1939. Aged 17, he became the editor of *Tarzan Adventures*. He was subsequently the editor of the controversial science fiction magazine *New Worlds* between 1964 and 1971 and again between 1976 and 1996. The magazine was responsible during the 1960s for developing the 'new wave' in science fiction in the UK; the magazine published writers such as J. G. Ballard and Brian Aldiss. Moorcock's first novel, *The Stealer of Souls*, the first novel in his Elric Saga series, was published in 1961. He has gone on to produce a huge number of stories and novels, publishing nearly 100 works of fiction and non-fiction. While best known in the US for his science fiction and fantasy, in the UK he came to prominence for non-genre work, winning the Guardian Fiction Prize in 1977 for *The Condition of Muzak*, the final book in his Jerry Cornelius Quartet. In the 1980s in particular, he concentrated on such non-genre writing, completing *Mother London* (1988), which was shortlisted for the Whitbread Award. A number of his novels, such as *Behold the Man* (1966) and *The Final Programme* (1969), have been read as non-genre work. All Moorcock's work expresses his political commitment, and he has been particularly critical of the misogynistic and escapist elements in science fiction and fantasy fiction. In the 1990s, Moorcock moved to the US. In 2002, he was inducted into the Science Fiction Hall of Fame. He has been the recipient of a great many awards and prizes.

Iris Murdoch

Iris Murdoch was born in Dublin in 1919. Her parents moved to London while she was still a baby. She studied Classics at Oxford, and between 1944 and 1946 she worked for the United Nations Relief and Rehabilitation Administration in Europe. She went on to study philosophy as a postgraduate student at Oxford, and eventually became a fellow of St Anne's College, Oxford. She published essays on philosophy and a monograph on Jean-Paul Sartre. Her first novel, *Under the Net*, was published in 1954. She went on to publish over 20 more novels, including *The Black Prince* (1973) and *The Book and the Brotherhood* (1987), and several more works of philosophy. Her novel *The Sea, the Sea* (1978) won the Booker Prize, and she won numerous other awards for her fiction. She was made a Dame Commander of the Order of the British Empire in 1987. Murdoch developed Alzheimer's disease in the mid-1990s, and the account of her husband, John Bayley, of her illness was adapted as a film, *Iris* (dir. Richard Eyre, 2001). She died in 1999.

Ravinder Randhawa

Ravinder Randhawa was born in India and grew up in the UK, in Warwickshire. She was a founder of the Asian Women Writers Collective in 1984, and contributed to two collections published by the collective, *Right of Way* (1989) and *Flaming Spirit* (1994). Her first novel, *Wicked Old Woman*, was published by The Women's Press in 1987, and was one of the first novels to be published by a British Asian writer in the post-war period. She has also published a novel for teenagers, *Hari-jan* (1992), another novel, *The Coral Strand* (2001), and numerous short stories. She has been a fellow at St Mary's College, University of Surrey, and at Queen Mary, University of London.

Joan Riley

Joan Riley was born in Jamaica in 1958. An immigrant to the UK in 1976, she studied social work at the University of Sussex and the University of London. Her first novel, *The Unbelonging*, was published by The Women's Press in 1985. This was followed by *Waiting in the Twilight* (1987), *Romance* (1988) and *A Kindness to the Children* (1992). Riley was the first women Afro-Caribbean writer to write about the experience of black women in the UK. Each of her novels offers an often painful account of the experiences of a young girl or woman who has migrated to the UK from the Caribbean, struggling with racism, sexism and poverty. Riley co-edited *Leave to Stay: Stories of Exile and Belonging*, published by Virago Press in 1996, a collection of writing on the theme of exile. She was awarded a prize for her fiction by the *Voice* in 1992, and the MIND prize for *A Kindness to Children* in 1993.

Salman Rushdie

Salman Rushdie was born in 1947 into an affluent Muslim family in Bombay (Mumbai), India. He attended the Cathedral School in Bombay from 1954 to 1961. In 1961 he was sent to Rugby School in England. In 1965 he went to study Islamic history at King's College, Cambridge. After graduating in 1968 he returned to Karachi, where he tried to begin a career in the television industry. Disgusted by the censorship he encountered, he moved back to England, where he worked as an advertising copywriter. Writing part-time, Rushdie abandoned two novels and had a third rejected before publishing his first parodic science fiction novel, *Grimas*, in 1975 to compete for a science fiction prize. In 1981 he published *Midnight's Children*, which won the Booker Prize (and the 25-year Booker of Bookers and 40-year best of the Booker) and catapulted him to international fame, allowing him to leave his job as a copywriter. His third novel, *Shame* (1983), offered a thinly disguised satire of Pakistan under Presidents Zulfikar Ali Bhutto and Zia-ul-Haq and was banned in that country. In 1988, Viking Penguin published *The Satanic Verses*, which quickly attracted the outrage of militant Muslims around the world. Ayatollah Khomeini, the Supreme Leader of Iran, issued a fatwa calling for Rushdie's execution that drove Rushdie into hiding for almost a decade. His next novel, *Haroun and the Sea of Stories* (1990), was directed at children. His subsequent novels are *The Moor's Last Sigh* (1995), *The Ground beneath her Feet* (1999), *Fury* (2001), *Shalimar the Clown* (2005) and *The Enchantress of Florence* (2008). In 2000 Rushdie moved to New York. His other books include a sequel to *Haroun and the Sea of Stories*, *Luka and the Fire of Life* (2010), two collections of his non-fiction – *Imaginary Homelands: Essays and Criticism 1981–1991* (1992) and *Step across This Line: Collected Nonfiction 1992–2002* (2002) – and a collection of short stories, *East, West* (1994).

Graham Swift

Graham Swift was born in London in 1949. He went to school at Dulwich College, in south London, and then to the Universities of Cambridge and York. Swift published his first novel, *The Sweet-Shop Owner*, in 1980, followed by *Shuttlecock* (1981), *Waterland* (1983) and *Out of This World* (1988). In 1983, Swift was included in the Granta 'Best of Young British Novelists'. *Waterland* won the Guardian Fiction Prize and the Geoffrey Faber Memorial Prize. His subsequent novels are *Ever After* (1992), *Last Orders* (1996), which won both the James Tait Black Memorial Prize for Fiction and the Booker Prize, *The Light of Day* (2003), *Tomorrow* (2007) and *Wish You Were Here* (2011). He has also published two volumes of short stories, *Learning to Swim* (1982) and *Chemistry* (2008). Two of Swift's novels have been adapted as films, *Waterland* (dir. Stephen Gyllenhaal, 1992) and *Last Orders* (dir. Fred Schepisi, 2001).

Emma Tennant

Emma Tennant was born in London in 1937, the daughter of Charles Tennant, 2nd Baron Glenconner, and Elizabeth, Lady Glenconner. She spent the war years in her family's house in Scotland, The Glen. She later worked as a travel writer for *Queen* magazine, and for *Vogue*. She published her first novel, *The Colour of Rain*, under the pseudonym Catherine Aydy in 1964. She became a full-time novelist in 1973, and between 1975 and 1979 she edited the literary magazine *Bananas*. Tennant has written many novels, biographies and autobiography. A number of her novels, such as *Two Women of London: The Strange Case of Ms Jekyll and Mrs Hyde* (1989), *Tess* (1993), *Pemberley: Or Pride and Prejudice Continued* (1993) and *Adele: Jane Eyre's Hidden Story* (2000), rewrite or continue the stories of well-known novels by other writers. Other novels, such as *Heathcliff's Tale* (2005), entwine the biographies of writers into new narratives.

D. M. Thomas

D. M. (Donald Michael) Thomas was born in Cornwall in 1935. He moved to Australia with his family in 1949. He returned in 1951, and did national service from 1953, when he learned Russian. He graduated in English from Oxford in 1958. He published in the science fiction magazine *New Worlds* in the 1960s (during Michael Moorcock's first stint as editor). He taught English until 1978, when he was made redundant, and published his first novel, *The Flute-Player* (1979). The best known of his novels, *The White Hotel*, published in 1981, was shortlisted for the Booker Prize. The novel won the Los Angeles Fiction Prize and became an international best-seller, particularly successful in Europe and in the US. It was translated into 30 languages. Thomas has not published a novel since 2000. His first love is poetry, and he has published 12 collections of poetry and translated Russian poetry. His biography of Alexander Solzhenitsyn won the Orwell Prize in 1998. He has also published two memoirs, *Memories and Hallucinations* (1989) and *Bleak Hotel: The Hollywood Saga of the White Hotel* (2008).

Jeanette Winterson

Jeanette Winterson was born in Manchester in 1959. She was adopted as a baby, and her adoptive parents, who were members of the Elim Pentecostal Church, brought her up in Accrington, not far from Manchester. She left home at 16, and went to Oxford to read English when she was 18. She wrote her first novel, *Oranges Are Not the Only Fruit*, while she was at Oxford, and it was published in 1985. It won the Whitbread First Novel Award, and Winterson adapted it for television in 1990. She published *Boating for Beginners* three months after *Oranges*' appearance, but wrote this for money, not considering it a serious work. *The Passion*, her second novel, was published in 1987. Winterson subsequently began to write full-time, publishing a further seven novels: *Sexing the Cherry* (1989), *Written on the Body* (1992), *Art and Lies* (1994), *Gut Symmetries* (1997), *The Powerbook* (2000), *Lighthousekeeping* (2004) and *The Stone Gods* (2007) She has also completed a book of essays, *Art Objects* (1995), a collection of short stories, *The World and Other Places* (1998), a number of novels for children and an autobiography, *Why Be Happy When You Could Be Normal?* (2011). She was made an OBE in 2006.

Index

1922 Committee 5
1970s stagflation 3
7/7 viii
9/11 viii

acceleration 32
Ackroyd, Peter 29, 133, 176,
    192, 208, 223, 229–30
  Chatterton 230
  Hawksmoor 229
Adam Smith Institute, the 2
Adams, Robert M. 192
addiction 53, 70
African American women writers 106–7,
    109–10
Agard, John
  'Palm Tree King' 104
aesthetics 23, 26
Akomfrah, John, *Handsworth Songs* 13
Ali, Monica 101
alienation 64, 70–2
  see also estrangement
Allesandrini, Anthony 182
ambivalence 10, 27, 36, 38, 43, 46
Amis, Kingsley 179
Amis, Martin 22, 33, 36–9, 46,
    48, 79, 82, 85, 87–8, 91–2,
    96, 98–100, 152–4, 160–4,
    169, 170, 172, 174, 177, 184,
    186–91, 208, 221, 223,
    228–30, 239
  Einstein's Monsters 230, 239
  London Fields 96, 152–4, 160–3, 168,
    170, 172–3, 229, 231, 239
  Money 36, 39, 43, 46, 85–8, 91, 95, 99,
    152, 172
  Other People 228, 239
Amos, Valerie, et al. (eds), 'Many Voices,
    One Chant: Black Feminist
    Perspectives' *Feminist Review* 104
Anderson, Benedict 10
Angry Young Men 210

Arana, R. Victoria 102, 117
Arts Council of Great Britain 104
Ascherson, Neal 128
Asian British fiction 114
Asian Women's Action Group
    (later Collective) 107, 114
Asian Women's Resource Center 107
Asian Women's Writers' Workshop 108,
    114
  Right of Way 114
avant-garde, the 51, 178, 207
Ayatollah Khomeini *see* Khomeini,
    Ayatollah

Babi Yar
  Don Giovanni 155–6
  Eugene Onegin 156
Bailey, David A. 11
Bakhtin, Mikhail 153–4, 163, 166
Ballard, J. G. 151
Banks, Carolyn 184
Banks, Iain (M.) 13, 36, 43, 51–3, 55, 59–60,
    63–4, 69, 73–4, 229–30, 239
  The Bridge 230, 239
  The Player of Games 230
  Walking on Glass 229, 239
  The Wasp Factory 229, 239
Banville, John 208
Barbican theatre, the 16
Barker, Pat 21, 36, 40, 46, 82, 88, 90–3,
    98–9, 228–30, 240
  Blow Your House Down 229, 240
  Liza's England 230, 240
  Union Street 21, 46, 228, 240
Barnes, Julian 152–3, 157–60, 165,
    170–3, 192–3, 208, 221, 223,
    229–31, 240
  A History of the World in 10½ Chapters
    231, 240
  Flaubert's Parrot 229, 240
  Staring at the Sun 230, 240
Barnes & Noble 194

Barth, John 175, 177, 179, 192, 194
Barthelme, Donald 175, 192
Basel, Marilyn K. 187
Baucom, Ian 196
   see also Bailey, David A.
Bellow, Saul 178, 187, 190–1
   Henderson the Rain King 190
Bennett, Andrew and Nicholas Royle 16
Bennism 14
Bergonzi, Bernard 6, 176
   The Situation of the Novel (1970) 6
Berlin Wall 21, 238
Berlinski, Claire 5
Bernard, Catherine 191
Bhabha, Homi K. 10
Bhopal 237
Big Bang, financial deregulation, 1986
   5, 234
Bildungsroman, the 41, 56, 163, 166,
   169, 181
Billington, Michael 190
Black British 10-13, 43
Black communities 11
Black Lesbian Group Birmingham 102
Black Womantalk 105, 106, 108, 109, 233
   Black Women Talk Poetry 109
   *Don't Ask Me Why: An Anthology of
      Short Stories by Black Women* 109
   Women 109
Blackness 11
   Britain, meaning of 11
   discourse of 11
   USA, meaning of 11
Blairism viii
Blaise, Clark 181
Blake, William 144
Bleasdale, Alan 1, 88, 90
   Boys from the Blackstuff, [television
      drama series] 1, 88, 90
Blitz, the London 140–6
body 56, 58–60, 70–2
Bogle, Marlene T. 102
Bogle L'Ouverture Bookshop 105
Bohm, David 35, 47
Bohr, Niels 33
book-selling, new approaches, 1980s
   Dillons 9
   Waterstones 9
   WHSmith group 10
   see also Booker Prize, publishing

Booker Prize, the [Man] 8–10, 43, 82, 100,
   136, 175, 178–80, 195, 232, 236, 240,
   244–8
   ceremony first televised, 1981 8
Bookwise 103
Borges, Jorge L. 178
Boyce, Sonya see Bailey, David A.
Boyd, William 192
Bracewell, Michael 80, 99, 230
   The Conclave 80, 99
   The Crypto-Amnesia Club 80, 99, 230
   Divine Concepts of Physical Beauty 99
Bradbury, Malcolm 36, 175–6,
   179–80, 191
Bragg, Melvyn 178
Brautigan, Richard 182
Brennan, Timothy 43–5, 47, 182
bricolage 15
bricoleur 163
Brideshead Revisited [TV series] 125, 136
Briggs, Raymond 79, 99
   When the Wind Blows 79, 99
Britain's industry, decimation of 3
British identity 103, 112, 120
British imperialism, legacies of 13
British Nationality Act 232
Britishness, changing viii
   Black British 10–13, 43
Brixton Black Women's Group 102
Brixton riots [uprising] 86, 171, 113
Brooke, Stephen 13
Brooke-Rose, Christine 33, 177–8
Brookner, Anita 179
Bryan, Beverly, Stella Dadzie and Suzanne
   Scafe, *Heart of the Race* 102, 108
Buford, Bill 176–7, 177–8
Burford, Barbara 11, 13, 105, 107–9,
   114–15, 117–20, 240, 241
   *Dancing the Tightrope: New Love
      Poems* 117
   A Dangerous Knowing 108, 117
   'Dreaming the Sky Down' 117
   Patterns 117
   'The Pinstripe Summer' 117–18
   *The Threshing Floor and Other
      Stories* 117
   'The Threshing Floor' 118–19
Burgess, Anthony 208
Busby, Margaret 108, 110

Daughters of Africa: An International Anthology of Words and Writings by Women of African Descent: From the Ancient Egyptian to the Present 108
Bush, George H. W., President 238
Butler, Judith 186

Callaghan, James 3
    motion of no confidence March 1979 3
Calvino, Italo 195
Cambridge University, English Faculty, Colin McCabe affair 1981
Cameron, David 125, 131
Cameron, Louise *see* Brooke, Stephen
Campañón, Carlos Silva 189
campus novel, the 36
capitalism 170
    global capitalism 7
carnivalesque 154, 163
Carter, Angela 33, 40, 91, 98–9, 133, 152–3, 163–9, 172–3, 177, 184–6, 188, 195, 229, 241
    Nights at the Circus 154, 163–6, 168, 172, 229, 241
Carter, President Jimmy 194
Charles, Prince 187
Chaudhuri, Una 180
Chernobyl 237
Chesterton, G. K. 137
Choong, Da 109
Chotina, Isaac 183
Christian, Mark 11
Churchill, Winston 140–3
Clark, Giles 6, 7
Clark, Roger Y. 182
Clarke, Becky Ayebia 119
class 16, 53, 61–2, 64, 67, 73, 85–6, 88, 89, 90–3, 101–2, 104, 106–7, 111–12, 114–15, 119
    class privilege 17
Coal Board, the National 5
Coe, Jonathan 76, 82–3, 85, 87, 99
    The Terrible Privacy of Maxwell Sim 99
    What a Carve Up! 82, 85, 99
Coetzee, J. M. 223
Cold War, the 152
Coleridge, Samuel Taylor 167
Collins, Merle, *Because the Dawn Breaks* 105

colonial 10, 13
    discourse 10
    'exoticized' other 43
    Mindset 182
colonialism 108, 111
comedy 160, 163–4, 169
Commonwealth literature 10
communism 8, 15, 79, 221–2
Communist bloc, collapse of viii, 15
Communist Party of Great Britain 210
    overthrow in Romania 206
community 36, 39, 41
Connor, Steven 9
Conservatism 21, 26, 32, 40, 43, 83–4, 96–7, 98
    free-market Thatcherite 26, 32–3
    realist literary 177
Conservative(s) 41
    1922 Committee 5
    attack on post-war consensus 77
    Central Council 130
    conference 77, 232–3
        1980 'Not for turning' speech 232
        Brighton bombing by IRA 233
    economics 41
    electoral victory 1979 60–1
    government(s) 4, 75–6, 126–7
        opposition to 1, 76
    policies 1, 25
Conservative values 12, 22, 25, 30, 32, 35, 77, 83, 93, 96, 125, 130, 141, 220
consumer 22, 26, 37, 39, 46
    capitalism 26, 39
    -ism 23, 25
    society 39
consumption 70
Continental philosophy 14
Cool Britannia viii
Cooper, James 5
Coover, Robert 192
cosmopolitan 44–6
Cowell, Ben 125
crisis, sense of, 1970s, 1980s 14
criticism 204–9, 211, 213, 215, 217–18, 220–5
cultural 22–4, 26–8, 36, 39–40, 48
    consumers 24

materialism 16–17
materialist 22
'culture wars' 14–15

Dadzie, Stella *see* Bryan, Beverly
Dalton, B. 194
Dangarembga, Tsitsi 11, 43
Daniels, Sarah 79, 99
　The Devil's Gateway 79
Davies, Pete 1–2, 95, 99–100, 230
　The Last Election 1–2, 95, 99, 230
Dayal, Samir 183
'death of the novel,' 1970s 6
deconstruction 153, 171
deconstructive approach 15
Deighton, Len 179
Deleuze, Gilles 14
Democracy 22
Derrida, Jacques 14, 23
Desai, Kiran 183
devolution 13, 51, 53, 60, 72, 74
Dhingra, Leena, *Amritvela* 108
dialogism 154
Diana, Princess 187
Dick, Kay 40
Dickens, Charles 169, 216, 220
　Dickensian technique 37
　Our Mutual Friend 169
Diedrick, James 187
Dirlik, Arif 10, 11
diversity 12
Doctorow, E. L. 131, 192
Dollimore, Jonathan 16
　Dollimore, Jonathan and Alan Sinfield,
　　*Political Shakespeare: Essays in
　　Cultural Materialism* (1985) 16
Douglas, Kirk 189
Downing Street 1
Drabble, Margaret 178
Drill Hall Arts Centre 117
Duffy, Maureen, 40
Duncker, Patricia 40, 42–3, 48
Dworkin, Andrea 185
dystopian 154

Eco, Umberto 192
Edgar, David 79, 99
　Maydays 79, 99
Edinburgh 58

Education Reform Act, the 235
Elias, Amy J. 191
Elphinstone, Margaret 52
Emecheta, Buchi 11, 13, 43,
　110–12, 114–15, 119–20, 229,
　231, 241–2
　Double Yoke 110, 120
　enemy within, the 5
　'Feminism with a Small "F"!' 111
　Gwendolyn 110, 112, 231
　Head Above Water 110–11
　In the Ditch 110
　Kehinde 112
　The New Tribe 112
　Ogwugwu Afor [publishing company] 110
　Our Own Freedom (with Maggie
　　Murray) 109
　The Rape of Shavi 229
　Second Class Citizen 110
English Heritage 127
English history 16
English, James 8, 10
Englishness 16, 22, 30
Enlightenment rationality, challenges to 15
Enright, D. J. 194
entrepreneurial 26
entropic 32
Epstein, Jacob 191
Equal Pay Act 102
estrangement 64
　see also alienation
Ethical 26, 31, 38
ethnicity 11–12, 16, 22
Evaristo, Bernadine 109
eventfulness 24
Ezenwa-Ohaeto 111

fabula 162
fabulation 158, 168
fairy tales 166
Falklands War, the 5, 78, 128, 232
　UK victory, 1982 5, 128
family values 26, 36
farce 169
father(s) 56, 59, 61–4, 70
Faulks, Sebastian 190
Fawcett, Farah 189
feminism 79, 92, 94, 99, 184–6
　Black feminism 101–2, 104, 111

Black feminist publishing 106–10
feminist publishing 103–7
Feminist Book Fortnight 106
Feminist Library 107
Feminist Review see Amos, Valerie
Fernihaugh, Anne 186
Fiedler, Leslie A. 182
financial markets, deregulation
  in UK, 1970s 7
financial markets, deregulation
  in US, 1970s 7
Finney, Brian 185
Fischer, Susan Alice 101, 105, 110,
  112–13
Foot, Michael 232
formal experimentalism 206
Forsyth, Frederick 179
Foucault, Michel 14, 28, 48, 50, 186
  The Order of Things 28, 48
Fowles, John 15, 170, 172, 191, 205–6, 208,
  215–29, 242
  The Collector 215–16, 219
  Daniel Martin 215, 218–20,
    225–7
  The Ebony Tower 215
  The French Lieutenant's Woman 170,
    172, 215, 218–19, 221, 223–4
  A Maggot 229, 242
  The Magus 215–17, 219
  Mantissa 215–16, 223, 225,
    228, 242
  The Tree 215
fragmentary, the 15
Frank, Soren 180
free market, the 22, 26
Freedman, Jean 140–1
Freud, Sigmund 155–7
  Beyond the Pleasure Principle 156
  Freudian case study 155, 157
Fryer, Peter, *Staying Power* 102
Fukuyama, Francis, 'The End of History?'
  15, 16
funding, public 104, 107

Gaddis, William 175, 177, 192
Galford, Ellen 52
Galloway, Janice 51–3, 55, 68–71, 73–4, 85,
  99, 231, 242, 243
  The Trick is To Keep Breathing 231, 243

Garnham, Nick 103
Gash, Norman 2
Gass, Joanne M. 186
Gass, William 177
Gates, Henry Louis 10
gay 40, 47, 107
Gee, Maggie 36, 151
gender 16, 22, 27–8, 39–3, 49, 152, 163,
  166–8, 171
Geng, Veronica 190
genre 29, 36–7, 43, 47, 153–4, 159, 163–4,
  167, 171–3
Gerzina, Gretchen 101
Gilroy, Beryl 12, 119–20, 231, 243
  Boy Sandwich 119–20, 231, 243
Gilroy, Paul 11, 24
  There Ain't No Black in the Union Jack
    11, 102
Glasgow 52, 55, 58, 65–7, 73
global capitalism 7, 170
Globe Theatre, the 16
Gomez, Jewelle 109, 118
Goodman, Alissa and Andrew Shephard 2
Gorbachev, Mikhail 237–8
Gordimer, Nadine 208
gothic 51–3, 62–3, 66, 73–4, 91–2,
  94, 98
  gothic fiction 163
grand narratives 15–16, 28–9, 166
  challenges to 16, 28–9, 166
Grass, Gunter 178, 181, 195
Gray, Alisdair 13, 36, 43, 52, 55–9, 68, 73,
  82–5, 87–8, 92, 94–5, 98–9, 151,
  228–9, 232, 243–4
  1982, Janine 229, 243
  The Fall of Kevin Walker 229, 243
  Lanark 228, 232, 243
Greater Access to Publishing (GAP) 108
Greater London Council (GLC) 107
  abolition by Thatcher government 234
  GLC Women's Committee 107
Green, Jonathan 130
Greenham Common 24, 116, 233
Grewal, Shabnam, et al. (eds), *Charting the
  Journey: Writings by Black and Third
  World Women* 108–9
Gross, John 178, 188
Grossman, Leo 187
grotesque body 166

grotesque realism 163, 166
Guptara, Prabhu 12, 105

Haffenden, John 188, 190
Hall, Stuart 11, 12–13, 24, 129, 141
   'New Ethnicities' 12
   Policing the Crisis 11
Hamilton, Ian 186
Hardt, Michael 33, 48
Harris, William 12
Harvey, David 26, 48
Hawkes, David 188
Hawkes, John 177
Hayton, Sian 52
Head, Dominic 6
Heinemann, African & Caribbean Series 119
Heisenberg, Werner 33
Heller, Joseph 191
Hemingway, Ernest 188
Hennegan, Alice 104
   'Home' 112–15, 120
Hensher, Philip 98–9, 147
   Kitchen Venom 98–9
herethics 40
heritage industry 125–8, 137
heterogeneity 23, 36, 45
   stylistic 6
Hewison, Robert 128
Higgins, Jack 179
Hills, John 4
Hillsborough disaster, the, 15 April 1989 235
historical fiction 175, 179, 181, 183–4, 187, 191–6
historiographic metafiction 125, 131–3
history 21, 28–32, 45–6, 48, 50
   historical 21–2, 28–33, 41–2, 45
   historiographical 28, 30
Hitler, Adolf 193
HM Treasury 4
   The Government's Expenditure Plans 1980–81 (1979)
Hobbes, Thomas 58
Hollinghurst, Alan 40, 147
hooks, bell 109
Huggan, Graham 10, 43, 48
Hulme, Peter 10
humanism 23

Hunt, Linda 107
Hussain, Ahmede 114
Hutcheon, Linda 23, 28–9, 48, 131–2, 155–7, 161, 173
   The Poetics of Postmodernism 23, 157
   The Politics of Postmodernism 161
Hutchinson, Colin 175, 176
Huxley, Aldous 57
hybridity 11, 23–4, 43, 101, 116, 119–20

identity 23, 28, 38–44, 47, 49, 52, 58, 62, 63, 65, 68–9
   national identity 54, 55
   see also nationalism
   politics 21, 23, 25–6, 38–40, 43–9
ideology 1, 4, 15, 21, 22–3, 36–7, 52, 54, 70, 88, 111, 140–3, 146, 154–5, 175, 206–7, 222, 225
   consumerist 37
   nationalist, Scottish 54
   neo-liberalism, Anglo-American 175
   patriarchal 155
   racist 23
immigrant communities 11
Immigration, migration 108, 114, 115
   British Nationality Act of 1981 102, 232–3
indeterminacy 33, 153, 207, 213
individualism 5, 16, 22–3, 25–7, 36, 78, 94, 175
   1960s 25
   market 22
   Thatcherite 26–7
inflation 3
   inflationary house price rises 3
inner-city riots, UK, 1981 3, 11, 13, 86, 171, 187, 232
Innes, C. L. 101
Institute of Fiscal Studies 2
International Fair of Radical, Black and Third World Books 105
International Feminist Book Fair 106–7
International Monetary Fund (IMF) crisis, 1976 3, 13
international relations, 'Common-Marketization' of 15–16
International Women's Year (1975) 111
IRA [the Irish Republican army] 232, 235
Irving, John 179, 182

Ishiguro, Kazuo 13, 22, 36, 43, 76, 99, 126,
    134, 136–9, 178, 183, 187, 192, 195,
    223, 228, 230, 244
  An Artist of the Floating World 230
  A Pale View of Hills 228
  The Remains of the Day 76, 99, 231, 244
Islam, Yusuf [Cat Stevens] 194

James, Henry 188
Jameson, Fredric 32, 35, 48, 137, 237
  The Political Unconscious 35–6, 48
  'Postmodernism, of the Cultural Logic
    of Late Capitalism' 237
Jarry, Alfred 165
  The Sadeian Woman 165, 172
Jin, Meling, *Gifts from My Grandmother:
    Poems* 109
Johnson, B. S. 177–8

Kafka, Franz 65, 168, 190
  The Metamorphosis 168, 190
Kakutani, Michiko 178–9, 184, 192–3, 195
Kappeler, Susanne 185
Karia Press 105
Kaufmann, K. 107
Kay, Jackie 11, 106, 108–9
Keen, Suzanne 191
Keitel, Harvey 189
Kelman, James 13, 51–3, 55, 64–70, 73, 151,
    229, 230, 231, 244
  The Busconductor Hines 229, 244
  A Chancer 229, 244
  A Disaffection 231, 244
  Greyhound for Breakfast 230, 244
Kendrick, Walter 186
Kennedy, A. L. 52
Kennedy, President Jack 195
Kennedy, Senator Bobby 195
Kermode, Frank viii
  *The Sense of an Ending: Studies in the
    Theory of Fiction* viii
Khan, Naseem, *The Arts in Britain* 103
Khan, Rashida 108
Khomeini, Ayatollah 170, 179, 194
  fatwa calling for death of Salman Rushdie
    170, 179, 194, 235, 238, 247
King, Bruce 102, 105
King Lear 16
King, Rev. Martin Luther 195

Kitson, Michael and Jonathan Michie 4
Knox, John 54
Konzelmann, Suzanne J., Marc Fovargue-
    Davies and Frank Wilkinson 2, 5
Kureishi, Hanif 11, 21, 40, 43, 47, 102
  My Beautiful Laundrette 102
  The Buddha of Suburbia 47
Kuznetsov, Anatoly 155

Lacan, Jacques 14
Lacayo, Richard 187
Lahirio, Jhumpa 183
Lamming, George 12
Landor, Liliane 109
language 23, 31, 39
Law of the Father 61, 63
Lawson, Mark 80–1, 98, 100, 125
  Bloody Margaret 98, 100
Lazarus, Neil 10
Le Carré, John 179
left liberal 23, 25, 27
Leigh, Mike 1
  High Hopes (1988) 1
  Life Is Sweet (1990) 1
  Meantime (1983) 1
Leithauser, Brad 196
Leonard, John 179
lesbian 40–3, 47, 102, 104,
    106–7, 117–19
Lessing, Doris 208
*Let It Be Told: Essays by Black Women
    Writers in Britain* 108
Leung, Linda 5
Levy, Andrea 101, 105
Lewis, Gail 104, 109
liberal ideology, 1980s criticism of 14
libertarians 16
linearity 34, 44
linguistic 42
literary 21–4, 26, 28, 41,
    43–4, 48–9
  criticism 22–3
  market 23
  marketing of culture 22
literary prizes, growth of, 1980s 8
Lively, Penelope 178
Liverpool 1
Lochhead, Liz 51–2, 54
Lockerbie bombing, the 235

Lodge, David 15, 36, 92, 100, 208, 221, 228-9
  How Far Can You Go? 228
  Nice Work 92, 100, 231
  Small World: An Academic Romance 229
London Borough Grants Scheme 107
'Loony left,' the 107
Lorde, Audre 106, 109
Lowenthal, David 126
ludic, the 15
Lyotard, Jean-François 15, 28, 35, 49, 158, 173
  The Postmodern Condition 28, 49

Macedo, Lynne 119-20
magic realism 36, 43, 115, 134, 163, 167-9, 184-6, 195, 205
Mahabarata 181
Malchow, Howard 127-8
Mallot, J. Edward 114, 116
Mansfield, Stephanie 189
Mantel, Hilary 147
Márquez, Gabriel Garcia 178, 181, 194
Marwick, Arthur 130
Marxist 23, 36
Marzorati, Gerald 195
masquerade 166
Massie, Alan 53, 73
McClintock, Anne 10
McEwan, Ian 22, 33-7, 39, 47-8, 49n. 1, 79, 82, 94-8, 100, 177, 184, 208, 221, 223, 227-8, 230, 245
  The Child in Time 33-6, 39, 47, 49n. 1, 94-8, 100, 184, 230, 245
  The Comfort of Strangers 228
  Or Shall We Die? 79, 95, 100, 245
McGrath, Patrick 191
McHale, Brian 23, 49
McLeod, John 10-11
  Beginning Postcolonialism 10
  Postcolonial London: Rewriting the Metropolis 11
McLiam Wilson, Robert 43
Menzies 103
Mercer, Kobena 12
metafiction 161, 172-3, 181, 184, 196
  metafictional 26, 29, 35
Michael, Magali C. 186
middle-class 27, 38, 44

Miners' strike, 1972 13
Miners' strike, 1984-5 viii, 233
  see also Orgreave miners' 'riot'
minority communities 11
Mitchell, David 78, 100
  Black Swan Green 100
Mo, Timothy 13, 43, 48-9, 183
modernism 225
  late modernism 207
Mohammad 193-4
Mojtabai, A. G. 195
Monaghan, David 1
monetarism 5
  monetarist 37
montage 32
Moorcock, Michael 139-46, 231, 245
  Mother London 231, 245
Moore, Alan 79, 100
  Watchmen 79, 100
morality 38-9
Morgan, Edwin 51-2, 54
Morris, William 126
Morrison, Jago 33
Morrison, Susan 187-8
Morrison, Toni 181
Morton, H.V. 138
Mota, Miguel 1
mother(s) 63, 69
Mount, Ferdinand viii
  'The Doctrine of Unripe Time' viii
Mudimbe, V. Y. 10
Muir, Edwin 53, 73
Mukherjee, Arun 182
Mulhern, Francis 14
Müller, Jan-Werner 15
multiplicity 22, 43, 45
Murdoch, Iris 15, 205-6, 208-16, 219-28, 230, 246
  The Bell 210, 224
  The Book and the Brotherhood 230, 246
  The Good Apprentice 210
  Nuns and Soldiers 214, 228
  The Philosopher's Pupil 210-11, 213
  The Sandcastle 209
  The Sea, the Sea 210-11, 213, 219, 246
  Under the Net 209-10, 214, 246
  A Word Child 210

Murray, Maggie 109
    see also Emecheta, Buchi
mystical 34, 35

Nabokov, Vladimir 178, 190–1
Naipaul, V. S. 12
Namjoshi, Suniti
    Aditi and the One-Eyed Monkey 109
    The Conversations of Cow 108
    Feminist Fables 109
narrative 26, 28–9, 31–3, 38, 40–2, 44–5
Nasta, Susheila 114–15
National Front 102, 113, 119
National Heritage Act, the 127, 233
National Heritage Memorial Fund, the 232
national identity 54–5
    see also nationalism
National Union of Mineworkers
        (NUM) 5
    MI5 infiltration of 5
nationality 28
    nationalism 10, 46, 54
        see also national identity
    nationalist sentiment 22
Nationality Act, UK, 1981 11
Negri, Antonio 33, 48
Neo-conservatism 4
Neo-liberalism 4
neo-realism 176, 180, 186, 188–9, 191–2
Net Book Agreement, the 80
New Beacon Books 105
New Cross fire, the 119, 232
new historicism 15–16
new historicists 16
New Physical 33
New Right 36, 77, 95
New Statesman 105, 110
Nichols, Grace 105, 108
Noakes, Lucy 141
Nora, Pierre 139
North [of England], the 84, 88, 98
Northern Irish 43
Northern Irish novelists 13
nostalgia 27, 31
novel, the 6
    of ideas 169
    'renaissance' of, 1980s 6
nuclear 30, 31
    anxiety 31

Oates, Joyce Carol 192
Office of National Statistics 3
oil crisis 1973–4 6
Okri, Ben 43
    apocalypse 31
One Thousand and One Nights 181
Onlywomen Press 105
oral narrative 169, 181, 182
OPEC crisis 21
Organization of Women of African and
        Asian Descent (OWAAD) 102
Orgreave miners' 'riot' 5, 233
Orwell, George 57
Orwell Prize 248
Orwellian distortion 34
Osler, Audrey, *Speaking Out: Black Girls in
        Britain* 109
Othello 169
Owusu, Kwesi 103–4

Palmer, Paulina 184
Paranjape, Makarand 108, 114–16
Parker, Gabriela 109
Parmar, Pratibha 104, 106, 109
parody 1–2, 36–7, 39, 41, 43, 70, 137, 139,
        158, 160, 164, 166, 192, 212, 247
Parry, Benita 43, 49
particularity 22, 65
pastiche 15, 32, 77, 136–7, 146, 166
patriarchal 24, 27, 41
patriarchy 163
Peace, David 147
Pearse, Gabriela 108–9
Peck, Brian V. 1
Peepal Tree Press 105
Peim, Nick 14
Penguin, losses 1979 7
Perera, Padma, *Birthday Deathday and
        Other Stories* 108
performance 23
    Performativity 40
permissive 25, 40–1
    society 40–1
personal 23, 26, 32–4, 37, 42
Peterson, Shirley 186
Pettinger, Tom 3
phallogocentrism 40
Phillips, Caryl 11, 43, 230–1
picaresque, the 163, 169, 181

picaro 163
Planck, Max 33
plural, the 15
plurality 27
police brutality 113
political 21, 23–4, 26–8, 30, 32, 35–6,
    38–43, 46, 48
Poll Tax, the 5
postcolonial 10, 13
    1970s periodization 10
    Britain 17
    immigration 13
postcolonial studies 10, 15
postcolonial theorists 11
postcolonialism 13, 28, 115
postmodern 23, 26–9, 31–3, 35–6, 39–40,
    42–3, 45–9, 153, 155, 158, 161–2,
    170, 172–3
    postmodernism 15, 23, 27, 32–3, 43,
        47–9, 175–6, 181, 184–6, 191, 196,
        203, 225–26
    postmodernity 37
postmodernist fiction 23, 49
poststructuralism 14–15, 185–6, 190
    poststructuralist 22, 28–30, 39–40
post-war Britain 1–3, 14, 22, 77, 84, 137–8,
    140–2, 144, 178, 204–5, 246
    failure 142
    mythologizing of 140–1
    rebuilding 144
post-war consensus 1, 2, 14, 77–8, 129–30,
    175
    demise of 14, 130, 175
    Thatcher's opposition to 77–8
post-war Keynesian inflationary
    economics 3
post-war settlement 22
pragmatism 25, 30
Pratt, Mary Louise 10
Prescod, Marsha 110
Priest, Christopher 36
private property 26
privatization *see* Thatcher, Margaret
prize culture 24, 82
Procter, James 12
progress 28, 30–1, 33
protest 23, 30, 38
provincialism 41

psychology 35
publishing 6–10, 76, 81, 88, 100
    1970s, rising costs 6
    book sales, 1980s, influence of
        television 9
    Dillons 9
    literary 6
    literary prizes, growth of, 1980s 8
    multinational conglomerates 7
    Penguin, losses, 1979 7
    Thatcherism, effects upon 7
    traditional bookshops struggling,
        1960s and 1970s 9
    Waterstones 9
    WHSmith group 10
Pynchon, Thomas 131, 175, 194

queer 40, 46–7
queer theory 15
quest romance 165–6
Quin, Ann 177

race 16, 102, 111–12, 119
    Race Relations Act of 1976 102
racism 10, 106, 109, 111, 113–15, 118, 120,
    160, 163, 168–9
racist 23
Rafferty, Terence 195
Randhawa, Ravinder 114–17, 120, 231, 246
    Right of Way 231, 246
    A Wicked Old Woman 114–17
rationalization 30
realism 15, 30, 51–2, 73, 103, 161, 163,
    166, 168, 171, 175–80, 184, 187–9,
    194–5, 203, 205–9, 212–14, 220–2, 226
    bourgeois 177
    dissociative 208
    grotesque realism 163, 166
    hyperrealism 221
    Iris Murdoch 220
    Jamesian 161
    journalistic 214
    psychological 214
    socialist 206, 208
    surrealism 221
    textual 208
    see also Magic Realism; neo-realism
Reder, Michael 180–181

referential 26, 29
  referentiality 205, 225
Regan, President Ronald 21, 175, 187, 236–8
Rehberger, Dean 191
Reichl, Susanne 114
relativism 26, 29, 31, 35
revitalization of the arts, 1980s 6
Rhys, Jean 208
right-wing 23, 34
Riley, Joan 11, 13, 110, 112–15, 120, 230–1, 246
  Romance 113, 231, 246
  The Unbelonging 110, 112
  Waiting in the Twilight 112–15, 230, 246
rioting 86, 234
Riviere, Francesca 189
Robertson, Bruce 131
Robinson, Sally 186
Romanticism 167, 173
Roth, Philip 191, 195
Roy, Arundhati 183
Royal Wedding 1981, Prince Charles to Lady Diana 86, 187, 232, 236
Royle, Nicholas *see* Bennett, Andrew
Rubens, Bernice 13, 43
Rushdie, Salman 11, 13, 22, 33, 36, 43–5, 47–9, 87, 97–8, 100, 131, 133, 152–4, 168–71, 173, 178–83, 187, 192–6, 208, 223, 228–9, 231–2, 247
  fatwa 170, 179, 194, 238, 247
  Imaginary Homelands 154, 168–71, 173, 247
  Midnight's Children 228, 232, 247
  Satanic Verses 97, 100, 231, 247
  Shame 229, 247
Ruskin, John 126

Sade, Donatien-Alphonse-François, count (marquis de Sade) 185
Said, Edward 10
Salyer, Gregory 192
Sam, Agnes, *Jesus is Indian and Other Stories* 108
Samuel, Raphael 128–30
satire 88, 95, 160, 169
Saville, John 5

Scafe, Suzanne *see* Bryan, Beverly
Scargill, Arthur 233
scepticism 23, 28, 46
Schiffin, André 9
scholarly 'turn to history,' 1980s 16
scientific 33
Scotland 52–6, 58–9, 61, 72–3
Scottish 43
Scottish novelists 13
Scottish Renaissance 51, 72
  second Scottish Renaissance 51–2, 61
Section 28 of the Local Government Act (1988) 107, 235
See, Carolyn 184
Self, Will [William Woodard] 131, 187
self-reflexivity 23, 26, 160, 166, 169–71, 183, 216, 218
Selvon, Sam 12
Seth, Viram 183
sexism 111–12, 114–15, 119, 163
sexual 27, 39–43
  asexual 41
  identity 39, 43
  repression 41
  sexuality 25, 28, 40, 42, 50, 152, 166, 171
Shakespeare, William 16, 189
  appropriation of, for right-wing ideological purposes 16
Sheba Feminist Publishers 105–9, 117, 232
Sheets, Robin Ann 185
Shepard, R. Z. 189, 191
Shephard, Andrew *see* Goodman, Alissa
Shields, S. 101
Siegel, Carol 185
simulacra 22, 32
Sinclair, Clive, 36
Sinclair, Iain 95, 98, 100, 130, 133, 142, 230
  Downriver 98, 100
  White Chappell, Scarlet Tracings 230
Sinfield, Alan 16, 22, 24–5, 49, 141–2
Sivanandan, A. 11, 102
Smartt, Dorothea 105, 109
Smith, Ali 52
Smith, Amanda 180
Smith, Joan 91, 100
  Misogynies 91, 100
Smith, Zadie 101, 105
Snider, Norman 188

Snow, C. P. 178
social disorder, sense of, 1970s, 1980s 14
Sorrentino, Gilbert 177
Sougou, Omar 112
Southall Black Sisters 102
Soviet Union, collapse of 15
space 52–3, 59, 62, 65–6, 68, 71, 72
Spare Rib 105
spectacular 23, 26
Spivak, Gayatri Chakravorty 10
Squires, Clare 9
St. Francis of Assisi 1
Star Wars [movie] 31
state of the nation, the 36
Stein, Mark 12
Stevens, Cat see Islam, Yusuf
Stevenson, Randall 6–9
Stevenson, Robert Louis 63, 74
Stoddart, Helen 185
Stone, Robert 182
Stop and Search ('Sus') Laws
  [section 4 of the Vagrancy Act 1824]
  102, 119
storytelling 31–2, 44, 47
Stout, Mira 187
structuralism 14
style 23, 25–6, 31–2, 37, 40, 44, 46
Su, John J. 115, 139
subaltern identity 11
subaltern theory 15
Swift, Graham 47, 132, 152, 164, 173, 192,
  208, 223, 228–9, 231, 247
  Out of This World 231, 247
  Shuttlecock 228, 247
  The Sweet Shop Owner 228, 247
  Waterland 30–1, 47, 152, 173, 229, 247
syuzhet, 162

Taylor, D. J. 38, 46, 49
television, central cultural role, 1980s 9
temporality 32
Tennant, Emma 40, 82, 91–5, 98, 100, 231,
  248
  Two Women of London 91, 93, 231, 248
Tew, Philip 2, 26–7, 49, 168
  The Contemporary British Novel 2, 26–7,
    49
  'Wintersonian Masculinities' 168
textual 22–3, 28–9, 37, 42–3
Thanatos 162

Thatcher, Margaret 2, 17, 21, 25–7, 30–1,
  36–7, 40–1, 43, 46, 49, 75–80, 84, 89,
  96–8, 125–31, 135, 137, 139, 140–2,
  145, 147, 151–2, 168, 175, 186–7,
  194, 232–5
  council houses, sale of 4
  creative artists and novelists,
    appalled by 2
  deregulation City of London 4
  electoral victories, 1983, 1987 3
  electoral victory 1979 60, 233
  enemy within, the 5
  government 107
  Iron Lady 6
  monetarism 5, 37
  monetarist policies, failings of 3
  National Union of Mineworkers
    (NUM), provocation of 5
  'No such thing as society' speech 26
  'Not for turning' speech 232
  oil revenues, dependence on 4
  parental figure for nation 96–7
  privatization of public assets 4, 78
  project 17
  property-owning democracy 5–6
  publishing, Thatcher's effect upon 7–8
  resignation 96
  share ownership, encouragement of 6
Thatcherism 1, 3, 7, 14, 75–86, 88–91,
  93, 95, 97–100, 107–9, 126–7, 131,
  135, 139, 145, 147, 151–2, 160–1,
  168, 186–7
  inconsistent ideology 4
Thatcherite 21–2, 24–6, 28, 30–2, 37–8
  Britain 2, 10, 135
  corruption 37
  nationalism 13
  neo-liberalism 26
  policies 10
  wets, relation to 5
Thatcherism / Thatcherite *see* Thatcher,
  Margaret
'theory,' 1970s literary and humanities
  scholarship 14
'theory wars' the 14
  see also Cambridge University
Thomas, D. M. 153, 155–7, 160,
  162, 173–4, 180, 208, 211, 223, 228, 248
  The White Hotel 153, 155–7, 160, 171,
    173–4, 228, 248

time 23–4, 28, 32–5, 37–8, 40, 47–50
Todd, Richard 8, 80–2, 100
Toryism 25
Towers, Robert 179, 180, 183
trades union legislation 5
tragedy 160, 169
translation 204, 208, 210–12, 214, 219, 221, 223–4, 227
Tremain, Rose 29, 151, 173
    Restoration 151, 173
Trewin, Ion 180

'unbelonging' 101, 110, 112, 114, 120
uncertainty 31
unemployed, the 1, 2, 83, 89
unemployment 2–4, 53, 83, 89, 127, 232–3, 235
    Liverpool 1
    North East 4
    North West 4
    Northern Ireland 3
    Scotland 4, 53
Union with England Act, the 54
United Kingdom 14, 237
    deindustrialization 4, 6
    economic decline 4
    public spending cuts 4
    tax rates, Institute for Fiscal Studies 4
universalizing 27
Unsworth, Barry 29

van der Poorten, Menika 109–10
'Victorian values' 128–30
Vidal, Gore 176, 179
Vietnam War 195
    Veterans Memorial, Washington 236
Virago Press 88, 105–9, 234, 246
von Hayek, Friedrich 5, 16
    The Road to Serfdom (1944) 5
Vonnegut, Kurt 175, 182

Wajsbrot, Cecile 180
Walden Books 194
Walker, Alice 181
Walters, Colin 192
Walton, David 192
Ward, Abigail 102
Warner, Alan 51
Warner, Marina 40, 184

Waugh, Evelyn 137
Waugh, Patricia 23, 27, 49, 224
    Harvest of the Sixties 27
    Metafiction 23, 49, 224
Weldon, Fay 40, 229, 231
welfare 22, 25
    capitalism 22
    state 'socialism' 25
welfarism 2
Welsh [the] 43, 103, 179
Welsh, Irvine 51
Welsh writers, novelists 13, 43
Western Europe
    'post-historical' 15
    'post-ideological' 15
Westlake, Michael 33, 228, 230
    Imaginary Women 230
    One Zero and the Night Controller 228
Westminster 54
White, Hayden 131
WHSmith 10, 103, 106
    see also book-selling, new approaches, 1980s
Wilson, Amrit, *Finding a Voice: Asian Women in Britain* 107–8
Wilson, Harold 3
Wilson, Jonathan 187
Wilson, Olivette Cole 109
Wilson, Robert McLiam 13
'Windrush generation,' of black writers, the 12
Winter of Discontent 1978–79 3, 13
Winterson, Jeanette 22, 33, 36, 40–3, 47–8, 76, 80, 91, 94, 100, 126, 133–5, 142, 146–7, 152–3, 166–9, 173–4, 184, 192, 230–1, 248–9
    Art Objects 167, 174, 249
    Elim Pentecostal Church 249
    Oranges Are Not the Only Fruit 40–3, 47, 230, 248–9
    Oxford University 248
    The Passion 76, 100, 153–4, 166–58, 171, 173–4, 184, 192, 230, 248–9
    Sexing the Cherry 126, 132–5, 184, 231, 249
Wise, V. 107
Wolfe, Tom 179
Women's Press, the 105–6, 108, 112, 114, 117, 235
Women's Press Bookclub, the 104

working class 11, 26, 44, 45, 46
Worpole, Ken *see* Garnham, Nick
Worrow, Eileen 117
Wright, Patrick 80, 90, 100, 127–8
Wright, Peter 79, 90, 100
   Spycatcher 79, 100

Yardley, Jonathan 188, 195
Young, E. 109–10
yuppie 80

Zeitgeist 8, 17, 52, 92, 125
Zora 108